Civic Insecurity:
Law, Order and HIV in
Papua New Guinea

EDITED BY VICKI LUKER AND SINCLAIR DINNEN

Civic Insecurity:
Law, Order and HIV in Papua New Guinea

EDITED BY VICKI LUKER AND SINCLAIR DINNEN

State, Society and Governance in Melanesia Program

Studies in State and Society in the Pacific, No. 6

E PRESS

Published by ANU E Press
The Australian National University
Canberra ACT 0200, Australia
Email: anuepress@anu.edu.au
This title is also available online at: http://epress.anu.edu.au/civic_insecurity_citation.html

National Library of Australia Cataloguing-in-Publication entry

Title:	Civic insecurity : law, order and HIV in Papua New Guinea / edited by Vicki Luker and Sinclair Dinnen.
ISBN:	9781921666605 (pbk.) 9781921666612 (eBook)
Notes:	Includes bibliographical references.
Subjects:	AIDS (Disease)--Papua New Guinea.
	AIDS (Disease)--Law and legislation--Papua New Guinea.
	AIDS (Disease)--Papua New Guinea--Prevention.
	HIV infections--Papua New Guinea.
	Law enforcement--Papua New Guinea.
	Crime--Papua New Guinea.
	Papua New Guinea--Social conditions.
	Papua New Guinea--Social life and customs.
	Papua New Guinea--Politics and government--1975-

Other Authors/Contributors:
Luker, Vicki.
Dinnen, Sinclair.

Dewey Number: 362.196979209953

Cover design and layout by ANU E Press

Cover image: Young boy at celebrations in Goroka for the 30th anniversary of Independence, 2005. Courtesy of photographer Kahunapule Michael Johnson, http://Kahunapule.org and http://worldoutreach.org

Contents

Introduction

Masculinity, Violence and HIV

Networking, Sex Working and the Law

Police, Prisons, Army and Mainstreaming HIV

Governance, Rights and Security

Cover and Section illustrations

Cover: Young boy at celebrations in Goroka for the 30th anniversary of Independence, 2005. Courtesy of photographer Kahunapule Michael Johnson, http://Kahunapule.org and http://worldoutreach.org

Introduction: 'Lukautim yu yet long AIDS': Mendi shopfront, Southern Highlands Province. Courtesy of photographer Richard Eves

Masculinity, Violence and HIV: pen drawing, Chris Kauage. From the collection of Sinclair Dinnen

Networking, Sex Working and the Law: 'Haiwe'. From the collection of Richard Eves

Police, Prisons, Army and Mainstreaming HIV: Prison inmates. Benjmain Lowy/ VII Network

Governance, Rights and Security: Tari road scene, Southern Highlands Province. Courtesy of photographer, Murray Lord

Conclusion and Epilogue: Child looks back. From Tari road scene, Southern Highlands Province. Courtesy of photographer, Murray Lord

Figures, Maps and Tables

Figures

Figure 1: Poster featuring Brad Fittler. PNG National AIDS Council. From the collection of Richard Eves

Figure 2: Poster featuring Mal Meninga, PNG National AIDS Council. From the collection of Richard Eves

Figure 3: Portrait of Gaitzman, from Kips Kaboni ('Red Devils'), Port Moresby, 2004. Courtesy of Stephen Dupont, www.stephendupont.com

Figure 4: Portrait of Shookman, from Kips Kaboni ('Red Devils'), Port Moresby, 2004. Courtesy of Stephen Dupont, www.stephendupont.com

Figure 5: Portrait of Mania, from Kips Kaboni ('Red Devils'), Port Moresy, 2004. Courtesy of Stephen Dupont, www.stephendupont.com

Figure 6: Haphap Meri bilong PNG. By Maik Yomba Kagi, 2000. www.Pazifik-Infostelle.org

Maps

Map 1: Papua New Guinea. By Karina Pelling, Coombs Cartography, College of Asia and the Pacific, Australian National University, Canberra, Australia

Map 2: Papua New Guinea and the Region. By Karina Pelling, Coombs Cartography, College of Asia and the Pacific, Australian National University, Canberra, Australia

Map 3: Southern Highlands Province. By Karina Pelling, Coombs Cartography, College of Asia and the Pacific, Australian National University, Canberra, Australia

Graphs

Graph 1: Proportion of all HIV and AIDS cases in different Pacific island countries and territories, 1984–2007. Source: UNAIDS, AIDS Epidemic Update, December 2009. Geneva: UNAIDS, 77

Glossary

AIDS	Acquired immunodeficiency syndrome
BAHA	Papua New Guinea Business Coalition against HIV and AIDS
Bilum	string bag
Buai	betel nut
Buriburi	magic by sorcery
CBO	Community-based organisation
CS	Correctional Services
DoH	Department of Health
EU	European Union
HAMP Act	The HIV/AIDS Management and Prevention Act of 2003
HIV	Human immunodeficiency virus
HR	Human resources
IMR	Institute of Medical Research
Kastom	custom
Kina	unit of PNG currency: 1 kina = 100 toea
Lain	line
Lainap	Pack rape, group sex
LRC	Law Reform Commission
Lukautim yu yet AIDS	Protect yourself against AIDS
Maket	market
NAC	PNG National AIDS Council
NACS	PNG National AIDS Council Secretariat
NGO	Non-government organisation
NHASP	National HIV/AIDS Support Program
Pamuk	'Prostitute'
Pasindia meri	'passenger women' who exchange sex for money
plet kaikai	plate of take-away food
PLHIV	People living with HIV
PLWHA	People Living with HIV/AIDS
PNGDF	Papua New Guinea Defence Force
PSP	Poro Sapot Project (Save the Children)

RPNGC	Royal Papua New Guinea Constabulary
Raskol	'rascal', lawless young man
Rot meri	woman of the streets
rabisman	'rubbish man', worthless man
sagapari	'small mangrove garden', around Daru also term with meaning similar to '*tu kina bus*'
STD	Sexually transmitted disease
STI	Sexually transmitted infection
SW	sex worker
Toea	unit of PNG currency: 100 toea = 1 kina
Tu kina bus	Outdoor setting where sex can be purchased cheaply
VCT	Voluntary Counselling and Testing
Wantoks	Kinsmen; people who speak the same language

Contributors

Peter Bamne—Director of Medical Services, Mt Hagen General Hospital, PO Box 36, Mt Hagen, WHP, Papua New Guinea

John Cartwright—Consultant, Centre of Criminology, Law Faculty, University of Cape Town, Private Bag X3, Rondebosch 7701, Republic of South Africa

Sinclair Dinnen—Senior Fellow, State Society and Governance in Melanesia Program, College of Asia and the Pacific, Australian National University, ACT 0200, Australia

Richard Eves—Research Fellow, State Society and Governance in Melanesia Program, College of Asia and the Pacific, Australian National University, ACT 0200, Australia

Karen Fletcher—Health Protection and Prevention and Population Health, Department of Health, Melbourne VIC 3001, Australia

Bomal Gonapa—Legal and Policy Adviser, Papua New Guinea National AIDS Council Secretariat, PO Box 1345, Boroko, NCD, Papua New Guinea

Nicole Haley—Convenor, State Society and Governance in Melanesia Program, College of Asia and the Pacific, Australian National University, ACT 0200, Australia

Lawrence Hammar—Anthropologist and Social Researcher, engaged on 'Positive Research for Positive People: strengthening HIV social research capacity in Fiji', in tandem with Pacific Islands AIDS Foundation and the Fijian Positive Network

Carol Jenkins—The late Carol Jenkins was an Anthropologist and Social Researcher, Director of Alternate Visions, Bangkok, Thailand

Madeleine Jenneker—Faculty of Law, University of the Western Cape, Private Bag X17 Bellville, Cape Town 7535, Republic of South Africa

Greg Law—Sexual Health and HIV/AIDS Prevention and Care Project, PO Box 1875, Port Moresby, NCD 121, Papua New Guinea

Vicki Luker—Visiting Fellow, State Society and Governance in Melanesia Project, College of Asia and Pacific, Australian National University, ACT 0200, Australia

Martha Macintyre—Associate Professor and Honorary Senior Fellow, School of Philosophy, Anthropology and Social Inquiry, University of Melbourne, VIC 3010, Australia

Paul Maia—Chairman, Saraga Peace, Good Order and Community Development Association, Six-Mile, NCD, Papua New Guinea

Abby McLeod—Coordinator, Policy and Governance, Australian Federal Police, Canberra, ACT, Australia

Michael Monsell-Davis—Anthropologist, PO Box 280, Galston, NSW 2159, Australia

Michael O'Keefe—Senior Lecturer, Politics and International Relations Program, School of Humanities and Social Sciences, La Trobe University, Melbourne, VIC 3086

Joachim Pantumari—Senior Medical Advisor, Papua New Guinea National AIDS Council, PO Box 1345, Boroko, NCD, Papua New Guinea

Ian Patrick—Director, Ian Patrick & Associates Pty Ltd, 16 Roemer Cres, Alphington, Melbourne, VIC 3078, Australia

Elizabeth Reid—Development Practitioner and Visiting Fellow, State, Society and Governance in Melanesia Project, College of Asia and Pacific, Australian National University, ACT 0200, Australia

Clifford Shearing—Professor of Criminology and Director of the Centre of Criminology, Law Faculty, University of Cape Town, Private Box X3, Rondebosch 7701, South Africa

Christine Stewart—Research Scholar, School of Culture, History and Language, College of Asia and Pacific, Australian National University, ACT 0200, Australia

Isaac Wai—Deputy Chairman, Saraga Peace, Good Order and Community Development Association, Six-Mile, NCD, Papua New Guinea

Acknowledgements

This collection is indebted, directly and indirectly, to many people. We would like to thank those whose conversation, assistance, comments and contributions in other ways have helped and inspired. Special thanks to Julie Airi, Bryant Allen, Dennis Altman, Isu Aluvula, John Ballard, Sister Rose Bernard, Kila Bulina, Marina Carman, Chris Chevalier, Elisabeth Cox, Anne Dickson-Waiko, Miriam Dogimab, Anna Dorney, Phillip Gibbs, Mike Bourke, Jack Caldwell, Mary Crewe, Berit Gustaffson, Christopher Hershey, Fiona Hukula, Terry Hull, Sister Tarcisia Hunhoff, Kal Indistange, Margaret Jolly, Mili Kaitani, Lesley Kaivalon, Evelyn King, Susan Kippax, Betty Koka, Litiana Kuridrani, Miriam and Steve Layton, Andrew Lepani, Kathy Lepani, Jenny Litau, Martha Macintyre, Clement Malau, Ros Morauta, Sister Mary McArthy, Sister Gaudentia Meier, John Millan, Ninkama Moiya, Florence Momo, Mark Mondia, Ili Movono, John Muke, Eileen Natera, Annmaree O'Keefe, Susan Paxton, Nii'ke Plange, John Reeder, Edward Reis, Father Jude Ronayne-Ford, Jimmie Rodgers, Peter Sapak, Ute Schumann, Orovou Sepoe, Jerry Singirok, Barbara Sivusia-Joyce, Barbara Smith, Tesse Soi, Rick Steele, Sharon Walker, Neva Wendt, Alan Whiteside, Heather Worth, Cammi Webb and Naomi Yupae.

Two organisations have materially supported this book: the State, Society and Governance in Melanesia Program (SSGM) in the College of Asia and the Pacific at the Australian National University; and the Australian Agency for International Development, AusAID. SSGM has been home or a home-away-from-home for many contributors to this volume. With AusAID's generous support, SSGM has organised several seminars, publications and other activities on HIV in the Pacific, including a workshop 'HIV/AIDS in PNG' held at the ANU in 2004, which first brought the movers behind this collection together. Our gratitude is owed to former SSGM convenor David Hegarty, current convenor Nicole Haley, administrative supremo Sue Rider, her adjutant Jean Hardy, editing wizards Helen Marshall and Maxine McArthur, and last but not least, Peter Elder. At AusAID, very deep thanks go to Peter Lindenmayer and his committed and tireless colleagues.

As editors we would like to express our gratitude to Alan Patience for editorial acumen, imagination and input; to Richard Eves for his famous generosity with his archive of texts and images; and to Lawrence Hammar for hospitality and memorable times in Goroka. Michael and Lori Johnson, Murray Lord and Stephen Dupont kindly permitted us to use their fine photographs.

Our thanks also go to Stewart Firth and members of the Pacific Editorial Board of the ANU E Press. In particular, we acknowledge the valuable insights and suggestions of our anonymous reviewers. At ANU E Press, we thank Duncan Beard and his team for their technical support.

Finally, we would like to pay tribute to the activism and research of the late Carol Jenkins, the unsung work of so many people working with their communities for health, safety and the future of PNG's children, and to those whose lives have been changed by HIV.

Joan's Story

Beaten and shunned because she had AIDS

A 27-year-old mother of three was beaten up, burned and left to die by her village people near Goroka town because she had AIDS.

Joan (not her real name), from Ketarobo village, was picked up by staff from the Papua New Guinea Institute of Medical Research two weeks ago after they were alerted by a friend of the women.

The woman was taken to Goroka hospital where she died a week later.

Phili Manove, a research officer with the IMR, was among four people who picked up Joan, including the IMR's HIV/AIDS sero-surveillance project coordinator Dr Lawrence Hammar and his wife. She said when Joan was found, she had fungus already growing in her mouth because she had not eaten for some time. Parts of her body were burnt and she had ulcers, obviously from beatings she had received from village men.

She was left under a shelter the people had put up near a stream away from the village.

'It was obvious that she had not eaten for days. She was extremely skinny and she was deteriorating because she had fungal growth in her mouth. Her house was burnt but she escaped being burnt,' she said.

She said the people refused to give a bucket to Dr Hammar and his team when they asked for one to wash Joan before taking her to the hospital. After Joan was brought to the hospital, her father came and told them that Joan must not be brought back to her village.

'When we took her to the hospital, the health workers were not helpful. Maybe because they thought that IMR was responsible. I don't know why but her sores were not treated although they gave her an injection. Maybe because she was deteriorating,' she said.

The villagers, through Joan's sister, asked later to compensate the IMR staff for caring for Joan, but Dr Hammar's team refused and asked only that Joan be buried in her village. The request was granted and her body will be buried in the village today.

Post-Courier
Wednesday, 7 July 2004

Introduction

Introduction

VICKI LUKER

This book explores the interaction between PNG's HIV and 'law and order' problems. We hope readers will take from it a richer appreciation of the potentially vicious spirals and virtuous circles that this interaction can create. Ultimately, we advance the cause of 'deep prevention' for these interlinked challenges, and the concept and goal of 'civic security' to embrace them both.

Joan's story, reprinted here from Papua New Guinea's largest daily newspaper, begins this collection. She represents one face of PNG's now endemic HIV that is so often described as undergoing 'feminisation'. She died with AIDS and she died in violence and abuse. She thus conjoins aspects of HIV and 'law and order' that this collection treats together. Joan had been a member of her community, a citizen of PNG and metaphorically a citizen of the world. But, if the term 'citizenship' can be used in both its strict and looser senses, Joan's belonging to these collectivities gave her no security of person. She lacked what we call here civic security. Of course, there are many stories like Joan's, reported and unreported, that could illustrate these features. But among the people touched by Joan's story was contributor Lawrence Hammar, who played a part in her 'rescue' and subsequent return to her village for burial. He has written about her elsewhere, in details never broadcast by media accounts (Hammar 2008, 71–76). One of the editors was also Lawrence's houseguest at the time. So it was Joan's story, more so than any of the others, that happened to be the seed for this book.[1]

We have tried to make this collection accessible to any curious reader. International discourse on AIDS, despite its conventions, comprises many dialects, and our authors speak from their different areas of expertise—in law, community work, medicine, consultancy, anthropology, development practice, international relations and so on—but we have edited to minimise dialectal differences. We also hope the book can communicate to those unfamiliar with PNG and the Pacific, but note that it was written within the context of Papua New Guinea's relationship with Australia and speaks to certain parochial

---

1　Several stories that, like Joan's, conjoin HIV and civic insecurity are referred to in chapter one and figure in chapters throughout the book, including Luker this volume, conclusion.

concerns. For a long time, PNG's largest source of aid has been its former colonial administrator, Australia, and PNG's HIV and 'law and order' predicaments have loomed large in Australia's perceptions of and policies towards PNG. This collection contributes to reflection on these interests.

The literature on conflict, violence, crime and regulation in PNG encompasses ethnographies of traditional rural and to a lesser extent urban societies; historical and legal studies of colonial law; and research undertaken to inform policy for the young nation of PNG in the areas of law and justice, development and economics.[2] As discussed in chapter one, concerns about PNG's law and order problems date from the years before PNG attained independence in 1975 and have intensified since then. A popular 'law and order' discourse is loaded with fears and linked to a large body of academic and policy-related literature.

The popular discourse on HIV is similarly loaded, but the academic and policy-related literature is less developed. A decade ago, despite longstanding interests of anthropologists in marital and sexual practices, the social roles of men and women, indigenous therapeutics and culturally specific theories of disease, relatively little research had addressed sexuality, gender or indigenous perceptions with respect to HIV—though many people had been deeply apprehensive about the possibility of a severe HIV epidemic in PNG even before the nation's first case of AIDS was notified in 1987. Several authors in this volume contributed significantly to the earliest research and commentary on HIV in PNG, most notably the late Carol Jenkins and (the still kicking) Lawrence Hammar.[3] Over the last decade, although the literature has broadened and deepened,[4] the need for a research base to underpin HIV policy in PNG continues to be acute.

Internationally, the last ten years could also be dubbed the decade of security and the decade of AIDS, since both have been major global preoccupations. Frequently alarms about each have been conflated, and researchers have cast and recast HIV as a security issue (see Luker and Dinnen this volume; O'Keefe this volume). While this collection resonates with these wider concerns, its origins are more specific. In PNG, the discourses on HIV and 'law and order' have been highly pronounced yet, though often superficially enmeshed, they remain somehow intellectually separate. In ordeals such as Joan's, however,

---

2   For useful discussions, see Dinnen 2001, 11–39; Dinnen 2009; Goddard 2009.

3   Jenkins' large output includes NSRRT and Jenkins 1994; Jenkins 1994; 1996a; 1996b; 1996c; Jenkins and Passey 1998. Hammar's includes Hammar 1992; 1996; 1998a; 1998b, 1998c; 1999.

4   For a listing of recent HIV research, and a discussion of items published in 2007–2008, see King and Lupiwa (n.d). Special mention should be made of Caldwell 2000; CIE 2002; Hammar 2004; HEMIS 2006; Jenkins and Buchanan-Aruwafu 2007; Dundon and Wilde 2007; Butt and Eves 2008; Spingler 2009; CAP 2009; Hammar 2010.

realities to which these discourses refer converge, and this convergence seemed to call for some more dedicated attempt to explore the themes of HIV and 'law and order' within the same big frame.

Readers should be aware that this book deals with sex and violence. The sexual transmission of HIV, in circumstances frequently involving or shaped by violence, and the violent response that HIV and AIDS can provoke, are central to it. Parts of the book are distressing. Chapters by Carol Jenkins, Joachim Pantumari and Peter Bamne, and Nicole Haley quote extensively from informants whose testimony can be disturbing. Overarching the whole volume are also issues about the risks of depicting sex and violence in a manner that can have the unintended effect of confirming negative stereotypes. Moreover, while it is common to hear workers within the internationally-funded AIDS response lament the reluctance of people in many host societies to talk about sex (and authors and informants within this collection attest to specific difficulties), it is less often admitted that the values, politics and decorum of the international response also make some aspects of sex and sexuality difficult to articulate or acknowledge. Finally, most people everywhere have some sense of what is in the range of social acceptability for talk on certain topics in any given setting. Some of the sexual subject matter here has been translated from a circumscribed context of communication into the public domain of this book, and will jar with the sense of many readers of what is publicly appropriate to say. Similar problems beset the discussion of violence. As Kathy Lepani has suggested, in some contexts, discussing violence is 'voicing the unspeakable' (Lepani 2005).

The book ahead falls into six parts that move from scene-setting; to masculinity; to sex work; to specific law and justice institutions; to meditations on governance, rights and security; and end with our conclusion and epilogue.

Part one, chapter one, establishes a context for the volume as a whole. Titled 'Entwined endemics' (we often use the term 'endemic' in preference to 'epidemic', as we explain), it surveys HIV in PNG and the country's 'law and order' problems, broadly discussing the roles of the state, community, and their interface in the governance of security. It then sketches the interaction between HIV and 'law and order', and the potential of a public health approach to improve the governance of security while 'law and order' measures may help prevent and manage HIV. Although, in theory, the state has a primary responsibility to ensure the security and welfare of its citizens, in PNG this responsibility is perhaps better recast as a question: how can the state best *promote* or *facilitate* civic security, especially in circumstances where its power is weak and the state is only one of many actors? We see one possible means in models of community governance, in effect a new civics, which later chapters and the conclusion will further explore.

Part two addresses masculinity. In AIDS research and policy circles, it is axiomatic that 'gender inequality' in countries such as PNG drives the predominantly heterosexual transmission of HIV and unevenly distributes the burdens of AIDS. Within these circles, 'gender inequality' is also widely understood as both expressed and effected, in large part, by 'gender violence', which in turn helps spread the virus. Such statements routinely highlight women and girls as those who suffer disadvantage and harm. Only recently have boys and men received more searching attention. Chapters two and three contribute to this re-visioning of men in the context of PNG's HIV and 'law and order' endemics.

The need to involve men in changing masculine norms is Richard Eves' central message in chapter two. He traces the links between masculinity, gender-based violence and the spread of HIV and, drawing on international literature and PNG-based studies of gender and violence (including his own body of academic and applied anthropological research), reviews recent efforts to rescript masculinity. In PNG these include initiatives that use Australian rugby-league icons to promote HIV awareness and demote, so to speak, violence against women. Eves advocates better programs for 'other ways of being men'—programs that enlist boys and men positively as partners in problem-solving. Eves stresses that gender is a key analytic for responding to HIV, but efforts stall if our thinking stops at 'women's vulnerability' or 'the empowerment of women', as if men are beyond reach and incapable of participation and change.

The *raskol*, or lawless young man in groups with other *raskols*, is probably *the* symbol of PNG's 'law and order' problem. *Raskols* also figure, less directly, in anxieties about the transmission of HIV, in part due to their association with pack-rape or *lainap*, in part because they belong to 'youth', a target population for HIV prevention. In chapter three, Vicki Luker and Michael Monsell-Davis review social changes relating to young men and tease out the tangle of associations that link *raskols*, crime, violence, youth and HIV. Without denying the importance of responding to *raskolism* and the plight of both male and female youth, they ask whether this tangle of associations can distract attention from other factors that need attention in relation to crime and HIV, including the role of transactional sex (in its broadest sense) and patterns of concurrency; 'white collar' crime and corruption; and older men.

Part three's interlocking themes are the legal status of prostitution in PNG, the policing of sex work, and the character of transactional sex within the diffuse dynamics of sexual networking. Internationally, 'sex work' is a fundamental domain of HIV prevention where improvements to policing practices and the legal status of this work may limit the spread of HIV and enhance the welfare of all parties (primarily sex workers, clients and police). Yet such agenda are complicated in PNG.

Lawrence Hammar's chapter four highlights certain basic complications. One is the dynamism of sexual networking, another is the pervasive and polymorphous transactional character of sexual relations. As editors we note that, in countries such as Thailand and Cambodia where HIV interventions in the sex industry have reported success, sex work is, by way of contrast, differentiated and formalised to a higher degree than in PNG. Hammar favours decriminalising prostitution, but argues against proposals for state regulation on grounds that in PNG capacity is lacking for any such initiatives to deliver public health benefits, while the 'regulated' women would only be subjected to further abuse. Data on sexual health and behaviour for this chapter were gathered at Lae, Daru, Port Moresby and the Southern Highlands Province by Hammar and colleagues at the PNG Institute of Medical Research from 2003-2006.

In chapter five, Karen Fletcher and Bomal Gonapa, both lawyers, discuss decriminalising prostitution. As demonstrated in the Three-Mile Guesthouse Raid in Port Moresby in 2004, when police rounded up 40 women and accused them of prostitution and spreading HIV, the persecution and criminalisation of 'prostitutes' create conditions that thwart HIV prevention efforts. The PNG National AIDS Council engaged Fletcher and Gonapa to research decriminalisation and here they address the provisions in the Summary Offences Act (1977); the 2002 amendments to the Criminal Code concerning the sexual exploitation of children and prostitution; and possible legal amendments to ensure that condoms are not taken as evidence of prostitution. While Fletcher and Gonapa strongly argue that decriminalisation would make certain preventive measures easier, they also indicate the legal intricacies, wider difficulties and inherent limitations of success. On the question of regulation the authors could come to no agreed position, while proposals to decriminalise prostitution remain contentious in PNG. NAC has announced that draft changes to legislation governing both sex work and homosexuality are ready for discussion in 2010.

The final chapter in this part, by Carol Jenkins, describes the component of PNG's pioneering Transex Project from 1994 to 1998 that specifically aimed to prevent HIV transmission by changing the way police treat sex workers. This was internationally innovative work, subsequently adopted by UNAIDS for its best practice collection (Jenkins 2000). Police and sections of the private security industry cooperated with the project because AIDS was already understood as an occupational health issue. Jenkins reports some success from interventions, measured in subsequently higher rates of condom usage, lower rates of *lainap* (pack rape) and some signs that the sex-workers involved were now prepared to take action against police mistreatment. But this chapter must be read alongside others in this collection, including the next chapter which suggests that these reported gains were temporary and, incidentally, that the promotion of 'safe sex' may inadvertently condone sexual violence (so long as condoms are used).

Part four looks more closely inside the police force, prisons and army, and considers their capacity to change from within in response to HIV.

Abby Macleod and Martha Macintyre in chapter seven, discuss the potential of the Royal Papua New Guinea Constabulary (RPNGC) to affect the spread and management of HIV both positively and negatively. They use a wider lens than Jenkins, and draw upon their work as RPNGC gender advisors to reflect on broader factors influencing police attitudes and behaviour. These include police working conditions, public expectations, and the values that police share with the general populace. The authors note that on some questions of violence and gender, these values are far from those enshrined in PNG's constitution or promoted by global rights discourse. While police generally know the laws they are required to enforce, are acquainted with principles of human rights, and have basic understanding of AIDS, translating awareness into change is a challenging and long-term undertaking that must also recognise practicalities and how analytic frames from outside often poorly 'fit'.

Prisons everywhere can be sites for the effective transmission of disease. In chapter eight, Sinclair Dinnen reviews PNG's prison system while Greg Law outlines the main modes for potentially spreading HIV within PNG's prison populations: tattooing, skin cutting (often involving circumcision or other forms of penile modification), and unprotected sexual intercourse. Greg Law speaks from his role as a visiting medical officer to Beon Prison outside Madang and from long health experience in PNG, including work for the National HIV/AIDS Support Program. As editors we note that the challenge of tackling HIV in PNG's prisons must be seen beside the range of other challenges and the generally dire state of health conditions for prisoners in the sector overall. An ambitious program of prison rebuilding and reform is currently under way. On the bright side, the highly efficient mode of HIV transmission mostly responsible for the spread of HIV among prisoners in many parts of the world— that is, injecting drug use with contaminated equipment—has not so far been a factor in PNG's prisons or the country at large.

Armies too have received special attention in international literature about AIDS and security. Soldiers can be prone to HIV infection, the circumstances of their work can sometimes favour their role in widely disseminating HIV, and the effects of HIV and AIDS can severely erode defence capacity. The authors of chapter nine, Joachim Pantumari and Peter Bamne, are medical doctors with jointly wide experience in health, military practice, and PNG's response to HIV. They discuss risk factors for HIV transmission within the PNG Defence Force and how informants perceive them. Working and living conditions for service personnel foster practices and ideals of masculinity that could interact harmfully with HIV, but Pantumari's and Bamne's informants, like police in previous chapters, express values widely held in PNG. Nevertheless, the authors note that some men are clearly ambivalent about certain masculine norms, while the army has in many ways responded admirably to HIV. As editors, we appreciate the testimony in this chapter from army wives, who speak of concerns, responsibilities and difficulties that many women must share.

Should organisations like police, prisons and armies adapt their core business to HIV prevention and mitigation? Can they? Consultant Ian Patrick broaches these questions in chapter ten on mainstreaming. This approach is endorsed by PNG's National AIDS Council, advanced by AusAID and advocated by UNAIDS. Against best practice principles, Patrick assesses HIV measures taken within two larger AusAID-funded projects with police and prisons. These measures were not designed as mainstreaming projects, yet Patrick demonstrates what, ideally, mainstreaming would involve and also the enduring challenges to this approach. One is the basic capacity of the institution concerned. Another is the competition of multiple needs for prioritisation by management. Moreover, an agency's leadership must move beyond basic AIDS awareness to an analytical appreciation of the role their agency plays or could play in the larger field of HIV. Patrick notes a tendency for attention to HIV to wax or wane in tandem with donor assistance.

Part five further explores broader themes in governance, rights and security. Nicole Haley's chapter eleven is set in the Southern Highlands Province around Lake Kopiago, where AIDS is experienced in and through the breakdown of state and community governance. The torture and killing of alleged witches or sorcerers is both a symptom and a factor of this breakdown—and an issue of mounting concern in PNG. In response to an apparent upswing in sorcery accusations, the nation's sorcery laws are currently under review. As Haley explains, mortality caused by AIDS, because death strikes adults in the prime of life, lends itself to explanations in terms of witchcraft beliefs. Paradoxically, while resource exploitation in the Southern Highlands Province is a major source of national income for PNG, the province itself scores among PNG's lowest by standard indices of development. This chapter demonstrates the potentially vicious spiral of PNG's entwined HIV and 'law and order' endemics, compounded by maldevelopment and malgovernance.

The next chapter offers a counterpoint to Haley's: it instances potentially 'virtuous circles'. John Cartwright, Madeleine Jenneker and Clifford Shearing give more detail on the Zwelethemba model of community governance introduced in chapter one, while Isaac Wai and Paul Maia describe the evolution of a loosely similar project for peace-building and community improvement in the Port Moresby settlement of Saraga. It is one of many examples of local ingenuity and resourcefulness in PNG that receive too little recognition. While both the Zwelethemba and Saraga initiatives primarily respond to community needs for better security and development, the peace dividend in each case promises health benefits: social environments that reduce the risks of disease, and enhanced capacity to respond to specific health and other needs. Sinclair Dinnen's opening remarks relate both case-studies to themes in this book and directions in development policy.

Christine Stewart, who drafted PNG's HIV/AIDS Management and Protection (HAMP) Act, addresses the role of law reform in the response to HIV. Although Fletcher and Gonapa tackled this in relation to PNG's prostitution laws, Stewart's terms of reference also include the legal status of homosexuality, abortion, rape of men, marital rape, sexual offences against children, the trafficking of children, and specific provisions of the HAMP Act. Stewart also notes how the 'enabling' and 'rights-based' approaches that inform the HAMP Act remain incompatible with much popular opinion that still favours repressive measures. Notwithstanding this and other factors that limit the influence of law, Stewart stresses the role it can play in shaping society and social action. Like Fletcher and Gonapa, she endorses the important if constrained contribution that law reform can make to the prevention and management of HIV.

Elizabeth Reid, in chapter fourteen, also argues for an HIV response that fosters human rights. She advocates however, an activism of praise, a focus on community, and an orientation towards the future. This approach contrasts to the more usual, but often counterproductive, global rights activism that tends to be state-focused, retrospective, and legalistic, while employing tactics of shame and condemnation. Through the methodology of community conversations, which she uses in PNG, speakers and listeners come to appreciate the challenges posed by HIV, know their collective resources, and acquire skills for change. Participants also become aware of structural violence: the larger and longer-term dynamics that shape gender relations and behaviour capable of transmitting HIV and worsening the impacts of AIDS. Such knowledge, Reid believes, can release the human capacity for goodness and banish from the minds of some people, especially outsiders, essentially ignorant tendencies to dismiss 'Others' as simply 'violent'.

The final chapter, by Michael O'Keefe, rehearses HIV in PNG through various security scenarios. He demonstrates the difference between traditional concepts of security centred on the state, its military power and its capacity to maintain borders and sovereignty, with more recent definitions that emphasise human security: people's welfare and survival. O'Keefe shows how, over the last few years, crude international anxieties about the threat of HIV to security in traditional senses of the word have been revised and complicated in the light of unfolding events; and though he warns against tendencies to 'Africanise' the Pacific and specifically PNG's experience with HIV, literature and data concerning the securitisation of AIDS in Africa provides an inevitable context.

O'Keefe argues that HIV in PNG primarily poses a threat to human security. While this does have implications for state governance, the greater potential damage is to the social fabric on which the state rests.

Our conclusion returns to Joan's story and the concept of civic security. The epilogue, 'Ela's question', illustrates the need, stressed in Reid's earlier chapter, to appreciate the larger processes and patterns of constraint that shape people's lives, perceptions of possibility, and choices. It also underscores the need for a 'whole of governance approach' to the challenges addressed in this volume.

References

Butt, Leslie and Richard Eves, eds. 2008. *Making Sense of AIDS: Culture, Sexuality, and Power in Melanesia*. Honolulu: University of Hawai'i Press.

Caldwell, John C. 2000. AIDS in Melanesia. Paper commissioned by AusAID. Available www.ausaid.gov.au

CAP (Commission on AIDS in the Pacific). 2009. *Turning the Tide: An OPEN Strategy for a Response to AIDS in the Pacific*. Suva: Commission on AIDS in the Pacific.

CIE (Centre for International Economics). 2002. *Potential Economic Impacts of an HIV/AIDS Epidemic in Papua and New Guinea*. Report prepared for AusAID. Available http://www.ausaid.gov.au (accessed 27 April 2010).

Dinnen, Sinclair. 2001. *Law and Order in a Weak State: Crime and Politics in Papua New Guinea*. Honolulu: University of Hawai'i Press.

Dinnen, Sinclair. 2009. Thirty Years of Law and Order Policy and Practice: 'Trying to Do too Much, too Badly, with too Little'? In *Policy Making and Implementation: Studies for Papua New Guinea*, ed. R. J. May, 233–260. Canberra: ANU E Press.

Dundon, Alison and Charles Wilde (guest editors). 2007. HIV and AIDS in Rural Papua New Guinea. Special issue, *Oceania*, 77: 1.

Goddard, Michael. 2009. *Substantial Justice: An Anthropology of Village Courts in Papua New Guinea*. New York and Oxford: Berghahn Books.

Hammar, Lawrence. 1992. Sexual Transactions on Daru: With Some Observations on the Ethnographic Enterprise. *Research in Melanesia* 16: 21–54.

Hammar, Lawrence. 1996. Bad Canoes and *Bafalo*: The Political Economy of Sex on Daru Island, Western Province, Papua New Guinea. *Genders* 23: 212–243.

Hammar, Lawrence. 1998a. AIDS, STDs, and Sex Work in Papua New Guinea. In *Modern Papua New Guinea*, ed. L. Zimmer-Tamakoshi, 257–296. Kirksville, MO: Thomas Jefferson University Press.

Hammar, Lawrence. 1998b. Sex Industries and Sexual Networking in Papua New Guinea: Public Health Risks and Implications. *Pacific Health Dialog*, 5 (1): 7–53.

Hammar, L. 1999. Staking out the Middle Range between Macro- and Micro-Disease in the Social Structure. *Pacific Health Dialog* 6 (1): 112–121.

Hammar, Lawrence (guest editor). 2004. Focus Issue on Sexual Health. *Papua New Guinea Medical Journal*, 47 (1–2).

Hammar, Lawrence. 2008. Fear and Loathing in Papua New Guinea: Sexual Health in a Nation under Siege. In *Making Sense of AIDS: Culture, Sexuality, and Power in Melanesia*, ed. Leslie Butt and Richard Eves, 60–79. Honolulu: University of Hawai'i Press.

Hammar, Lawrence. 2010. *Sin, Sex and Stigma: A Pacific Response to HIV and AIDS*, Wantage: Sean Kingston Publishing.

HEMIS (HIV Epidemiological Modelling Impact Study). 2006. Impacts of HIV/AIDS 2005–2025 in Papua New Guinea, Indonesia and East Timor: Final Report of the HIV Epidemiological Modelling Impact Study February 2006. Canberra: AusAID.

Jenkins, Carol. 1994. An Epidemic with a Future? *Pacific AIDS Alert Bulletin*, 8, 11.

Jenkins, Carol (guest editor). 1996a. Focus Issue on HIV and AIDS. *Papua New Guinea Medical Journal*, 39 (3).

Jenkins, Carol L. 1996c. The Homosexual Context of Heterosexual Practice in Papua New Guinea. In *Bisexualities and AIDS: International Perspectives*, ed. Peter Aggleton, 191–206.

Jenkins, Carol. 2000a. HIV, Development and Unhealthy Institutions. *Development Bulletin* 52, 12–13.

Jenkins, Carol. 2000b. Female Sex Worker HIV Prevention Projects: Lessons Learnt from Papua New Guinea, India and Bangadesh. UNAIDS Best Practice Collection. Geneva UNAIDS.

Jenkins, Carol. 2002. *Situation Analysis of HIV/AIDS in Papua New Guinea*. September 2002. Global Fund Proposal.

Jenkins, Carol. 2005. *HIV/AIDS in the Pacific*. Manila: Asian Development Bank.

Jenkins, Carol and Michael Alpers. 1996b. Urbanization, Youth and Sexuality: Insights for an AIDS Campaign for Youth in Papua New Guinea. *Papua New Guinea Medical Journal*, 39 (3): 248–251.

Jenkins, Carol and Holly Buchanan-Aruwafu. 2007. *Cultures and Contexts Matter: Understanding and Preventing HIV in the Pacific*. Manila: Asian Development Bank.

Jenkins, Carol and Megan Passey. 1998. Papua New Guinea. In *Sexually Transmitted Diseases in Asia and the Pacific*, ed. T. Brown, R. Chan, D. Mugrditchian, B. Mulhall, D. Plummer, R. Sarda, and W. Sittitrai, 230–354. Armidale: Venereology Publishing.

King, Evelyn and Tony Lupiwa. (n.d.). *A Systematic Literature Review of HIV and AIDS Research in Papua New Guinea 2007–2008*. Available National AIDS Council of PNG, www.nacs.org.pg

Lepani, Katherine. 2005. Voicing the Unspeakable: How to Articulate the Realities of Violence in HIV Awareness and Prevention. Paper presented to forum 'Reproductive Health and HIV/AIDS in Papua New Guinea', hosted by Australian Reproductive Health Alliance, Canberra, Australian National Botanical Gardens, 13 October 2005.

NSRRT (National Sex and Reproductive Knowledge Research Team) and Jenkins, C. 1994. *National Study of Sexual and Reproductive Knowledge and Behaviour in Papua New Guinea*. Goroka: Papua New Guinea Institute of Medical Research.

Spingler, Hermann, ed. 2009. AIDS: Belief and Culture in Papua New Guinea. Special Issue of *Catalyst: Social Pastoral Journal for Melanesia*, 39 (2).

1. Entwined Endemics: HIV and 'Law and Order'

VICKI LUKER AND SINCLAIR DINNEN

Papua New Guinea has two entwined endemics: a complex 'law and order' problem and entrenched HIV. Each has serious implications for the nation's future. Together they pose joint challenges and joint opportunities, most fundamentally for efforts to realise 'civic security' that may confer some immunity to both.

This chapter surveys HIV and 'law and order' in PNG. It scopes broader dynamics in the governance of security, and the contributory roles of state, community, and their interface. It highlights how synergies of HIV and 'law and order' can create vicious spirals or virtuous circles. The potentials of a public health approach for improving the governance of security and of 'law and order' measures for helping prevent and manage HIV are also stressed. While in theory the state is primarily responsible for the security of its citizens, in PNG we suggest that it may be more fruitful to ask: how can this young, postcolonial state best *promote* or *facilitate* civic security? We see one possible means in models of community governance.

HIV in PNG: Epidemic, Epidemics, Endemic?

HIV contributes to Papua New Guinea's difficult mix of challenges for health and development. In mid-2010, PNG was home to roughly 6.7 million people (SPC 2010), speaking some 800 languages and living mostly in small, dispersed communities, heavily dependent on a mix of cash-cropping and subsistence activities. About 85 percent of the population is classed as 'rural' (NSO 2003). On the United Nations' human development index, PNG ranks 145 out of 177 listed countries and is the least developed of the Pacific Island states and territories (UNDP 2008). Despite PNG's great wealth of natural resources, the gulf between 'haves' and 'have nots' is wide and widening; and much of PNG's population is poor, and growing poorer (see Bourke 2008; Haley this volume). Roads and government services have deteriorated. About 40 percent of men and 50 percent of women are illiterate (PNG 2003, 52). Life expectancy at birth is the lowest in the Pacific: 54 years (SPC 2008).

PNG's first notified case of AIDS was in 1987: a policeman who had been serving in Bougainville; his wife and child were subsequently found to have HIV too (Pantumari, pers. comm.). But the virus was probably in PNG before that date (CAP 2009, 22) and in the 1990s spread rapidly (UN 1996, 13). HIV nevertheless remains difficult to track or quantify because surveillance, while improving, is still weak (NACS 2008, 75–77). At the end of 2008, cumulative notifications numbered 28,294 and estimates of prevalence, as this volume goes to press, seem to range between 1.5 percent and the projected figure of roughly 3 percent for 2010 (CAP 2009, 20; UNAIDS 2009a; NACS and NDoH 2007, 25), though some informed observers 'feel' this range, particularly the bottom end, is too low (Reid 2009).[1] Whereas injecting drug use (IDU) and sex between men are important means of HIV transmission in many south east Asian nations and in Australia and New Zealand, IDU is negligible in PNG, while sex between men seems to play a small, but perhaps underestimated role (see Luker with Monsell-Davis, this volume).[2] The main mode of transmission is heterosexual, with secondary transmission from mother to child. For ages 2-29 years, cumulative notifications are higher for females than males and Papua New Guinea is experiencing the 'feminisation' of HIV and AIDS—with respect both to transmission and impacts (CAP 2009, 22; NACS 2008, 21; UNAIDS 2008, 168-169).

HIV is also believed to be ruralising.[3] AIDS has always been most noticed in the National Capital District, other urban centres, along transport routes such as the Highlands Highway and, more recently, in the vicinity of development enclaves (see Map 1). But in 2007, for the first time, rural HIV prevalence was estimated to have surpassed urban and very high prevalence has been found in some localities—for instance, 40 percent of 15–45 year olds sampled from Tari in the Southern Highlands (NACS 2008, 19–20; Anon. 2006; WB 2007, 85, 86; see Haley this volume). This ruralisation and feminisation pose a double challenge for the response to HIV—of reaching the most disadvantaged members of what are many of the most disadvantaged communities in PNG.

---

1   At the time of going to press, the results of PNG's recent national demographic and health survey were not yet published.

2   See Jenkins 1996; NACS and NDoH 2007, 18. Molecular epidemiology has found the predominant subtype of HIV in PNG is most closely related to East African strains (CAP 2009, 22) and correlated with heterosexual transmission.

3   Studies that have deepened understanding of the cultural dimensions of rural HIV in PNG include Dundon and Wilde 2007; Butt and Eves 2008; Spingler 2009.

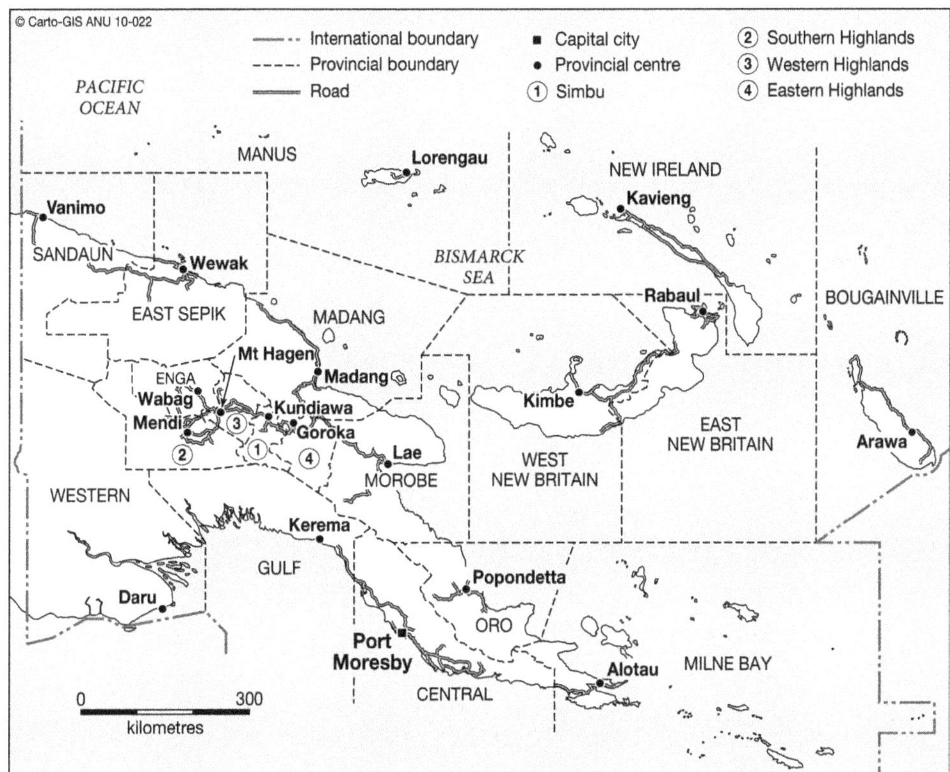

Map 1: Papua New Guinea. By Karina Pelling, Coombs Cartography, College of Asia and the Pacific, Australian National University, Canberra, Australia.

Among the conditions favouring the spread of HIV is PNG's predominantly youthful and rapidly growing population, poor and in many parts of the country deteriorating health services, and the co-presence of other sexually transmitted infections that can assist transmission. As several chapters in this collection indicate, high levels of rape and sexual abuse, domestic violence, and multiple sexual partners have contributed to HIV's spread. The relationships between development and HIV are complex. Sizeable urban populations and uneven development, conducing to migration, social stress, widening disparities along axes of location, class and sex, and the commodification of female sexuality (HELP 2005) have shaped environments and patterns of human interaction in which the risk of infection is heightened (PNG 2006, 10).

PNG has been routinely described as experiencing a 'generalised' epidemic, meaning that prevalence has reached or exceeded 1 percent and HIV has spread beyond so-called high-risk groups and settings. In the wider Asia-Pacific, PNG is one of only two nations currently so classified. (The other is Thailand, but its estimated prevalence is marginally lower than PNG's (UNAIDS 2009b, 37; UNAIDS 2009b)). Among the member states and territories of the South Pacific

Community, PNG accounts for 95 percent of the total reported cases of HIV and AIDS (see Graph 1). Among PNG's neighbours, the Indonesian province of Papua, comprising the western half of island of New Guinea, comes closest to PNG in the scale and prevalence of HIV (see Map 2). In 2006, among a population of roughly two million, prevalence was calculated to be 2.4 percent (SI and MoH 2007, i), perhaps 15 times higher than Indonesia's national average (UNAIDS 2009c, 38).[4]

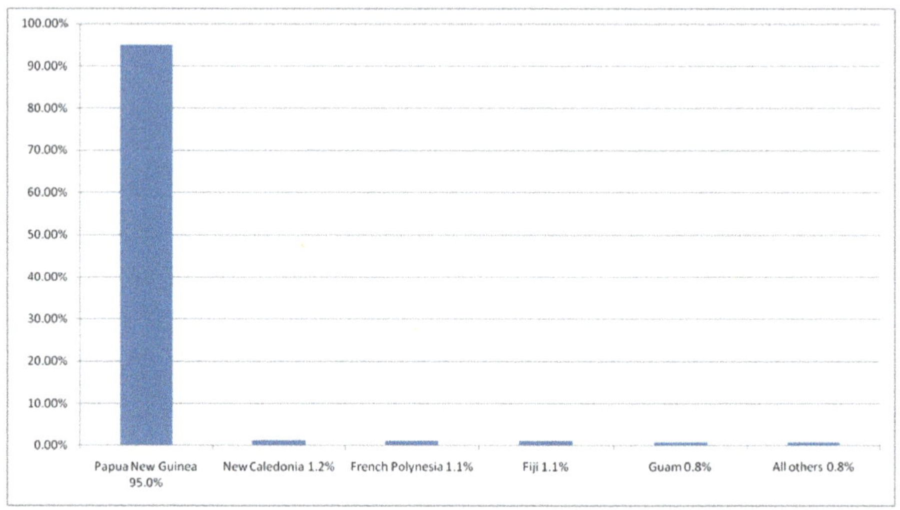

Graph 1: Proportion of all HIV and AIDS cases in different Pacific island countries and territories, 1984–2007. Source: UNAIDS, *AIDS Epidemic Update*, December 2009. Geneva: UNAIDS, 77.

But is 'generalised epidemic' the best description? As indicated above, while PNG's national epidemic may be described as 'generalised', subnationally it has 'concentrated' and 'micro' epidemics within certain networks and locales. Some connotations of the word 'epidemic' can be misleading too. Consider speed and infectiousness, two qualities often implied. Epidemic HIV however, unlike for instance epidemic influenza, is not so easily passed from one person to another and is even less infectious than most common STIs. Consider transience. Unlike, say, the 1918-19 'flu, which swept across the globe in several rolling waves and then completely petered out, HIV is now deeply rooted in the world and in PNG, embedded in the very means by which humans reproduce. Finally, 'epidemic' triggers fight or flight. This reaction can be useful in the immediate response to HIV, but we also need to tackle HIV's 'non-epidemic' qualities, to prevent and mitigate, in the very long term, a disease that is difficult to dislodge.

---

4   Sadly, few studies have considered HIV in the Indonesian province of Papua and the nation of PNG together. One is Butt et al., 2004.

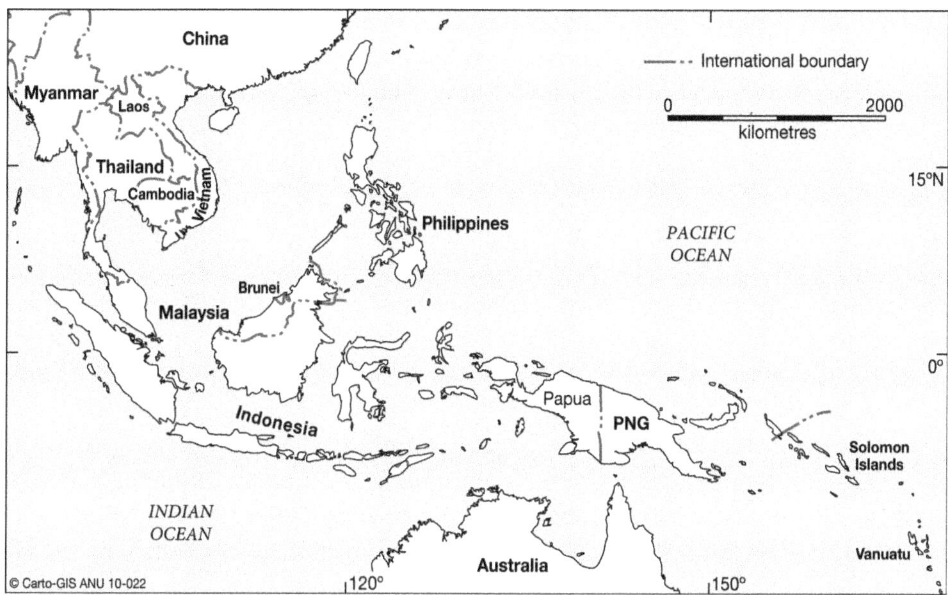

Map 2: Papua New Guinea and the Region. By Karina Pelling, Coombs Cartography, College of Asia and the Pacific, Australian National University, Canberra, Australia.

Some researchers have tried to epitomise the non-epidemic characteristics of HIV in new metaphors. Barnett and Whiteside have described HIV as a 'long wave' and 'multi-wave' event (Barnett and Whiteside 2002). De Waal has pictured it as a structural and structuring component of our social and biological evolution (de Waal 2005). But a catchy formulation that counters some of the misleading connotations of 'epidemic' seems elusive. In this book, though the conventional parlance of 'epidemic' is used, as editors we prefer, following Barnett, to describe PNG as experiencing an 'HIV endemic' (Barnett 2008). This reminds us that HIV is here to stay, at least for the foreseeable future.

Several studies have modelled the medium- and longer-term social and economic impacts of AIDS on PNG (e.g., CIE 2002; Hauquitz 2004; HEMIS 2006). These studies depend on underlying projections of AIDS-related morbidity and mortality, in turn dependent on calculations of HIV prevalence. According to recent projections, HIV will stabilise around the year 2012 at a prevalence of 5.07 percent (Hayes 2007). While certain impacts on the formal sector—on hospital beds, gross domestic product, salaried labour force and so forth—can be relatively easily calculated, the harshest damage affects individuals, households, and the informal sector, with repercussions for possibly generations. This damage is difficult to track and quantify (Barnett and Whiteside 2002, 182–195). Indeed, some of the human costs of AIDS—such as grief, or a parent's love that orphans may never know—are unquantifiable.

The national response to HIV has many achievements (Ballard and Malau 2009; WB 2008, 96–106). These include the formation of the National AIDS Council and a network of Provincial AIDS Committees, a series of public education campaigns, national strategic planning and policy development, workplace reforms, and the passage of the HIV/AIDS Management and Prevention Act in 2003. In recent years, the contribution of churches, non-government organisations (NGOs) and the private sector—through such bodies as the PNG Business Coalition Against HIV and AIDS (BAHA)—has strengthened (see, e.g., ADB 2008, 14–29), as has leadership at national and subnational levels of government. Since 2004, care and treatment services have also rapidly extended, and at the end of 2007, close to 35 percent of people who need antiretroviral therapy were estimated to be receiving it (NACS 2008, 11–13, 39). Great weaknesses in the response remain, some indicated by recent scandals engulfing the National AIDS Council Secretariat and in reasons for the Global Fund's rejection, in 2009, of PNG's application for continued financial assistance (Fox 2009). Nonetheless many recent initiatives appear to have answered to the call 'for renewed energies and directions to contain a fast spreading epidemic', guided by 'the rights of all PNG citizens, as enshrined in the national constitution' (PNG 2004, ix, 3; PNG 2006, 1, 3).

Finally, this short survey of HIV in PNG would be incomplete without some reflection on the term itself. As many readers will know, since 2006 UNAIDS has discouraged the usage 'HIV/AIDS' (UNAIDS 2006). Either 'HIV' or 'HIV and AIDS' are preferred. With some regret, this volume uses HIV very elastically, depending on context, to refer to: stages 1–3 of HIV disease; stages 1–4 (that is, including AIDS) (WHO 2007); the HIV endemic; the broader historical, social, cultural, and political phenomenon centred on HIV and AIDS; and finally, to imply specific issues associated with the progress of the disease through individuals and collectivities. But the retention of 'HIV/AIDS' is warranted in some contexts.

'Law and Order'

At the heart of the phrase 'law and order' is a concept of 'civic security'—that is, the safety and liberty of citizens in a modern nation-state. As the preamble of the PNG constitution proclaims, all citizens are entitled to 'life, liberty, security of person and the protection of the law…' (quoted in Brunton and Colquhoun-Kerr 1984, 24). In principle, civic security remains first and foremost a responsibility of the state and its various agencies of law and justice. The police are accorded a central role in the deterrence and detection of crimes or, as the constitution puts it, in the preservation of 'peace and good order'.

Yet the reality for most PNG citizens is very different. Formal law and justice resources are concentrated in the urban centres and suffer from a chronic lack of capacity. For nearly everyone, and especially the rural majority, challenges of personal security are more likely to be mediated through an individual's membership of an extended family, sub-clan or other local association rather than through citizenship in the state.

In this collection, we use the term 'law and order' broadly to implicate the full range of conditions and factors that affect, or are seen to affect, civic security, including: 1) criminal acts and violence (particularly sexual violence); 2) state law (as provided in written laws and judicial precedents); 3) the 'arms of the law'—that is, the institutional enforcers and interpreters of state law, notably the police and other uniformed services, courts and prisons; 4) myriad methods of informal community-based social regulation, including customary law and community norms whose authority is not derived primarily from the state, and that prevail at local levels throughout PNG.

Papua New Guinea's 'law and order' difficulties were noted before Independence in 1975 (Nelson 2000; Levantis 2000b, 134–5). Since then they have grown. Alphonse Gelu voices a number of common, current perceptions: that rising rates of crime and violence in both urban and rural settings threaten the democratic process, prey on lawful business, cause health and other services in parts of the country to shut down, subject women and girls to sickening abuse, and defy church and government countermeasures (Gelu 2003, 46). These anxieties are amply aired in the local press. Recent national surveys attest to widespread concerns about personal safety, crime, corruption and violence while a signficant proportion of informants have also been victims. Women more often report and fear intimate and sexual violence, but men are prone to other forms of assault (PNG JAG, 32; see also Sims 2004; Hukula 1999, 19). At a recent symposium on 'Culture and Violence' in Madang, Powes Parkop, governor of the National Capital District, complained that violence 'is like a cancer destroying our nation and retarding our social and economic progress' (Anon. 2009a). Port Moresby is repeatedly classed as one of the world's unsafest cities (though recent data suggest that it is not the worst in PNG (PNG JAG 2008,17)) and, like Parkop, many outside commentators identify PNG's law and order problems as major impediments to development (see Levantis 2000a, 13; Windybank and Manning 2003; Hughes 2004: White and Wainwright 2004).

Discussing 'violence', 'corruption' and 'lawlessness' in PNG, whether from inside or outside, is beset by difficulties, dangers and distortion, to which the introduction and several chapters allude. But these pitfalls do not alter the fact that PNG indeed faces great challenges in the governance of security. 'Governance' can be taken to mean the organisations and norms, state and non-state, that collectively regulate social life, and, if the metaphor is not taken too far, it can be helpful to think of governance in PNG by analogy with an hourglass.

The top half of the hourglass is the state. PNG's state is less than 40 years old. It was built on the spare skeleton of a colonial administration largely—but rapidly and minimally—fashioned after World War II. Many people in PNG today are little touched by the state; they live beyond its geographic reach. Where the state does operate, dysfunction is common. While PNG has the usual panoply of state law and state agencies, many ideals and attributes associated with the Western-cum-liberal state in countries with longer traditions of statehood (by which criteria, of course, many older states also fall short), do not altogether apply. These include the state's spatial permeation of the nation; state capacity to fulfill crucial responsibilities, such as the rule of law; impersonal bureaucratic principles; and the depersonalised exercise of power (Dinnen 1998, 11–39). (The rich literature on the concept of the Melanesian 'big man', though debated, attests to the vitality and operation, at every political level in PNG, of a contrasting ideal of personalised power (see May 2001)). The constitution, state laws, the bulk of law and justice agencies and the military are to be found in this half of the hourglass.

The bottom half of is 'community'—a tricky word that in PNG as elsewhere can refer to a variety of flexible social configurations (Nelson 2009; Goudsmit 2008; James et al. 2009). For this volume, it applies to people who recognise 'ties that bind' through relations of reciprocity, often embodied and symbolised in common language (*wantoks*), kinship and cultural observations; joint interests in a physical locality; and a sense, in certain contexts, of common interests in survival. While these interests and relations can accommodate much change, diversity, 'insider' manipulation and fission, they can also provide prompts and platforms for people's cooperation—for their coming together to sort things out—and, as PNG's Social Welfare and Development Minister Dame Carol Kidu and others argue, constitute PNG's major social resource (Kidu 2008). The vast majority of everyday disputes, within and between communities, tends to be managed informally through community-based mechanisms.

The narrow waist of the hourglass is the conduit and intermediate zone between the two. For the governance of security, two state institutions are crucial here: police and village courts. The national force of some 5,000 police can be imagined as an arm of state law that reaches down to community. The village court system, currently comprising around 14,000 courts that serve over 90 percent of PNG's villages, was introduced by Australian colonial administration in 1973 but designed in part as an extension of community governance that could reach up and interlock with the national court system and bridge different legal and social worlds. The village court system and police are stressed (see Goddard 2009, esp. 67–71; Dinnen 2006). Similar observations could be made for crucial state institutions at this interface in other areas, such as health (aidposts) and education (schools) (Nelson 2003).

Civil society affiliations can also serve as bridging tissue. In PNG, vertical civil society linkages, as well as those that horizontally knit people from different primary communities of place and kin—through for instance common pastimes, causes, professions, or educational experience—are increasing, but still relatively scarce. An important exception is the churches that, in the language of social capital, often have intensive and extensive, horizontal and vertical networks (Luker 2004; Hauck et al. 2005). Heterogeneous though the churches are, their presence and influence are pervasive. Secular NGOs operating in the intermediate zone include organisations that have abilities to engage with government policy and project a public profile, but many draw their greatest strength from international networks while their roots in communities at large are relatively weak.

Business can act as a state-and-community 'go between' too. The formal business sector in PNG, however, employs only a tiny proportion of the working population (according to 2000 census figures, 10.4 percent (NSO 2003, 56)), and tends to be dominated by very large companies. These can be admirable corporate citizens, engage in dialogue with the state, feature in national media, do important work with their employees and the communities where they operate, and sometimes they constitute 'mini states within the state' by providing services in education, health and security to 'their people'. But again, the bulk of Papua New Guineans remain outside such constituencies.

This metaphor of 'hourglass governance' thus points to the narrowness of the conduit that both joins and separates state and community. It can also be useful to think about the pressures on this slender waist. From the top comes the requirement to observe the principles of law, the values they enshrine, assumptions of how state and citizenry should behave, and operational dictates. From below comes the imperative to meet the expectations and values of local communities, or what Michael Goddard terms 'local sociality' that may variously draw upon ancestral traditions, Christianity and other sources (Goddard 2009, esp. 13–21). From many angles, but probably most powerfully from the side, come the demands of a global discourse on rights, often most vigorously promoted by NGOs, international organisations, and development partners. Global rights discourse harmonises most readily with the underlying Western-cum-liberal morality of the state, but can make common ground with Christian teachings and also with elements of local socialities. Yet in many parts of the world, PNG not excepted, the promotion of rights is often heard as an exogenous Western discourse of criticism (see Macintyre and Macleod this volume; Reid this volume; cf. de Waal, 2003).

Violence is an attribute of many issues featured in this collection, and deserves reflection within this sketch, beginning with some general reflections on violence in the modern state according to Western, liberal ideals. In Weberian theory, the state has a monopoly on the exercise of legitimate violence. Theoretically, it is also ultimately responsible for dealing with illegitimate violence in its midst (though, in practice, some forms of violence, such as domestic violence, have been, and continue to be, largely left alone). Only minimal levels of state-sponsored violence necessary should, ideally, be used (though, again, instances of excessive state-sponsored violence occur and proponents of punitive state violence continue to be vigorous). And lastly, while deterrence has always been part of the state's responsibility to 'ensure peace and good order'—and is an ancient justification for its use and exploitation of violence—that responsibility has been subjected to more recent reassessment and reemphasis. Forms of state violence, such as public hanging, have been argued to be both immoral and demonstrably ineffective as deterrents, while conventional state responses to violence and crime are said to often reproduce the problem—for example, when a convicted young man reemerges from prison more hardened and violent than before. As a corollary to these arguments, the moral value and economic benefits of deterrence have been emphasised. Consequently, interest in the state's promotion of nonviolent forms of prevention has grown, both in theory and practice.

For the young, postcolonial state in PNG, these broad statements are qualified somewhat by consideration of state capacity, resources, and community attitudes—attitudes that state officers may share with the wider community and which also shape their working environment. In PNG, even if opportunity avails, some forms of domestic violence and sexual assault are even less likely to be reported to or pursued by police than they are in many Western countries, as several chapters here attest. Other forms of violence, such as 'community sanctioned' assaults, killings, or intergroup fighting may not be investigated properly because police believe that the violence was warranted or they lack the means. Some crimes are kept from police and the formal justice system by parties who prefer to exact and pay compensation, or because benefits—such as stolen goods—are distributed. And the vast majority of violent acts that are illegitimate according to law simply occur far from the eyes, ears and arms of the state (see Haley this volume). In PNG, the arguments for the involvement of police in the prevention of violence before the fact therefore have particular force, if only because so little is or can be done after.

Police also reportedly use violence and, on occasion, exploit its spectacle. The rough treatment of suspects, raids on settlements or the torching of villages are examples (Anon 2008; HRW 2006, 2005). Such police violence may be justified as retribution, deterrence, the best option for action with limited resources, or a fair response to the perceived failure of courts to deliver justice. Some police may also commit acts of violence primarily as a perquisite and expression of masculinity (Macintyre and MacLeod this volume). For the same reasons that many legal responses to violence and crime by police and other law and justice agencies can be criticised for reproducing the problems they are supposed to limit, policing practices such as these, while in themselves illegal, also add to the sum of violence.

In societies everywhere violence has accepted roles, and traditional cultures of PNG are no exception.[5] For instance, warfare was a means for securing group resources (and a mechanism for the redistribution of land). The term 'payback' also implies an acceptably violent retaliation for a wrong. Witchcraft and sorcery have been understood as an effective means of oblique violence; and untimely death and other personal misfortunes continue to be commonly attributed to such practices. Overt violence could be used to punish wrongdoers for an offence or to remove individuals deemed to pose a threat to the group. In many (but by no means all) parts of PNG, forms of gender or intimate violence have been considered justified in certain circumstances. While much has been written about traditional precedents for man-to-woman violence and its role in structuring masculine dominance (see, e.g., Eves this volume), woman-to-man and, more often, woman-to-woman violence could also as be seen as sometimes justified (cf. Macintyre and Macleod this volume).

The traditional exercise of violence may have been costly in human life, but appears to have been regulated (see, e.g., Luker with Monsell-Davis this volume). It must also be seen alongside complementary tendencies to form relationships of reciprocity between groups and individuals, and to respond to wrongs through non-violent compensation and reintegration. As Richard Sikani has written, the restorative impulse is strong in many PNG traditions (Sikani 1996, 192–194). This tends to be reinforced by indigenised Christianity and was a feature, for instance, in grassroots reconciliation in the Bougainville peace process (Howley 2002). In some cases, however, the payment of compensation and reintegration of an offender can be interpreted as violating principles of Western justice, women's rights or the interests of the victim, and failing to repudiate the crime (see, e.g., Kewa 2007, 31). In other circumstances, cycles of retribution are difficult to stop (e.g., Ward 2000).

Various factors currently favour violence, while weakening traditional and modern checks. Laments are often heard that elders have lost authority while young men have lost their way (see Luker with Monsell-Davis). The

---

5   The word 'traditional' is used loosely in this context to describe cultures that existed before interaction with mission, colonial and other influences; and cultures that continued to be shaped to a high degree by the practices and values from that time.

retreat of police and other government services from some areas has left a space where traditional responses, for instance, to persons accused of witchcraft, have assumed new, more violent forms (see Haley, this volume). Links between male violence and, since the 1960s, alcohol consumption or, more recently, marijuana are keenly perceived (Iamo and Ketan 1992; Haley this volume). Guns have changed the rules of violent engagement and, with deteriorating medical services, made it more deadly. Social change has eroded many customs that regulated contact between the sexes and which, in some communities, both authorised but checked violence against women (Wardlow 2002). Crowding, due to population growth or immigration, has accentuated tensions over resources in various urban and rural locales (see, e.g., Beer 2008, 100–3). The need for money can dispose a victim's kin to seek financial compensation rather than challenge the wrong itself (Kewa 2007, 31), while poverty can encourage crime and opportunistic sexual relations (often leading to domestic and other violence) for material gain (see Haley this volume). Trafficking in girls, guns, and marijuana has emerged, and the use of girls as currency (Alpers 2004). Indeed, certain forms of crime and conflict appear to follow (as do directions for the spread of HIV) broader development processes—hence the concentration of organised crime in expanding urban centres, armed hold-ups along arterial highways, and inter-group conflict near major resource development (see, e.g., Badi 2008; Hammar this volume; Haley this volume). Critics of PNG's huge liquid natural gas project, at AUD$15.6 billion the Pacific's largest ever business investment, predict it will only fuel corruption, conflict and HIV on a hitherto unprecedented scale (Callick 2009).

PNG's law and order problems are not simply problems of violence, but these highlight the weakness of the PNG state with respect to what is theoretically its cardinal responsibility: the governance of security. Yet many communities also struggle with this same task, while cooperation between state and community is often less than it could be. Phrases such as 'an epidemic of violence' are commonplace, but just as the term 'epidemic' is in some ways misleading with respect to HIV, in PNG it can disguise the many etiologies of violence, their implication in broader processes of governance and development, and the differing moral analyses that converge on its regulation. Like endemic HIV, PNG's law and order problems pose a long-term challenge.

Connecting HIV and 'Law and Order'

Certain connections between HIV and 'law and order' figure in everyday talk, the media, and documents relating to PNG's national response. Despite awareness campaigns and legal provisions, people living with HIV still often suffer abuse and cases similar to Joan's (see frontispiece, this volume) continue to be reported. The HIV-positive 'Hagen lass', burned alive on top of tyres at a rubbish dump in early 2009, is one recent example (NACS 2009; see Luker this volume, conclusion). She was also alleged to be a witch, further suggesting the part of HIV in the perceived surge of witch-killings that has prompted the current review of PNG's sorcery laws (Anon. 2009b; cf. Haley this volume). Other allegations of deliberate attempts to transmit HIV, and incidents of child abuse and rape that spread the virus, excite anxieties about a range of occasions for possibly reckless, willful, or violent transmission (Anon. 2003a; Kewa 2004). 'Gays' and 'lesbians' are sometimes accused (John 2003), but more often 'prostitutes' are described as spreading HIV while tales abound of HIV-positive girls who set out to infect men (see Fletcher this volume; Anon. 2003b). The tendency to blame women is marked (see Eves this volume; Haley this volume; MacPherson 2008; cf. Lepani 2007, 122–144). Yet women in safe houses for people living with HIV are targets for rape (Gerawa 2009). Reports of 'street kids' orphaned by AIDS and the selling of sex for survival loosely suggest how crime, poverty and HIV entangle (Gerawa 2004a, b). The nation's AIDS strategy states too that 'urban migration, squatter communities and high levels of crime' foster favourable conditions for HIV, a diagnosis with which many ordinary people would agree (PNG 2006, 9; cf. Beer 2008, 103). The press has aired fears that AIDS could unman the military and police (Steven 2004). Meanwhile, the National AIDS Council itself stands accused of gross corruption (Nalu 2009). Against this background and reports of systemic failure in the national response to HIV, the 2009 rejection of PNG's application to the Global Fund jeopardized the funding for antiretroviral treatment that keeps some 7,000 Papua New Guineans alive (Fox 2009; see also Aggleton et al. 2008, 29–31).

Such talk, stories and perceptions suggest a multitude of links between HIV and 'law and order', but our central thesis of their two-way interaction is embedded more deeply in the literature on how social, political and economic factors can determine health and, vice versa, how a population's health influences its social and economic conditions. Thus it is widely acknowledged that medical services, though they play an extremely important part in the response to diseases, have very limited ability to remedy their social causation. As John Kemm and Jayne Parry remark, 'Major improvements in population health are more likely to be achieved through interventions in economic, industrial, housing, transport, agriculture, education, law and order, and other 'non-health' areas than in policy areas with which ministries of health are involved' (Kemm & Parry 2004, 5). Conversely development agencies invest in measures to improve health not just as a good in itself, but because this investment delivers other social and economic dividends.

A similar point about the importance of deeper determinants can be made in respect of 'law and order'. Conventional responses to 'law and order' problems have tended to depend on the coercive role of law enforcement agencies. However, policing responses or indeed longer-term capacity-building in the formal law and justice sector will not address underlying and structural factors contributing to high levels of conflict, crime and violence. Such arguments have forcefully emerged from efforts to address crime and conflict in South Africa, among other countries (see, e.g., DSS 1996; Emmett and Butchart 2000). In PNG, the National Law and Justice Policy observes, '(t)he failure of official responses [to crime] has in part been because we have been concentrating on applying 'band aid' solutions in an essentially ad hoc manner. We have been focusing on the symptoms of much deeper problems that are inextricably bound up with broader processes of social, economic and political change' (PNG 2000, 9).

Public Health Approaches to HIV and Security

As David Hemenway remarks, public health approaches 'can be contrasted to the often reactive, individual focus of therapeutic medicine and traditional criminal justice' (Hemenway 2004, 8–9). But public health approaches can differ widely among themselves. For instance, from the early years of the international response to HIV, a stark difference emerged between 'classic' public health approaches and those described as upholding human rights (Scheper-Hughes 1994). The former rely on active case-finding, contact-tracing and the isolation of infected individuals, and were widely employed in past efforts to control tuberculosis, leprosy and STIs. The latter emphasises public education, the implementation of certain universal precautions, and the capacity of individuals, once they are equipped with knowledge and means, to change. While theoretically, both approaches can be construed as pragmatic, and each ultimately appeals to the commonweal, they are often morally contrasted. The former tends to accord with retributive proclivities on the part of majorities against individuals and minorities, the latter with the celebration and assertion of individual and minority rights. In terms of limiting HIV, each approach has its success stories. Australia, for example, is one for the second; Cuba for the first (Bowtell 2005; Scheper-Hughes 1994; Arazoza et al. 2007). Yet success depends enormously on contextual factors. Cuba's cannot be replicated in many contexts, and neither can Australia's.

Along the spectrum of public health approaches to HIV, contributors to this volume all cluster towards the 'rights' end. The 'rights' approach broadly characterises PNG's national strategy, the policy of most of PNG's development partners, including Australia, and the global response promoted by UNAIDS.

Yet chapters ahead reflect many of the challenges to this kind of response in PNG. These include limited state capacity, limited community mobilisation, local values apparently at odds with those of the AIDS agenda, difficulties in translating 'AIDS awareness' into preventive or ameliorative action, and the sense that larger processes and structures are untoward. Of course, similar challenges are found in other countries; and those working with HIV in PNG are not alone in targeting 'barriers' to effective programs, and stressing the need to create 'enabling environments'. As Jenkins and Sarkar noted, 'Effective HIV prevention not only requires targeted interventions that foster behavior change in individuals and communities at risk, but also requires creating environments that support people in their efforts to change, rather than punishing them or driving them away' (Jenkins and Sarkar 2004, 3).

For this volume, an article by Sevgi Aral, Scott Burris and Clifford Shearing (2002) has been particularly helpful for thinking about public health approaches that respond conjointly to HIV and 'law and order', but at two levels. One might be called the level of 'barrier removal' and 'enablement'; the other, while also operating on that plane, goes deeper: to the progressive structuring of social and cultural environments which deliver, almost incidentally and unconsciously, benefits for HIV prevention and the amelioration of AIDS.

Aral and her coauthors use two case studies—the policing of sex work in Moscow and an example of community governance in South Africa—and employ a standard epidemiological model for the rate of an STI's spread. Its three determinants are: 1) the rate of exposure between infected and susceptible persons; 2) the probability that infection will occur from one of these sexual encounters; and 3) the duration of infectiousness. Drawing on research relating to the policing of sex-work in Russia (where prostitution per se is not a crime) they demonstrate the effects of laws, political directives, and police practices upon these determinants.

A few examples can illustrate. Russian police reportedly use a woman's possession of condoms as grounds for persecuting her as a prostitute. This could discourage the use of condoms, increase the likelihood of unprotected intercourse, and thus affect the second determinant. Because immigrants are not legally entitled to free medical treatment in Moscow, immigrants who sell sex are likely to delay or forego medical treatment for STIs that are co-factors of HIV transmission. This affects the second determinant. Police actions that clear sex workers from one site of work to another may disrupt existing sexual networks and promote new networks in new locations. This could affect the first determinant. The sexual services that are routinely demanded by police from these women could also affect the first determinant.

Obviously, these illustrations could have been taken from policing in many countries, including PNG, while this model can be used to think about the possible epidemiological effects of a range of state laws, enforcement practices, related conditions and events—from prison sentences, mass prison breakouts, curfews and area-specific crime control measures, the criminal status of homosexuality, retributive practices by uniformed services, conditions of service for law and order personnel, and so forth. Similarly, the model can be used to analyse the possible epidemiological consequences of non-formal methods of social regulation, such as warfare, various forms of 'pay-back' and punishment.

While Aral, Burris and Shearing demonstrate how certain law and order factors can promote the spread of HIV, conversely they show how, within the formal sector, the reform of specific laws, policies, and crime-control practices could reduce transmission. It would be theoretically possible, for instance, to educate Russian police not to demand sexual services from sex-workers nor persecute them for carrying condoms, and so on. Their discussion also mentions, more generally, other areas where reforms can help limit infection: in, for instance, prisons, or by diverting offenders from detention.

Similarly, a number of initiatives in PNG—in community policing, restorative justice programs, juvenile justice reform, HIV prevention and support programs within the uniformed services and prisons, the involvement of law and order personnel in educating communities about HIV, and the provisions of the HIV/AIDS Management and Prevention Act to name a few—suggest ways in which the uniformed services, courts, prisons, and state law can make a beneficial difference to the management of HIV, converting the same abilities for (unintentionally) facilitating the spread of HIV to the cause of prevention (see Patrick this volume). However, as Aral and her co-authors note, such state initiatives can be difficult to effect where state capacity or resources are limited (see Law this volume; Patrick this volume). Also, reforms mainly dealing with the formal law and justice sector do not fully exploit co-present methods, or potentials, for governing civic security that exist beyond the (often short) reach of state agencies.

So perhaps the greatest value of their article is, finally, its advocacy of a deeper preventive approach in the Zwelethemba model for community governance, from South Africa's Community Peace Program. Cartwright, Jenneker and Shearing describe it in greater detail later in this volume. Briefly, it brings community members together in 'peace-making' that prevents the escalation of conflicts and in 'peace-building' that prevents conflicts from starting. The model makes use of the community's resources: time and knowledge. It obliges participants to observe South Africa's constitution. They also receive a financial incentive: participants earn a small payment, part of which goes to each while a proportion is reserved for the community to invest in 'peace-building' projects of its own devising. The process involves women and youth. It develops community skills and capacity. While the model fully recognises the limited role that the state can play, it also stimulates thinking about how best the state can play its hand. Finally, the authors argue that the higher resulting levels of social cohesion can be predicted to correlate with better health and also to facilitate effective health programs. They specifically suggest that this model could contribute to lower levels of HIV transmission and more effective community management of HIV. The Zwelethemba model, in effect, promises a new civics of security that offers HIV benefits, 'accidentally' through 'deep prevention' and deliberately by enabling self-conscious initiatives that target HIV.

As Dinnen stresses in his preface to chapter twelve, where both the Zwelethemba model and Port Moresby's Saraga project are featured, the former's value for this collection lies in its clearly articulated rationale and design, and in its resemblances to the Saraga and other such local initiatives (Jacka 2007, 51–52.). PNG's National Law and Justice Policy also recognises the importance of social cohesion for improved community safety and health. This recognition in turn underlies the Policy's emphasis on community engagement in crime prevention and dispute resolution, as reinforced in the White Paper on Law and Justice (Dinnen 2006; PNG 2007). Recent thinking on democratic engagement at the community level in PNG resonates with features of this model too (e.g., Goudsmit 2008), while the Integrated Community Development Program introduced by Dame Carol Kidu envisions 'inside out' community governance that inherently involves the reduction of both HIV and crime (Kidu 2008).

Entwined Endemics, Prevention and the State

Endemic HIV and 'law and order' entwine in PNG, and it is possible to tabulate ways in which each may exacerbate or moderate the other (Table 1). But this chapter has also argued that public health approaches to the governance of security have potential to prevent and ameliorate each and their interaction, at 'shallow' and 'deep' levels.

What then is the role of the PNG state in the governance of security? Our discussion has underlined two irresistible facts. First, PNG's young state, though nominally responsible for civic security, does not have the reach or capacity that many older states can flex and, for the foreseeable future, will have only limited ability to discharge this responsibility. Second, for the foreseeable future, communities will continue to do most of 'the work' of civic security, though clearly many currently struggle.

Tendencies in thinking that polarise state and community, and stress solutions to the governance of security that focus on one to the occlusion of the other, must be resisted. The international interest, over the last decade, in improving national and international security by 'building' states described as failed, fragile or flailing, has contributed to fresh thought on both the potentials (for instance, through 'a whole of government' approach) and limitations of state-centric conceptions of governance and security (see, e.g., Wood and Dupont 2006). These debates have special point for the Island Pacific, where several nations, including PNG, have been dubbed as failed, fragile or failing states and have been targeted, notably by Australia, for urgent state-building measures (Fry and Kabutaulaka 2008; Wood 2007). Both globally and with respect to the Pacific, the escalation of these 'state-building' and security concerns also roughly coincided with a steep increase of interest in and funding for interventions in HIV (Schneider and Garrett 2009; CAP 2009, 61–62).

The critiques of so-called 'state-centric' approaches to development in PNG (see, e.g., Dinnen 2008; Patience 2008), and the renewed, creative attention that 'community' is now receiving (see, e.g., Jacka 2007; Kidu 2008; Goudsmit 2008; James et al. 2009; Boege et al. 2008; Macdonald 2009), at least partly as a consequence of such critiques, do not lessen the necessity, or the moral imperative, for the state to discharge its specialised tasks in the governance of security as effectively and strategically as it can. Many of these—in policing, prisons, defence, legislation—place the state in positions from which it can advantageously intervene in both the concentrated and generalised dynamics though which 'law and order' and HIV play out and entwine. Nor should the potential for state agencies—police, village courts, but also institutions in other areas such as health and education—to contribute to local civic evolution be underestimated. Even if, in such settings, representatives of the state are only one of many actors and have circumscribed local roles, the state can provide vital long-term, stabilising and strategic elements to local endeavours. This 'whole-of-governance' vision calls for less talk of a fragile, failed or failing state, and continuing effort to back an enabling one.

Postscript: While this collection was in press, new figures were released for HIV prevalance in PNG. In 2009, 0.9% of PNG's adult population was estimated to be infected. Prevalance in the Highlands and Southern regions exceeded the national figure. UNAIDS. 2010. 'Papua New Guinea releases new HIV prevalance figures'. 26 August 2010. http://unaids.org/en/KnowledgeCentre/ Resources/

Table 1: Entwined endemics

<table>
<tr><td>

Potentially detrimental impacts of HIV and AIDS on 'law and order'

- A new mode of inflicting or attempting to inflict harm now exists in cases where individuals deliberately try to infect others with HIV—whether through sexual contact or via other means.
- Community responses to HIV and AIDS may involve acts (such as murder or torture) or inflame pre-existing conflicts so as to increase demands upon the resources of law and order agencies and tax community capacities to ensure the safety of members.
- HIV, through its effects on law and order personnel and consumption of resources, may further reduce the capacities of uniformed services to combat crime and safeguard order.
- Because HIV can impoverish individuals and families now and in succeeding generations, the endemic can drive more people into criminal activities for economic survival, often thereby promoting conditions or behaviours that favour the further spread of the virus.

Potentially harmful effects of 'law and order' factors on HIV and AIDS

- Acts of sexual violence can spread HIV and make their consequences (sometimes for the perpetrator as well as the victim) fatal.
- The criminalisation of certain sexual acts can facilitate the spread of HIV by impeding prevention efforts.
- Policing and related practices—sometimes supported or required by law, sometimes not—can promote transmission.
- Law and order personnel, and the inmates of prisons, can constitute populations with a high prevalence of HIV and may also serve as bridges of infection to other populations.
- Failings of law and order can exacerbate the suffering of people affected by HIV or accused of causing AIDS, and render them vulnerable to acts of violence.
- Violence can prevent the delivery of or access to health and other services for people affected by HIV.
- Corruption and the misappropriation of funds can undermine the work of HIV agencies.

Potentially beneficial effects of law and order factors on HIV and AIDS

- Law and order responses may help to safeguard people affected by HIV and prevent the mistreatment of persons accused of causing AIDS.
- Initiatives within law and order populations—among men and women in the uniformed services and the inmates of prisons—may reduce the levels of HIV infection within these groups and the dangers of further transmission beyond them.
- Reforms to law and policing practices can both discourage actions that transmit HIV and enable interventions to change behaviour (see Stewart this volume).
- More fundamentally innovative, community-based approaches to the governance of civic security may help create 'safer environments' where occasions for infection occur less frequently, while simultaneously enhancing the capacity of communities to effect preventive measures and deal with the impacts of AIDS.

</td></tr>
</table>

References

ADB (Asian Development Bank). 2008. *Profiles of Progress: Papua New Guinea.* Manila: Asian Development Bank.

Aggleton, Peter, Shalina Bharat, Felecia Dobunaba, Robert Drew and Steve Wignall. 2008. Independent Review Group on HIV/AIDS: Report from an Assessment Visit 27 August- 9 September 2008.

Alpers, P. 2004. Gunrunning in Papua New Guinea: From Arrows to Assault Weapons. A Special Report from AusAID and the Small Arms Survey, First Draft, 12 October 2004.

Altman, D. 2003. HIV and Security. *International Relations* 17 (4): 417–427.

Altman, D. 2008. State Fragility, Human Security and HIV. In *The Politics of AIDS: Globalization, the State and Civil Society,* ed. Maj-Lis Follér and Håkan Thörn, 17–26. Houndmills, Basingstoke: Palgrave MacMillan.

Anon. 2003a. Man Held for Injecting Wife with Contaminated Blood. *The National*, 18 September 2004.

Anon. 2003b. Churches Oppose Prostitution Calls. *Post-Courier*, 25 September 2004.

Anon. 2007. Buried Alive. *Post-Courier*, 27 August 2007.

Anon. 2006. HIV/AIDS Prevalence could be Higher. *Post-Courier*, 26 September 2006.

Anon. 2008. Rights Abused. *Post-Courier*, 22 September 2008.

Anon. 2009a. Violence Hindering Growth, Says Parkop. *Post-Courier*, 27 August 2009.

Anon. 2009b. Battle for Sorcery Killings. *Post-Courier*, 7 April 2009.

Australia, Government. 2008. *Papua New Guinea Strongim Gavman Program.* Attorney-General's Department. http://www.ag.gov.au/www/agd/agd.nsf (accessed 27 April 2010).

Aral, S., S. Burris and C. Shearing. 2002. Health and the Governance of Security: A Tale of Two Systems: Crime Control and Sexually Transmitted Diseases in Russia. *Journal of Law, Medicine and Ethics* 30: 632–643.

Badi, Dennis. Police Play Big Role in SHP. *Post-Courier*, 2 January 2008.

Ballard, John and Clement Malau. 2009. Policy Making on AIDS, to 2000. In *Policy Making and Implementation: Studies from Papua New Guinea*, ed. R. J. May, 369–378.

Barnett, T. and A. Whiteside. 2002. *AIDS in the Twenty-First Century: Disease and Globalization*. Houndmills, Basingbroke: Palgrave.

Barnett, Tony. 2008. A Long Wave Event: HIV/AIDS, Politics, Governance and 'Security': Sundering the Intergenerational Bond? In *The Politics of AIDS: Globalization, the State and Civil Society*, ed. Maj-Lis Follér and Håkan Thörn, 27–46. Houndmills: Palgrave Macmillan.

Beer, Bettina. 2008. Buying Betel and Selling Sex: Contested Boundaries, Risk Milieus, and Discourses about HIV/AIDS in the Markham Valley, Papua New Guinea. In *Making Sense of AIDS: Culture, Sexuality, and Power in Melanesia*, ed. Leslie Butt and Richard Eves, 97–115. Honolulu: University of Hawai'i Press.

Boege, Volker, Anne Brown, Kevin Clements and Anna Nolan. 2008. On Hybrid Political Orders and Emerging States: State Formation in the Context of Fragility. Berghof Research Center for Constructive Conflict Management. [no place of publication given] www.berghof-handbook.net

Bourke, R. M. 2008. The Poorest People Stay in Rural PNG. *The National*, 11 Jun 2008.

Bowtell, Bill. 2005. *Australia's Response to HIV/AIDS 1982–2005*. Sydney: Lowey Institute. Available www.lowyinstitute.org

Bradley, Christine. 2001. *Family and Sexual Violence in PNG: an Integrated Long-Term Strategy*. Report to the Family Violence Action Committee of the Consultative Implementation and Monitoring Council. Port Moresby: Institute of National Affairs.

Brown, M. Anne. 2007. Security and Development: Conflict and Resilience in the Pacific islands Region. In *Security in the Pacific islands: Social Resilience in Emerging States*, ed. M. Anne Brown, 1–32. London and Boulder: Lynne Rienner Publishers.

Brunton, B., and D. Colquhoun-Kerr. 1984. *The Annotated Constitution of Papua New Guinea*. Port Moresby: University of Papua New Guinea Press.

Butt, Leslie, Jenny Munro and Joanna Wong. 2004. Border Testimonials: Patterns of AIDS Awareness across the Island of New Guinea. *Papua New Guinea Medical Journal*, 47 (1–2): 65–76.

Butt, Leslie and Richard Eves, eds. 2008. *Making Sense of AIDS: Culture, Sexuality, and Power in Melanesia.* Honolulu: University of Hawai'i Press.

Callick, Rowan. 2009. Corruption Fear in PNG Project: Luke Fletcher. *The Australian.* 20 October 2009.

CAP (Commission on AIDS in the Pacific). 2009. *Turning the Tide: An OPEN Strategy for a Response to AIDS in the Pacific.* Suva: Commission on AIDS in the Pacific.

CIE (Centre for International Economics). 2002. *Potential Economic Impacts of an HIV/AIDS Epidemic in Papua New Guinea.* Report prepared for AusAID. Available http://www.ausaid.gov.au/ (accessed 27 April 2010).

De Waal, Alex. 2003. Human Rights Organizations and the Political Imagination: How the West and Africa have Diverged. *Journal of Human Rights,* 2 (4): 475–494.

De Waal, Alex. 2005. The Challenge of HIV/AIDS. In *Towards a New Map of Africa,* ed. Ben Wisner, Camilla Toulmin and Rutendo Chitiga, 113–127. London: Earthscan.

Dinnen, S. 1998. In Weakness and Strength: State, Societies and Order in Papua New Guinea. In *Weak and Strong States in Asia-Pacific Societies,* ed. P. Dauvergne, 38–59. St Leonards, NSW: Allen and Unwin.

Dinnen, S. 2000. Breaking the Cycle of Violence: Crime and State in Papua New Guinea. In *Developing Cultural Criminology: Theory and Practice in Papua New Guinea,* ed. C. Banks, 51–78. Sydney Institute of Criminology Monograph Series No. 13.

Dinnen, S. 2001. *Law and Order in a Weak State: Crime and Politics in Papua New Guinea.* Honolulu: University of Hawai'i Press.

Dinnen, S. 2006. Restorative Justice and the Governance of Security in the Southwest Pacific. In *Handbook of Restorative Justice,* ed. Dennis Sullivan and Larry Tifft, 401–421. London and New York: Routledge.

Dinnen, S. 2008. Beyond State-Centrism: External Solutions and the Governance of Security in Melanesia. In *Intervention and State-Building in the Pacific: The Legitimacy of 'Cooperative Intervention',* ed. Greg Fry and Taricisius Kabutaulaka, 102–118. Manchester: Manchester University Press.

DSS (Department of Safety and Security, South Africa). 1996. *National Crime Prevention Strategy: Summary.* Pretoria, SA: Department of Safety Security.

Dundon, Alison and Charles Wilde, eds. 2007. HIV and AIDS in Rural Papua New Guinea. Special Issue, *Oceania* 77:1.

Elbe, Stefan. 2009. *Virus Alert: Security, Governance and the AIDS pandemic*. New York: Columbia University Press.

Emmett, Tony and Alex Butchart, eds. 2000. *Behind the Mask: Getting to Grips with Crime and Violence in South Africa*. Cape Town: HSRC Publishers. Available online from www.hsrcpress.ac.za.

Fourie, Pieter. 2007. The Relationship between the AIDS Pandemic and State Fragility. *Global Change, Peace and Security*. 19: 3, 281–300.

Fox, Liam. 2009. 'PNG's HIV Pledge on Shaky Ground'. Australian Broadcasting Commission, 5 Dec. 2009.

Fry, Greg and Tarcisius Tara Kabutaulakan, eds. 2008. *Intervention and State-Building in the Pacific: The Legitimacy of 'Cooperative intervention'*. Manchester: Manchester University Press.

Garap, S. 2004. *Kup Women for Peace: Women Taking Action to Build Peace and Influence Community Decision-Making*. Discussion Paper 2004/4. Canberra: State, Society and Governance in Melanesia Project, Research School of Pacific and Asian Studies, The Australian National University.

Gelu, A. 2003. A Democratic Audit for Papua New Guinea. In *Building a Nation in Papua New Guinea: Views of the Post-Independence Generation*, ed. D. Kavanamur, C. Yala, and Q. Clements, 25–50. Canberra: Pandanus Books.

Gerawa, M. 2004a. AIDS Cause of Kids Living on Streets. *Post-Courier*, 6 January 2004.

Gerawa, M. 2004b. Kids' Centre Mooted. *Post-Courier*, 21 December 2004.

Gerawa, M. 2009. NACS Upset on Rape. *Post-Courier*, 8 September 2009.

Goddard, M. 2009. *Substantial Justice: An Anthropology of Village Courts in Papua New Guinea*. New York and Oxford: Berghahn Books.

Goudsmit, Into A. 2008. *Nation Building in Papua New Guinea: A Local Alternative*. State, Society and Governance in Melanesia Project Discussion Paper 2008/9. Canberra: State Society and Governance in Melanesia Project, Research School of Pacific and Asian History, Australian National University.

Haley, Nicole. 2008. When There's No Accessing Basic Health Care: Local Politics and Responses to HIV/AIDS at Lake Kopiago, Papua New Guinea. In *Making Sense of AIDS: Culture, Sexuality, and Power in Melanesia*, ed. Leslie Butt and Richard Eves, 24–41. Honolulu: University of Hawai'i Press.

Hemenway, David. 2004. *Private Guns, Public Health*. Ann Arbor: University of Michigan Press.

Hemenway, David. 2009. *While We were Sleeping: Success Stories in Injury and Violence Prevention*. Berkeley: University of California Press.

Hauck, V., A. Mandie-Filer and J. Bolger. 2005. *Ringing the Church Bell: The Role of Churches in Governance and Public Performance in Papua New Guinea*. Discussion Paper 57 E. Maastricht: European Centre for Development Policy Management.

Hauquitz, A.C. 2004. Looking Down the Barrel of a Cannon: The Potential Economic Costs of HIV/AIDS in Papua New Guinea. *Papua New Guinea Medical Journal* 46 (4).

Hayes, Geoffrey. 2007. The Demographic Impact of the HIV/AIDS Epidemic in Papua New Guinea, 1990–2030. *Asia-Pacific Population Journal*, 22: 3, 11–30.

Hegarty, David and Pamela Thomas (eds). Effective Development in Papua New Guinea. *Development Bulletin* No.67 April 2005. Canberra: Development Studies Network.

HELP. 2005. A Situational Analysis of Child Sexual Abuse and the Commercial Sexual Exploitation of Children in PNG. [no place cited]: HELP Resources, Inc., with the support of UNICEF PNG.

HEMIS (HIV Epidemiological Modelling Impact Study). 2006. Impacts of HIV/AIDS 2005–2025 in Papua New Guinea, Indonesia and East Timor: Final Report of the HIV Epidemiological Modelling Impact Study February 2006. Canberra: AusAID.

Hill, Bruce. 2008 'Australia and PNG Ministers Resurrect Version of the ECP'. Australian Broadcasting Commission, Pacific Beat, 24 April 2008. http://www.radioaustralia.net.au/programguide/stories/200804/s2226260.htm (accessed 27 April 2010).

Howley, Pat 2002. *Breaking Spears and Mending Hearts: Peacemakers and Restorative Justice in Bougainville*. London and Annandale, NSW: Zed Books/ Federation Press.

HRW (Human Rights Watch). 2005. 'Making Their Own Rules': Police Beatings, Rape, and Torture of Children in Papua New Guinea. New York: Human Rights Watch. www.hrw.org

HRW (Human Rights Watch). 2006. Still Making Their Own Rules: Ongoing Impunity for Police Beatings, Rape, and Torture in Papua New Guinea. New York: Human Rights Watch. www.hrw.org

Hughes, Helen. 2004. Can Papua New Guinea Come back from the Brink? *Issue Analysis* No. 49. St Leonards NSW: Centre for Independent Studies.

Hukula, Fiona. 1999. *Women and Security in Port Moresby*. NRI Discussion Paper No. 92. Boroko: National Research Institute.

Iamo, Wari and Joseph Ketan. 1992. How Far under the Influence? Alcohol-related Law and Order Problems in the Highlands of Papua New Guinea. Boroko: National Research Institute.

Ivoro, J. 2003. Conflict Resolution in a Multi-Cultural Urban Setting in Papua New Guinea. In *A Kind of Mending: Restorative Justice in the Pacific Islands*, ed. Sinclair Dinnen, 108–113. Canberra: Pandanus Books.

Jacka, Marion. 2007. Local Solutions: Security and Development in Papua New Guinea. In *Security in the Pacific islands: Social Resilience in Emerging States*, ed. M. Anne Brown, 33–64. London and Boulder: Lynne Rienner Publishers.

James, Paul, Victoria Stead, Yaso Nadarajah, Karen Haive. 2009. Introduction: Projecting Community Life. In Projecting Community Life, by Paul James et al. *Local Global: Identity, Security, Community* 5: 6–16.

Jenkins, C., & Alpers, M. 1996. Urbanization, Youth and Sexuality: Insights for an AIDS Campaign for Youth in Papua New Guinea. *Papua New Guinea Medical Journal* 39 (3): 248–251.

Jenkins, C., & Passey, M. 1998. Papua New Guinea. In *Sexually Transmitted Diseases in Asia and the Pacific*, ed. T. Brown, R. Chan, D. Mugrditchian, B. Mulhall, D. Plummer, R. Sarda, & W. Sittitrai, 230–254. Armidale: Venereology Publishing.

Jenkins, C. 2000. HIV, Development and Unhealthy Institutions. *Development Bulletin* 52: 12–13.

Jenkins, C., & Sarkar, S. 2004. Creating Environments that Care: Interventions for HIV Prevention and Support for Vulnerable Populations (draft): Policy Project (USAID) and UNAIDS.

Jenkins, C.L. 1996. The Homosexual Context of Heterosexual Practice in Papua New Guinea. In *Bisexualities and AIDS: International Perspectives*, ed. P. Aggleton, 191–206. London: Taylor and Francis Inc.

John, M. 2003. Gays Promoting Sex Hatred. *Post-Courier*, 28 August 2003.

Kemm, J., and J. Parry. 2004. What is HIA? Introduction and Overview. In *Health Impact Assessment*, ed. J. Kemm, J. Parry, and S. Palmer, 1–14. Oxford: Oxford University Press.

Kewa, C. 2004. Child Sex Shock. *Post-Courier*, 1 September 2004.

Kewa, Christina. 2007. *Being a Woman in Papua New Guinea: From Grass Skirts and Ashes to Education and Global Changes*. Nelson, NZ: The Copy Press.

Kidu, Carol, 2008. The Power of Partnerships: Reflections on Addressing Papua New Guinea's Social Challenges. Presentation to the Lowy Institute, Sydney, 7 May 2008. Available http://lowyinstitute.org/Publication.asp?pid=797 (accessed 27 April 2010).

Lepani, Katherine. 2007. 'In the Process of Knowing': Making Sense of HIV and AIDS in the Trobriand Islands of Papua New Guinea. PhD thesis. Canberra: Australian National University.

Levantis, T. 2000a. *Papua New Guinea: Employment, Wages and Economic Development*. Canberra and Port Moresby: Asia Pacific Press and the Institute of National Affairs.

Levantis, T. 2000b. Crime Catastrophe—Reviewing Papua New Guinea's most Serious Social and Economic Problem. *Pacific Economic Bulletin*. 15 (2): 130–142.

Luker, V. 2004. Civil Society, Social Capital and the Churches: HIV/AIDS in Papua New Guinea. Working Paper 2004/1. Canberra: State Society and Governance in Melanesia Project, Australian National University.

MacDonald, Rosita. 2008. *Safety, Security, and Accessible Justice: Participatory Approaches to Law and Justice in Papua New Guinea*. Pacific Islands Policy No. 3. East West Center. Honolulu: University of Hawai'i.

MacPherson, Naomi. 2008. SikAIDS: Deconstructing the Awareness Campaign in Rural West New Britain, Papua New Guinea. In *Making Sense of AIDS: Culture, Sexuality, and Power in Melanesia*, ed. Leslie Butt and Richard Eves, 207–224.. Honolulu: University of Hawai'i Press.

May, R. J. 2001. (Re?)Discovering Chiefs: Traditional Authority and the Restructuring of Local-Level Government in Papua New Guinea. In *State and Society in Papua New Guinea: The First Twenty-Five Years*, by R. J. May, 203–236. Adelaide: Crawford House Publishing.

NACS (PNG National AIDS Council Secrerariat). 2005. National AIDS Council Secretariat and Department of Health HIV/AIDS Quarterly Report December 2004. Boroko, NCD: National AIDS Council Secretariat.

NACS (PNG National AIDS Council Secretariat) and NDOH (National Department of Health). 2007. The 2007 Estimation Report on the HIV Epidemic in Papua New Guinea. [Boroko, NCD: National AIDS Council Secretariat].

NACS (PNG National AIDS Council Secretariat). 2008. UNGASS 2008 Country Progress Report. Reporting Period January 2006–December 2007. [Boroko, NCD: National AIDS Council Secretariat].

NACS (PNG National AIDS Council Secretariat), 2009. NACS and Special Parliamentary Committee on HIV and AIDS have Condemned the Brutal Murder of Young Hagen Lass. Media Release, Wednesday, 7 January 2009.

Nalu, Malum, 2009. Massive Scam within AIDS Council: Barter. *The National*. 6 March 2009.

Nelson, H. 2000. Perspectives on Crime and Blame. In *Australia and Papua New Guinea: Crime and the Bilaterial Relationship*, ed. B. Boeha and J. McFarlane, 280–289. Canberra: Australian Defence Studies Centre, Australian Defence Force Academy.

Nelson, H. 2006. *Governments, States and Labels*. State, Society and Governance in Melanesia Project Discussion Paper 2006/1. Canberra: State Society and Governance in Melanesia Project, Research School of Pacific and Asian History, Australian National University.

Nelson, H. 2009. *Mobs and Masses; Defining the Dynamic Groups in Papua New Guinea*. State, Society and Governance in Melanesia Project Discussion Paper 2009/4. Canberra: State Society and Governance in Melanesia Project, Research School of Pacific and Asian History, Australian National University.

NSO (National Statistical Office). 2003. *Papua New Guinea 2000 Census*. Port Moresby: National Statistical Office.

NSRRT (National Sex and Reproduction Research Team) and C. Jenkins. 1994. *National Study of Sexual and Reproductive Knowledge and Behaviour in Papua New Guinea*. Goroka: Papua New Guinea Institute of Medical Research.

O'Collins, M. 2000. Images of Violence in Papua New Guinea: Whose Images? Whose Reality? In *Reflections on Violence in Melanesia*, ed. S. Dinnen and A. Ley, 19–34. Leichardt: Hawkins Press and Asia Pacific Press.

Patience, Alan. 2008. Cooperation between Australia and Papua New Guinea: 'Enhanced' or Enforced? In *Intervention and State-Building in the Pacific: The Legitimacy of 'Cooperative Intervention'*, ed. Greg Fry and Taricisius Kabutaulaka, 102–118. Manchester: Manchester University Press.

Patrick, Stewart and Kaysie Brown. 2007. *Greater than the Sum of Its Parts? Assessing 'Whole of Government' Approaches to Fragile States*. New York: International Peace Academy.

PNG (Papua New Guinea). 2000. National Law and Justice Policy and Plan of Action - Toward Restorative Justice. Independent State of Papua New Guinea, 2000.

PNG (Papua New Guinea). 2004. *Papua New Guinea National Strategic Plan on HIV/AIDS 2004-2008*. [Port Moresby]: National AIDS Council.

PNG (Papua New Guinea). 2006. *Papua New Guinea National Strategic Plan on HIV/AIDS 2006-2010*. [Port Moresby]: National AIDS Council.

PNG (Papua New Guinea). 2007. A Just, Safe and Secure Society. A White Paper on Law and Justice in Papua New Guinea, 2007.

PNG (Papua New Guinea) JAG (Justice Advisory Group). *Urban Crime Victimisation in Papua New Guinea, 2004–2008: A Synthesis*. 17 November 2008.

Prins, G. 2004. AIDS and Global Security. *International Affairs* 80 (5): 931–952.

Reid, Elisabeth. 2009. *Interrogating a Statistic: HIV Prevalence in PNG*. State Society and Governance in Melanesia Discussion Paper, 2009/1. Canberra: State Society and Governance in Melanesia Project, Research School of Pacific and Asian History, Australian National University.

Scheper-Hughes, Nancy. 1994. An Essay: AIDS and the Social Body. *Social Science and Medicine*, 39 (2): 991–1003.

Schneider, Kammerle and Laurie A. Garrett. The Evolution and Future of Donor Assistance for HIV/AIDS. Working Paper. New York: Council on Foreign Relations.

SI (Statistics Indonesia) and MoH (Ministry of Health). 2007. *Risk Behaviour and HIV Prevalence in Tanah Papua 2006*. [Jakarta]: Statistics Indonesia.

Sikani, Richard Charles. 1996. Dealing with Deviance in Contemporary Papua New Guinea Societies: The Choice of Sanctions in Village and Local Court Proceedings. Masters thesis. Melbourne: University of Melbourne.

Sims, P. 2004. How the Poor Die in the Settlements of Port Moresby, 2003–2004. *Papua New Guinea Medical Journal*, 47 (3-4): 192–201.

Spingler, Hermann. ed. 2009. AIDS: Belief and Culture in Papua New Guinea. Special Issue of *Catalyst: Social Pastoral Journal for Melanesia*, 39 (2).

SPC (Secretariat of the Pacific Community). 2010. Pacific Island Populations - Estimates and Projections of Demographic Indicators for Selected Years. Updated February 2010. Noumea: Secretariat of the Pacific Community. www.spc.int

Steven, C. 2004. Epidemic Threatens Grave Ravages for our Defence. *Post-Courier*, 8 July 2004: 16.

Tacon, Dave, 2009. As Things Fall Apart. *The Age*, 4 July 2009.

UN (United Nations). 1996. *Time to Act: The Pacific Response to HIV and AIDS*. Suva: United Nations.

UNAIDS. 2000. Female Sex Worker HIV Prevention Projects: Lessons Learnt from Papua New Guinea, India and Bangladesh. In UNAIDS Best Practice Collection. Geneva: UNAIDS.

UNAIDS. 2004. AIDS Epidemic Update: December 2004. Geneva: UNAIDS.

UNAIDS. 2005. AIDS Epidemic Update: December 2005. Geneva: UNAIDS.

UNAIDS, 2006. UNAIDS' Editors' Notes for Authors (May 2006).

UNAIDS. 2008. Report on the global AIDS epidemic. Geneva: UNAIDS.

UNAIDS. 2009a. Papua New Guinea. www.unaids.org/en/CountryResponses/Countries/papua_new_guinea.asp (accessed 6 February 2010).

UNAIDS. 2009a. Thailand. www.unaids.org/en/CountryResponses/Countries/papua_new_guinea.asp (accessed 6 February 2010).

UNAIDS. 2009c. AIDS Epidemic Update: December 2009. Geneva: UNAIDS.

UNDP. 2008. Human Development Index. Available http://hdrstats.undp.org/indicators/1.html. (accessed 27 April 2010).

Ward, Michael. 2000. Fighting for *Ples* in the City: Young Highlands Men in Port Moresby, Papua New Guinea. In *Reflections on Violence in Melanesia*, ed. Sinclair Dinnen and Allison Ley, 223–238.

Wardlow, Holly. 2002. Passenger-women: Changing Gender Relations in the Tari Basin. *Papua New Guinea Medical Journal* 45 (1–2): 142–146.

Wardlow, Holly. 2008. 'You have to Understand: Some of Us are Glad AIDS has Arrived': Christianity and Condoms among the Huli, Papua New Guinea. In *Making Sense of AIDS: Culture, Sexuality, and Power in Melanesia*, ed. Leslie Butt and Richard Eves, 187–205. Honolulu: University of Hawai'i Press.

WHO (World Health Organization). 2007. WHO Case Definitions of HIV for Surveillance and Revised Clinical Staging and Immunological Classification of HIV-related Disease in Adults and Children. Geneva: World Health Organization.

White, Hugh and Elsina Wainwright. 2004. *Strengthening our Neighbour: Australia and the Future of Papua New Guinea*. Barton ACT: Australian Strategic Policy Institute.

Windybank, Susan and Mike Manning. 2003. Papua New Guinea on the Brink. *Issue Analysis* No. 30. St Leonards NSW: Centre for Independent Studies.

Wood, Jennifer and Benôit Dupont, eds. 2006. *Democracy, Society and the Governance of Security*. Cambridge: Cambridge University Press.

World Bank. 2007. Strategic Directions for Human Development in Papua New Guinea. Washington, D.C.: The World Bank.

Masculinity, Violence and HIV

2. Masculinity Matters: Men, Gender-Based Violence and the AIDS Epidemic in Papua New Guinea

RICHARD EVES

Introduction

Gender has been a key category of enquiry into the AIDS pandemic for many years. Today, every major international authority involved in the response to AIDS recognises that a gendered approach is essential to success (UNAIDS 1999, 2000a; UNAIDS, UNFPA and UNIFEM 2004; UNAIDS and KIT 2005; UNDAW 2000; WHO 2003). Programmes to reduce gender inequalities are considered to be crucial to HIV prevention (see Carovano 1995; Gupta 1995; Jewkes, Levin and Penn-Kekana 2003, 132). So, there is a broad consensus that gender matters, but is it so clear that masculinity matters?

In 2001, the United Nations General Assembly adopted a Declaration of Commitment on HIV/AIDS which stressed that gender equality and the empowerment of women were fundamental to reducing the spread of HIV (para. 14) and that there was a dire need to challenge gender stereotypes, attitudes and inequalities (para. 47). Recognising that women and girls were disproportionately affected by HIV and AIDS, the Declaration emphasised the need to accelerate the implementation of national strategies to promote men's and women's shared responsibility to ensure safe sex (para. 59) (UNDAW 2004, 5–6).

Despite this recognition that greater equality of men and women is vital to HIV prevention, many programs worked solely with women, trying to empower them in sexual relationships (Rivers and Aggleton 1999). This was partly due to a tendency to view gender as synonymous with the feminine and the issue of gender equality as a women's problem—as a matter of helping women themselves to change their circumstances. The practice of addressing only women also developed because it was women who were disproportionately impacted by the epidemic. It was realised that female biological vulnerability made women more likely to be infected than men, and also that women's social and economic marginalisation increased their exposure to HIV.

At least in retrospect, this focus on women seems naïve and it left the masculine as the unquestioned status quo. Its rationale has some similarity to blaming the victim. Some argue that it 'actually served to undermine women by making them responsible for HIV risk reduction' (Campbell 1995, 197; Giffin 1998, 151; Mane and Aggleton 2001, 3). It meant that two vital factors were neglected: the part played by men and the part played by broader social circumstances in the spread of HIV (Rivers and Aggleton 1999). Of course I am not suggesting that women do not need particular attention, but that it is wrong to leave men outside the equation. Largely due to the activism of homosexuals, men have been a central focus of prevention efforts in the developed world, but this has not usually been the case in the developing world, where heterosexually driven epidemics predominate. While the focus on women is of the utmost importance, especially with the increasing feminisation of the epidemic, it is evident that a strong and constructive focus on men is required in these countries. Gender, after all, does not simply equate with women; it concerns men as well, something that is often forgotten (Dowsett et al. 1998, 305; Barker and Ricardo 2005, 1).

It is now increasingly recognised that attempts to empower women in sexual relationships are based on the highly questionable assumption that they have the power and ability to control their sexual and reproductive lives (Gupta and Weiss 1993; Rivers and Aggleton 1999; Wood and Jewkes 1997). The nature of gender roles and gender relations often mean that women have far less control over these and other aspects of their lives than men, and in particular are severely constrained in their ability to negotiate safe sex.

Broad agreement now exists that men (and boys) must be involved in prevention work if HIV transmission rates are to be reduced (Campbell 1995, 207; Mane and Aggleton 2001, 26; Rivers and Aggleton 1999). Internationally, there has been a growing body of academic literature and policy documents addressing men and HIV (Campbell 1997; Carovano 1995; Foreman 1999; Hunter 2005; Setel 1996; UNAIDS 2000b, UNAIDS 2000c, UNAIDS 2001; UNAIDS/Panos Institute 2001; UNFPA 2000; Wardlow 2007). An important starting point in this response was the 2000 and 2001 World AIDS campaigns coordinated by UNAIDS under the themes of 'Men Make a Difference' and 'I Care—Do You?' which recognised the need to involve men and boys as allies in stemming the global HIV pandemic.

One consequence of the research on men that followed these initiatives has been a more complex understanding of gender and its relationship to HIV, though much more work is needed. It is now widely recognised that it is important to examine the conceptual underpinnings of masculinity, its assorted meanings and values, and how and why it generates behaviours which contribute to the spread of the virus. Particularly pertinent here is the relationship between masculinity and gender-based violence, which is receiving increased interest internationally (see Campbell 1992; Barker and Ricardo 2005; Medrado 2003; Walsh and Mitchell 2006).

Gender-based violence is any form of violence used to define or keep in place strict gender roles and unequal relationships (UNDAW 2004, 31). Thus, it constitutes a 'policing mechanism' to 'keep women (or different types of men) in their place', to assert 'who makes the decisions' in a relationship or 'who holds the power' (UNDAW 2004, 31; and see UNFPA, UNIFEM and OSAGI 2005; UN 2006). Though it generally refers to men's violence towards women and girls, it also refers to violence toward other men and boys who are considered to challenge prevailing masculine gender ideologies. Importantly, making distinct the gender dimension helps to firmly ground the concept in gender and directs attention to the cultural dimensions of gender and the way children are socialised to become adults. Especially, it highlights the ways that masculine socialisation often authorises violence against women.

Until recently, male violence towards women was largely taken to be a separate problem from HIV, but now that such violence is known to play a prominent role in the spread of HIV, they are usually treated as dual and interconnected epidemics which should be addressed in an integrated way (Global Coalition on Women and AIDS and WHO 2004; Nduwimana 2004; Maman et al. 2000; Jewkes et al. 2003; Rothenberg and Paskey 1995; WHO 2001, 2004).[1]

The topic of this chapter is the constructions of masculinity which affect the perpetuation of gender-based violence and the spread of HIV, in particular in Papua New Guinea (PNG). I begin by examining from this angle the government response to the epidemic in PNG. I then outline the theory of the cultural construction of masculinity and describe the cultural influences that contribute to the dominant form of masculinity in that country. Next, I describe the extent of violence against women in PNG and explain how gender relations legitimate this. The extent to which the cultural constructions of gender which give men power limit women's ability to engage in safe sex is an important theme that follows. Next, I analyse and critique attempts that have been made to address the issue of gender-based violence through prevention messages which seek to

---

1 The issue of violence against women has for some time regularly been on the agendas of international forums, and international legal and policy frameworks for addressing it have been developed. Landmark achievements to this end include the UN Declaration on the Elimination of Violence Against Women (1993), the Dakar Platform for Action (1994), the Beijing Platform for Action (1995) and UN Resolution 1325 on Women Peace and Security (2000). Violence against women was identified as one of the twelve critical areas of action in the Beijing Platform for Action, and at the eleventh session of the Convention on the Elimination of All Forms of Discrimination against Women (CEDAW) (1992), General Recommendation No. 19 was formulated especially to address the issue.

re-define masculinity. I conclude by suggesting more considered approaches that are more likely to be successful in reducing gender-based violence and HIV transmission.

Engendering a Response to HIV

Cultural constructions of gender have a major impact on the way the epidemic is unfolding in PNG (Eves and Butt 2008; Haley 2008, 33; Beer 2008, 105), but there has been very little appreciation of this by those at the forefront of the national response. Overall, recognition of gender and the need to examine it in the context of gender-based violence and HIV transmission has been slow and largely donor-driven.

The response to the epidemic in PNG is currently guided by the National Strategic Plan (NSP) 2006–2010, which barely acknowledges the gendered nature of the epidemic (PNG NAC 2006a). A UNDP gender audit of the plan notes that it does not identify gender as one of its several focal areas nor as one of its cross-cutting themes to be addressed through the other focal areas (UNDP 2005, 8). Its recognition of gender is limited mainly to a rather brief discussion in the context of national vulnerability. It acknowledges to some extent gender inequality and the low status of women, referring to their much lower levels of literacy than men, limited employment opportunities, heavy health burden and very limited representation at all levels of the economy and government (UNDP 2005, 7). However, it fails to take seriously the need to assess the differential impact of the epidemic on men and women infected or affected by the epidemic (UNDP 2005, 8). The plan pays scant attention to the widely recognised connections between men, violence and HIV. While it acknowledges the violence men use against women to maintain their authority and the high incidence of sexual assault including rape (PNG NAC 2006a, 10), which exposes women to HIV, it sees gender in terms of women's vulnerability. This is a lop-sided definition of gender which includes women as a category but not men.

The UNDP gender audit found 'only a rudimentary level of understanding of gender on the part of a majority of stakeholders and most certainly only very basic level of knowledge of how gender intersects with the epidemic and what might be its relevance for strategies and activities identified in the NSP' (2005, 27). Even more disturbing was the claim by some of the stakeholders interviewed during the audit research that there were 'no gender issues in PNG's HIV epidemic' (UNDP 2005, 27). The higher levels of infection of female teenagers was put down to promiscuity and the 'greed for quick money' (UNDP 2005, 27).

The tendency among some, mostly male, stakeholders was to attribute blame to girls rather than to relate it to the economic and social susceptibility of girls to sexual advances by older men (see Luker with Monsell-Davis this volume).

Attempts have been made to rectify the inadequate focus of the NSP by developing a specific gender policy and plan, the National Gender Policy and Plan on HIV and AIDS 2006–2010, as a complement to the NSP (PNG NAC 2006b). This significantly advances the plan's gender policy component by clearly acknowledging that 'the biggest single factor affecting a person's risk of contracting HIV, and the consequences of infection, is gender' (PNG NAC 2006b, vi). However, there still appears to be very little developed action in this regard. For example, the PNG report to the United Nations General Assembly Special Session in 2008 comments that while a gender policy has been launched, 'there is a common misunderstanding in PNG that gender refers to women and girls. Few programs address gender roles and relations, gender power configurations, masculinity, male aggression and gender-based violence, sexual coercion and rape, and trans-generation sex' (PNG NACS and Partners 2008, 65).

Masculinity and the Making of Men

Theoretical understandings of masculinity have moved beyond taken-for-granted and universal conceptions of 'men' across cultures, regardless of histories and contexts. More considered historical and cultural study reveals that the nature of masculinity is fluid, depending on its setting, which is everywhere constantly reshaped by new influences. Indeed, within any society multiple forms of masculinity co-exist, reflecting different factors and different groups. That particular forms of masculinity are culturally elevated above others at various times and places, is another indication that considerable variation exists (Cleaver 2002, 7).

With the development of theory, new concepts and terms have been needed to point to and differentiate the various forms of masculinity. Recent writings on masculinity argue that within any one society there are ways of being a man that are dominant and considered exemplary, while others are seen as less than ideal. The former are termed 'hegemonic masculinities', while the latter are 'subordinate variants' (Cornwall and Lindisfarne 1994, 3; Connell 1995). Hegemonic masculinities exert pressure on men to behave in particular culturally and socially sanctioned ways. They legitimise and enforce the roles not only of women but also of men, 'constraining what they can and cannot think and do … [They] for example, have an important role to play in policing the boundaries of heterosexuality' (Mane and Aggleton 2001, 29; see also Brown, Sorrell and Raffaelli 2005, 586; Courtenay 2000; Larkin, Andrews and Mitchell 2006, 217).

The rituals associated with the transition from childhood to adulthood have been a major focus of anthropological studies of masculinity in PNG (Herdt 1981, 1992). These rituals confirm the point that gender, in this case masculinity, is cultivated through ritual and other cultural means. So far, however, insufficient effort has been made to understand the broad significance of masculinity and especially the rise of plural, and often competing masculinities, that have come about as a result of social and cultural change (but see Brison 1995; Eves 2006; Wilde 2003). Many changes that have had a profound impact on gender have occurred, such as Christianisation, Western education, exposure to modern media and labour migration. Significantly, some of these changes have seen the emergence of new forms of masculinity, such as those based on Christianity, which often eschew violence against women. On the other hand, these changes have sometimes brought the reinscription of 'traditional' conceptions of masculinity, which legitimate new forms of power in the contemporary context.

Generally, people in PNG are valued for their achievements. Although this applies both to men and women, the general rule is that women serve to assist a man to achieve renown. Women are valued for their role of raising children and producing the kinds of wealth (such as pigs, garden produce and artefacts) that are exchanged during the ceremonies and presentations where men gain political power and prestige. Women have an important role in maintaining social relations between groups, since the exchanges on which men build their prestige depend on the kinship relationships gained through marriage (Brown 1988, 125). It remains true that 'in the final analysis, the idea which men hold of themselves is based on what men do rather than what they have at birth' (Read 1982, 70). Men must try to prove themselves economically, socially and politically, which usually requires self-assertion and public accomplishment in the form of oratory, conspicuous displays of wealth, political office or other public status. The 'big man', who has achieved renown, is respected, while the man who has not, is contemptuously labelled *rabisman* (rubbish man). This renown depends on a man's ability to cultivate and harness pre-existing kinship and social relationships, rather than being 'self-made'.

The chief characteristics that make up the dominant, exemplary form of masculinity are assertiveness and powerfulness. Traditionally, the masculine ideal is 'a strong warrior and orator, a "big man" directing and leading a group of men in warfare and ceremony' (Brown 1988, 128). Though men may no longer be socialised to become warriors, they are still socialised to be extremely assertive, to the point of aggressiveness (McDowell 1990, 174). Consequently, anger and violent redress are considered natural and appropriate responses to insult or challenge. There is a general inclination to avenge perceived or actual insults, since these are perceived as injuries to one's person that need to be reciprocated. Anger is sometimes valued because it enables things to be done that could not normally be done. For example, in some places it is regarded as a motivating and energizing force, which has made possible men's great acts of warfare (Nash 1990, 138).[2]

Engendering Violence

Because of their desire to raise successful sons who will be big men who control and dominate over others, PNG boys are frequently socialised from early childhood to interact assertively and aggressively with others. This was also often a feature of male initiation rituals in parts of PNG (Herdt 1982). These 'rituals of manhood', as they have been called, involved the radical separation of boys from any contact with women and fostered male sociality and bonding. Though it is unclear whether these rituals continue to be practised, the belief continues to be strongly held that women, especially their bodily secretions, are dangerous and undermine men's power. In contexts such as hunting, preparation for dances and warfare, avoidance of women is considered essential to success. In circumstances where young men and boys are socialised to believe that women are antithetical, it is perhaps hardly surprising that violence against women is taken for granted as acceptable.

Currently, as McLeod observes, women in PNG enjoy neither freedom of movement nor equal protection by the law (2005, 115). Many women live under the threat of violence and this restricts their ability to move freely in the community, to use public transport, to access health and education services, and to travel to market or to the workplace (AI 2006, 1; NRI and JAG 2005, 6). Women are ill-served at all levels of the male-dominated law and justice sector, ranging from the village court system to the police, where cultural assumptions about male superiority are commonly embraced, and issues that affect women, such as sexual and domestic violence, are either ignored totally or not seriously pursued. Village courts also demonstrate 'excess traditionalism', espousing a timeless and strongly masculine concept of tradition (McLeod 2005, 115). [3] Moreover, the threat of violence from intimate partners and husbands means women are often unable to earn an income, or if they do, to control its use, rendering them financially dependent. Neither, as I show below, do women have control over their bodies and their sexual and reproductive health, very often being unable to determine whether, when and with whom they have sex and whether or not they become pregnant.

---

2   In the past, a man could be turned into an angry killer, a *pikonara*, with great strength through the ingestion of a magical powder, which included human bones. Any boy child showing unusual belligerence was believed likely to grow up to be a pikonara (Nash 1990, 135).

3   In some contexts, though, women are very successful users of village courts (Goddard 2004).

The Papua New Guinea Constitution has a stated commitment to equal human rights, and PNG is a signatory to the Convention on the Elimination of All Forms of Discrimination against Women (CEDAW). [4] PNG is also a signatory to other relevant international and regional platforms for action committing the government to promoting the advancement of women by eliminating family and sexual violence. [5] However, like many other countries, PNG has not matched this international level of progress by developing policies at the national level. The good work done by the Law Reform Commission (LRC) in the 1980s and 1990s, in formulating appropriate recommendations for legislative reforms and for broader action to address violence against women in PNG, was largely ignored by politicians. [6] This failure, and many others since, has led Amnesty International to conclude recently that the PNG state 'is doing very little to promote and fulfil the realisation of women's rights or to protect women from human rights abuses. In fact, State agents themselves are often directly implicated in perpetrating violence against women' (AI 2006, 3; HRW 2005, 2006; Eves and Butt 2008, 19). Numerous reports on the issue of gender-based violence in PNG have appeared over the years (AI 2006; Bradley 2001; HRW 2005, 2006; INA 2001; LRC 1992). [7]

The full extent of the problem of gender-based violence in PNG today is difficult to gauge, because no nation-wide generalisable research has been undertaken since the Law Reform Commission's research in the 1980s. This found widespread violence against women in the form of wife-beating, 67 percent of women in rural areas and 56 percent of women in urban areas having been abused by their husbands (Bradley 2001, 7). It also found considerable regional variation, ranging from a maximum of 100 percent in the Western Highlands Province to a minimum of 49 percent in Oro Province. For urban-dwellers, it showed that 56 percent of wives of low income earners and 62 percent of elite wives had been physically assaulted by their husbands (LRC 1987, 2).

In the absence of recent comprehensive data, statistics from the police, reports in the media, and anecdotal evidence show that gender-based violence, and especially violence against women, is still widespread and in epidemic proportions. Week after week, horrific reports appear in the national media of

---

4   PNG ratified the convention in January 12, 1995. So far, PNG has not submitted reports as required of signatories. For a more detailed account of PNG's commitments, see Bradley (2001, 4–5) and Amnesty International (2006, 25–6).

5   Including the Pacific Platform for Action on Women and Sustainable Development, 1994, and the Revised Pacific Platform for Action on the Advancement of Women and Gender Equality, 2004.

6   For more detail, see Amnesty International (2006, 26–7). Some legislative reforms have been introduced by Lady Carol Kidu, though the majority of the LRC recommendations are yet to be implemented (AI 2006, 27).

7   These reports make suggestions about what the state should be doing through legislative reform and the law and justice sector, and about support mechanisms the state should provide for the victims of violence. None of these, however, focuses on the issue of masculinity or recognises the need to work closely with men and boys in addressing the problem.

women being killed by intimate partners or of cases of violent rape. Other forms of violent crime also appear to be at epidemic proportions and this may indicate the emergence of a new masculine ethos, the origins of which have hardly been investigated.

Research in 2005, as part of the PNG Armed Violence Assessment in the National Capital District (NCD) and the Southern Highlands Province (SHP), also confirms that a significant proportion of the violence in communities in PNG occurs in households among intimates and kin. Evidence from household surveys suggests that serious domestic violence is rising and that this is a primary contributor to feelings of insecurity, though other factors such as social conflict and armed criminality are also considered important (Haley 2005, 30; Haley and Muggah 2006, 166). The researchers found that in the six months prior to the survey, domestic and family violence affected 18 percent of surveyed households in the NCD and 26 percent in the SHP. Moreover, they indicate considerable under-reporting, since the respondents made it clear that they reported only the more serious cases, such as those involving broken limbs (Haley 2005, 30; Haley and Muggah 2006, 170–172). Significantly, they also found that domestic violence was not evenly represented in all areas of the NCD, with a greater number of cases occurring in the settlements. They also found a correlation between the provincial origins of NCD households and the preponderance of domestic violence. For example, domestic violence marked 24 percent of the households originally from the Highlands or Gulf Provinces and 23 percent of those from Central Province, while those households with origins in the Momase and Islands regions reported no domestic violence (Haley and Muggah 2006, 172).

Sexual violence is a major problem in much of PNG and has been for many years (NSRRT and Jenkins 1994; Bradley 2001, 13; Banks 2000). Violence and coercion, including verbal threats and forced sex, are common features of young people's sexual experiences and of adult intimate relationships. The Interim report of the Law Reform Commission reported that of the rapes and sexual assaults reported to Port Moresby General Hospital for the first three months of 1985, 22 percent were of girls aged between 11 and 15 years old, 12 percent of girls between eight and 11 years old, and 13 percent of girls under eight years old (1987, 6). In the research conducted by the NSRRT and Jenkins, 60 percent of men reported having participated in a gang rape (known as line-ups), at some time in their lives, involving an average of ten men at a time (1994, 102).

More recently, the Port Moresby Community Crime Survey found in 2004 that females were most likely to suffer sexual assault, followed by property crime with force and vehicle theft (NRI and JAG 2005, 3). The Port Moresby Diagnosis of Insecurity Report also reports high levels of sexual violence. In a summary of the criminal activities of 1,097 male youths, it reports 74 had committed rape (UN Habitat 2004, 24). [8] Although not disaggregated by sex, this research reports 22 percent of the youth sample had been a victim of physical abuse and 16 percent of sexual abuse (UN Habitat 2004, 24).

As with domestic violence, accurate and up-to-date figures on the extent of sexual violence in PNG are hard to come by, although the PNG Armed Violence Assessment confirms that it remains a major concern. In the six months prior to the survey, over 8 percent of the respondents in the SHP and 3 percent of respondents in the NCD reported that someone in their household had been the victim of sexual assault or rape, often involving the use of weapons, such as firearms and bush knives (Haley 2005, 35; Haley and Muggah 2006, 170, 174). In the SHP, 89 percent of the incidents occurred in the Hela region (the western end of the province), while in the NCD 60 percent occurred in the settlements (Haley 2005, 35). In rural PNG, most sexual assaults and rapes occurred in the village, often in the home, and the perpetrators were generally known to the victim (Haley and Muggah 2006, 174). They also found that young and very young girls make up a greater percentage of rape victims than occurred two decades ago (Haley and Muggah 2006, 174).

These findings are generally supported by Lewis and colleagues, who found high levels of sexual abuse among respondents in their survey undertaken in 2005 and 2006 among 415 women, mostly between 20 to 30 years of age, attending antenatal, STI and VCT clinics in four provinces. [9] They found that 27.5 percent (114 of 415) of women had been sexually abused under the age of 16 years (Lewis et al. 2007, 5, 57). The abuse women were subjected to included unwanted sexual talk (18.5 percent or 77 women); unwanted sexual touching (13 percent or 54 women); sexual penetration (10 percent or 40 women) and sexual exposure by the offender (1 percent or 4 women) (Lewis et al. 2007, 57). Those subject to sexual assault included some who were gang-raped. As other research has also shown, the offenders were mostly known to the victims, being relatives or neighbours (Lewis et al. 2007, 5).

The ramifications of this kind of experience for these women are major. Those who were subject to sexual abuse were more likely: to be in relationships that were violent (70 percent compared to 54 percent) and sexually abusive (65.5 percent compared to 38 percent); to have sex at a much younger age (16.9 years compared to 18.24); to work away from home (37 percent as opposed to 21 percent); to be involved in the exchange of sex for money (29 percent as opposed to 2.7 percent), goods or gifts (18.6 percent compared to 2.7 percent) or favours (21 percent compared to 3 percent); to have more sexual partners (16.7 percent compared to 5.9 percent having two current partners); to participate in

---

8   Also 31 murders, 130 assaults, 136 car-jackings and 59 cases of unspecified violence (UN Habitat 2004, 24).

9   National Capital District, Western Highlands Province, Morobe Province and Western Province.

casual sex (25 percent compared to 10 percent) than those who were not subject to sexual abuse. Women who have been abused as children are more likely to be HIV positive, with 28 percent of women who were abused being HIV positive (Lewis et al. 2007, 5, 57).

Legitimating Violence

Violence is seen as legitimate only if the woman is perceived to have failed to behave in the manner proper to a wife. As one man remarked to me, 'We don't fight for nothing, there must be a reason' (*mipela no pait nating nating, i mas got as*). Women are also generally in agreement with this view; as one woman said, 'Husbands don't hit their wives for no reason' (*man i no paitim meri nating*). Thus it seems that though violence is condoned, unprovoked violence is not.

Unquestionably, the prevailing gender ideology in PNG is that violence is an entirely appropriate corrective to even the slightest failure of wives to fulfil their perceived marital duties and proprieties. The research by the Law Reform Commission found that the wife's failure to carry out her duties was stated by 63.2 percent of men as leading to problems in marriage (this was followed by sexual jealousy at 62.1 percent) (Toft and Bonnell 1985, 20, 45, 46). [10] According to the literature, this belief remains widespread in PNG. For example, it underlies Tolai domestic violence: 'The general rationalisation for coercive violence against wives is that it is "corrective", "educational", "informative", or "for teaching a lesson"' (Bradley 1985, 50). It exists also among the Abelam of East Sepik Province, where the men believe that 'occasional beatings are sometimes "necessary" in order to socialise women properly' (Scaglion 1990, 189). Among the Bun, also in East Sepik Province, the reason men gave for hitting their wives was that the wife did not prepare food or did not carry out her work (McDowell 1990, 180). Similarly, the Kewa of the Southern Highlands say that a husband hits his wife when she disobeys him or fails to do his bidding (Josephides 1985, 94).

By far the commonest 'mistake' I found during fieldwork in Chimbu was for a wife to refuse her husband sex. One woman, a member of an interdenominational women's group who often counsels women who have experienced domestic violence, suggested that regardless of what men may say in public about the causes of violence, the main one from her experience was women refusing their husbands sex. She went so far as to say that there wasn't a night that went by when such violence, often including marital rape, did not occur.

---

10   Female respondents gave less priority to the wife's failure to meet obligations (36.4 percent) and more to sexual jealousy (69.4 percent) (Toft and Bonnell 1985, 20).

This has also been found by research in other parts of PNG. Lewis and colleagues found that 52.2 percent (217 of 415) of women felt that they could not refuse sex to their partners (2007, 118; see also Pantumari and Bamne this volume). This lack of control over sex was even greater in relationships marked by physical violence and 71 percent of women who said they were subject to this kind of violence could not refuse sex (Lewis et al. 2007, 118). Women who were sexually abused were also in a similar situation, with 72 percent of sexually abused women unable to say no to sex with their partners. There were also high figures for emotional abuse and women who were socially isolated by their husbands or partners, with 51 percent of emotionally abused women, and 71 percent of women socially isolated, being unable to refuse sex (Lewis et al. 2007, 6). Refusing sex was the biggest trigger for violence in the relationships with 176 women of 415 (Lewis et al. 2007, 6).

Far from being simply impetuous and irrational, the violence that men inflict on women is an execution of power which has the effect of keeping women in their place, subservient to men. Women's subordination is most clearly marked in the marriage relationship, since a woman is bound to obey her husband by virtue of the bride-price that has been transferred to her relatives from her husband's relatives (Bradley 1985, 34). Thus the payment of bride-price is used to justify the husband's authority over his wife, entitling him to her labour, her sexual services, and her full obedience. Put bluntly, the underlying and general objection is to any exercise of agency on the part of a woman. [11] What is at issue, then, are the traditional relations of power and the continuation of the control that men have held over women. This has the logical consequence of legitimating violence, since having authority means exercising authority and, ultimately, using punitive means to enforce this.

Tok Pisin expressions, such as *baim meri* (buying a woman) fail to convey the complexity of the exchange relationship and have the effect of reinforcing the belief that the woman now becomes the property of the man. It appears that under various modern influences, perhaps especially the commodification of exchange, the traditional meaning and practice of bride-price has been eroded and largely forgotten, a simplified version taking its place. Rather than being seen as an exchange which creates a relationship between two social groupings, and the bride's kin being compensated for her loss, the bride-price exchange is now widely understood quite literally as a simple property transaction, in

---

11 It should be stressed that women are not always passive victims of male domination and violence, but in many instances are agents who develop strategies and responses to the situations they find themselves in (see Wardlow 2004, 2006). Unfortunately, the agency women express is often reactive, being defined by the parameters of the masculine culture in which they live. The domestic violence that takes place in polygynous households, for example, often sees wives fighting between themselves.

which a woman becomes the property of a man. This is expressed by women, for example as: *em baimim mi pinis* (he's bought me), *em ownim mi* (he owns me), or *mi properti bilong en* (I'm his property).

Having 'purchased' a woman, a man believes he owns her, as though she is little more than an object. This was put by one woman in the following way: 'He feels he has paid bride price and he owns me. I can't do anything else. I have to sleep with him' (Lewis et al. 2007, 121). As Zimmer-Tamakoshi remarks, men have variously portrayed women as men's 'hands', 'tradestores', 'tractors' and 'capital assets' (1997, 541). Such dehumanising designations point to women's roles as labourers and assets for the creation of wealth. During field research in Chimbu Province, one woman explained it this way: 'When a man has exchanged bride-price (*baim em*), he is the boss now. So he claims her as his property, or something like that, and the woman will be his labourer until he dies'.

However, it is important to note that violence against women is by no means confined to wedlock and that many cases of physical abuse occur in relationships where bride-price has not been exchanged (see Toft 1985). While many of the rationales for men's power and control over women are given added weight by marriage, to understand marital violence, 'it is essential to see it in the context of relations between men and women in general, and between husbands and wives in particular' (Bradley 1985, 33). Violence against women is legitimated not only by the exchange of bride-price but also by men's general domination over women.[12]

The normalisation of violence that is generally a cultural feature of PNG society has specific implications for HIV transmission rates. Jenkins has stressed that gang-rape or *lainap* results in a very high rate of HIV transmission; recent work has also highlighted the sexual abuse of very young girls and children as a cause of HIV transmission (HRW 2005; HELP 2005; Luluaki 2003); however sexual violence—as discussed below—is a standard feature of marriage. Even where certain forms of violence against women are not directly related to HIV transmission, as directly as say sexual violence, it underpins the severely diminished sexual agency that women possess (see Scheper-Hughes 1994, 993; Liguori and Lamas 2003). With so little control over their lives and their bodies, they are extremely vulnerable to infection.

---

12   Some commentators have suggested that male angst and confusion in the face of rapid change have led to violence against women. Josephides, speaking of the Kewa of the Southern Highlands, refines this view, saying that these changes are giving rise to a comparative lessening of male power in relation to women which sees women slipping from men's grasp (1994, 187). The changes, such as the Constitutional recognition of rights of equality, the availability of education and new career opportunities, that have brought a new independence to women, disturb the traditional gender roles. Much violence against women is motivated by fear because of the resultant weakening of men's ability to control them (Josephides 1994, 190).

Negotiating Safe Sex: Is It as Easy as ABC?

PNG's intervention to stem the epidemic has been based on the ABC (A for abstinence, B for be faithful, and C for condoms) model of prevention, which is widely employed in many countries (Eves and Butt 2008, 6, 19; Wardlow 2008, 203–204). [13] Such recommendations are gender-blind since they assume a subject who is in a position to control his or her body and sexual health, oblivious to the fact that while this may sometimes be the case for men, it is rarely so for women. Failing to recognise that sexual encounters are arenas in which the unequal power relations between men and women are played out, they assume that the agent of prevention is an independent person who can make decisions irrespective of the opinions and actions of others and of the wider social context in which they live (Wood and Jewkes 1997, 43–44; see Ellison, Parker and Campbell 2003, 5).

Exhortations to practise safe sex raise the perplexing question of how this might be achieved in the context of unequal power relationships, where social and economic conditions severely limit women's ability to control their sexual activity. [14] Further, these HIV prevention messages promote the myth that being faithful in marriage makes one immune from HIV, leading people to disregard potential risks (Bujra 2000, 72). A great deal of research is suggesting that far from being immune to HIV infection, married women are more susceptible because their husbands often do not follow the injunctions of the ABC. Women are often not aware of the past or even the present sexual history of their husbands and so do not perceive themselves as potentially at risk of HIV infection. Even when they are aware of their husband's other sexual relationships, they often can do little (cf. Pantumari and Bamne this volume; McLeod and Macintyre this volume). This has led some commentators to remark that marriage is a high-risk setting. In PNG there exist many instances of women who have practised marital fidelity being infected by their husbands (Aeno 2005; Hammar this volume). As noted above, sex is seen by husbands as their prerogative to which 'no' is never an acceptable answer, and as I describe below, it is a brave woman who asks her husband to use a condom.

In the context of unequal power, it is invariably men who determine the timing of sexual intercourse and its nature, including whether a woman should try to conceive, and whether or not condoms will be used (Eves and Butt 2008, 9; Campbell 1995, 197; Gupta and Weiss, 1993; WHO 2001, 11; Wood and Jewkes 1997, 41; Wood, Marforah and Jewkes 1998, 235). Evidence from around

---

13 More recently, this has been expanded by the addition of a D, signifying 'do other things (than penetrative sex)' (PNG NAC 2006b, iii, 5).

14 As Seidel and Vidal noted some time ago, married women are not even regarded as being at risk in some national intervention programs, suggesting 'a glaringly inadequate construction of sexuality' (1997, 64).

the world suggests that conditions where women have little power and men exercise control in intimate relationships are associated with increased HIV risk behaviours and infection (Dunkle et al. 2004; Chege 2005, 115). As Maman and colleagues suggest, 'as long as traditional gender norms for sexual relationships persist, defined by men pressuring women and women resisting, negotiation of condom use by women remains difficult' (2000, 473; Jewkes, Levin and Penn-Kekana 2003, 126).

Violence, of course, intensifies the problematic nature of existing HIV prevention strategies that are promoted globally (Maman et al. 2000, 461). [15] Violence or the ever-present threat of violence severely constrains women's ability to adopt safe sex practices, women who live in abusive relationships being unable to negotiate condom use or even to suggest using them (Eves and Butt 2008, 19; Campbell 1995, 197; Chege 2005; Johnson 2001, 126; Larkin, Andrews and Mitchell 2006, 209; UNFPA, UNIFEM and OSAGI 2005, 18). HIV prevention programs will have limited impact unless they somehow take into account the role of violence in women's lives (Maman et al. 2000, 476).

The study by Lewis and colleagues found that women in PNG are also limited in their ability to negotiate condom use due to lack of knowledge and experience, which are generally seen as men's business, and due to misinformation about the effectiveness of condoms. This study found that women who attempt to negotiate condom use are likely to experience anger and physical violence from their husbands or partners (Lewis et al. 2007, 9, 139–40). Asking their sexual partner to use condoms was one of the three most common triggers for men to use violence. As one woman remarked: 'If I tell him to use condom he will bash me up, he says I am his wife and don't need condom' (Lewis et al. 2007, 109). Even women who assessed their own risk of being infected with HIV as high, because of their partners' other sexual relationships, were unable to use condoms. For example, 64 percent who see themselves as 'at risk' do not use condoms (Lewis et al. 2007, 6).

Much international research has shown that while women are willing to use condoms with their non-regular partners, they are less likely to do so with their regular partners (Heise and Elias 1995, 936, 938). In the United States, for example, condom use is much more likely in fully commercial sex than it is in longer-term or more intimate relationships, and it is almost unknown in marriage (Maman et al. 2000, 473). This also appears to be the case in PNG where women use condoms at a higher rate when exchanging sex for gifts, goods or money (Lewis et al. 2007, 131). Condom use is more likely if the woman experienced some form of childhood sexual abuse. Forty percent of women who

---

15   Research in South Africa has found that more frequent condom use was associated with lower levels of violence for women in their primary relationships (Harrison et al. 2006, 716).

were sexually abused as children say that they use condoms with their partners compared to 24 percent of non-sexually abused women (Lewis et al. 2007, 134). The reasons for this correlation are unclear and research to investigate why and how this is so may be worthwhile.

As in many parts of the world, efforts to promote the use of the male condom have failed to reduce HIV rates in PNG. As elsewhere, this is largely because of men's resistance to behavioural change and especially their reluctance to use condoms. PNG men prefer sex which is 'skin to skin' as it is sometimes called (see Lewis et al. 2007, 139). More generally, there is a widespread perception in PNG that the distribution of condoms has licensed pre-marital sex and sex outside of marriage and that condoms are associated with sex-work. Far from containing sexuality and confining it to marriage, condoms are viewed as unleashing it and, as a consequence, spreading HIV (see also Lewis et al. 2007, 137; Wilde 2007, 62 and below).

The research by Lewis and colleagues found that while there was more condom use by women today than in some figures cited in the literature (see for example UNDP 2005, 7), it was still not very high or regular (2007). Out of the 409 women who answered the question 'Do you use a condom with your partner?' 73 percent (299) said they did not. Of those who did use them, 19 percent (76) used them sometimes, 6 percent (23) used them often and 3 percent (11) used them always. Significantly, and of concern, is that 63 percent who were HIV positive reported that they do not use condoms (Lewis et al. 2007, 129–30).

Recent research among men has found that men's use of condoms is higher but also not very regular and is accompanied by the same kinds of concerns and misinformation that Lewis and her colleagues found. [16] A survey undertaken by Wilde, in 2004, on condom use in Western Province, found that many respondents were concerned that condoms were not 100 percent effective, with more than 30 percent believing that even when they were used properly they would not prevent the transmission of HIV (Wilde 2007, 64). Despite this, many men believed nevertheless that condoms were effective for family planning and could prevent pregnancy. This appears to be a widely held belief, and I came across a similar idea during fieldwork in the Southern Highlands Province in 2007.

------

16   In the last three years, 91 of the total surveyed said they were sexually active, with 22 of the 71 married men admitting they had extramarital affairs and of these 13 saying they did not use a condom. A total of 26 men who had one or more sexual relationships said condoms were not used (Wilde 2007, 64).

Redefining Masculinity and the Language of Prevention

In recognition of the extent to which masculine attitudes and standards prevent them from practising safe sex, efforts to understand and target these have begun to increase. In PNG in recent years, some attempts have been made to put out prevention messages targeting the general issue of violence against women and the more specific issue of violence and HIV. A number of these interventions have endeavoured specifically to convert masculinities founded on violence to those that embrace a respect for women as well as the practice of safe sex. Here I review some of these initiatives, focussing initially on interventions targeting violence against women, before discussing those that address violence and HIV.

Internationally, campaigns against violence have tried to promote non-violence as a desirable masculine trait. As Flood writes, anti-violence campaigns directed at men have adopted three broad strategies. The first of these is to promote alternative constructions of masculinity which displace the positive cultural association between violence and masculinity. This has meant appropriating the cultural expectations of manhood to give non-violence a masculine face. He refers to this as a 'rescripting' of masculinity. An example was the production of the slogan, 'Real men don't bash or rape women', used internationally including in PNG. The second strategy draws on stereotypically masculine culture, particularly sport, to appeal to men. The slogan, 'Violence Against Women—It's against the rules', used in an anti-violence campaign in New South Wales is one instance. The third strategy has been to show men speaking out, or standing together, against violence. Such campaigns have sometimes used men who have a public profile, such as celebrities or sporting figures, whose opposition to violence, it is hoped, will be emulated (Flood 2002–3, 28). Other campaigns have sought to appeal to ordinary men by utilising unknown men who have no public profile, but with whom men are likely to identify because of their ordinariness.

In PNG, campaigns addressing violence against women have followed some of the strategies Flood identifies. Some simply employ declarative statements, mirroring the slogan used internationally: 'Stop Violence against Women'. For example, a t-shirt produced by National AIDS Council Secretariat (NACS) has a red hand on a yellow background with the statement 'Stop the Violence Against Women'. The international NGO, Save the Children, has produced two posters that involve the kind of 'rescripting' of masculinity that reinforces gender difference. These feature a married couple on one, and young couple on the other, with the couples in intimate proximity. Both carry the main message of *Bel isi imas stap oltaim*, which translates as an imperative: 'Always be calm and coolheaded'. The poster with a married couple is about wife-beating, with man saying that when he and his wife have a disagreement they sit down and sort it out (*Taim mitupela igat bel hevi, mitupela i save sindaun isi na stretim*). He adds, 'I'm a real man, I don't beat women' (*Mi trupela man, mi no save paitim meri*). [17] The second poster with the young couple addresses the issue of non-consensual sex or rape, with the man saying, 'If she says no, I say that's alright, we're together on that' (*Taim en tok nogat mi tok em orait, wanbel i stap*). This poster also redefines what constitutes a real man by declaring, 'I'm a real man, I don't ruin (rape) women' (*Mi trupela man, mi no save bagarapim meri*). [18]

Organisations such as AusAID, the Australian government aid organisation, are increasingly using sport as means to promote important health and social messages. This sporting diplomacy has involved sponsoring matches between Papua New Guinea and Australia and visits by high-profile sporting figures from Australia to communities to discuss issues such as HIV and violence against women. The game of rugby league, which is hugely popular throughout PNG, has been at the forefront of this sporting diplomacy and in March 2008 the Prime Minister of Australia announced a $260,000 package of support to develop sport, with a significant proportion being assigned to rugby league (Australian Government 2008).

Rugby league, the only sport in PNG to run a full national competition, is considered the national sport and is often put forward as a medium for national unity, a way of uniting the diverse cultures of the PNG nation. Perhaps incongruously, Australian rugby league is followed fanatically by tens of thousands of PNG fans. Even in the remotest villages one can come across men wearing Australian Rugby League jerseys and people knowing the names of ARL teams and players. The annual series of three 'State of Origin' rugby league matches between the teams of the Australian states of Queensland (who wear the colour maroon) and New South Wales (who wear the colour blue) are major events in PNG. Everyone tries hard to get to the nearest town or city in the hope of viewing the match on television. Fans paint their faces and don the colours of their respective teams, PMVs (Public Motor Vehicles) are decorated with flags and other paraphernalia, and supermarkets sell boxes of sugary breakfast cereals in blue and maroon and saveloys and matching buns in either blue or maroon colours!

---

17   The website of *The National* newspaper used a similar slogan on its Weekender page during 2006. In this case, the message, 'Real men don't hit women' was superimposed on a photo of a young woman with a thick bandage on her right eye and her arm in a sling. The newspaper had used the same photograph previously on a poster distributed with the printed edition, but bearing the words, 'This could be your sister ... wife bashing is wrong!' On seeing this poster, a senior police officer at a meeting with others working in the Law and Justice sector in Buka, remarked, 'It is good to see that men are still in control' (reported by an Australian Advisor present at the meeting). Thus it is easy to see why many women do not believe that it is worthwhile to report domestic violence to the police.

18   There is also a third poster, featuring a married couple and a young girl, which addresses the issue of violence against children. This one does not seek to redefine masculinity.

For a number of years AusAID has sponsored rugby league matches in Port Moresby between the respective Prime Ministers' teams. The first of these took place in 2005 as part of the 30th anniversary celebrations of PNG independence. As the Australian High Commissioner to PNG commented at the reception to welcome the visiting Australian team: 'Sport can bring individuals and communities together to discuss tough issues' (Potts 2006). The High Commissioner echoed the theme of playing by the rules that has been a feature of anti-domestic violence messages in Australia when he remarked: 'One of [the players'] key messages is that violence against women is against the rules. We all need to respect women, stop the violence against them and protect them from the spread of HIV and AIDS—here, in Australia, and internationally' (Potts 2006). [19] He also reiterated a key message of some of the National AIDS Council posters about staying safe on and off the field: '[The players] will also discuss the importance of playing by the rules—this includes staying safe on and off the field and respecting other people, especially women' (Potts 2006).

During a visit to a community in Port Moresby while the Australian team was on tour, the coach, Mal Meninga (the former Canberra Raiders player and more recently coach of the Queensland State of Origin team) reminded listeners: 'There can be no rugby league players in the future if this terrible disease isn't stopped now' (AusAID 2006, 19). Elsewhere he is reported as saying: 'HIV and AIDS needs to be tackled in Papua New Guinea and the message needs to reach every village that sexual violence against women is not acceptable and only increases the spread of the disease' (Meninga 2006). Through its aid support project to the National AIDS Council AusAID has also produced and funded posters featuring Meninga and Brad Fittler (Captain of the Sydney Roosters and Captain of Australian Kangaroos Rugby League team). The first poster (see Figure 1) showed Fittler wearing a cap with the slogan *Lukautim yu yet AIDS* (Protect yourself from AIDS) and featuring the slogan 'Play Safe … Stay Safe': 'To be World Champions we need to play hard, but we also play it safe. And in life, like sport you have to play safe to stay safe … from AIDS'. Later posters featured Fittler and Meninga (see Figure 2) more directly promoting the use of condoms, each holding a packet of the socially marketed condoms, Karamap. Again, these put the play safe, play hard message: 'You know life is like sport, you need to play hard, but also play safe in order to stay safe … from AIDS'. The message concluded by reminding the viewers that if they were thinking about sex to think about using Karamap condoms.

---

19   An almost identical message was voiced by the next Australian High Commissioner in 2007 (*Sydney Morning Herald*, 16 August 2007).

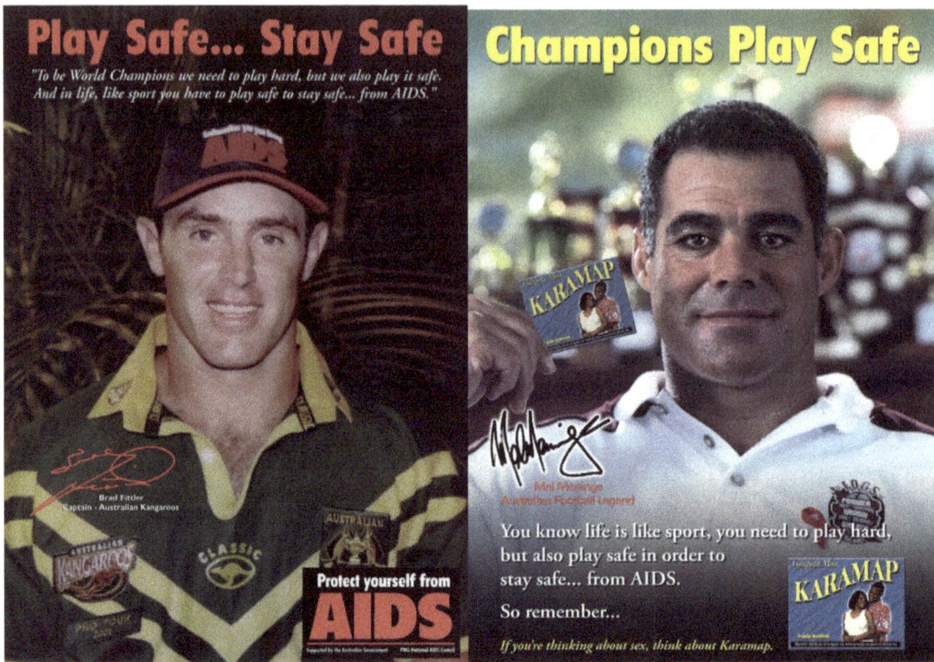

Figure 1 (left): Poster featuring Brad Fittler. PNG National AIDS Council. From the collections of Richard Eves.

Figure 2 (right): Poster featuring Mal Meninga. PNG National AIDS Council. From the collections of Richard Eves.

An effort to rescript masculinity was also made in two early AIDS prevention posters promoting the use of condoms. The first featured a spear-wielding warrior in traditional highlands dress holding a body-sized condom in front of himself instead of a shield. The message on the poster declared that he was not afraid because he has protection (*Mi no poret, Mi gat banis*). The second poster had an identical message but featured a warrior in coastal dress. Rather than being ready for battle, these warriors were ready for sex. As Campbell has noted, internationally some HIV prevention programs have often considered it 'useful to associate condom use with masculinity, promoting the idea that a man proves his masculinity by using condoms' (1995, 206). While this strategy may sometimes be effective, it is based on traditional notions of manliness and reinforces associations between masculinity and strong sexual performance (Campbell 1995, 206; Eves and Butt 2008, 6). Rather than displacing forms of masculinity that encourage violence or predatory sexual behaviour, such approaches encourage the very aspects of masculinity that need to be displaced. This leads Flood to caution against approaches that appeal to men's sense of 'real' manhood or that invite them to 'prove themselves as men', since they may in fact actually intensify men's investment in the status quo. These are even more problematic if they represent certain qualities as uniquely male, thus assigning particular qualities such as strength and courage to men and effectively denying them to women (Flood 2002–3, 27).

Posters featuring sporting stars and which emphasise 'playing hard' run into the same problems that Campbell and Flood point out, especially when considering that sport often encourages and values dominant masculine traits, such as extreme competitiveness and aggression. Indeed, one has to look no further than the history of rugby league in PNG, which as one commentator has remarked is a history of violence (Foster 2006, 753). Far from being a 'universal language that can bring people together, no matter what their origin, background, religious beliefs or economic status' (Kofi Annan in AusAID 2006, 15), it can be a divisive force. The expatriate chairman of PNG Rugby League, alluded to this divisiveness when he commented prior to a State of Origin series that, 'it's almost a substitute for rival warfare, or for showing dominance of my clan over your clan' (cited in McLeod 2003).

Violence has often marred the State of Origin series that is so enthusiastically supported in PNG. The celebrations accompanying the watching of the games often degenerate into drunkenness and violence in which people are sometimes killed. [20] Not only does violence take place in the public settings where the game is watched, but also within homes where husbands and wives fight amongst themselves if they support opposing teams. This has led political leaders to call for the broadcasts to be banned (Foster 2006, 753).

Violence has also marred domestic PNG rugby, with the 2007 premier rugby league competition being suspended due to violence, including a referee being beaten senseless by a supporter. On this 'rugby league disgrace' the editorial writer of *The National* newspaper wondered what had turned 'team sports into a minefield of blood and potentially deadly confrontations?', commenting that the game is 'regularly transformed into bloody clashes' (*The National*, 9 May 2007).

Conclusion: Preventing Violence

The Declaration on the Elimination of all forms of Violence Against Women (DEVAW) calls for states and civil society to develop 'in a comprehensive way, preventive approaches and all those measures of a legal, political, administrative and cultural nature that promote the protection of women against any form of

---

20   During the colonial period the annual match between Papua and New Guinea, rather than cultivating a sense of national unity, emphasised division, with the 1969 match leading to looting and rioting. Eventually, in 1972 the match was abandoned (Foster 2006, 753).

violence' (UN General Assembly 1993). Speaking about the worldwide problem of violence towards women, Michau calls for the implementation of a primary prevention approach that focuses on preventing violence before it occurs. This means not only creating a legal and policy environment supportive of women's rights, but fostering a culture which promotes non-violence and relationships based on equity, and supporting individuals to take a public stand against abuse (2005, 3). This, says Michau, requires moving beyond programs that focus on one sector (such as health, police, education or judiciary) or one group (such as policy makers, battered women or youth), since effective change requires a critical mass of institutions and people who aspire to these ideals and are prepared to put their beliefs into practice. An essential first step, she argues, is to develop a gender-based analysis of why violence occurs and to recognise that women's low status, the imbalance of power, and rigid gender roles are root causes of violence against women (2005, 3).

As I stated at the start of this chapter, the automatically accepted notion that gender equals women has meant that programs to eliminate gender-based violence have concentrated on women as victims or potential victims. Men, meanwhile, have generally been taken for granted as the problem, and excluded from any positive consideration. This problem, then, was addressed mainly in negative terms, particularly the need for greater criminal justice interventions such as restraining orders and prosecution (UNDAW 2005, 30–31). In PNG, for example, most of the solutions recommended by the Law Reform Commission focused on legal changes intended to extend the protection of the law to women (Bradley 2001, 21). While an obvious need does exist for a much stronger law and justice sector approach, gender-based violence is a complex problem which cannot be solved by this alone. This is not merely because much gender-based violence is not brought to the notice of the law and justice sector but because legal and judicial measures do not address the root causes of violence. Those attempts made so far to target men through public education campaigns have also rested on easy assumptions, running the risk of reinscribing the very behaviour that needs to be eliminated, since they fail to interrogate masculinity, often appealing to existing hegemonic masculine ideals. The lesson to learn from this is that there are no simple solutions; all assumptions need to be closely interrogated. Detailed knowledge and skill, solid research and careful thought are needed to produce worthwhile programs.

As I noted at the outset, it is now more widely appreciated that if gender-based violence is to cease and the AIDS epidemic to be contained and reversed, fundamental changes are needed in men's attitudes and beliefs about women and their roles in society. Indeed, it is more and more being argued that efforts to prevent violence against women 'will fail unless they undermine the cultural and collective supports for physical and sexual assault found among many men'

(Flood 2002–3, 25). Flood and other researchers are saying that an essential way to deal with unequal gender relations and violence against women is to challenge and change dominant models of masculinity (UNDAW 2005, 32). In other words, the relationships between violence, masculinity and gender need to be understood and challenged. Since the problem of violence, and particularly violence by men against women, is clearly a category of gender, then male socialisation and what it means to be a man becomes a central aspect of any solution. It appears that many men see their manhood as dependent on their control over women and they use violence to achieve this. This has obvious ramifications for HIV prevention, as the examples presented in this chapter illustrate.

The role of men and boys in challenging and changing unequal power relations is essential (UNDAW 2005, 3; Barker 2001, 94). If gender-based violence and HIV transmission is to be seriously tackled and eliminated, men and boys must be included in the project, since they are not only part of the problem, they are part of the solution (Flood 2001, 42). In short, the aim must be to inspire men and boys to take responsibility for their actions and to adopt more constructive and cooperative behaviour. Men and boys should be seen as allies and partners who will participate in redefining manhood (Kaufman 2001, 10). In this positive approach, men should not be seen as the problem, or as criminals who should be punished, but as participants in solving the problem (UNDAW 2005, 32). Since not all successful and manly men are aggressive, and many positively reject and condemn violence, it cannot be argued that violence is an essential aspect of the male identity. The rejection of violence by some men clearly suggests that alternative models of masculinity exist and, indeed, in some traditions for a man to strike a woman is considered most unmanly. [21] This also occurs in PNG where, although violence often constitutes a pervasive manifestation of masculinity, many men are rejecting this in favour of more equitable and non-violent relationships. The challenge is to find ways of making these alternative masculinities mainstream. [22]

Acknowledgements

The field research for this chapter was undertaken during a consultancy for Caritas Australia: Exploring the role of men and masculinities in PNG in the 21st century: Finding solutions to address violence that generates empowerment for both men and women. It was written while I was an Australian Research

---

21   The Bena Bena of the Eastern Highlands have an expression which means that if a man beats his wife her blood will cover him up, he will not be able to see and will behave like an animal (pers. comm. Naomi Yupae).
22   The Caritas report suggests many practical initiatives to encourage alternative, more cooperative ways of men relating to women as equal partners (Eves 2006).

Council QE II Research Fellow in the State Society and Governance in Melanesia Program and I thank SSGM and the ARC for their institutional and funding support. The piece has benefited greatly from the constructive comments and editorial suggestions of Roe Sybylla.

References

Aeno, H. 2005. Marriage, Sex and STDs: Transmission Risks of Papua New Guinean Women as Assessed Through HIVab Counselling. Paper presented at the Annual Meeting of the Association for Social Anthropology in Oceania, Kauai, Hawai'i, February 2–6.

AI (Amnesty International). 2006. Papua New Guinea Violence Against Women: Not Inevitable, Never Acceptable! AI Index: ASA 34/002/2006.

Anon. 2007. Fittler, Meninga to Coach PM's XIII. *Sydney Morning Herald*, 16 August, 2007. http://www.smh.com.au/news/Sport/Fittler-Meninga-to-coach-PMs-XIII/2007/08/16/1186857670449.html (accessed 27 April 2010).

AusAID. 2006. Playing the Game. *Focus* Jan.-April 2006: 15–19. Canberra: AusAID.

Australian Government. 2008. Media Release: *Australian Support for PNG*. 7 March 2008.

Banks, C. 2000. Contextualising Sexual Violence: Rape and Carnal Knowledge in Papua New Guinea. In *Reflections on Violence in Melanesia*, ed. S. Dinnen and A. Ley, 83–104. Leichhardt and Canberra: Hawkins Press (Federation Press) and Asia Pacific Press.

Barker, G. 2001. 'Cool Your Head, Man': Preventing Gender Based Violence in Favelas. *Development* 44 (3): 94–98.

Barker, G. and C. Ricardo. 2005. Young Men and the Construction of Masculinity in Sub-Saharan Africa: Implications for HIV/AIDS, Conflict, and Violence. *World Bank Social Development Papers: Conflict Prevention and Reconstruction, No. 26.* Washington: World Bank.

Beer, B. 2008. Buying Betel and Selling Sex: Contested Boundaries, Risk Milieus, and Discourses about HIV/AIDS in the Markham Valley, Papua New Guinea. In *Making Sense of AIDS: Culture, Sexuality, and Power in Melanesia*, ed. L. Butt and R. Eves, 97–115. Honolulu: University of Hawai'i Press.

Bradley, C. 1985. Attitudes and Practices Relating to Marital Violence among the Tolai of East New Britain. In *Domestic Violence in Papua New Guinea*, ed. S. Toft, 33–71. Law Reform Commission of Papua New Guinea Monograph No. 3. Port Moresby: Law Reform Commission of Papua New Guinea.

Bradley, C. 2001. *Family and Sexual Violence in PNG: An Integrated Long-Term Strategy*. Report to the Family Violence Action Committee of the Consultative Implementation and Monitoring Council. Discussion Paper No. 84. Port Moresby: Institute of National Affairs.

Brison, K. 1995. Changing Constructions of Masculinity in a Sepik Society. *Ethnology* 34 (3): 155–175.

Brown, P. 1988. Gender and Social Change: New Forms of Independence for Simbu Women. *Oceania* 59 (2): 123–142.

Brown, J., J. Sorrell and M. Raffaelli. 2005. An Exploratory Study of Constructions of Masculinity, Sexuality and HIV/AIDS in Namibia, Southern Africa. *Culture, Health and Sexuality* 7 (6): 585–598.

Bujra, J. 2000. Risk and Trust: Unsafe Sex, Gender and AIDS in Tanzania. In *Risk Revisited*, ed. P. Caplan, 59–84. London: Pluto Press.

Campbell, C. 1992. Learning to Kill? Masculinity, the Family and Violence in Natal. *Journal of Southern African Studies* 18 (3): 614–628.

Campbell, C. 1997. Migrancy, Masculine Identities, and AIDS: The Psychosocial Context of HIV Transmission on the South African Gold Mines. *Social Science and Medicine* 45 (2): 273–281.

Campbell, C. A. 1995. Male Gender Roles and Sexuality: Implications for Women's AIDS Risk and Prevention. *Social Science and Medicine* 41 (2): 197–210.

Carovano, K. 1995. *HIV and the Challenges Facing Men*. Issues Paper No. 15. UNDP: HIV and Development Programme.

Chege, J. 2005. Interventions Linking Gender Relations and Violence with Reproductive Health and HIV: Rationale, Effectiveness and Gaps. *Agenda: Special Focus on Gender, Culture and Rights* (special issue): 114–123.

Cleaver, F. 2002. Men and Masculinities: New Directions in Gender and Development. In *Making Men Matter: Men, Masculinities and Gender Relations in Development*, ed. F. Cleaver, 1–27. London: Zed Books.

Connell, R. W. 1995. *Masculinities*. Berkeley: University of California Press.

Cornwall, A. and N. Lindisfarne. 1994. Introduction. In *Dislocating Masculinity: Comparative Ethnographies*, ed. A. Cornwall and N. Lindisfarne, 1–10. London: Routledge.

Courtenay, W. H. 2000. Constructions of Masculinity and their Influence on Men's Well-Being: A Theory of Gender and Health. *Social Science and Medicine* 50 (10): 1385–1401.

Dowsett, G. W., P. Aggleton, S. Abega, C. Jenkins, T. M. Marshall, A. Runganga, J. Schifter, M. L. Tan, and C. M. Tarr. 1998. Changing Gender Relations among Young People: The Global Challenge for HIV/AIDS Prevention. *Critical Public Health* 8 (4): 291–309.

Dunkle, K. L., R. K. Jewkes, H. C. Brown, M. Yoshihama, G. E. Gray, J. A. McIntyre and S. D. Ha. 2004. Prevalence and Patterns of Gender-based Violence and Revictimization among Women Attending Antenatal Clinics in Soweto, South Africa. *American Journal of Epidemiology* 160 (3): 230–239.

Ellison, G. T. H., with M. Parker and C. Campbell. 2003. Introduction: Learning from HIV and AIDS: From Multidisciplinary to Interdisciplinarity. In *Learning from HIV and AIDS*, ed. G. Ellison, M. Parker and C. Campbell, 1–31. Cambridge: Cambridge University Press.

Eves, R. 2006. Exploring the Role of Men and Masculinities in Papua New Guinea in the 21st century: How to Address Violence in Ways that Generate Empowerment for Both Men and Women. Sydney: Caritas Australia.

Eves, R. and L. Butt. 2008. Introduction. In *Making Sense of AIDS: Culture, Sexuality, and Power in Melanesia*, ed. L. Butt and R. Eves, 1–23. Honolulu: University of Hawai'i Press.

Flood, M. 2001. Men's Collective Anti-Violence Activism and the Struggle for Gender Justice. *Development* 44 (3): 42–47.

Flood, M. 2002–3. Engaging Men: Strategies and Dilemmas in Violence Prevention Education among Men. *Women Against Violence: A Feminist Journal* 13: 25–32.

Foreman, M., ed. 1999. *AIDS and Men: Taking Risks or Taking Responsibility?* London: The Panos Institute and Zed Books.

Foster, R. J. 2006. From Trobriand Cricket to Rugby Nation: The Mission of Sport in Papua New Guinea. *The International Journal of the History of Sport* 23 (5): 739–758.

Giffin, K. 1998. Beyond Empowerment: Heterosexualities and the Prevention of AIDS. *Social Science and Medicine* 46 (2): 151–156.

Global Coalition on Women and AIDS and WHO 2004. Violence Against Women and HIV/AIDS: Critical Intersections—Intimate Partner Violence and HIV/AIDS. *Information Bulletin Series No. 1*. Geneva: WHO.

Goddard, M. 2004. *Women in Papua New Guinea's Village Courts*. State, Society and Governance in Melanesia Discussion Paper 2004/3. Canberra: State, Society and Governance in Melanesia (SSGM), Research School of Pacific and Asian Studies, Australian National University.

Gupta, G. R. 1995. Integrating a Gender Perspective in UNAIDS Policies and Programmes: A Proposed Strategy. Geneva: UNAIDS.

Gupta, G. R. and E. Weiss. 1993. Women's Lives and Sex: Implications for AIDS prevention. *Culture, Medicine and Psychiatry* 17 (4): 399–412.

Haley, N. 2005. *PNG Armed Violence Assessment*. Port Moresby: UNDP.

Haley, N. 2008. When There's No Accessing Basic Health Care: Local Politics and Responses to HIV/AIDS at Lake Kopiago, Papua New Guinea. In *Making Sense of AIDS: Culture, Sexuality, and Power in Melanesia*, ed. L. Butt and R. Eves, 24–40. Honolulu: University of Hawai'i Press.

Haley, N. and R. Muggah. 2006. Jumping the Gun: Armed Violence in Papua New Guinea. In *Small Arms Survey 2006*, 165–187. Oxford: Oxford University Press.

Harrison, A., L. F. O'Sullivan, S. Hoffman, C. Dolezal and R. Morrell. 2006. Gender Role and Relationship Norms among Young Adults in South Africa: Measuring the Context of Masculinity and HIV Risk. *Journal of Urban Health* 83 (4): 709–722.

Heise, L. L. and C. Elias. 1995. Transforming AIDS Prevention to Meet Women's Needs: A Focus on Developing Countries. *Social Science and Medicine* 40 (7): 931–943.

HELP Resources. 2005. A Situational Analysis of Child Sexual Abuse and the Commercial Sexual Exploitation of Children in Papua New Guinea. Port Moresby, PNG: HELP Resources, Inc. with the support of UNICEF PNG.

Herdt, G. H. 1981. *Guardians of the Flutes: Idioms of Masculinity*. New York: McGraw Hill.

Herdt, G. H., ed. 1992. *Rituals of Manhood: Male Initiation in Papua New Guinea*. Berkeley: University of California Press.

HRW (Human Rights Watch). 2005. 'Making their Own Rules': Police Beatings, Rape, and Torture of Children in Papua New Guinea. New York: Human Rights Watch.

HRW (Human Rights Watch). 2006. Still Making their Own Rules: Ongoing Impunity for Police Beatings, Rape, and Torture in Papua New Guinea. New York: Human Rights Watch.

Hunter, M. 2005. Cultural Politics and Masculinities: Multiple-Partners in Historical Perspective in KwaZulu-Natal. *Culture, Health and Sexuality* 7 (4): 389–403.

INA (Institute of National Affairs). 2001. *A Life Free From Violence—It's Our Right*. Proceedings of the Family Violence Workshop 13 and 14 September 2000. Port Moresby: Institute of National Affairs.

Jewkes, R. K., J. B. Levin and L. A. Penn-Kekana. 2003. Gender Inequalities, Intimate Partner Violence and HIV Preventive Practices: Findings of a South African Cross-Sectional Study. *Social Science andMedicine* 56 (1): 125–134.

Johnson, F. C. 2001. Strategies to End Gender Based Violence: The USAID Approach. *Development* 44 (3): 125–128.

Josephides, L. 1985. The Politics of Violence in Kewa Society (Southern Highlands). In *Domestic Violence in Papua New Guinea*, ed. S. Toft, Law Reform Commission of Papua New Guinea Monograph No. 3, 92–103. Port Moresby: Law Reform Commission of Papua New Guinea.

Josephides, L. 1994. Gendered Violence in a Changing Society: The Case of Urban Papua New Guinea. *Journal de la Société des Océanistes* 99: 187–196.

Kaler, A. 2003. 'My Girlfriends Could Fill A Yanu-Yanu Bus': Rural Malawian Men's Claims About Their Own Serostatus. *Demographic Research*, Special Collection 1: 350–372.

Kaufman, M. 2001. Building a Movement of Men Working to End Violence Against Women. *Development* 44 (3): 9–14.

Larkin, J., A. Andrews and C. Mitchell. 2006. Guy Talk: Contesting Masculinities in HIV Prevention Education with Canadian Youth. *Sex Education* 6 (3): 207–221.

Lewis, I., B. Maruia, D. Mills and S. Walker. 2007. *Final Report on Links Between Violence Against Women and the Transmission of HIV in PNG*. Port Moresby: National AIDS Council.

Liguori, A. L. and M. Lamas. 2003. Commentary: Gender, Sexual Citizenship and HIV/AIDS. *Culture, Health and Sexuality* 5 (1): 87–90.

Luluaki, J. Y. 2003. Sexual Crimes Against and Exploitation of Children and the Law in Papua New Guinea. *International Journal of Law, Policy and the Family* 17 (3): 275–307.

LRC (Law Reform Commission). 1987. Interim Report. Port Moresby: Papua New Guinea Law Reform Commission.

LRC (Law Reform Commission). 1992. *Final Report on Domestic Violence*. Report No. 14. Port Moresby: Papua New Guinea Law Reform Commission.

Maman, S., J. Campbell, M. D. Sweat and A. C. Gielen. 2000. The Intersections of HIV and Violence: Directions for Future Research and Interventions. *Social Science and Medicine* 50 (4): 459–478.

Mane, P. and P. Aggleton. 2001. Gender and HIV/AIDS: What Do Men Have to Do with It? *Current Sociology* 49 (6): 23–37.

McDowell, N. 1990. Person, Assertion, and Marriage: On the Nature of Household Violence in Bun. *Pacific Studies* 13 (3): 171–188.

McLeod, A. 2005. Violence, Women and the State in Papua New Guinea: A Case Note. *Development Bulletin* 67: 115–118.

McLeod, S. 2003. Papua New Guinea Falls Victim to State of Origin Fever, 11 June 2003. http://www.abc.net.au/pm/content/2003/s877613.htm (accessed 27 April 2010).

Medrado, B. 2003. *Men, Masculinities and Gender Violence*. United Nations Division for the Advancement of Women (DAW) in Collaboration with International Labour Organization (ILO) Joint United Nations Programmes on HIV/AIDS (UNAIDS) United Nations Development Programme (UNDP) Expert Group Meeting on 'The Role of Men and Boys in Achieving Gender Equality', 21–24 October 2003, Brasilia, Brazil.

Meninga, M. 2006. Big Mal and Boys Land in Cairns. The World of Rugby League, Rleague Grandstand Forumshttp://forums.rleague.com/showthread.php?t=19470 (accessed 27 April 2010).

Michau, L. 2005. Good Practice in Designing a Community-Based Approach to Prevent Domestic Violence. Paper at the Expert Group Meeting Workshop 'Violence Against women: Good Practices in Combating and Eliminating Violence Against Women', Organized by UN Division for the Advancement of Women, May 2005, Vienna, Austria.

Nash, J. 1990. Factors Relating to Infrequent Domestic Violence among the Nagovisi. *Pacific Studies* 13 (3): 127–140.

Nduwimana, F. 2004. *The Right to Survive: Sexual Violence, Women and HIV/ AIDS*. Montreal: International Centre for Human Rights and Democratic Development.

NRI (National Research Institute) and JAG (Justice Advisory Group). 2005. *Port Moresby Community Crime Survey, 2004*. Waigani: National Research Institute.

NSRRT (National Sex and Reproduction Research Team) and C. Jenkins. 1994. *National Study of Sexual and Reproductive Knowledge and Behaviour in Papua New Guinea*. Monograph No. 10. Goroka: Papua New Guinea Institute of Medical Research.

PNG NAC (Papua New Guinea National AIDS Council). 2006a. *Papua New Guinea National Strategic Plan on HIV/AIDS 2006–2010*. Port Moresby: National AIDS Council.

PNG NAC. 2006b. National Gender Policy and Plan on HIV and AIDS 2006– 2010. Port Moresby: National AIDS Council.

PNG NACS (Papua New Guinea National AIDS Council Secretariat) and Partners. 2008. UNGASS 2008 Country Progress Report. Papua New Guinea Reporting Period: January 2006–December 2007. http://data.unaids.org/pub/ Report/2008/papua_new_guinea_2008_country_progress_report_en.pdf (accessed 27 April 2010).

Potts, M. 2006. Speech at the Australian High Commissioner's Reception for the Visiting Prime Minister's XIII Australian Rugby League Team. 28 September 2006. http://www.png.embassy.gov.au/pmsb/PMXIII.html (accessed 27 April 2010).

Read, K. 1982. Male-Female Relationships among the Gahuku-Gama: 1950 and 1981. *Social Analysis* 12: 66–78.

Rivers, K. and P. Aggleton. 1999. *Men and the HIV Epidemic, Gender and the HIV Epidemic*. New York: UNDP HIV and Development Programme.

Rothenberg, K. H. and S. J. Paskey. 1995. The Risk of Domestic Violence and Women with HIV Infection: Implications for Partner Notification, Public Policy, and the Law. *American Journal of Public Health* 85 (11): 1569–1576.

Scaglion, R. 1990. Spare the Rod and Spoil the Woman? Family Violence in Abelam Society. *Pacific Studies* 13 (3): 189–204.

Scheper-Hughes, N. 1994. An Essay: AIDS and the Social Body. *Social Science and Medicine* 39 (7): 991–1003.

Seidel, G. and L. Vidal. 1997. The Implications of 'Medical', 'Gender in Development' and 'Culturalist' Discourses for HIV/AIDS Policy in Africa. In *Anthropology of Policy: Critical Perspectives on Governance and Power*, ed. C. Shore and S. Wright, 59–87. London: Routledge.

Setel, P. 1996. AIDS as a Paradox of Manhood and Development in Kilimanjaro, Tanzania. *Social Science and Medicine* 43 (8): 1169–1178.

Toft, S. 1985. Marital Violence in Port Moresby: Two Urban Case studies. In *Domestic Violence in Papua New Guinea*. Law Reform Commission of Papua New Guinea Monograph No. 3, ed. Susan Toft, 14–31. Port Moresby: Law Reform Commission of Papua New Guinea.

Toft, S. and S. Bonnell. 1985. *Marriage and Domestic Violence in Rural Papua New Guinea*. Occasional Paper No. 18. Waigani: Law Reform Commission.

UN (United Nations). 2006. *Report of the Secretary-General In-Depth Study on all Forms of Violence Against Women*. Sixty-First Session. Advancement of Women: Advancement of Women A/61/122/Add.1. New York: United Nations.

UNAIDS (Joint United Nations Programme on HIV/AIDS). 1999. *Gender and HIV/AIDS: Taking Stock of Research and Programmes*. Geneva: UNAIDS.

UNAIDS. 2000a. *Gender and AIDS Almanac*. Geneva: UNAIDS.

UNAIDS. 2000b. Men Make A Difference: Objectives and Ideas for Action. Geneva: UNAIDS.

UNAIDS. 2000c. Men and AIDS—a Gendered Approach: 2000 World AIDS Campaign. Geneva: UNAIDS.

UNAIDS. 2001. Working with Men for HIV Prevention and Care. Geneva: UNAIDS.

UNAIDS and KIT (Royal Tropical Institute). 2005. *Operational Guide on Gender and HIV/AIDS: A Rights-Based Approach*. Amsterdam: UNAIDS Inter-Agency Task Team on Gender and HIV/AIDS, KIT Publishers.

UNAIDS/The Panos Institute. 2001. *Young Men and HIV: Culture, Poverty and Sexual Risk*. Geneva and London: UNAIDS/The Panos Institute.

UNAIDS, UNFPA (United Nations Population Fund) and UNIFEM (United Nations Development Fund for Women). 2004. *Women and HIV/AIDS: Confronting the Crisis.* New York: UNAIDS/UNFPA/UNIFEM.

UNDAW (UN Division for the Advancement of Women). 2000. *The HIV/AIDS Pandemic and its Gender Implications.* Report of the Expert Group Meeting Windhoek, Namibia, 13–17 November 2000. New York: Division for the Advancement of Women.

UNDAW in collaboration with Economic Commission for Europe (ECE) and World Health Organization (WHO). 2005. Violence Against Women: A Statistical Overview, Challenges and Gaps in Data Collection and Methodology and Approaches for Overcoming Them. Report of the Expert Group Meeting Geneva, Switzerland, 11–14 April 2005.

UNDAW. 2004. *The Role of Men and Boys in Achieving Gender Equality.* Report of the Expert Group Meeting Brasilia, Brazil, 21–24 October 2003, Final Report. New York: UNDAW.

UNDP (United Nations Development Programme). 2005. *A Gender Audit of the National Strategic Plan on HIV/AIDS 2006–2010.* Port Moresby: United Nations Development Programme.

UNFPA. 2000. Partners for Change: Enlisting Men in HIV/AIDS Prevention. New York: UNFPA.

UNFPA, UNIFEM and OSAGI (Office of the Special Adviser on Gender Issues and Advancement of Women). 2005. *Combating Gender-Based Violence: A Key to Achieving the MDGS.* New York: UNFPA, UNIFEM and OSAGI.

UN General Assembly. 1993. Declaration on the Elimination of Violence Against Women (DEVAW). UN General Assembly Resolution 48/104.

UN HABITAT and UNDP. 2004. *Port Moresby Diagnosis of Insecurity Report.* Port Moresby: UN HABITAT and UNDP.

Walsh, S. and C. Mitchell. 2006. 'I'm Too Young to Die': HIV, Masculinity, Danger and Desire in Urban South Africa. *Gender and Development* 14 (1): 57–68.

Wardlow, H. 2004. Anger, Economy, and Female Agency: Problematizing 'Prostitution' and 'Sex Work' among the Huli of Papua New Guinea. *Signs:Journal of Women in Culture and Society* 29 (4): 1017–1040.

Wardlow, H. 2006. *Wayward Women: Sexuality and Agency in a New Guinea Society.* Berkeley: University of California Press.

Wardlow, H. 2007. Men's Extramarital Sexuality in Rural Papua New Guinea. *American Journal of Public Health* 97 (6): 1006–1014.

Wardlow, H. 2008. 'You Have to Understand: Some of Us Are Glad AIDS Has Arrived': Christianity and Condoms among the Huli, Papua New Guinea. In *Making Sense of AIDS: Culture, Sexuality, and Power in Melanesia*, ed. L. Butt and R. Eves, 187–205. Honolulu: University of Hawai'i Press.

WHO (World Health Organization). 2001. Violence Against Women and HIV/AIDS: Setting The Research Agenda. Geneva: WHO.

WHO. 2003. Integrating Gender into HIV/AIDS Programmes. A Review Paper. Department of Gender and Women's Health Family and Community Health. Geneva: World Health Organization.

WHO. 2004. Gender Dimensions of HIV Status Disclosure to Sexual Partners: Rates, Barriers and Outcomes. A Review Paper. Geneva: WHO.

Wilde, C. 2003. Men at Work: Masculinity, Mutability, and Mimesis among the Gogodala of Papua New Guinea. Ph.D. Thesis, University of Sydney.

Wilde, C. 2007. 'Turning Sex into a Game': Gogodala Men's Response to the AIDS Epidemic and Condom Promotion in Rural Papua New Guinea. *Oceania* 77 (1): 58–71.

Wood, K. and R. Jewkes. 1997. Violence, Rape, and Sexual Coercion: Everyday Love in a South African Township. *Gender and Development* 5 (2): 41–46.

Wood, K., F. Marforah and R. Jewkes. 1998. 'He Forced Me to Love Him': Putting Violence on Adolescent Sexual Health Agendas. *Social Science and Medicine* 47 (2): 233–242.

Zimmer-Tamakoshi, L. 1997. 'Wild Pigs and Dog Men': Rape and Domestic Violence as 'Women's Issues' in Papua New Guinea. In *Gender in Cross-Cultural Perspective*, ed. C. Brettell and C. Sargent, 538–553. Englewood Cliffs: Prentice-Hall.

3. Teasing out the Tangle: *Raskols*, Young Men, Crime and HIV

VICKI LUKER WITH MICHAEL MONSELL-DAVIS

Introduction

This chapter revolves around the *'raskol'*, a term first used in the mid-1960s to describe young men, usually in groups, who engaged in petty theft and vandalism around Port Moresby, but later became associated with more serious property crime, violence and rape (Harris 1988, 3–16). Deriving from the English word 'rascal', *raskolism* referred to a new development in the growing town life of what was then the administrative centre of the Australian territories of Papua and New Guinea. Though *raskolism* still preserves certain connotations of urbanisation and opportunism, so-called *raskols* are now found in many rural areas while the nature and complexity of criminal activity, including *raskolism*, has evolved.

Using the *raskol* as a pivot of discussion here has several justifications for this volume. *Raskols* remain perhaps *the* symbol of PNG's 'law and order' problems (see figures 3, 4 and 5; Dupont 2005; Borrey 2000, Dinnen 2001, 55–110) and figure, if less directly, in important contexts for HIV. As adolescents or young men (though some so-called *raskols* are older and others younger), they belong to the category 'youth' that is a target population for HIV prevention in PNG and globally (Monasch and Mahy 2006; NAC 2006, 12–13; 21, 34, 32). In media accounts and the fears of many women, *raskols* are also vividly associated with rape, particularly *lainap* or pack-rape[1] (see, e.g. Hukula 1999, 8–9; Banks 2000, 93; Borrey 2000, 105). These practices are of intense concern as crimes in themselves but have serious additional implications for HIV transmission that will be

---

1   In some circumstances, *lainap* may involve some kind of 'consent' from the woman and its status as rape can be questionable. This chapter uses the term *lainap* to apply to cases of group-rape as distinct from group-sex.

discussed. Moreover, the *raskol* offers one window onto broader questions of masculinity that, as Eves (this volume) argues, warrant more searching consideration in relation to HIV.

We will argue that some concerns inherent in the *raskol* tangle of associations distract from other factors that deserve more attention in responses to PNG's law and order challenges and HIV. These include: other dimensions of crime, including 'high end' organised crime and corruption; rape by perpetrators who are not *raskols*; the broader implications, for HIV, of seemingly non-violent sex (particularly transactional sex broadly defined) and the character of concurrent sexual networks; and, in contrast to vivid anxieties about male youth and *raskols*, there is a deep need to come to grips with the epidemiologically more significant role of older men in HIV transmission—who are also, arguably, a bigger worry in relation to crime. Finally, while it has long been recognised that HIV prevalence is higher among PNG's female than male youth, this difference must be underscored.

Yet such observations do not weaken the imperative to respond to *raskolism* in the original senses of the term, or the plight of youth both male and female. The challenges involved are great, not least the difficulty of facilitating new economic opportunities for young people, a point stressed in our conclusion. Many reflections in this chapter draw upon Michael's experience over decades in Papua New Guinea, and his time in Fiji, Samoa and Kiribati, where much of his work has involved youth and witnessed painful social changes (Monsell-Davis 1998a; Hezel 2001; Rubinstein 1994; UNICEF 1995; UNICEF 1998).[2] This chapter therefore begins with a survey of some of these.

---

2   This paper was informed by discussions with Michael Monsell-Davis and ideas from his unpublished paper, 'Reflections on Cultures, Social Change and the Spread of HIV in PNG and Oceania'.

Figure 3: Portrait of Gaitzman, from Kips Kaboni ('Red Devils'), Port Moresby, 2004. Courtesy of Stephen Dupont, *www.stephendupont.com*

Figure 4: Portrait of Shookman, from Kips Kaboni ('Red Devils'), Port Moresby, 2004. Courtesy of Stephen Dupont, www.stephendupont.com

Figure 5: Portrait of Mania, from Kips Kaboni ('Red Devils'), Port Moresy, 2004. Courtesy of Stephen Dupont, www.stephendupont.com

A Composite Picture

The great changes experienced in PNG over the last 50 years are often represented as 'shifts' from subsistence to cash; from governance on the bases of autonomous, small scale, non-literate communities to the politics and machinery of a modern state; from the moralities and worldviews fitting the one to those fitting the other. In fact, the word 'shift' is misleading, implying a universal movement in one direction.

A varied composite picture might better capture present realities. Cash has spread rapidly since the 1960s and nearly everyone has a pressing need for it, yet the subsistence economy still feeds and shelters the vast majority of the population, roughly 85 percent of which is rural (SPC 2010). While some of PNG's citizens are among the Pacific's wealthiest individuals, most languish at the low end of the Human Development Index and have limited participation in the cash economy (Bourke 2008; Baxter 2001). Also, although PNG has been an independent nation, with its laws, bureaucracy and elected representatives since 1975, for most citizens the state has little presence in their lives, government services have receded here and there, and people continue to rely (in some places even more so than formerly) on kin- and community-based governance. New worldviews, moralities and desires have been fashioned from Christian teachings, schooling, communication and interaction with worlds beyond immediate localities and via consumption, but again, opportunities for this vary while the political and moral economies that support subsistence have some kind of continuing, practical rationale for most people.

These changes nonetheless have implications for youth, beginning with the concept itself. In most bureaucratic definitions, youth is defined by numbers of years: according to global HIV policy, youth comprises persons between the ages 15 to 24 (e.g. UNAIDS ITTYP 2006); and according to PNG's National Youth Commission (NYC), youth consists of citizens aged 12 to 25 (NYC 2007). But the NYC also acknowledges cultural definitions of youth that rely on the person's attainment of social responsibilities: 'youth' is the phase after childhood but before marriage and parenthood (cf. Renkin and Hughes 2006). Older people who remain unmarried may therefore still be regarded as 'youth', and usually 'youth' lasts longer for men than women who tend to marry and have children at an earlier age. Most Pacific languages have a word for youth in the sense of young, unmarried men. In PNG, many people do not know exactly how old they are and these cultural definitions matter more.

The 'shifts' outlined above also implicate physiological and demographic effects. Some studies suggest that even small alterations in diet due to purchased foodstuffs (especially protein) have resulted in young people growing bigger faster than their forebears, and this probably involves an earlier onset of puberty (Jenkins 2007, 35; Worthman 1998, 29–36). Also, chiefly owing to reduced rates of infant mortality, PNG's population has more than trebled since Independence to an estimated 6.7 million (SPC 2010) and a larger proportion than previously is comprised of people aged 12–25: about 28 percent (NYC 2007, 17). The median age in PNG is 20 in contrast, say, to the European region, where it is 37 (WHO 2008, 96, 102). In more senses than one, PNG is a 'young' country.

Changes Affecting the Roles and Integration of Young Men

Changes since the onset of colonialism have affected young men with respect to their warrior function, productive and economic value, education, integration into surrounding society, and sexual relations. Colonialism arrived relatively late in PNG: from the second half of the 19th century in the lowlands, from the interwar era in the populous Highlands, and as late as the 1980s for some extremely isolated communities. Perhaps in no other nation has the colonial experience been so brief and uneven. Change has multiplied and accelerated in the last half century.

The Warrior Function

Traditionally,[3] young men were essential for the defence of their communities. Before church and colonial administrations fostered peace, warfare was endemic and young men constituted every community's principal fighting force. They were largely segregated from female society, living in the men's house or accommodation for male youth and spent much time in ritual cultivation and physical readiness for war (see Herdt 1982; Herdt 1984; Jenkins 1996). Throughout PNG and the Pacific, sexual abstinence and avoidance of women were understood as necessary, at least for certain periods, to ensure masculine efficacy in warfare and other vital tasks.

Today young men, in theory, are no longer needed as warriors. Under the modern state, in principle the task of external security belongs to defence, internal

---

3　Tradition is a difficult term. In this chapter, it is used without inverted commas when it refers to values, practices or conditions as they existed prior to interaction with missionaries, colonial administrations or capitalist economies (even though there can still be some historical uncertainty), while 'tradition' with inverted commas is used to indicate more problematic usages. It must be stressed that traditional societies and cultures were nowhere unchanging; many practices labelled 'traditional' are recent products of creative historical processes, including processes that combine heterogeneous elements; much scholarship is very uncomfortable with habits of contrasting 'tradition' with 'modernity'; and yet, at the same time, to many people, such contrasts capture a kind of truth, or signify keenly felt change. For an entry into the huge Pacific literature and debates on tradition, Jolly and Thomas 1992 and Jolly 1992 remain classics.

security to police, and intergroup warfare should no longer exist. But in PNG as elsewhere traditional values exalting warriors persist and are reinforced by icons of aggressive masculinity in popular culture (Macintyre 2008). Intergroup warfare has also re-emerged in places, returning many youths to the warrior vocation, which in turn fosters warfare. Other opportunities can be taken to express the warrior ethos too, one of them *raskolism*. In Stephen Dupont's photographic portraits, Koboni *raskols* from Port Moresby invoke both local and global symbols of the warrior ideal (Dupont 2005; cf. Macintyre 2008). In the absence of robust alternatives, some variation of the warrior appears to offer young men a ready, flexible and recognised masculine role.

The Productive and Economic Value of Young Men

Traditionally, even if their supreme value was as warriors, young men's labour was also essential for the community economy. In neo-traditional societies under colonial rule, although warfare had ceased and the warrior ethos was challenged by missions and colonial administrations (Fife 1995, 279–287), young men's productive labour continued to be valued. While young (and older) men who worked for periods on plantations were the main means for many communities of tapping the cash economy, life still largely centred on village subsistence and needs for money were few.

Today their economic and productive value has declined in several respects. Most male youth of course live rurally where their contribution to subsistence activities, if reduced, remains important, in contrast to youth in urban areas where such opportunities are scarce. But since the 1960s parents have acquired new economic expectations for their children: that they bring in money. As Barker has remarked, this expectation overlaid the economic values traditionally placed on them (Barker 1987, 98; Monsell-Davis 1998b, 317–318). The expense of school fees, particularly for boys, has often been offset against the promise of financial returns from the job that schooling would lead to. Unfortunately, jobs in the formal sector remain scanty. Only about 15 percent of men of working age have paid jobs (NSO 2003, 56) and even in urban areas more than 60 percent of adults are formally unemployed (PNG JAG 2008, 63). Also some salaried men do not pass their earnings on to their families, preferring to spend it on masculine pastimes like drinking (see, e.g. Macintyre 2008, 188–190). Michael has noted how young men in Port Moresby, whether employed or unemployed, equally drain their households (cf. Abbott 2007, 70). Large numbers of young men now probably represent a net economic cost to their families.

By striking contrast, girls and young women remain 'useful' and their economic value has appreciated. They continue to do much caring and household work, the needs for which remain relatively constant. More importantly, girls now embody a mighty asset that can convert into *kina*. In the cash economy, young women are at the peak of their market value for sex or reproductive relations. This can be leveraged by kin demanding bride-price or in a variety of other transactions (see Hammar this volume; HELP 2005). This process of commodification has been underway for several decades. More than 30 years ago Bernard Narokobi remarked: 'Parents now breed their girls like pigs in order to have them sold for a handsome price' (Narokobi et al. 1980, 130). Many families lacking daughters are keen to adopt girls for bride-price later on. As Hammar notes, terms used for a woman's vagina include her *kina* or *goldmain* (Hammar this volume; see also Hammar 2008).

Education

Education is also a vexed issue for boys. Traditionally, it was kin-based and brought benefits to the community there and then, as male youths acquired skills in, say, clearing actual land or building a real house. Now school-based learning is removed from kin and such locally useful work. Ideally, it lays foundations for modern competencies, but in practice causes many disappointments (Herdt and Leavitt 1998, 22–25).

Some problems are general. PNG has made great gains in schooling by some criteria (see, e.g. PNG 2004, 16; cf. UNDP 2009), but too many people never acquire a sound primary education. Fundamental skills in literacy and numeracy are necessary for participation in the formal economy above the lowest echelons and also for success in many areas of the informal economy. These skills also give access to a range of information and empower men and women as citizens. Yet nearly half a million people in PNG between the ages 12–25 have never been to school (NYC 2007, 18). Others have only patchy education for many reasons— school disruptions and closures; deteriorating access due to ambient violence, decay of roads, increased transport costs; and the difficulties of paying school fees. Some data suggest that today a smaller proportion of PNG youth (combined male and female) receives formal education than in the past (NYC 2007, 18). While the 2000 census reported that literacy levels had increased to nearly 60 percent of adults, others put levels of functional literacy much lower (NSO 2003; Kidu 2008a).

But perturbing gender patterns appear. PNG's predicted failure to meet the Millennium Development Goal (MDG) of universal primary education by 2015 is often mainly attributed to barriers against girls (see, e.g. PNG 2004, 15). Yet, while families may prioritise their sons' education, Michael recalls many instances of resentment by male youths whose fees were not paid: one Papuan boy ran away, angry and ashamed, to be found six months later with strangers on a Port Moresby dump. The gap between the proportion of male youth (30.2 percent) who have never been to school and the corresponding female (35.7 percent) also suggests a high degree of common disadvantage. Perhaps curiously, over time male literacy has been declining while female literacy—notwithstanding gender-specific impediments to girls' schooling—has trended up. In 2000, approximately 35 percent of male youth aged 15–24 was estimated to be illiterate which was less than the female proportion; but on unchanging trajectories the proportion of illiterate male youth has been predicted to exceed female by 2010 (PNG 2004, 18). These data hint at complicated patterns of gendered disadvantage while pointing to some structural factors affecting male and female students fairly equally.

The gendered effects of post-school unemployment are grave. Less than 10,000 jobs are available for the circa 80,000 boys and girls who leave school every year, while the number of employees in industry since 1990 shows a real decline (NYC 2007, 19). No one expects job opportunities in the formal sector to suddenly, massively expand.[4] Only about 5 percent of working age women have formal employment (a third of the male proportion) (NSO 2003, 56) and a de facto alternative to employment and formal education for girls is often early motherhood. Unfortunately, this can bring grief to the young women and their children, including elevated maternal and infant mortality (PNG's are the highest in the Pacific (NZPPD 2010, 29)), and hampers national development in other ways. For many young men, as Michael observes, their inability to find a job causes a particular kind of masculine pain. They are brought up with expectations that they succeed, perhaps like the 'big man' in a suit with a car, and should contribute to their kin, yet when they leave school vast numbers have no means to contribute anything (Monsell-Davis 1998b, 318–319; 2000, 218–219; cf Fife 1995, 294–296). The lack of jobs for young people is perceived by some experts and most ordinary citizens as the main driver of young women into prostitution and young men into crime (Levantis 2000, 136; HELP 2005, 14; HELP 2005, 14; PNG JAG 2008, 75).

The Social Integration of Young Men

Traditionally a web of relations, with its ideological supports, granted young men their own social space while integrating them into surrounding society and leading to full adulthood. This web is now not so tight and can be considered in terms of the 'family'. Though a fuzzy word (Monsell-Davis 1994), the 'family' is arguably the model for traditional authority structures in PNG and much of Oceania, with the senior male (more rarely female) by age, heredity or achievement as head.[5] Earlier, missionary teachings and colonial administrations challenged aspects of traditional gender relations and authority (Jolly and Macintyre 1989),

---

4   Some analysts, who diverge profoundly in other ways, agree that the massive Exxon-Mobil liquid natural gas project, which is expected to accelerate PNG's economic growth, will create few jobs and perpetuate existing poverty (Fletcher quoted in Callick 2009; Chandy 2009, 1).

5   In some chiefly societies female chiefs could and can occupy the highest positions.

but the greater challenges to local authority over the last 50 years have come from the formation of the nation state and PNG's further incorporation into global politics, economies and cultures. These processes have in some ways broached the integrity of extended family structures and weakened kin-based authority (which vice versa has often compromised state authority at local level).

One kind of weakness derives from ideological disjunction. The interests and norms of the 'family' can clash with those of other entities. In John Waiko's words, 'In ethical terms, whatever helps the group maintain itself and the land is right, and whatever goes against the group is wrong' (Waiko 1993, 235).[6] At the extreme, a community may believe that killing a person accused of sorcery is just, while according to state law it is murder. A family may believe that arranging a daughter's marriage that rewards them with bride-wealth is proper, while from a human rights perspective, she is violated. A trader must make money for his business, but also share with his community (Monsell-Davis 1985; 1993b). A manager must appoint on merit but also find jobs for *wantoks*. As Waiko further remarks, 'Many people find it difficult to continue to identify with village society and at the same time become members of modern institutions' (Waiko 1993, 246). While creative processes of combination, transformation and continuity can be celebrated, Michael has also observed how feelings of disconnection from both 'traditional' and 'modern' worlds can significantly affect behaviour and inchoate notions of masculinity among young men (Monsell-Davis 1998a; 2000).

Traditional authority structures also indicated routes that young men could take to positions of adult influence. These routes differed, loosely speaking, across the Pacific and within PNG along the spectrum from 'big man' styles of leadership to those of the hereditary chief (Sahlins 1963). 'Big men' have been described as 'leaders of groups, coalitions and factions in pursuit of competitive ends' (Strathern 1993, 42); hereditary chiefs as descendants of gods and essential for the fertility of land, sea and people. The societies of the former are characterised as small-scale, fundamentally egalitarian for men, while comprehensively subordinating women as a class; the latter as hierarchical and often on a larger scale, in which principles of heredity, seniority and female descent create complex relations of status whereby women can sometimes outrank men. In practice a range of leadership styles combining varying degrees of achievement and heredity manifested throughout the Pacific region and in PNG too where, as Herdt and Leavitt (1998, 16; cf. McLeod 208) observe, the ranking systems of Trobriand culture differ significantly from the 'big man' politics of the Highlands. Yet 'big man' styles have tended to predominate in PNG. Whereas the path to status in hierarchical societies was often through reverential service, in PNG young men built up their

---

6   For a searching discussion of 'justice' from the vantages of state law and local socialities, see Goddard 2009.

own influence and networks and so in time could openly challenge dominant men. Women's productive and reproductive work supported men in their pursuit of renown—unmarried men would get nowhere.

Because 'big man' leadership styles lend themselves to continual challenge, this kind of leadership, in changing conditions, may be so fluid and aggressive that a stable ethical environment for integrating male youth is lacking. In some communities, older men now feel powerless in the face of aggressive young men, often with guns (e.g. Dinnen and Thompson 2009; cf. Haley this volume). In some circumstances the violent and wayward behaviour of male youth has been explained as their seeking the traditional status of older men, but, with the waning of traditional institutions, having to beat modern pathways to it. Some researchers have broadly interpreted *raskolism* in this way (Goddard 2005; Dinnen 2001; cf. Leavitt 1998).

The 'family' has also been changing. The change commonly remarked is the supposed 'shift' from the rural extended family to the urban nuclear family. In fact, a complex series of urban and rural changes has been underway. In the past the extended family was of central importance throughout Oceania. It formed a labour pool (cf. Finney 1973). All members contributed in various ways to household and community welfare and each faced sanctions if he or she failed to fulfill reciprocal obligations (cf. Belshaw 1964, 21). This arrangement is still vital for the subsistence activities on which most PNG citizens depend. Nevertheless there is evidence in rural areas of a trend towards the nuclear household, particularly in day-to-day affairs (Monsell-Davis 2005; cf. Finney 1973; Kay 1971; Hezel 2001). This is partly in response to Christian emphases on the nuclear family, but increasingly to the greater use of cash.

In urban areas extended families are somewhat different. Government authority housing was built with the nuclear family in mind, but numerous accretions are common, as children of the original couple raise their own families under the same roof (cf. Pantumari and Bamne this volume) or relatives come to stay. And many people crowd into settlement dwellings. Urban households thus tend to be larger on average than their rural counterparts, even if couples have fewer children.[7] They also frequently contain members who are less closely related and often centre on a woman as its stable core (cf. Kay 1971). As someone said to Michael, 'in town the woman is boss!'—and the relatives who come to stay are frequently hers. An elderly man in a village outside Port Moresby added 'Why do you think I never go to my son's house in town? It is always crowded with his wife's relatives'.

---

7   The national average is 5.4 persons per household (NSO 2003, 70), but recent surveys found 9.6 in Port Moresby, 8.8 in Lae and 8.3 in Mt Hagen (PNG JAG 2008, 62, 63).

The commitment of household members to household welfare is often less uniform in urban centres too. First, unemployed members may be unable to constructively contribute; and second, even where several members are salaried, it is not uncommon to find them spending money on their own interests. This can be especially true of young men who want to drink and party and purchase personal property. Disputes arise from overcrowding, failure to contribute, and conflict over resources. Michael recalls married brothers and sisters in Port Moresby hiding food from each other's families, outbursts of domestic violence, and young people leaving to seek refuge with other kin or friends. Increasing numbers of children and young people live together in shacks, drains or on the streets (Buchanan-Aruwafu et al. 2002, 8).

In urban communities that are not physically and socially so tightly bounded, collective opinion and authority can be harder to shape and enforce. While many people live in settlements[8] surrounded by *wantoks* , ethnically mixed areas are increasing and it is common to hear about difficulties caused by 'outsiders' (see, e.g. James et al. 2009, 25); the number of individuals whose parents come from different areas or whose first language is Tok Pisin is also increasing (Goddard 2005, 7; HELP 2005, 15–16); the range and coverage of community institutions, such as churches, peace committees, village courts and youth groups vary, and the abilities of communities to handle internal difficulties through kin mechanisms or such institutions vary too (James et al. 2009, 17–62). This variation in social bonds and the structures of local urban authority (whether rooted in kin, state, church or business) results in gaps and weaknesses that hamper the regulation and integration of young men. Some forms of *raskolism* are arguably, in part, one symptom of these difficulties.[9] So is the private security industry, a major source of formal urban employment for young men within the limited number of jobs on offer.

Sexual Relations

Finally, how has change affected young men and sexual relations? Contemporary sexual practices involve great tensions and confusing trends. It may be helpful initially to consider, very broadly, the role of sex in subsistence and cash economies as they coexist and interact in PNG.

PNG's traditional sexual cultures have been said to range from 'sex positive' to 'sex negative'. The former are described as celebrating sexuality (especially

---

8   A settlement strictly speaking refers to an unplanned residential area, in contrast to a government-planned suburb. 'Settlement' is used more loosely in this chapter to refer to urban residential areas where many poor and ordinary people live.

9   This line is consistent with the 'culturalist' interpretations of *raskolism* by Goddard (2005) and Dinnen (2001), which stress how *raskol* activities can represent an adaptation of traditional politics and economics to modern conditions.

youthful sexuality), often correlate with political styles that favour principles of hereditary rank (which in turn tend to accommodate more complex articulations of female status by descent) and seem to grant a lesser role for gender and sexual violence—the Trobriands for instance have often been depicted in such terms (Malinowski 1929; Lepani 2007). 'Sex negative' cultures are said to stress the dangers of sex, particularly to male potency; to correlate with a masculine politics of egalitarianism and open competition (predicated on the subordination of women and entailing a certain 'sex antagonism'), and to grant a greater role for gender and sexual violence—some traditional sexual cultures of the Highlands are often so described (Zimmer-Tamakoshi 1997; Meggitt 1964). Of course, these are caricatures, but perhaps indicate some dimensions of traditional difference in the big picture.

Commonalities however are more important. Traditional cultures in PNG and throughout Oceania fundamentally valued fertility and reproductive efficacy, in people and their environment. These were preconditions for survival and social generation—and human sexuality and the children it produced were, among other things, economic and political assets. The collectivity had vested interests in managing the reproductive potential of young people that, in important senses, 'belonged' to their clan or line. Even cultures that allowed young people latitude for (usually clandestine) sexual liaisons circumscribed youthful sexuality in various ways. Another widespread assumption—found beyond Oceania too—held men's sexual urges to be almost impossible to control from within. Spatial segregation of the sexes and social mores governing interaction between them were important forms of sexual regulation.

The sexual cultures linked with the cash economy in PNG implicate, by contrast, some globalised ideologies that value individualism, choice, mobility and consumerism.[10] In some strands of thought, reproduction is not necessarily a central sexual value, even for heterosexual activity (and indeed, children can represent considerable costs in many cash economies); sexuality is in important senses the rightful property of the individual and a medium through which individuality can be realised; and people are expected to manage their sexual desires in their interactions with others and in the various mundane social spaces where different genders mix.

---

10   For a broad treatment of this theme, see Altman 2001.

In Papua New Guinea, these broadly contrasting economies, with some of their implications and ideological supports, overlap in the lives and consciousness of many people as depicted so evocatively by contemporary Papua New Guinean artists (see Figure 6).[11] The gendered cartography of everyday life was already being redrawn under colonialism, as new principles for the Christian family were enjoined and new social spaces created by administrative and money-making activities. But these processes have enlarged over the last 50 years, and the kinds of places and activities that throw people together who would have traditionally had fewer or no opportunities for contact, including sexual contact, have proliferated. Sexual values, rooted in very different sexual economies, can mingle in the same social zones, hybridise, and adapt to the opportunities offered by the other.

Figure 6: Haphap Meri bilong PNG. By Maik Yomba Kagi, 2000. www. Pazifik-Infostelle.org

---

11   Another splendid graphic representation of this overlap is the painting *Boi pren na girl pren. Tupelo lusim tingting long pasin bilong wait man* (Boyfriend and girlfriend. They no longer think about their local customs and instead have taken the customs of the Europeans) by John Siune, 1999, from Clive Moore Private Collection, but reproduced on the dustcover of Moore 2003.

Much attention has focused on women in this interaction, particularly concerning the multivalent commodification of female sexuality. Kin manage some modes of this commodification along loose analogies with the traditional management of female sexual and reproductive assets. Financial demands by kin for bride-price and the like are arguably adaptations of the traditional economy to the cash economy, and similar explanations can be offered for compensation claims and acquisitive *raskolism* (cf. Goddard 2005; Dinnen 2001).

Other modes of commodification, exercised by the woman herself, reveal a range of possible motivations. Sometimes a woman's resort to 'sex work' is retaliation against immediate family. Holly Wardlow's work among Huli *pasindia meri* (women who travel around and sell sex) found that for many this was primarily a way of 'getting back' at kin who had failed in their responsibilities: the woman was therefore denying them what was theirs—her sexuality and its economic returns (Wardlow 2006, 134–165). For other women, sex work can be a means to economic autonomy and the exploration of possibilities that would otherwise be closed to them (such as the young girl who explained that she wanted to be a prostitute 'and get feelings. Get feelings like happiness' (Jenkins 2007, 45)). But for most, sex work seems a brute financial necessity: whether housewives, sisters or daughters needing to feed their families; school girls seeking money to pay school fees; university students needing cash for soap and tampons; or uneducated, abused women, alienated from subsistence supports, without other means for survival.

Many PNG women (see, e.g. Garap 2000; Kewa 2007) believe that women and girls are now more vulnerable to abuse than before. The commodification of female sexuality has in many circumstances enabled men to hurt girls and women with untraditional immunity. Wives can be mistreated as bought objects (Kewa 2007, 46–49). A sexually abused child may be paid afterward by her abuser, retrospectively 'regularising' the act as a transaction (HELP 2005, 43, 45). Compensation to kin for a daughter's rape does little to repair the damage to her and sometimes offers the offender a way of avoiding a severer traditional penalty, such as death (e.g. Banks 2000, 92). Money also gives a few men a fast track to status and a scale of prerogatives that would be harder to earn and exercise traditionally, including a much greater capacity to buy sex, women and wives. Clement Malau has observed that the modern cashed-up 'big man' is removed from former restraints and the obligations of traditional polygamy (Malau quoted in Guy and Crofts 2000).

On the other hand, the degree of independence and affluence that some young women may derive from sex with moneyed men can anger other men, particularly those without money, and prompt a punitive response. Other women totally dependent on selling sex earn very little and lack any measure of safety that may be offered by kin. In the absence of state or other protection, such women can be mistreated with impunity. Several cases in this volume describe abused women who evidently had no kin who could or would effectively assist (Luker and Dinnen introduction this volume; Haley this volume; Luker conclusion this volume). Many women routinely raped by police appear to be in this predicament (Jenkins this volume).

Two key points about young men can be stressed. First, several factors seem to favour their involvement in rape—and a high proportion of male youth state that they have used force to have sex: for example, 49.3 percent of unmarried, 61.4 percent of married young men in one sample (Millan et al. 2006, 42). Some offer an economic explanation. Most male youth have difficulty 'buying' sex, as discussed above, and their sexual rebuff or exclusion on the perceived grounds of pennilessness can cause resentment that, in Michael's experience, not infrequently leads to rape. Similarly, Jenkins and Alpers found that many young men 'justified rape on the grounds that they could not compete financially for sex. Therefore, whenever an opportunity arose … it had to be acted upon' (Jenkins and Alpers 1996, 248; cf. Banks 2000, 93; 98–100). Rape in this sense is analogous to theft, and seems often understood as such (Jenkins 2007, 60). Thus the theft, robbery and rape committed by *raskols*, that researchers tend to put in two different boxes (one marked 'property crime', the other 'sexual violence') can be considered in some contexts within the same frame as economic acts.

A cultural consensus around rape that might offer young men (and everyone else) consistent guidelines is wanting. Certain sexual acts that state law defines as rape are 'traditionally' accepted in many cultures: such as rape for punishment, in war, as 'payback', of women who don't count, or because circumstances permit. Indeed, a concept and term for rape is absent from many PNG vernaculars (Strathern 1975; Borrey 2000; Banks 2000). Researchers have also noted that where ordinary sex resembles rape, one can be hard to distinguish from the other (e.g., Borrey 2000, 107). For many men and women, rape within marriage is normal too, tallies with beliefs about uncontrollable male desire, and is further justified in modern understandings (at odds with equally modern concepts of human rights) that bride-price entitles husbands to treat wives as purchased property (cf. Eves this volume; Macleod and Macintyre this volume). While one must emphasise that rape has little traditional precedent in parts of PNG (Zimmer-Tamakoshi 1997, 539; Lepani 2007) and the nation's progress towards addressing violence against women has been described as now 'on a strong upswing' (Ellsberg et al. 2008, 120), contemporary values and ideas concerning rape could still be described as 'pluralistic'. As Hukula has noted, an act of rape can occur simultaneously in several different social realities (Hukula 2005, 14).

The same general remarks for rape apply specifically to *lainap*, which, though pack rape happens all over the world, seems unusually prevalent in PNG. A national survey in the early 1990s found that 60 percent of male informants had participated in *lainap* (NSRRT 1994, 102); countless reports testify to routine occurrences in town and village (Jenkins 2007, 62); and the practice appears normal within some masculine occupations (see, e.g. Pantumari and Bamne this volume; Jenkins this volume; McLeod and Macintyre this volume). Jenkins has argued that *lainap* expresses intense masculine homosociality traditional in many PNG societies that persists into the present (Jenkins 1996). Occurrences traditionally related to men's house and warfare provide seeming precedents both for its practice within the army and police today (see Jenkins this volume; McLeod and Macintyre this volume; Pantumari and Bamne this volume).[12] Traditionally, pack rape may often have been a young warrior's sexual initiation, and older men can use *lainap* today as a way of rewarding younger men and introducing them to sex (NSRRT 1994, 104; Jenkins 1996 203–204; Hukula 2005; cf. Pantumari and Bamne this volume). Common forms of *raskolism* accommodate these features: by invoking the warrior ideal, taking rape for granted as an intrinsic activity (*raskols* who dislike rape seem exceptional (e.g., Goddard 2005, 103–104; Werf 2009, 89)), and using *lainap* for these purposes.

Secondly, young men—and women—are caught up in wider, diffuse changes of sexual mores not captured in the spotlight here on certain types of commodified sexual relationships or on rape. While sexual values prizing reproduction, the family, and community still have a strong basis in subsistence economies and in church teachings, generally a certain relaxation of earlier cultural constraints have been noted (but see Jenkins 1996, 193–194). For instance, in the villages on the central Papuan coast where Michael has worked, a boy's sexual adventures were once curbed by the crucial need for sometimes lengthy sexual abstinences as ritual preparation for warfare, trading expeditions, competitive dancing or canoe racing, and to a lesser extent before hunting or fishing and continued to be practised for special undertakings. Such restrictions have eased significantly over the last 40 years. Certain research also sees several modern factors strengthening the formation of a gender inclusive 'youth culture', that is, a 'horizontal' social entity meshing young men and women according to age in contrast to youth divided 'vertically' by kin or gender (Herdt and Leavitt 1998). Schooling is a major factor in this; so is identification with symbols of local or global youth culture that become markers of that cohort's identity; and also are other shared activities, which may involve sexual intimacy and relatively recent patterns of consumption (such as drinking alcohol, smoking marijuana, viewing videos and DVDs). These changes contribute importantly to portrayals of youth—as unemployed, inadequately educated, suffering family breakdown, abusing substances, watching pornography, engaging multiple sexual partners, alienated

---

12   It should be noted, however, that 'traditional precedents' are not necessarily explanations.

from community, and lacking access to public goods—in which juvenile crime and the risk of HIV to youth also figure (e.g. Sikani 1997; Buchanan-Aruwafu et al. 2002; HELP 2005; Jenkins 2007).

Such dystopic visions tend to have an urban setting, but need not be confined to town. Poverty is entrenched in some rural areas; the imbalances between enclave capitalism and economies heavily dependent on subsistence can cause huge distortions for affected communities; while generally, rural PNG has suffered most from retreating services, deteriorating infrastructure, and neglect—and remains of course sensitive to natural hazards (Baxter 2001; Bourke 2008; Ninkama 2009). A Papuan community that Michael has known for decades had experienced several years of increasing poverty on his last visit (Monsell-Davis 2005): crayfish—the principal money-earning resource—were gone, and a long drought combined with poor soil had killed the gardens. Anxieties about sickness were rife, and sorcery accusations appeared to be on the rise. People were also troubled by the withdrawal of chiefs from village leadership, how once cooperating households were now behaving independently, and by *raskols* and 'law and order'. In contrast to the early years of Independence (Monsell-Davis 1987), their own male youth were causing problems too. Sexual activity among young people was also perceived to have increased and teenage pregnancies from casual liaisons seemed more common.

Nicole Haley provides another example. Around Lake Kopiago, in the Southern Highlands Province, an elderly informant shared songs that he had once sung with fellow youths to celebrate their land and their own splendor. This age-group had reached adulthood before 1955, after which colonial rule began extending, indigenous ritual activity died away, and the bachelor cult was abandoned (Haley 2008, 220). By sad contrast, today's songs reflect the 'untraditional' gun and gender violence now pervasive, and the poor estimation young men have of themselves, their ground, their competence: 'impoverished with nothing to offer'. The words of a 2002 election chant translate as 'Kopiago, truly the last place development occurs' (Haley 2008, 222, 225; cf. Haley this volume).

These evocations of maldevelopment, which frame negative depictions of youth, challenge common tendencies among many Papua New Guineans and outside observers to idealise the village as opposed to town (Zimmer-Tamakoshi 1990) when in practice, a line between rural and urban life is often hard to draw. Other caveats are worth noting. Although rural maldevelopment can be acute and rural poverty hidden from view, subsistence still manages to support most citizens on their land with kin; while hardships in town are prone to grim stereotype, they can mask the more complex realities of settlement existence (Goddard 2005, 2–8). As Allen observes, the 'youth problem' is nothing new (Allen 1987, 33, 36–39; Barker 1987) and in cultures that allowed for dominant men to be openly challenged, young men have perhaps always been a source of disturbance especially during times of stress. Finally, against lurid pictures of today's youth, some research throws up countervailing data: for instance, a generally later age of sexual debut and fewer sexual partners in some sampled populations than darker depictions of sexual mores might suggest; a relatively small number of girls in a high-risk setting selling sex; the appeal to young people of quite 'traditional' sexual and reproductive aspirations; and the continuing support and integration provided by structures of kin (e.g. Sivusia-Joyce 2004, 10–11, 14; Naemon 2009, 93; Kelly et al. 2008, 10; NCY 2007, 12).

Teasing out the Tangle

The tangle of associations that link young men, *raskols*, property crime, rape, youth HIV nonetheless seem to emerge naturally from these visions of maldevelopment, but its elements can be usefully teased out, reassessed and perhaps repositioned in both the response and the rhetoric relating to HIV and 'law and order' in PNG.

First, *raskols*, as already indicated, are not all young men. Some labelled as such are younger or much older (see, e.g., portraits in Dupont 2005). There is also a difference between youths who play to the *raskol* image without strong criminal commitment or experience and the *raskols* in Goddard's and Dinnen's influential studies (Goddard 2005; Dinnen 2001). They were older or married with children, in some cases even educated men who once had enviable jobs, but had become accomplished criminals committed to the *raskol* road.

Second, property crime broadly defined[13] and rape cannot be reduced to *raskolism* in the original scope of the term. Rape, as discussed above, covers sexual coercion in a range of contexts by a range of perpetrators. The special media and women's anxiety over rape by *raskols* may owe partly to its ability to evoke a sense of urban anomie and indiscriminate vulnerability (cf. Borrey 2000; PNG JAG 2008). The character of *raskol* collectivities has also evolved—to encompass very loose gatherings, tighter networks, and integration within formalised business structures—and this reflects a range of property crime too: from 'low end' opportunistic and street crime, to 'high end' heists and organised commercial enterprises that can involve leading politicians, businessmen and international players (Harris 1988; Goddard 2005; Dinnen 2001; Levantis 2000; Bashir 2009). The youthful face of *raskolism*, with its persisting connotations of the low end, does not capture this spectrum. Nor does it invoke 'white collar' crime and corruption, with their frequent accomplice, mismanagement.

---

13 Property crime is broadly defined here to include theft and robbery (that is stealing both with and without force); and also 'white collar' crime and corruption.

However, *raskolism* in its original connotations of theft and robbery may represent the kinds of crime people are most likely to have personally suffered (PNG JAG 2008, 14–40).

Yet 'high end' activities, 'white collar' crime, corruption and mismanagement pose huge challenges for both PNG's governance of security (see, e.g. INA 2004) and experience of HIV. Respecting the latter, the possible effects on HIV's spread from criminal enterprises—in particularly narcotics or sex—are known from other countries, but perhaps more pertinent is the role of corruption and mismanagement in weakening PNG's government response. Thus, for instance, though mothers' needs for antiretroviral prophylaxis are largely unmet and increasing, the number of women who received it dropped when these services were transferred from church to government health services (NACS and Partners 2008, 42). The Department of Health failed to distribute millions of condoms that consequently passed their use-by date (Joku 2009). The National AIDS Council was suspended and restructuring commenced in response to, among other concerns, a scandal involving millions of kina (Nalu 2009). Corruption and mismanagement were considerations in the 2009 decision of the Global Fund not to renew assistance to PNG that, inter alia, funded antiretroviral treatment (ART) for 7000 Papua New Guineans (Fox 2009). Cessation of drugs would not only kill these patients, but jeopardise ART as a pillar of the national response.

Third, the contribution of rape to HIV transmission must be seen in the broader context. In much expert literature, rape figures as a major spreader of HIV. Transmission from male rapists to female victims is highlighted with stress also on rape of women by their husbands and regular partners (cf. Eves this volume; Hammar this volume). The dangers of infection to female rape victims are not just due to their difficulties negotiating condom use (Lewis 2009): because the vaginal male-to-female route for HIV is so much more effective than female-to-male (Whiteside 2008, 30), because rape often involves vaginal abrasion and injury that increases the chances of female infection, and because young rape victims are more attractive targets and their immature vaginal lining is more susceptible, HIV is a grave risk from rape for women, particularly young women. And this risk is very widely experienced (see, e.g. Lewis 2009).

Rape, specifically *lainap*, does however pose a particular HIV risk to men, and perhaps to young men. This is tricky to discuss, because the information may be taken to confirm beliefs that women cause infection; to support tendencies, reflected in newspaper accounts (see, e.g. Luker this volume conclusion; Anon. 1994; 1998), to sympathise with rapists; and to condone rape so long as condoms are used (cf. McLeod and Macintyre this volume; HELP 2005, 21) Yet, as Jenkins has stressed, much greater than the risk of contracting HIV from any woman they rape is men's risk of contracting HIV in *lainap* by making contact in the woman's vagina with infected fluid from another man in the line (Jenkins

1996, 204). While the likelihood of an uninfected woman receiving HIV in such circumstances is even higher, a larger number of men can be exposed to elevated risk in a single act of *lainap* (Jenkins 1996, 204; NSRRT 1994, 105). Perhaps *in toto* more men than women contract HIV through *lainap* and if some male youth are more likely to participate in *lainap* than in other modes of sexual intercourse, this practice could represent a proportionately higher risk of HIV to young men.

But overall, is rape a major driver of HIV's spread in PNG? Some researchers (Barnett 2008, 8; cf. Epstein 2007, 245–246) have suggested that in countries with high levels of heterosexually transmitted HIV, rape and intimate partner violence may prove ultimately less important than transactional sex, which as Hammar (this volume) demonstrates, can encompass very diverse relationships beyond strict definitions of sex work. For epidemics mainly reliant on sexual transmission, Epstein and others also suggest that the nature of an unprotected sexual act perhaps matters less in the wider frame of reference than the character of the sexual network in which it occurs: to reach high prevalence, HIV requires far-reaching concatenations of concurrent sexual relations (as distinct from strings of serial multi-partnering), whereby a significant proportion of both men and women have more than one regular sexual partner at the same time (Epstein 2007, 54–95). The implications of these theses require more thought in regard to PNG.

The role of young men in the spread of HIV in PNG requires more thought too. Assessing their involvement is hampered by the fact that young men are the least likely of any adult group between the ages 15–45 to be tested. More is known about their female counterparts through young mothers at antenatal clinics. Yet available statistics suggest that HIV levels for young men in PNG are relatively low, even allowing for under-reporting. Those aged 15–19 account for the fewest HIV infections detected for any sex-specific adult cohort under the age of 45; and the total for young men 20–24 is relatively low too. The biggest contrast is between these figures for young men and those for girls and women of the same age, which are extremely high (CAP 2009, 29). This discrepancy between female and male youth is found in other countries with generalised prevalence of heterosexually transmitted HIV (Monasch and Mahy 2006, 23).

For global HIV policy, youth has been central to prevention (Monasch and Mahy 2006). As Buchanan-Aruwafu notes, this category cuts across groups identified to be at higher risk of HIV: men who have sex with men (MSM); those involved in injecting drug use (IDU); and sex workers and their clients. Young people may also facilitate the wider spread of HIV by moving between different sexual networks and risk-settings (Buchanan-Aruwafu 2007, 82–83). Social mapping in PNG has identified some localities, such as the settlements of Hanuabada and Joyce Bay in Port Moresby, where youth intersects with more than one of these higher risk groups (Millan et al. 2006, 17, 38–55; NHASP 2006, 59–62).

How do young men in PNG fit into this generic framework? IDU is negligible in PNG, though tattooing, scarification and penile modification can carry some risk of HIV transmission (Buchanan-Aruwafu et al. 2002, 8, 12; cf. Law this volume). The MSM factor and its epidemiological significance are difficult to ascertain. Although the ritual homosexuality practised in a handful of PNG societies has passed (Jenkins 1996), sex between men occurs in institutions such as prisons (see Law this volume); sometimes between men in *lainap* (NSRRT 1994, 105); in male to male sex work (Jenkins 1996, 196; Buchanan-Aruwafu et al. 2002, 9; HELP 2005, 61–62); and nearly 12 percent of young men in one survey reported having had sex with another male (SCiPNG 2008, 22). Because men, including young men, who have sex with men usually also have heterosexual relations (Jenkins 1996; Buchanan-Aruwafu et al. 2002, 9) and very few socially identify by an exclusive homosexual preference (e.g., NHASP 2006, 59; Engels 2008, 9), the MSM factor is camouflaged. Nevertheless the predominantly heterosexual dynamic of transmission in PNG seems both pronounced and corroborated by molecular epidemiology.[14] Finally, how do young men participate in the risk category of commercial sex workers and their clients? Aside from some youths engaging in homosexual sex work and scanty evidence of transactional sex with older women (Millan et al. 2006, 43), young men appear primarily excluded from one of the major epidemiological flows of HIV in PNG: from older men with 'purchasing power' to younger women with sexual goods.

Within this generic framework, the risks of HIV to young men seem much smaller than to young women, and the role in HIV transmission played by older men of more concern than by younger men. As Kalichman observes, whether dealing with heterosexually or homosexually transmitted HIV, in general 'Older men are more likely to have HIV, resist condom use, and have sex with multiple younger partners' (Kalichman 2009, 125). The *dakglas kar man* (dark glass car man), as Lepani remarks, is the *pisin* equivalent of the sub-Saharan 'sugar daddy' stereotype, and evokes 'the businessman, politician or landowner with plenty of disposable income who drives a car with tinted windows' (Lepani 2008, 152). The travesties and dangers of the *dakglas kar man* stereotype are of less interest here than the fact that, despite perhaps the odd allusion in local media (e.g. Muri 2009; Anon. 2004) very little public concern attaches to it, in contrast to the widespread blame of 'prostitutes' as sources of infection (see especially Fletcher and Gonapa this volume; Stewart this volume) and explicit anxieties about the sexual predations of young *raskols*. Certainly the moneyed older man can be

---

14　The predominant subtype of HIV in PNG is most closely related to East African strains (CAP 2009, 22) and correlated with heterosexual transmission.

difficult to challenge—a point David Lornie has made well with the character of Dennis in his HIV novel, *Vavine's Curse*, set in Port Moresby (Lornie 2008). PNG is not alone however in tending to focus away from older men and generally from people aged over 25. UNAIDS has observed that internationally 'relatively few prevention programmes have specifically focused on older adults' (UNAIDS 2009, 9). Older men are arguably a greater challenge than young men in relation to HIV and probably ditto in relation to crime.

Conclusion: A Chance Encounter

These observations upon teasing out the *raskol* tangle perhaps highlight some other angles on masculinity, youth, crime, sex, and HIV that also need bringing into focus. But they do not negate the need for responding to the plight of youth, female and male, or specifically reducing the involvement of young men in property crime and rape, or minimising the exposure of all youth, and particularly young women, to HIV. This is not the place to review many measures and proposals that currently target young people.[15] Instead, we would like to finish with a story and reflections on three of its themes.

Carol Kidu's autobiography recalls a chance encounter. In 1997 she was running for parliament on an 'intellectual campaign' that would explain her policy platform and background. She knew she would need to use pictures, because many languages were spoken in her Port Moresby electorate and illiteracy levels were high. With the help of an unemployed artist and sheets of plastic donated by a local business, she used charts to cover such questions as 'What is the work of a politician?', 'What is the power of your vote?', 'How does a budget work?', and 'What is development all about?'

> I will always remember well one incident. I had completed an educational campaign in a very poor settlement, notorious for its law and order problems. As usual a few young men hung around in the shadows of the trees listening to me. I encouraged them to join the other people in the small audience, but they did not do so.

---

15   Renewed efforts have been taken to involve young men in sport and community policing (NYC 2007, 3; PNG 2007, 35). Youth groups have proliferated, and The National Youth Policy observes that those including older members and tied into kin structures tend to endure. (NYC 2007, 3). A range of initiatives have been taken by the NAC, churches, universities, schools and others to equip youth to deal with HIV (NYC 2007, 31–32). Alongside expanded formal schooling and tertiary education, Kidu has advanced the idea of community centres that would serve as hubs for information, referral and life-long learning for the benefit of all, including disadvantaged youth (Kidu 2008a, 2008b). While no one expects a swift expansion of formal employment for young people, some see in the informal sector scope to increase opportunities for legitimate cash livelihoods (Levantis 2000, 141; NYC 2007, 31–32).

Unexpectedly, one of the young men came over to me when I was leaving, and looked into my eyes and simply said, 'Thanks for giving me hope.'

In him I saw the skinny, hollow-eyed look of poverty with his pants slipping below non-existent buttocks. But beyond those hollow eyes was a young man with dreams—unattainable dreams. There was a softness in his voice that betrayed his attempt to look like the gang and portrayed a gentleness that did not match the gang image. As soon as he had spoken, he slipped back into the small crowd of people to disappear forever (Kidu 2002, 155–6).

This young man might have passed as a *raskol*. He was a child of Independence: perhaps a few years younger, probably no older, than the nation of Papua New Guinea. The talk he listened to explained basic relationships between government, citizen and development. These are the themes for our final reflections.

First, citizen: while this was the young man's official status, in some senses it was unreal. The concept of citizenship, implicated in the notion of civic security central to this volume, has been discussed in youth studies since the 1990s (e.g. France 1998; Helve and Wallace 2001) with respect to rights, duties, responsibilities, participation and access to society's institutions. But as Sister John-Paul Chao reflected 20 years ago, on a settlement nine miles from Port Moresby's central business district—where many households lacked adequate food for days at a time; had no money to obtain medical help or to catch buses; were repeatedly searched by police without warrants; failed to enrol their children in school; in other words, resembled many households today—there is a 'hopeless gap' between people's aspirations and realities. 'Until they stop standing on the periphery... citizenship will remain an empty word devoid of meaning. If there is no participation, [there can be] no real sense of citizenship' (Chao 1989, 104)—and, one might add, an accompanying sense of responsibility to wider society.

Second, government: although Kidu's interlocutor lived in the capital, close to the central institutions of national politics and bureaucracy, this encounter between a candidate and a voter suggests a gulf between the worlds of state and local life that is even wider in most parts of the country. While some commentators stress the separation between the political elite and ground-level settlements and villages, unfortunately government institutions connecting these worlds have in many places weakened or receded during this young man's lifetime. As many recognise, and this book also stresses (see Luker and Dinnen this volume chapter one; Luker this volume conclusion), institutions in this connecting zone, and their infrastructure, need strengthening—some have argued in terms of hubs (Kidu 2008a; 2008b; Anon. 2008), a reconstrued *kiap* model (Dinnen and Braithwaite 2009), cross-sectoral partnerships (Hayward-Jones 2008), generalised systemic reform and, as advanced in this volume, 'whole of governance' approaches (Luker and Dinnen this volume, chapter one and Luker this volume, conclusion). The people who work in this zone—teachers, police, health workers, agricultural personnel, alongside workers in churches and nongovernment sectors—need fostering. They have a special potential for cultivating public goods, providing constancy, assisting community energy and initiative, and supporting processes of local understanding and innovation. Problems facing communities, including lawlessness and such challenges as HIV, must be understood in the wider context and longer term of very broad change, looking back and to the future (cf. Reid this volume, ch. 13).

Finally, development: what is it? Carol Kidu's presentation and the hope it kindled in the young man suggests that he understood development as something closely bundled with government and politics. And perhaps among his dreams was a hope for a livelihood. The lack of economic opportunity haunts the condition of young people today discussed in this chapter, but goes beyond *raskolism* and HIV. As Abbott remarks, youth unemployment, however we define it, is one of the most critical issues for governments of the Pacific region (Abbott 2007, 69)—and for the hopes of people, young and old, rural and urban, that their efforts will sustain a future for themselves and their families.

References

Abbott, David F. 2007. Poverty and Pro-poor Policies for Pacific Island Countries. *Asia-Pacific Population Journal* 22 (3): 59–74.

Allen, Bryant. 1986. Five Generations of Youth at Dreikir. In *Youth and Society: Perspectives from Papua New Guinea*, ed. Maev O'Collins, 33–42. Canberra: Department of Political and Social Change, Australian National University.

Altman, Dennis. 2001. *Global Sex*. Crows Nest, NSW: Allen and Unwin.

Anon. 1994. Compensation for Who? *Pacific AIDS Alert Bulletin*, 8, 13.

Anon. 1998. Rapists warned of AIDS Risk. *Pacific AIDS Alert Bulletin*, 15, 11.

Anon. 2008. Kidu Opts for New PNG Community Policy. Radio New Zealand International, 18 March 2008.

Anon. 2004. Shocking News. *Post-Courier*, 29 September 2009.

Banks, 2000. Contextualising Sexual Violence: Rape and Carnal Knowledge in Papua New Guinea. In *Reflections on Violence in Melanesia*, ed. Sinclair Dinnen and Allison Ley, 83–104. Annandale: Hawkins Press and Canberra: Asia Pacific Press.

Barker, John. 1986. In *Youth and Society: Perspectives from Papua New Guinea*, ed. Maev O'Collins, 81–108. Canberra: Department of Political and Social Change, Australian National University.

Barnett, Tony. 2008. *Hoping or Discounting the Future: A New Perspective on the Transmission of HIV/AIDS*. WDP 2008/8. Helsinki: World Institute for Development Economic Research, United Nations University.

Bashir, Mohammad. 2009. Asian Crime Syndicates Invading PNG—Officers. *Post Courier*, 3 April 2009.

Baxter, Michael. 2001. Enclaves or Equity: The Rural Crisis and Development Choice in Papua New Guinea. *International Development Issues* No. 54. Canberra: AusAID.

Belshaw, C. S. 1964. *Under the Ivi Tree: Society and Economic Growth in Rural Fiji*. London: Routledge and Kegan Paul.

Borrey, Anou. 2000. Sexual Violence in Perspective: The Case of Papua New Guinea. In *Reflections on Violence in Melanesia*, ed. Sinclair Dinnen and Allison Ley, 105–118. Annandale: Hawkins Press and Canberra: Asia Pacific Press.

Bourke, R. M. 2008. The Poorest People Stay in Rural PNG. *The National*, 11 June 2008.

Buchanan-Aruwafu, Holly, with Albert Komara, Gennie Koronos, Rory Sitapai, Rosely Roy Nana. 2002. Strategies and Framework for Targeting Youth: Advising with PNG Youth on HIV/AIDS. Milestone No. 37. November 2002. National HIV/AIDS Support Project (NHASP)

Buchanan-Aruwafu, Holly. 2007. Youth Vulnerability to HIV in the Pacific. In Carol Jenkins and Holly Buchanan-Aruwafu, *Cultures and Contexts Matter: Understanding and Preventing HIV in the Pacific*, 71–130. Manila: Asian Development Bank.

Callick, Rowan. 2009. Corruption Fear in PNG Project: Luke Fletcher. *The Australian*, 20 October 2009.

CAP (Commission on AIDS in the Pacific). 2009. *Turning the Tide: An OPEN Strategy for a Response to AIDS in the Pacific*. Suva: Commission on AIDS in the Pacific.

Chandy, Laurence. 2009. *Linking Growth and Poverty Reduction in Papua New Guinea*. Lowy Institute Analyses, September 2009. Sydney: Lowy Institute.

Chao, Sister J. P. 1989. A New Sense of Community: Perspectives from a Squatter Settlement. In *The Ethics of Development*, 17th Waigani Seminar, vol. 5: *In Search of Justice*, ed. C. Thirlwall and P. J. Hughes, 88–106. Port Moresby: University of Papua New Guinea Press.

Dinnen, S. and John Braithwaite. 2009. Reinventing Policing through the Prism of the Colonial Kiap. *Policing and Society*, 19 (2): 161–173.

Dinnen, S. and E. Thompson. 2009. State Society and the Gender of Gun Culture in Papua New Guinea. In *Sexed Pistols: The Gendered Impacts of Small Arms and Light Weapons*, ed. Vanessa Farr, Henri Myrttinen and Albrecht Schnabel, 143–176. Tokyo, New York and Paris: United Nations University Press.

Dinnen, Sinclair. 2001. *Law and Order in a Weak State: Crime and Politics in Papua New Guinea*. Adelaide: Crawford House Publishing.

Dupont, Stephen. 2005. *Raskols*. Limited edition of photographic portraits, held in the National Library of Australia, Canberra. www.stephendupont.com

Ellsberg, Mary, Christine Bradley, Andrew Egan, Amy Haddad. 2008. Violence against Women in Melanesia and East Timor: Building on Global and Regional Promising Approaches. Canberra: AusAID.

Engels, John. 2008. *Success Stories from Papua New Guinea: Tingim Laip*. Waigani: Family Health International.

Epstein, Helen. 2007. *The Invisible Cure: Why We are Losing the Fight against AIDS in Africa*. New York: Picador.

Fife, Wayne. 1995. Models for Masculinity in Colonial and Postcolonial Papua New Guinea. *The Contemporary Pacific* 7 (2): 277–302.

Finney, B. 1973. *Polynesian Peasants and Proletariats*. Cambridge, Massachusetts: Schenkman Publishing Company.

Fox, Liam. 2009. PNG's HIV Pledge on Shaky Ground. Australian Broadcasting Commission, 5 December 2009.

France, A. 1998. 'Why Should We Care?' Young People, Citizenship and Questions of Responsibility. *Journal of Youth Studies* 1 (1): 97–111.

Garap, Sarah. 2000. Struggles of Women and Girls. In *Reflections on Violence in Melanesia*, ed. Sinclair Dinnen and Allison Ley, 159–171. Leichardt and Canberra: Hawkins Press and Asia Pacific Press.

Gerawa, Maureen. 2004. Shocking News. *Post-Courier*, 29 September 2004.

Goddard, M. 2005. *The Unseen City: Anthropological Perspectives on Port Moresby, Papua New Guinea*. Canberra: Pandanus Books.

Goddard, M. 2009. *Substantial Justice: An Anthropology of Village Courts in Papua New Guinea*. New York and Oxford: Berghahn Books.

Guy, Sandy and David Crofts. 2000. Papua New Guinea: Epidemic on Our Doorstep. *The Mercury*, 26 February 2000.

Haley, Nicole. 2008. Sung Adornment: Changing Masculinities at Lake Kopiago, Papua New Guinea. *The Australian Journal of Anthropology*, 19 (2): 213–229.

Hammar, L. 1998. AIDS, STDs, and Sex Work in Papua New Guinea. In *Modern Papua New Guinea*, ed. Laura Zimmer-Tamakoshi, 257–296. Kirksville, MO: Thomas Jefferson University Press.

Harris, Bruce M. 1988. *The Rise of Rascalism: Action and Reaction in the Evolution of Rascal Gangs*. IASER Discussion Paper No. 54. Port Moresby: Institute of Applied Social and Economic Research.

Hayward-Jones, Jenny. 2008. Beyond Good Governance: Shifting the Paradigm for Australian Aid to the Pacific Islands Region. Policy Brief, September 2008. Sydney: Lowy Institute for International Policy.

HELP (HELP Resources Inc.). 2005. A Situational Analysis of Child Sexual Abuse and the Commercial Sexual Exploitation of Children in Papua New Guinea. Prepared by HELP Resources, Inc., with the support of UNICEF PNG. January 2005.

Helve, Helena and Claire Wallace. 2001. *Youth, Citizenship and Empowerment*. Aldershot: Ashgate.

Herdt. G., ed. 1982. *Rituals of Manhood: Male Initiation in Papua New Guinea*. Berkeley: University of California Press.

Herdt,. G. 1984. Ritualized Homosexual Behavior in the Male Cults of Melanesia, 1862–1983: An Introduction. In *Ritualized Homosexuality in Melanesia*, ed. G. Herdt, 1–81. Berkeley: University of California Press.

Herdt, Gilbert and Stephen C. Leavitt. 1998. Introduction: Studying Adolescence in Contemporary Pacific Island Communities. In *Adolescence in Pacific Island Societies,* ed. Gilbert Herdt and Stephen C. Leavitt, 3–26. Pittsburgh: University of Pittsburgh Press.

Hukula, Fiona. 1999. *Women and Security in Port Moresby*. NRI Discussion Paper no. 92. Boroko: National Research Institute.

Hukula, Fiona. 2005. *Rape and Social Identity*. NRI Discussion Paper No. 100. Boroko: The National Research Institute.

INA (Institute of National Affairs). 2004. Report of the Royal Papua New Guinea Constabulary Administrative Review Committee to the Minister for internal Security Hon. Bire Kimisopa. Port Moresby: Institute of National Affairs.

James, Paul, Victoria Stead, Yaso Nadarajah, Karen Haive. 2009. Projecting Community Life, themed issue, *Local Global: Identity, Security, Community*, 5.

Jenkins, C. 1996. The Homosexual Context of Heterosexual Practice in Papua New Guinea. In *Bisexualities and AIDS: International Perspectives*, ed. P. Aggleton, 191–206. London: Taylor and Francis.

Jenkins, C and M. Alpers. 1996. Urbanization, Youth and Sexuality: insights for an AIDS Campaign for Youth in Papua New Guinea. *PNG Medical Journal*. 39 (3): 248–251.

Joku, Harlyne. 2009. 2 Million Condoms Go to Waste! *Post-Courier*, 4 March 2009.

Jolly, M. 1992. Spectres of Inauthenticity. *The Contemporary Pacific*, 4 (1): 49–72.

Jolly, M. and M. Macintyre, eds. 1989. *Family and Gender in the Pacific: Domestic Contradictions and the Colonial Impact*. Cambridge: Cambridge University Press.

Jolly, M. and N. Thomas. 1992. Introduction. In The Politics of Tradition in the Pacific, ed. M. Jolly and N. Thomas, special issue of *Oceania*, 62 (4): 241–248.

Kalichman, Seth. 2009. *Denying AIDS: Conspiracy Theories, Pseudoscience and Human Tragedy*. New York: Copernicus Books.

Kay, P. 1971. Urbanisation in the Tahitian Household. In *Polynesia: Readings on a Culture Area,* ed. A. Howard, 319–329. Scranton: Chandler Publishing Co.

Kelly, Angela, Frances Akuani, Barbara Kepa, Lawrencia Pirpir, Agnes Mek, Martha Kupul, Rebecca Emori, Somu Nosi, Lucy Walizopa, Brneda Cangah, Kritoe Keleba. 2008. *Young People's Attitudes towards Sex and HIV in the Eastern Highlands of Papua New Guinea*. Monograph 1/2008. Sydney: National Centre for HIV Social Research.

Kewa, Christina. 2007. *Being a Woman in Papua New Guinea: From Grass Skirts and Ashes to Education and Global Changes*. Nelson, NZ: The Copy Press.

Kidu, Carol. 2002. *A Remarkable Journey*. Sydney: Longman.

Kidu, Carol. 2008a. Challenges and Opportunities for Papua New Guinea: A Reflection on Changing Times. Presentation to the Oceanic Connections Conference, Australian National University, Canberra, 18 April 2008.

Kidu, Carol. 2008b. The Power of Partnerships: Reflections on Addressing Papua New Guinea's Social Challenges. Presentation to the Lowy Institute, Sydney, 7 May 2008. Available http://lowyinstitute.org/ (accessed 27 April 2010).

Leavitt, Stephen C. 1998. The Bikhet Mystique: Masculine Identity and Patterns of Rebellion among Bumbia Adolescent Males. In *Adolescence in Pacific Islands Societies*, ed. Gilbert Herdt and Stephen C. Leavitt, 173–194. Pittsburgh, PA: University of Pittsburgh Press.

Lepani, 2007. 'In the Process of Knowing': Making Sense of HIV and AIDS in the Trobriand Islands of Papua New Guinea. PhD thesis, Canberra: The Australian National University.

Lepani, Katherine. 2008. Mobility, Violence and the Gendering of HIV in Papua New Guinea. *The Australian Journal of Anthropology*, 19 (2): 150–164.

Levantis, Theodore. 2000. Crime Catastrophe—Reviewing Papua New Guinea's most Serious Social and Economic Problem. *Pacific Economic Bulletin* 15 (2): 130–142.

Lewis, Ione. 2009. How is HIV transmission in PNG influenced by violence against women and attitudes towards condoms? In AIDS, Belief and Culture in PNG, ed. Hermann Spingler, special issue of *Catalyst*, 39 (2): 29–55.

Lornie, David. 2008. *Vavine's Curse*. Darnum, VIC: Dwyers Pacific Press Pty Ltd.

Macintyre, Martha. 2008. Police and Thieves, Gunmen and Drunks: Problems with Men and Problems with Society in Papua New Guinea. *The Australian Journal of Anthropology*, 19: 2, 179–193.

Malinowski, Bronislaw. 1932. *The Sexual Lives of Savages in North-western Melanesia: An Ethnographic Account of Courtship, Marriage and Family Life among the Natives of the Trobriand Islands*. London: Routledge and Kegan Paul.

McLeod, Abby, 2008. *Leadership Models in the Pacific*. State Society and Governance in Melanesia Discussion Paper, 2009/6. Canberra: Australian National University.

Millan, John, William Yeka, Walter Obiero, Joachim Pantumari. 2006. HIV/AIDS Behavioural Surveillance Survey within High Risk Settings: Papua New Guinea: BSS Round 1. [Port Moresby]: National AIDS Council Secretariat and National HIV/AIDS Support Project.

Monasch, Roeland and Mary Mahy. 2006. Young People: The Centre of the HIV Epidemic. In *Preventing HIV/AIDS in Young People: A Systematic Review of the Evidence from Developing Countries*, UNAIDS Inter-agency Task Team on Young People, 15–36. Geneva: World Health Organization.

Monsell-Davis, M. 1987. At Home in the Village: Youth and Community in Nabuapaka. In *Youth and Society: Perspectives from Papua New Guinea*, ed. Maev O'Collins, 65–80. Canberra: Department of Political and Social Change, Australian National University.

Monsell-Davis, M. 1985. *The Village Entrepreneur: Business Man or Villager?* Extension Studies Department. Port Moresby: University of Papua New Guinea [An abridged version appeared as: Rural Entrepreneurs need Expert Advice, *The Times of PNG*, 7 April 1985].

Monsell-Davis, M. 1993a. Urban Safety-net or Disincentive? *Wantoks* and Relatives in the Urban Pacific. *Canberra Anthropology* 16 (2): 45–66.

Monsell-Davis, M. 1993b. *Micro-enterprises and Rural Development: Global Economy, Local Initiatives and Local Constraints*. Department of Anthropology. Port Moresby: University of Papua New Guinea.

Monsell-Davis, M. 1994. What is this Thing Called 'Family'? Discussion Paper for Symposium on 'The Family'. Sociology Department. Suva: University of the South Pacific.

Monsell-Davis, M. 1998a. Youth and Social Change in the Pacific. Draft paper. MacMillan Brown Centre for Pacific Studies. Christchurch: Canterbury University.

Monsell-Davis, M. 1998b. Education and rural development: social considerations in expanding high school education to all. In *Modern Papua New Guinea*, ed. Laura Zimmer-Tamakoshi, 315–332. Kirksville, MO: Thomas Jefferson University Press.

Monsell-Davis, M. 2000. Social Change, Contradictions, Youth and Violence. In *Reflections on Violence in Melanesia,* ed. S. Dinnen and A. Ley, 209–222. NSW and Canberra: Hawkins Press/Asia Pacific Press.

Monsell-Davis, M. 2005. 'Don't Ask for Biscuits': Economic Decline and Social Change in a Coastal Papuan Village. In *A Polymath Anthropologist: Essays in Honour of Ann Chowning,* ed. Claudia Gross, H. Lyons and D. Counts, 121–130. Auckland: Research in Anthropology and Linguistics, Monograph Series Vol. 6.

Moore, Clive. 2003. *New Guinea: Crossing Boundaries and History.* Honolulu: University of Hawai'i Press.

Muri, David. 2009. 'I was raped.' 'Big man' lures school girl, 17. *The National,* 12 February 2009.

Naemon, Anna Sirimai. 2009. Behaviours that Put Female Youth at Risk of Human Immunodeficiency Virus and Sexually Transmitted Infections in Gerehu, Port Moresby, Papua New Guinea. Masters thesis. Wellington: Victoria University.

Nalu, Malum. 2009. Massive Scam within AIDS Council: Barter. *The National,* 6 March 2009.

Narokobi, Bernard, et al. 1980. *The Melanesian Way: Total Cosmic Vision of Life.* [Port Moresby]: Institute of Papua New Guinea Studies.

NACS (National AIDS Council Secretariat) and Partners. 2008. Papua New Guinea: UNGASS 2008 Country Progress Report: Reporting Period: January 2006–December 2007. Port Moresby: National AIDS Council.

NSO (National Statistical Office). 2003. *Papua New Guinea 2000 Census.* Port Moresby: National Statistical Office.

Ninkama, Kristoffa. 2009. 40 Years of Complete Neglect. *Post-Courier,* 12 March 2009.

NSRRT (National Sex and Reproduction Research Team and Carol Jenkins). 1994. *National Study of Sexual and Reproductive Knowledge and Behaviour in Papua New Guinea.* Goroka: PNG Institute of Medical Research, Monograph 10.

NYC (National Youth Commission). 2007. *National Youth Policy of Papua New Guinea 2007–2017.* Port Moresby: National Youth Commission of Papua New Guinea.

NZPPD. 2010. Making Maternal Health Matter: Report of the New Zealand Parliamentarians' Group on Population and Development. Open Hearing on Maternal Health in the Pacific. [Wellington]: The New Zealand All-Party Parliamentary Group.

PNG (Papua New Guinea). 2007. *A Just, Safe and Secure Society: A White Paper on Law and Justice in Papua New Guinea*. March 2007. Presented to Parliament by the Minister for Justice Bire Kimisopa. Port Moresby: Office of the Secretary for Justice and Attorney General.

PNG (Papua New Guinea) and UN (United Nations). 2004. Millennium Development Goals: Progress Report for Papua New Guinea. [place of publication, publisher, not specified]

PNG (Papua New Guinea) JAG (Justice Advisory Group). 2008. Law & Justice Sector: Urban Crime Victimisation in Papua New Guinea, 2004-2008: A Synthesis. [place of publication, publisher, not specified]

PNG (Papua New Guinea) NSO (National Statistical Office), 2003. *2000 National Census: National Report*. Port Moresby: National Statistical Office

Renkin, Lisa and Chad Hughes. 2006. HIV: The Predicament and the Potential of Young People in Papua New Guinea. Youth Advisors' Report. (unpublished report, reprinted with permission from the National AIDS Council of PNG).

Rubinstein, D. 1994. Changes in the Micronesian Family Structure Leading to Alcoholism, Suicide and Child Abuse and Neglect. *Micronesian Counsellor*, Occasional Paper 15.

SCiPNG (Save the Children in Papua New Guinea). [2008]. Youth Outreach Project: Knowledge, Attitude and Practice Survey in the Eastern Highlands and Madang Provinces of Papua New Guinea. Unpublished report.

Sahlins, M. 1963. Poor Man, Rich Man, Big Man, Chief: Political Types in Melanesia and Polynesia. *Comparative Studies in Society and History* 5 (3): 285–303.

Sikani, Richard. 1997. 'Live to Steal and Steal to Live': Juveniles and Economic Crime. Preliminary Paper No. 3. Port Moresby: Political and Legal Studies Division, National Research Institute.

Sivusia-Joyce, Barbara, Henry Koi, Hazel Mamae. 2004. Evaluation of the Impact and Effectiveness of the PNG HIV/AIDS Awareness Program in Selected Secondary Schools and High Schools in the National Capital District. [Port Moresby]: National Research Institute.

SPC (Secretariat of the Pacific Community). 2010. Pacific Island Populations—Estimates and Projections of Demographic Indicators for Selected Years. Updated February 2010.

Strathern, A. 1993. Violence and Political Change in Papua New Guinea. *Pacific Studies* 16 (4): 41–60.

Strathern, M. 1975. Report on Questionnaire Relating to Sexual Offences as Defined in the Criminal Code, Report Prepared for the Department of Law, New Guinea Research Unit, Boroko.

UNAIDS ITTYP (Inter-agency Task Team on Young People). 2006. Preventing HIV/AIDS in Young People: A Systematic Review of the Evidence from Developing Countries. Geneva: World Health Organization.

UNAIDS. 2009. AIDS Epidemic Update December 2009. Geneva: UNAIDS.

UNDP (United Nations Development Program). 2009. MDG Scorecard: MDG Status at a Glance. Suva: UNDP Pacific Centre.

UNICEF. 1995. The State of Pacific Children 1995. Suva: UNICEF.

UNICEF. 1998. State of Pacific Youth Report 1998. Suva: UNICEF.

UNICEF. 2005. Children and HIV/AIDS in Papua New Guinea. Port Moresby: UNICEF.

Waiko, John Dedamo. 1993. *A Short History of Papua New Guinea*. Melbourne: Oxford University Press.

Wardlow, Holly. 2006. *Wayward Women: Sexuality and Agency in a New Guinea Society*. Berkeley: University of California Press.

Werf, Janko van der. 2008. 'We Live like in a War': An Anthropological Investigation into Criminal Gangs in the Rural and Urban Areas of Papua New Guinea. *Melanesian Mission Studies* No. 3. Goroka: Melanesian Institute.

Whiteside, Alan. 2008. *HIV/AIDS: A Very Short Introduction*. Oxford: Oxford University Press.

Worthman, Carol M. 1998. Adolescence in the Pacific: A Biosocial View. In *Adolescence in Pacific Islands Societies*, ed. Gilbert Herdt and Stephen C. Leavitt, 27–52. Pittsburgh, PA: University of Pittsburgh Press.

WHO (World Health Organization). 2008. *World Health Statistics 2008*. Geneva: WHO.

Zimmer-Tamakoshi, L. 1990. Nationalism and Sexuality in Papua New Guinea. *Pacific Studies* 16 (4): 20–48.

Zimmer-Tamakoshi, L. 1997. Wild Pigs and Dog Men: Rape and Domestic Violence as 'Women's Issues' in Papua New Guinea. In *Gender in Cross-Cultural Perspective*, ed. C. Bretteland and C. Sargent, 538–553. Upper River: Prentice Hall.

Networking, Sex Working and the Law

4. From Gift to Commodity . . . and Back Again: Form and Fluidity of Sexual Networking in Papua New Guinea

LAWRENCE HAMMAR

Because, when you are a woman, you don't just sit still and do nothing—you have lovers . . . One man gives you only one kind of food to eat. But when you have lovers, one brings you something and another brings you something else. One comes at night with meat, another with money, another with beads. Your husband also does things and gives them to you (Nisa, to Shostak 1981, 271).

Hey little girl, ooh, sweet little Honey.
I'm gonna give you, all of my money.
All I'm asking is, give it to me when I come home
(Otis Redding, the original 'Respect').

The mature and sexually experienced [chimpanzee] female trades upon her ability to satisfy the sexual urges of the male (Yerkes 1943, 86).

With all my worldly goods I thee endow [the Bride, who then replies to the Groom:] With my body I thee love (traditional marriage vow).

Introduction

In this essay I want to contribute to longstanding discussions about sexism and marriage, gender relations and sexuality, and prostitution and public health in Papua New Guinea (PNG). My contribution is aimed at two overlapping developments and discourses. First, since at least the late 1970s, calls have been made for the PNG state to erect and regulate brothels, ostensibly as a 'public health' measure to prevent the transmission of STDs, but also to sequester the signs of sexuality away from public view. Sex is bad, but prostitution is lust, being both unproductive and wasteful. Prostitution-related topics appeared throughout the 1970s in newspapers such as *The Independent*, the *Post-Courier*, and the *Wantok* (in Tok Pisin). They set the stage for the first several years' worth of AIDS-related coverage and the current struggles over the question of brothels. Four of the first six articles published in the *Post-Courier*, after the first HIVab+ case had been reported (in 1987), implicated prostitution (July 2, 3, 6, 10, 22, and 24). As would be the case throughout the following 20 years, letter-writers, editors, and public health officials blamed prostituted women for the growing HIV crisis without presenting any evidence of transmission dynamics. Nor did they show concern for the women, their sexual partners and families, or the conditions under which they might have been infected, including through rape.

Significant protest against the erection of brothels continues to come from the church and other authorities, although few voices and even fewer authorities protest from feminist principles or concern about possible human rights violations. Nevertheless, proposals are increasingly being made by high-ranking politicians, businessmen and health officials (sometimes one and the same) to erect brothels as a response to the emerging AIDS crisis. It is true that state-sponsored brothels *can be argued to* 'work' well in preventing STD and HIV transmission elsewhere, for example, in Thailand, Melbourne, or certain counties in the American state of Nevada. Nevertheless, state-sponsored brothels in PNG would require 'regulation' by members of the 'disciplined' forces (who aren't) and whose 'force' is often greatest when their 'discipline' is weakest.[1] For this reason alone—one of the many paradoxes engendered in weak states—they will not 'work' in PNG.

There are other reasons, too, however, which this essay explores. In addition to the shortfall of truly disciplined powers and the corresponding excess of male dominance in such matters, proposals to erect and maintain brothels dramatically understate the medical and regulatory powers that would be required of the PNG state to ensure an increase in levels of condom usage in the brothels sufficient to dent fast-rising rates of HIV transmission and, in many places, near-epidemic levels of untreated STDs. My colleagues at the Institute of Medical Research (IMR), for instance, routinely demonstrate STD prevalence rates that approach or exceed 30 percent, in 40 percent or more of communities sampled (e.g. Tiwara et al. 1996; Gare et al. 2005; Hammar 2006). As well, state-sponsored brothels would surely increase already significant female sexual exploitation. As sexual minorities, women and girls already take rhetorical and literal poundings daily in 'prostitution' and in plain-old 'marriage', both terms which here gloss truly

---

1   See works by Luker and Dinnen, Stewart, Shearing, Fletcher, and Jenkins here in this volume, and those of these fine scholars plus also Bradley, Clark, Gillett, Hammar, Hughes, Knauft, Macintyre, Reid, Wardlow, Zimmer-Tamakoshi and others, elsewhere.

stupefying diversity in form and meaning of styles, locations and outcomes of sexual networking. Most Christian and customary doctrines and practices regarding land, money, reproduction and sex, assume that males have God- or ancestor-given rights to control the sexual and reproductive health of females with more or less unhindered male sexual access. This is neither healthy nor morally just. As I have argued at length elsewhere (e.g. Hammar 2004a, b; 1998), and as others have argued in other ways, it constitutes the widespread and deeply entrenched sexually transmitted dis-ease (the hyphen is intentional) on the level of social structure that is nevertheless felt also at the level of the individual. Few church, political, health or donor voices wish unblinkingly to examine such premises in thinking afresh about the origins of the 'current' AIDS crisis, which are in fact longstanding.

Second, in this essay I touch upon the historical and other forces that have shaped, and been shaped by, changes in sexual networking forms. I present data that I and others collected previously, and that I and my colleagues collected from 2003–2006 while undertaking a nationwide study of HIV/AIDS, STDs and sexual health and human behaviour for the Papua New Guinea Institute of Medical Research (PNGIMR) (Hammar 2006). Most examples are drawn from four locales: Lae (2004); Daru (1990–2, 2003–4); Port Moresby (1991, 2003–5); and Moro, Southern Highlands Province (2005, 2006). Throughout the essay I suggest that the differences between 'prostitution' and 'marriage', not being self-evident, require sociological analysis. The absence of social scientific perspectives in informing policy and public health debates in PNG cannot stand,[2] for the very future of PNG—weak state or not—hangs in the balance.

From Gift to Commodity . . . and Back Again

Each of the four quotations that appear at the outset imagine ideal gender relations, among European peasants, chimpanzees, African-Americans and the !Kung San hunter-gatherers of the Kalahari desert. Despite differences in space, time and political economy, each example suggests that the differential access that females have to the means of production—be they arrows, jobs, termite mounds, or land—is (but is only partly) mitigated by, through and because of sex, whether given, traded, bought or sold. Insofar as hunter-gatherers represent the primordial human subsistence strategy, and given that the !Kung San are held to be gender-egalitarian, Nisa's fuller story affirms the universal nature of

---

2   I do not mean that social science research hasn't been done or done sufficiently well as to inform such debates, but rather, that the response to HIV and AIDS in PNG since 1987 has been to stack national- and local-level bodies with physicians and public health workers, politicians and church leaders at the expense of sociologists, activists, and anthropologists.

sexism and male prerogative. In exchange for sex, her foraging skills and a little piece of her heart, Nisa expects meat, money and beads from different kinds of sex partners, including her husband.

To some researchers, that Nisa receives goods for sex constrains her value as a woman and marks her second-class status as a person, even amongst this seemingly egalitarian people. If she were allowed to string a bow, fire an arrow, or earn wages, that is, she wouldn't need a husband. To others, Nisa's sexual agency expresses the complementary nature of labor divisions (between hunting and gathering, in this case) and indexes the high value of women. Nisa's suitors get sex, mongongo nuts and trading partners (what they need), while she receives beads, food and money (what she needs).

Similar disputes abound regarding the degree to which male breadwinner-headed households cause, correlate with, or help mitigate male domination in commerce, religion and culture. The traditional marriage vow cited above ('With all my worldly goods . . .') seems to verbalise the structural imbalance of compulsory heterosexuality and the fact that women's options are fewer and more bodily than men's. Crossing the human/non-human primate divide, some early claims made about chimpanzee sociality by the famous primatologist, Robert Yerkes, so projected male fantasy—how would he know anything about female chimpanzee sexual skills?—that an extremely mature female chimpanzee, 'Josie', savaged him in the glorious satire, *Adam's Rib* (Hershberger 1948). Papua New Guinean readers might appreciate knowing that lengthy genealogies exist in primatology and kindred fields that tried in racist fashion to argue for similarities between the real and imagined sexual behaviours of chimpanzees, gorillas and baboons and those of the human beings living nearby—indeed, to many, more darkly complected peoples. In 'Respect', Otis Redding's R&B classic, the protagonist expects 'it' (sex) in exchange for his paycheck. The song was covered and punctuated rather differently ('R-E-S-P-E-C-T'), however, by Aretha Franklin, whose second-wave feminist anthem tellingly contains a mumbled acronym: 'T.C.B.' ('Takin' Care of Business'). The infectious refrains of 'Whip it ta me' and 'Sock-it ta me, sock-it ta me . . .' seem further to nudge open the envelope of male economic power, female desire and the ease with which the gifts of love turn into the commodities of sex.[3] Chris Gregory, in his ground-breaking treatise on Melanesian sociality, *Gifts and Commodities* (1982, 116), notes that 'a thing is now a gift, now a commodity, depending on the social context of the transaction'.

---

3 Indeed, fascinating debates too lengthy and complicated to pursue here have turned on this question of 'gift' and/or/versus 'commodity' in Melanesian sociality (see works by especially Marilyn Strathern, Aletta Biersack, Chris Gregory and others).

PNG is a particularly good country with which to put some of these ideas to the test. Both older (e.g. Sinclair 1981) and more recent (e.g. Gammage 1998) narratives demonstrate that, on contact with Westerners and other kinds of Melanesians, Papua New Guinean men and male corporate groups were already trading female sexual access and that women were themselves sexually networking in diverse, complicated ways. The 'Professional Beauties' of Normanby Island, the Bukan cargo cult-related 'Baby Gardens', the Sepik river area 'war captives' and the shell-earning canoe tours that some new brides made in the Papuan Gulf (see Hammar 1998, n.d.) are just some of the many types that can be found in the ethnological, colonial administrative and mission literature.

In only a few decades post-Contact, sexual networking outside marriages made formally in churches (which are themselves statistically rare) has come to include:

- formal or quasi-brothels, patronised by 'disciplined' forces and male landowners;

- *kastom marit*, in which parents quickly consume bride-price paid by often much older workmen or landowners;

- informal brothels and male social clubs, such as are operated in villages adjacent to sites of resource extraction or in the settlements of Port Moresby;

- gentlemen's clubs in Port Moresby's lounge-bars and members' rooms where young Papuan females earn commissions by convincing men to buy high-priced drinks;

- temporary marriages around sites of resource extraction involving expatriate workers, some of whom leave children behind;

- streetwalking or freelance prostitution near motel front-gates, betel-nut selling stands, male workers' quarters, black-market liquor shops and along roads;

- motels and guest-houses, where sex is facilitated by security guards, bar managers and taxi-cab drivers, who draw from well-known females nearby;

- 'wet lunches' in which mid-level public servants solicit high-school girls and younger female colleagues for in-office sex;

- *tu kina bus*, or cheap, quick, largely anonymous sex in outdoor bush locales;

- *rot meri* (in the rural areas) and road runners (in Port Moresby) who stand arms and legs akimbo adjacent to roads and streets, sometimes advertised by male handlers;

- *pasindia meri*, who were first sold by families as the Highlands Highways was nearing completion, but who later entered sexual networking in protest against ill treatment by male relatives; and

- *plet kaikai*, in which women sell sex in exchange for takeaway food.

Sexual networking in PNG is driven by the gendered antagonisms of social structure and political economy, but also by significant female agency. Rules of kinship and land ownership, marriage and religious expression, sexuality and political representation, and schooling options and post-marital residence patterns, express existing tensions between structure and agency and bring new tensions to the surface. It is men, not women, who get security guard positions, receive royalty payments and become political leaders, but usually women, not men, who sell sexual services and bear the brunt of spousal drinking and violence.

The following examples are familiar enough. A Balimo girl is enticed into sex with her 8th-grade teacher, which allows her to pay school fees and receive better marks. However, she becomes pregnant and is forced to leave school and her village, and ends up selling sex in Port Moresby. A 45 year-old Daru widow has sex with a hotel employee to gain long-distance telephone access with which to beg a potential suitor to return home. A 17 year-old girl in Moro is plucked from *tu kina bus* and married by an oil pipeline worker but who will likely leave her when he learns of her previous marriage (at age 11), current infections and seeming infertility. Goroka secretaries suffer sexual harassment so as to keep a job, and would-be clerks have to sell themselves to Malaysian shop-owners just to get one. Bingo- and 7 Card-addled 'housewives' near Tububil slink off to the bush for furtive sex with young fellows so as to get back into the game. At roadside stands (known in Tok Pisin as *kakaruk maket*) along the Highlands Highway, women sell sex (or extend 'credit') to keep Self and Family afloat. Girls and women in Lae are forced into sex with warders in lieu of bail money. Tari women know as early as do landowners the timing and amounts of royalties to be paid out and so seek help from policemen getting there, even if they have to 'give' sex to them to do so. Police cars in Vanimo are known as *pamuk teksi* (taxis for promiscuous females), which suggests something of the kind and extent of involvement in prostitution by this arm of the disciplined forces. If asked, any Port Moresby taxi driver can tell you from which Papuan settlement he procures females for businessmen, tourists and political leaders.

Sexual networking therefore tracks along lines of inequality and accepted sociality. 'Nobody answers a job ad to become a *pamuk*', but lacking available 'sexual scripts' that would instruct them in sexual physiology and performance, many Papua New Guinean girls must cement sexual knowledge and improve sexual skills 'through direct experience' (Delta 2005). Some network sexually to obtain alcohol and transportation or to bring food into the house. Others engage in it to escape dreary settlements, mitigate low wages, or avoid greedy male relatives and love-sick, *toea*-short boyfriends. Rules and norms of sociality in PNG mean that the non-material 'gifts' of sexual expression preceding sanctioned relationships can easily turn into 'commodities' (expected rice-packets, rides and telephone bill payments), but then back again into the 'gifts' of ongoing material support and social status ('housewife', 'married') that is imagined to offset the gendered imbalances of political economy.

Like political economy, marriage and compulsory heterosexuality exhibit many structural contradictions. Men can marry concurrently while women cannot. Widow*er*hood is not onerous compared to widowhood. Men commit sexual violence with virtual impunity, especially in marriage. Physically and otherwise immature females are routinely married against their will to much older husbands. For many married women shelter, food and an acceptable social status come dearly: some husbands whip out the Bible and read from the Book of Ephesians to justify their 'right' to 'use' their wives, and others say *'Em putim pe pinis, ya'*! ('He already paid brideprice'!).

Both marriage and prostitution exhibit stupefying diversity of form and evince complicated social processes. Not surprisingly, one begets the other begets the other on a continuum of connectedness. When Christian missionaries in PNG forbade polygyny and dissolved the 'married' status of all but the first wife, they sometimes consigned the remainder to prostitution because of double standards about divorce and sexually 'used' bodies (Willis 1974). Having refused marriage altogether, having preferred women sexually, or having refused to re-marry following abusive relationships, many English women became political prisoners aboard the Botany Bay-bound 'floating brothels' of 1788 and thereafter (Rees 2002). The boyfriends and husbands they often found aboard, however, just as do husbands in many PNG cultures, for example, the Kiwai, Hanuabada, Kikori and Bamu, also pimped them both aboard and upon disembarkation. A clinic in Tokyo that treats long-married women found that 26 percent of their clients had not had sex *in the previous year* with their husbands, who have 'pornography and the sex industry to take care of their needs' (Kim, in McCurry 2005). The clinic finds paying boyfriends for the wives. Some highlight the degree of affectivity involved to distinguish marriage from prostitution. However, just as not every customer is nice, neither are all husbands, if statistics regarding marital rape and wife-battering in PNG are even half-right (e.g. Zimmer-Tamakoshi 2004).

In short, it is not so simple to parse between, on the one hand, culturally acceptable (*because* they are not nakedly commercial) forms of sexual networking that *ideally* occur between two affective spouses who will have sex with each other again, and on the other hand, the more obviously commercialised forms of sexual networking but which can nevertheless feature greater duration, love and respect, and less anonymity than some 'successful' marriages. Many women come to marriage following stints in prostitution. Many women come to prostitution following miserable marriages and/or sexually abusive childhoods— sex they neither asked for nor were paid for. Men are persons *qua* men, but because women have second-class (or worse) access *qua* women to the means of production, they must sell their *kina* (in Tok Pisin, the national currency, a shell traditionally used to pay bride-price, but also vagina). Without allowing access to their *golmain* (gold-mine) or opening their *maket* (both meaning vagina), many women in PNG would simply die. Neither are renewable resources, as timber might someday be in PNG. In terms of prevailing public health messages and campaigns, and given settings of ubiquitous sexual networking and sexual violence, should women even be asked, much less be expected to 'stay faithful' to a single partner so as to avoid AIDS? Readers may judge for themselves whether such messages, common in PNG, were ever *really* about preventing transmission. I believe that they were not, but even assuming that they were, they haven't worked. They haven't worked for fairly predictable sociological reasons, for fundamentally misunderstanding of the nature and function of sex industries in PNG and the tenor of marital relationships.

Sex Industries in Papua New Guinea

Cross-cultural and historical studies of sex industries elsewhere show clearly that new and/or transformed types of sexual networking, such as those in PNG mentioned above, tend to simultaneously maintain existing and forge new gender, ethnic and other relations. Dreams of a *post*-colonial PNG are dashed at any number of clubs, hotels and other venues throughout Port Moresby and elsewhere. Faltering colonial and masculine ideologies are massaged there— often quite literally—as middle-aged (and older) working-class expatriates are paired with young Papuan females. Male drinkers, on the other hand, are separated into opposing classes of private 'members' (expatriates) and 'public' drinkers (nationals), though there are exceptions.

Sex industries thrive also on male privilege in sex, kinship and marriage, and in 'tradition'—and religion-induced shame about sex, communication and bodies. Inter-tribal relations and historical forces also matter. It was Gumine women (and not Gogodala) who first migrated to Port Moresby *en masse* with male relatives in the early to –mid-1970s and set up and operated quasi-brothels because Simbu already predominated in security firms, motel management, long-distance trucking and taxi-cab driving—locales and services crucially important to prostitution. Highlands women generally and Simbu women specifically, currently predominate in Lae (and not Port Moresby) for the same reason. Bamu women have since the mid- to late 1960s been exploited sexually on Daru in a form of sexual networking commonly found throughout PNG and known as *tu kina bus*, or two-kina bush prostitution, known locally as *sagapari* or 'small mangrove garden' (Hammar n.d.). That ethnic majority Kiwai and to a lesser extent, Suki and Gogodala women, predominated in *other* forms of sexual networking on Daru but did *not* engage in *tu kina bus* (until just recently), speaks to common ethnic/tribal/racial segmentations of local sex industries. Papuan females have quickly come to 'rule' in Port Moresby's motels and night-clubs and the agency they exhibit (Delta 2005) is laudable, but it seldom undermines, as it tussles with, the structural forces that put them there.

Daru

Daru has been an administrative center since 1893, hosting since that time sailors and missionaries, sea cucumber and pearl-shell collectors and traders, and members of probably 30 different tribes. Economic downturns, the flight of expatriates following Independence (1975), traditional sexual license, and worsening access to health and educational services have produced five different, although overlapping forms of commercial sexual networking.

In the 'family' form male relatives and 'intimates', mostly from Kiwai and Bamu tribes, find generally older, mostly married, wage-earning sexual partners for their daughters, sisters, wives and girlfriends, aged 15 to 45. Subsequent sexual activities that take place in their own houses, at public drinking locales and in nearby bush areas put food in the pot, money in the pocket (including of the male relatives and intimates), and tellingly, beer on the verandah. *Rotmeri* are poor, young, and pushed by parents, boyfriends and husbands into extremely opportunistic sex along streets. Mostly unmarried, somewhat older Kiwai, Bamu, Suki and Gogodala women engage in a 'freelance' form of sexual networking (though no one in PNG is ever fully independent) for money (or promise thereof), alcohol and food from public servants, sailors and crocodile skin and sea cucumber buyers. The 'women with sex broker' form involves Kiwai, Gogodala, Bamu and Suki women who also work freelance, but on whose behalf sex brokers solicit customers from amongst businessmen and visiting mainland villagers, especially public servants. In 1990–2, it was provincial- and national-level government workers who predominated as customers by a long stretch. In exchange for free alcohol, food, tobacco, betel-nut and 20 percent of the women's earnings, sex brokers provided escort and a modicum of protection. They also brokered marriages and sold sexually their own wives and female relatives.

The most starkly patterned form is called *sagapari*, which is also a public toilet and rubbish dump, which once involved only Bamu women as sellers and non-Bamu as buyers of sex that was had on the ground, standing up and atop impromptu beds. For the first time, though, it now involves Kiwai women and costs K5–10 or more. Daru informants said that things changed when 1) *sagapari* moved to its new location (away from Bamu settlements, toward Kiwai) on the other side of the island between swamp and cemetery, and 2) a Bamu woman was decapitated and dismembered there. It was for decades located adjacent to either wharf or to hospital (hence another indicative name *Dokta Point*).

Lae, Morobe Province

Sexual networking in Lae is similarly ubiquitous, but the more commercialised forms involve almost no local females, most being highlander, and specifically Simbu. Quasi-brothels exist in a medium-covenant house near the Milfordhaven Road roundabout (Delta 2005) and in *Top-Town* at ½ Street in a house that until recently doubled as an NGO office. Girls and women solicit in town at well-known betel-nut selling stands and at the autoport-based *kai-bars* (PNG 'fast-food' joints). Some are directed by *'was-man'*, the male relatives who 'pull' customers from streets and public drinking locales. Caucasians and Asians drive around town looking for females who, like their counterparts in Port Moresby, can communicate much (sexual availability) with little (hand and eye 'actions'), including their desire to become temporary girlfriends and 'wives'. At dusk the sexual and other activities of the orphaned and otherwise abandoned youth emerge starkly. Bush areas, doorways and stairwells are used by truckers, security guards, policemen and others, who purchase oral sex and more from boys and girls. Many guest-houses are popular hubs of sexual networking, and both 'freelance' women and room cleaners and associated female staff will accept *bas fe* (literally 'bus-fare', but more than 70 *toea*) in exchange for sex. At the Lae Football Association club-house reside 10–12 young highlander females (again, mostly Simbu) who are sexually available on-site and off. The lounge-bars inside several upper-end hotels bustle with women mostly from Simbu and Western Highlands Province, again, available for one-off sex or temporary relationships, and just opposite the front-gate at one particular hotel nightly cluster 5–15 females and *was-man*. At one motel near the hospital, girls and women seek entrance through the security gate or lounge at poolside, both soliciting customers on their own and engaging security guards and drivers who, for money, small goods or free sex, will also solicit for the women. The Planet Rock night-club allows women free entrance each Wednesday. Sexual networking there involves mostly younger nationals, but at each venue other favours, gifts and commodities are given, received, bartered, or sold, such as gate-fees, pitchers of beer, money, transportation, accommodation and clothing, among other things, and services that serve to heighten the promise of relationships.

Lae has the country's second-largest *tu kina bus ples*, located opposite ANGAU Memorial Hospital. At any one time a dozen or more 35–45 year-old highland women, many bearing literal stigmata in the form of cuts, bruises, scars and broken and missing teeth, solicit on the edges thereof and along the road. They also visit betel-nut selling stands, play cards and themselves sell betel-nut and other small goods to solicit customers. Police harassment and customer violence are common. Many women emerged from unhappy, often violent marriages, though they seek marriage again, preferring possible biological death to likely social leperhood.

Port Moresby

Only the danger-loving would attempt to nail down precisely all of the forms and locations of Port Moresby's exploding sex industry. Most observers accept the presence of at least a dozen or so formal or quasi-brothels. One is located in Boroko behind the canteen opposite the main entrance of the Port Moresby General Hospital, another being located near the Manu autoport, and many more *pamuk haus* (residences of women and girls dubbed prostitutes) are sheltered behind 'legitimate' motels, clubs, tradestores and guest-houses (Delta 2005; see also Fletcher and Gonapa this volume; Stewart this volume). One popular guest-house rents rooms on both nightly and 'transit' bases and is attached to a disco. Sex is easily available to mostly national clientele, cheap and like many other sex industry locales, very much a family affair (Lepani 2004). As is statistically frequent and culturally normative, sellers and buyers are related by the admirably diverse array of blood, marriage and 'fictive' forms of kinship. Connecting another motel to Bampton Street, until 2006, was a string of *faiv kinahaus* in each of which reside six to eight Papuan females mostly from Kerema and eastern Gulf villages 'along the highway connecting villages of Iokea, Moveave and Lilifaru' (Delta 2005). They served mostly national public-servant and clerk clientele, especially at lunch time, for K5–10. Many sexual assignations to hotel guests were until recently handled by a highlands female manager who also distributed condoms and protected the women from legal and customer violence.[4] Each place is also connected to nearby betel-nut and marijuana-selling operations. Male intimate 'pullers' also solicit for these 'road-runners', who are decidedly not *rot meri*. A quasi-brothel operates about 500 meters away near the AON House office tower, whose occupants then solicit sexual services in nearby parks, directly on the street and at supermarket fronts and the Post Office (Delta 2005). The Wanigela round-about is a popular pick-up spot in the evenings, and cell phones are used.

At such venues, the relations of class, culture, race and gender don't so much melt as clash. With wife and daughter in tow, on my first visit to one of Port

---

4 Following its sale and takeover by new management, the Ela Beach Hotel seems less enabling now of prostitution.

Moresby's several venues at which British expatriates cavort with young, on-site resident Papuan females, a drunken patron was allowed twice (but only once accurately) to blast away with shot-gun at a cardboard-cutout of Osama bin Laden displayed above the back-bar. To take a female out of the lounge-bar and disco area into one's guest-house room or off-premises altogether is to make a 'champagne arrangement' with the manager and purchase for K100 a bottle of champagne (in essence, the 'bar fines' of Okinawa, Thailand and the Philippines). In this and other clubs catering to expatriates, young resident Papuan females earn commission on high-priced drinks they convince men to purchase. They complain of perpetual hunger and also of beer bellies.

Moro, Southern Highlands Province

> When it's time for the [male] landowners to get their royalty payments [for owning the ground atop which sets the oil pipeline], that's when we charge more steeply . . . Okay, some of the [oil pipeline] workers, the security guards and so forth, they leave lunch for us [i.e., put take-away food on the ground] and then tell us, tell us: 'you and I go have sex' . . .[5]

This 35-year-old Huli woman recounts desperately hungry women—not housewives, though many are married—who have migrated to the Moro base camp from Tari villages and who will have sex with security guards and kitchen staff for as little as *plet kaikai*, a plate of take-away food. Just as Huli men have 'followed the money' available along the Lake Kutubu oil pipeline by 'marrying in' and seeking employment (some Foi/Foe and Fasu/Faso villages are now half-Huli), so have Huli women pursued workmen and landowners through sex to earn money but also by trying their best to arrange temporary or more permanent relationships. Huli women were 'traditionally' wooed by evocative poetry and singing in *dawe anda* (house/men), but many of these have since turned into quasi-brothels and contested sites of 'modern' masculinities (Wardlow 2006, see also Haley this volume). Now they can be had sexually for as little as K5–10 in Moro's *tu kina bus ples* though they sometimes charge K50–100 when the monies are flowing. Despite the stigma they suffer socially and corporeally, and however unrealistic it may be, their goal is most often a 'stable' relationship, one from which springs forth gifts, money and commodities. This is why so few women charge money up-front for sexual services, precisely the female agency that men see as provoking beatings. Of Holly Wardlow's *pasindia meri* informants in the Tari Basin, not one said that she charged money up-front (2004, 1032).

---

5   Audiotaped, transcribed focus group discussion conducted in Tok Pisin by Herick Aeno and Phili Manove, Moro, Southern Highlands Province, February 7, 2005.

As such, the strategies that Tari, and to a lesser extent, Mendi and Mt Hagen women follow are clear and consonant with those of their counterparts elsewhere. Moro *maket* bustles with activity from Monday night until Thursday morning. Trucks and PMVs filled with people and cargo go to and come from Mt Hagen, Mendi, and especially Huli villages adjacent to the main highway and those connected by feeder roads. At, inside of, and due to the Moro *maket*, sexual networking connects men to women, cargo to destination, tribe to resource, and of course, pathogen to infectee. Security guards, policemen, local landowners, visiting villagers and company workmen constitute the bulk of the clientele, although base-camps at Ridge and Moro are theoretically locked-down and prohibitive sexually. Oil Search Limited (OSL) states a policy of zero-tolerance for in-room, cross-gender socialising, designed to protect not only female privacy and safety but also the potential transmissive risks of fly-in, fly-out shift work. Nevertheless, many workers from OSL (and virtually all male employees of the local landowner companies) come and go as they please. Another Huli woman explained that 'they just suck the cocks of the security', meaning that the workers don't bribe security guards to let women inside the camp, but rather, to allow them passage to Moro *maket* and multiple adjacent *tu kina bus ples*.[6] Sexual networking is so intimately tied to the political economy— as is prostitution to marriage—that women come to know precisely the timing and location of the next pay-out. There is a 'guest-house' along the main road that is managed by a male intimate and that functions as a brothel. It is owned by a Port Moresby-based man from a nearby village, Kaipu, that has erected both fence and sign-board so as to prevent the entrance of sin and risk in the form of darts, Bingo, cards-playing, betel-nut chewing, alcoholic beverages and *pasindia man/meri* (those who engage in commercialised sex).

Let's Talk about Sin

Private citizens and state and church representatives have for more than two millennia discussed the merits and drawbacks of prostitution. Far less tolerant church pressure put recently upon the state in Australia and elsewhere to stamp it out 'has largely hidden the compromises of the past' (Perkins 1991, 18), including direct church complicity. In PNG, in many ways 'the church' supersedes 'the state' in terms of financial resources, the delivery of services and moral force. Due to the arrival of AIDS to PNG, calls have been made increasingly to decriminalise if not also to legalise prostitution in the form of state-sponsored brothels. One strand of discourse (not quite yet activism) claims (not quite yet argues) that lowered transmission risks would result, and that the innocence of youth, chastity of wives and public health of the nation would

---

6   Author's fieldnotes, 26 January 2005, Moro base camp.

thereby would be protected. You can't make sexual desire go away, prostitution is 'the world's oldest profession' and the state would profit from its taxation—so say proponents. These claims are voiced on the street, uttered by the well-educated, enunciated by higher-ranking health officials, and published in newspaper letters and editorials. At least one parliamentarian supports this (see Fletcher and Gonapa this volume).

A second discursive strand suggests that state sponsorship of brothels would yet further compromise if not altogether disqualify PNG as being 'a Christian country'. Along with alcohol, marijuana, Em-TV (and MTV), and the rise of two dangerous things—*raskolism* and women's consciousness—this most recent call further to secularise a nation that was supposed to have been founded on Christian principles—and which are stated in the national Constitution—is just going too far. This rhetoric comes from churches, community-based organisations, activist housewives and village elders. The writer ('Who Is the Man Indeed' of a letter to the editor entitled 'Gender equality could cause more harm than good' argued that 'empowering women' just isn't common sense: 'Whoever heard of men's days or men's awards?', he complained (*Post Courier* 14 April 2008). Few of them, however, comment much about nearly unchecked forms of misogyny—that is, 'unchristian behaviour'—ranging from the torture and killing of suspected witches and pack-rape, to wife-bashing and sexual molestation committed by male relatives, school-teachers, family friends and, if newspapers are to be believed, church leaders.

A third strand of commentary suggests that not everyone is so sad to see AIDS come to PNG. That is, *sikAIDS, em i kam long Bikpela, em i pe bilong sin bilong ol*, meaning that AIDS is God's *just* punishment of foul sinners as we approach the End Times. 'AIDS' helps to reveal the sin on which Christian doctrine and activity feed, just as unemployment helps to perpetuate capitalism. In April 2006 I interviewed a hospital CEO in the highlands who provided a pick-up truck and a loudspeaker to those recently diagnosed as HIV positive, so that they could warn their communities of their new status. Since Holly Wardlow first alerted me to this discourse among health workers in the Tari area, I have heard other health workers express the desire that a few religious leaders die from AIDS so as to reveal their far more damaging hypocrisy (see also Wardlow 2008).

I believe and predict here that despite the moral force exhibited by the numerically superior proponents of the second and third strands of discourse, proponents of the first one will win out. I say this for essentially two reasons. First and most obviously, the legalisation of prostitution and the state sponsorship of brothels would enshrine and further support male sexual privilege. Had male sexual privilege not been protected at all costs, then public health messages and campaigns would have intruded upon companionate marriage a long time ago and legal authorities would have begun to take sexual violence seriously. They haven't. Condoms would have emerged as *de rigeur* in sex per se, not just in 'high-risk' anonymous sex. They haven't. Second, the erection of brothels would provide two kinds of extremely powerful object lessons: 1) regarding the reality of sexual desire outside the bounds of the marital chambers, locating and attempting to channel it in known and finite places where by definition the sexually incontinent would go, and 2) regarding the continuing rhetorical usefulness of the existence of the two Marys in Christian discourse, one a sexually inexperienced Madonna, the other (not my term), a whore (Mary Magdalene). I am not a supporter of state-sponsored brothels, though I support decriminalisation. However well state-sponsored brothels express dialectical tensions in PNG regarding social structure, desire, political economy, culture, Westernisation, Christianity and psyche, they make a poor public health response.

Brothels, Harm and the Politics of AIDS

I contend that calls for the state to erect and regulate brothels are ill-conceived. Most obviously, brothels would neither decrease nor deflect putative male sexual excess so much as re-channel and re-locate it, just as zoning regulations don't make sex work disappear so much as move it around. By similar logic, *if* it is true that Em-TV and MTV titillate prurient interest, that 'blue-movies' make men want to rape, and that Australia's *People* magazine is pornographic,[7] then brothels would surely make male sexuality run riot. As I see it, and *even if* one grants (as I do not) that state-sponsored brothels could theoretically decrease HIV transmission appreciably in a country such as PNG, this is what would have to come about:

- the building and adequate maintenance (in terms of structural, aesthetic and hygienic considerations) of many more brothels than the state can afford to erect; 20–25 brothels would need to be erected in medium-sized provinces, at least 15–20 in the low-density provinces, 20–30 in Lae and Mt. Hagen alone, and perhaps 80–100 in the NCD;

- the complete overhauling, re-tooling and constant monitoring of the efficacy of the requisite medical and statistical–regulatory services, far in excess of what the state can afford; the state would need to test and re-test, treat and re-treat both the females conscripted into public health duty and, of course, their customers, and for surveillance to work, compare all such data collected as against those collected about sexual networking occurring outside brothels;

---

7   It is, in fact, specifically banned by Oil Search Limited.

- political re-education of the 'disciplined' forces who would police and regulate such brothels away from tyrannical misogyny; additional funds would be required, of course, to address the monetary and other interests such forces currently have in informal sexual networking, including sexual gratification and bribery (how many Papua New Guinean women would let their husbands work 'security' there?);

- more political re-education regarding the necessity of 100 percent condom usage, especially with regular customers, would-be boyfriends and husbands, and especially *wantoks* (people who share tribal, geographic, and especially linguistic affiliation); public health campaigns have yet even *specifically* to target *commercial* transactions (beyond excoriation of 'the *pamuku*'), much less those in a companionate setting;

- the building of brothels that would be equal parts geographically well-placed and aesthetically pleasing, sufficient to usurp and absorb the function of other forms of sexual networking, such as *tu kina bus* and street-walking; not only is this extremely unlikely to happen (what to do with the brothel when the timber camp shifts or with the employees when the owner is deported?), but it would price sex well beyond the abilities of vast legions of PNG men to pay;

- added protection ('policing the police') provided to the women regarding the sexually predatory nature of many who would 'regulate' prostitution;

- a collective coming to terms with the fact that state-sponsored brothels would further disable awareness that HIV is firmly established in marriage and other forms of companionate relationship; it would require a brave political act to acknowledge the role of expatriates (Caucasian and Asian) in sexual networking.

Conclusions

By looking at sexual networking as being ultimately *a social process* that has undetermined outcomes—instead of as *a thing* that is opposed to heterosexual monogamy—my argument to this point has been four-fold. First, I have underscored the obvious value of ethnographic data in informing such important public policy debates as this. Unfortunately, despite such relevant data having been collected in abundance for nearly three decades, and despite frequent calls that more be collected, extremely few of them have been put directly to use, and only rarely have critical theory and social research perspectives been aired.

What such data and perspectives show is the painfully obvious fact, that, second, we have a *Papua New Guinean* epidemic on our hands, one that is as little Ugandan as it is Australian. Just because brothels in Nevada can demonstrate

99.9 percent rates of condom usage doesn't mean that such will happen in PNG, although that would, of course, be a wonderful thing. If they ever get there in the first place, condoms are purposely allowed to expire in health facilities (Hammar 2006, 2008b). Susan Hunter's analysis of the structure and movement of the AIDS epidemic in PNG is at many points dead-on in this regard. She concludes in a recent report, for example, that, '[u]nlike Thailand and Cambodia, small states where aggressive condom promotion campaigns through relatively organised sex industries have contained the epidemic, knowledge of AIDS among PNG's citizens is low, condom use and availability is not widespread, and commercial sex is largely informal' (Hunter 2005, 14). Papua New Guinean modes of kinship and marriage were so fundamentally misunderstood by the application of 'African models' that one anthropologist asked: 'Are there Groups in the New Guinea Highlands?' Many now are lamenting what Ben Reilly calls the 'Africanisation of the South Pacific' (2000) in regards to expectations about liberal democracy's centralising tendencies when situated within decentralising social formations (see O'Keefe this volume). I have yet to hear Zambians say that 'if we don't look out, we'll have a Papua New Guinean epidemic on our hands'.

Indeed, the Papua New Guinean flavour and pace of the expanding and overlapping STD and HIV epidemics are being overlooked in favour of the application of models from elsewhere that are known more by acronym and abbreviation (e.g., 'ABC', '3X5', 'MSM', 'HRS' etc.) than by careful conceptualisation and operationalisation. In the final analysis, the national-level response to AIDS in PNG has been a centralised one, driven by internal PNG politics and the needs of external donors, specifically for the placement of structures, not the forging of sustainable relationships. Unfortunately, the social, economic, sexual, religious and pathogenic forces that propel AIDS forward are decentralising, centrifugal ones. If 85 percent or thereabouts of the total population still live in rural areas but for countless reasons travel and migrate far and wide, that's how infections must also be occurring. The site of detection (NCD) has been fetishised all out of proportion to the real complexity of transmission dynamics. People from A get infected in B, C and D, and get tested in E and even F at a bare minimum.

Third, there is merit to accepting the functions, the social origins and the likely continuance of a 'weak state' in PNG. I don't want (and I certainly don't expect) the PNG state to be 'strong'; I want it to be just. *Papua New Guinea*, on the other hand, not the state, is strong in ways that are neither addressed, nor valourised in the fight against AIDS. PNG is characterised by a multiplicity of Christian denominations, by extreme linguistic diversity, by pronounced cultural pluralism and by behavioural promiscuity in the neutral sense of less determined options of residence, work and sexuality. These are the kinds of factors that have been the hallmarks of effective, humane and above all, sustainable responses to AIDS elsewhere, for example, Brazil, and among gay and lesbian communities. Brooke Schoepf, among others writing about Uganda's 'success story', has highlighted that President Museveni's government takeover in 1986 'fostered a vibrant civil society of voluntary associations that eventually included more than 1,000 AIDS NGOs . . . This exemplary openness created an enabling context for change, with debate, dialogue and action' (Schoepf 2003, 553). This has not yet been allowed to happen in PNG.

Fourth, expecting the state to sponsor brothels wildly overestimates the statistical– and medical–regulatory powers requisite to bring about the kind of individual and community changes that, say, the People's Republic of China fomented in quickly eradicating gonorrhea. Such calls fail to question the 'discipline' of the police, landowners, soldiers, public servants and security guards who already drive the 'demand' side of the ledger insofar as they pay directly for sex (although not always with money); facilitate sexual networking by providing venues, vehicles, other customers, 'security', privacy and alcohol; and hyper-exploit women and girls by soliciting free sex in a 'disciplined' setting (such as in the back of a police vehicle, in an office at lunch time, or in a jail cell), by committing individual and pack-rape (sometimes alongside other policemen), and by not fulfilling their duty to prevent, investigate and successfully prosecute cases of sexual violence.[8]

In conclusion, one cannot much improve upon the words of Friedrich Engels of more than a century ago, which noted the inherent gendered double standards of the culture and political economy of the time as regards sex. Were the state in PNG to sponsor and attempt to regulate prostitution, women would become 'ostracised and cast out of society in order to proclaim once more the fundamental law of unconditional male supremacy over the female sex' (quoted in Perkins 1991, 178). In PNG, calls to erect brothels fail to acknowledge both rampant male sexual privilege and painfully sex-negative attitudes formed equally by church and more 'traditional' sources and practices. Were they finally and squarely to address the clear risks of the 'gift' of unprotected sex, public health campaigns and practitioners would usefully expand, not further narrow, sexual repertoire and partner choice. Church and community leaders, politicians and businessmen, athletes and expatriates, not to say doctors and nurses, too, should be targeted, not just 'CSW' (Commercial Sex Workers) and 'MSM' (Men who have Sex with Men). Their charge should be to help foster sex-positive, not sex-negative attitudes. Their mandate must be that PNG needs more sex, clearly, but that which is better and more protected *because* it is more consensual, certainly more pleasurable and hopefully less infected.

---

8   Not all policemen are bad, of course, and not all of them take part in prostitution and pack rape. Wardlow (2001, 3), for example, writes that 'until the [Tari] hospital ran out of money, it was regular practice for the STD clinic to hire a band of policemen to burn down dawe anda sites [i.e., quasi-brothels]'. In Moro, however, by various means we can confirm intimate engagement and facilitation of prostitution, including in poor facsimile of Wardlow's dawe and near work-camps.

Acknowledgements

Two readers have to be acknowledged pseudonymously for their input: *Gamo*, my colleague at the IMR, because she is my sister-in-law and has helped me understand sexual networking and shown exemplary style in investigations thereinto; and *Kikori Delta*, a well-placed expatriate financial advisor whose specific knowledge of sexual networking issues is too great and whose insight into places and people I describe here is too keen to be published openly at this time. Thanks go, too, to three colleagues I *can* acknowledge by real names— Vicki Luker, Sinclair Dinnen and Susan Hunter—whose continual support, sharp analytical eye and ongoing friendship mean a lot to me. Holly Wardlow's exemplary work among Huli *pasindia meri* ('passenger women' who exchange sex for money in protest at male relatives who have failed them) also deserves a round of applause (see especially *Wayward Women: Sexuality and Agency in a New Guinea Society* 2006; see also Hammar 2008b). Ross Hutton from Oil Search Ltd. sponsored my trip to the Tari Basin in 2006, for which I am extremely grateful.

References

Delta, Kikori (a pseudonym), 2005. Personal communication.

Gammage, Bill. 1998. *The Sky Travellers: Journeys in New Guinea, 1938–1939*. Melbourne: The Miegunyah Press (for Melbourne University Press).

Gare, Janet, Tony Lupiwa, Dagwin Suarkia, Michael Paniu, Asibo Wahasoka, Hannah Nivia, Janet Kono, William Yeka, John Reeder and Charles Mgone. 2005. High Prevalence of Sexually Transmitted Infections among Female Sex Workers in the Eastern Highlands Province of Papua New Guinea. *Sexually Transmitted Diseases* 32 (3):466–72.

Gregory, Chris. 1982. *Gifts and Commodities*. London: Academic Press.

Haley, Nicole. 2008. When there's No Accessing Basic Health Care: Local Politics and HIV/AIDS at Lake Kopiago, Papua New Guinea. In *Making Sense of AIDS: Culture, Sexuality, and Power in Melanesia*, ed. Leslie Butt and Richard Eves, 24–40. Honolulu: University of Hawai'i Press.

Hammar, Lawrence. n.d. Sex and Secrecy in the South Fly: *tu kina bus* in historical perspective. Manuscript submitted to *Oceania*.

Hammar, Lawrence. 2008. Rhetorics of Risk and Foreign Object(ion)s. *Pacific AIDS Alert Bulletin* 33.

Hammar, Lawrence. 2006. *'It's in Every Corner Now': A Nationwide Study of HIV, AIDS and STDs*. Final Report of a three-year study. Operational Research Unit. Goroko: Papua New Guinea Institute of Medical Research.

Hammar, Lawrence. 2004a. Sexual Health, Sexual Networking, and Sexually Transmitted Disease in Papua New Guinea and West Papua. *Papua New Guinea Medical Journal* 47:1–2.

Hammar, Lawrence. 2004b. 4,275 and Counting: Telling Stories about Sexually Transmitted Diseases on Daru Island, Western Province. *Papua New Guinea Medical Journal* 47 (1–2).

Hammar, Lawrence. 1998. AIDS, STDs, and Sex Work in Papua New Guinea. In *Modern Papua New Guinea*, ed. Laura Zimmer-Tamakoshi, 257–296. Kirksville, Missouri: Thomas Jefferson University Press.

Hershberger, Ruth. 1948. *Adam's Rib*. New York: Harper and Row.

Hunter, Susan. 2005. HIV/AIDS, Women and Children in PNG. Part II of Families and Children Affected by HIV/AIDS and Other Vulnerable Children in Papua New Guinea: a national situation analysis. Draft report, used by permission of the author.

Lepani, Katherine. 2004. Personal communication.

McCurry, Justin. 2005. Solace for Virgin Wives of Japan. *Guardian Weekly*, April 15–21, 18.

Perkins, Roberta. 1991. *Working Girls: Prostitutes, their Life and Social Control*. Canberra: Australian Institute of Criminology.

Rees, Sian. 2002. *The Floating Brothel: The Extraordinary True Story of an Eighteenth-Century Ship and its Cargo of Female Convicts*. London: Hyperion.

Reilly, Ben. 2000. The Africanisation of the South Pacific. *Australian Journal of International Affairs* 54 (3): 261–8.

Schoepf, Brooke Grundfest. 2003. Uganda: Lessons for AIDS Control. *Review of African Political Economy* 98: 553–72.

Shostak, Marjorie. 1981. *Nisa: The Life and Words of a !Kung Woman*. Harvard: Cambridge University Press.

Sinclair, James. 1981. *Kiap: Australia's Patrol Officers in Papua New Guinea*. Sydney: Pacific Publications.

Tiwara, S., M. Passey, A. Clegg, C. Mgone, S. Lupiwa, N. Suve and T. Lupiwa. 1996. High Prevalence of Trichomonal Vaginitis and Chlamydial Cervicitis among a Rural Population in the Highlands of Papua New Guinea. *Papua New Guinea Medical Journal* 39: 234–8.

Wardlow, Holly. 2001. 'Free Food, Free Food!': 'Traditional' Rituals of 'Modern' Manhood among the Huli of Papua New Guinea. Presented at the 3rd Annual IASSC conference, October 1–3.

Wardlow, Holly. 2008. 'You Have to Understand: Some of Us are Glad AIDS has Arrived': Christianity and Condoms among the Huli, Papua New Guinea. In *Making Sense of AIDS: Culture, Sexuality, and Power in Melanesia*, ed. Leslie Butt and Richard Eves, 187–205. Honolulu: University of Hawai'I Press.

Willis, Ian. 1974. *Lae: Village and City*. Melbourne: Melbourne University Press.

Yerkes, Robert. 1943. *Chimpanzees*. New Haven: Yale University Press.

Zimmer-Tamakoshi, Laura. 2004. Rape and Other Sexual Aggression. In *The Encyclopedia of Sex and Gender*, ed. Carol Ember and Melvyn Ember, 230–243. Amsterdam: Kluwer.

5. Decriminalisation of Prostitution in Papua New Guinea

KAREN FLETCHER AND BOMAL GONAPA

Prostitution, as the concept is understood in Western law, was criminalised in Papua and New Guinea in the early 20th century by the colonial governments of Queensland and Australia. [1] The Queensland Criminal Code of 1889 was imported into the laws of Papua in 1902 [2] and, in a slightly different form, into New Guinea in 1921. [3] With independence in 1975 the two codes were replaced with a single code to apply throughout Papua New Guinea. [4] That code and its associated criminal laws, with their quaint British references to the keeping of 'bawdy' and 'disorderly' houses and 'houses of ill-repute', are still in force today and remain largely foreign to the experiences, customs, traditional laws and cultural norms of the vast majority of people living in PNG. Like so much of the criminal law of PNG, they were grafted onto the colony and, with Independence, onto the nation. [5]

This chapter deals with these relatively recent laws (which we will refer to as 'formal' or 'written' law) rather than with the plethora of much older traditional laws and customs that still operate, to some degree, to regulate sexual and economic behaviour in PNG's constituent societies (see Eves this volume; Hammar this volume; Haley this volume). To that extent the chapter is, like so much legal writing on PNG, inadequate to the complex task of comprehensively exploring the new nation's intricate and pluralistic legal environment.

---

1   Papua, the southern half of present-day Papua New Guinea, was annexed by Britain in 1884 but effectively administered as an extension of the Colony of Queensland until the Commonwealth of Australian assumed responsibility in 1906. Australia took military control of the German colony of New Guinea, in the northern half of present-day Papua New Guinea, in 1914 and administered it as a mandated territory of the League of Nations from 1921 till World War II. During the war and until independence, the Australian administrations of both territories were combined, but their legal codes remained distinct.

2   Criminal Code Ordinance 1902.

3   Laws Repeal and Adopting Ordinance 1921.

4   Criminal Code Act (No. 78 of 1974).

5   Bruce Ottley, a Magistrate in the National Capital District from 1976 to 1977, and Jean Zorn, Principal Projects Officer with the PNG Law Reform Commission from 1975 to 1976, produced an interesting account of attempts to give recognition to customary law in the colonial criminal courts and under the 1975 Constitution. (Ottley and Zorn, 1983).

The purpose of the legal research upon which this chapter is based was very specific. It was initiated by the PNG National AIDS Council (NAC) in 2003/4 to explore the possibilities for reform of national prostitution laws in the context of NAC's central mission: to control and prevent the transmission of HIV in PNG. Following further work supported by NAC, civil society organisations and interested parliamentarians, changes to legislation criminalising sex work and homosexuality have been drafted for preliminary discussion in 2010 and the sensitisation of key stakeholders (Papik 2010).

The NAC, and other agencies involved in work to reduce the transmission of HIV in PNG, such as the Institute for Medical Research (IMR), the Department of Health (DoH) and a range of CBOs and NGOs, acknowledged grave difficulties in attempting to carry out HIV prevention with and amongst people identified, or who self-identify, as 'sex workers' and 'clients' of sex workers (Temu 2000). In her report on the Transex Project, which was funded by AusAID in cooperation with DoH from 1996 to 1998 to promote HIV prevention among sex workers and their clients in the transport and security industries, Jenkins noted:

> Rapport building with sex workers proved to be a long and delicate process, as police continued to harass them, even arresting them for prostitution. The sex workers thought the project was contributing to their problems. After one such arrest of nineteen sex workers in November 1996, many of whom had become involved with the project, they scattered, some leaving the city... (Jenkins 2000; see also Jenkins this volume).

The original intention was for the Transex Project eventually to be implemented through an urban, community-based NGO with the IMR acting as a major adviser. However, attempts from 1995 to 1997 to find an NGO willing to take on the fully funded project were unsuccessful because of the stigma, as well as security and legal problems, involved in working with sex workers (Jenkins 2000).

Today, Save the Children in PNG (SCiPNG) is the main NGO working among sex workers and their clients to prevent HIV, mainly through its Poro Sapot Project (PSP), meaning 'friends who help friends'. SCiPING operates 'drop-in' centres for sex workers in Port Moresby, Goroka and other centres that provide condoms, information on HIV and AIDS and basic training for peer educators and is currently implementing a project to reduce STI prevalence in the Eastern Highlands Province. Yet SCiPNG continues to face difficulties arising from the status of sex workers. The Three-Mile Guesthouse raid offers one widely publicised illustration (see also Stewart this volume; Stewart 2006).

On Friday 12 March 2004, two weeks after the authors had visited the PSP to interview staff and participants about the way prostitution laws affect their HIV-related work, a number of the peer educators supported by the PSP (including some we had met) were caught up in a police raid on a licensed club, the Three-Mile Guesthouse, which police alleged was a brothel. The raid occurred around 3 pm when patrons were enjoying a few drinks and a live band, Keke, at the end of the working week. According to witness statements gathered by the legal defence team (which included the authors), around 20 Mobile Squad police officers broke down the gates to the venue with hammers and pushed past guesthouse security to gain access. Several witnesses said that some of the police seemed drunk and they were all armed with guns, police batons and rubber implements that appeared to be car fan belts. Once inside the officers rounded up all the women on the premises (around 40) and ordered them to sit in a circle in a cement courtyard. The 40 to 50 men were ordered to stand behind them. Those who resisted were beaten with batons, sticks and other implements.

According to statements taken later that night by the legal defence team, the women seated on the cement were showered by police with food, soft-drink and masticated *buai* (betelnut) from the small market stalls that had been operating in and around the guesthouse. Each of them was issued with two or three Karamap condoms and ordered, under threat of further bashings, to chew and swallow one or more of them and inflate the others. Several of the women reported that cash was stolen from them by officers. Residents of the guesthouse reported that police looted 45 cartons of beer, three cases of whiskey and a number of electronic appliances. There were also reports that several young girls were raped by police at the premises (cf. HRW 2006; 2005).

The prisoners were then force-marched as a group several kilometres to the Boroko police station, women in front and men behind. According to witness statements, the police jeered at the women as they marched, ordering them to hold the inflated condoms above their heads and inciting bystanders to deride them as *pamuks* (prostitutes) and carriers of AIDS. When they arrived at the station they were videoed and photographed by a waiting media throng who had been summoned by police to observe the arrests. According to *The National* newspaper the next day, Metropolitan Superintendent Emmanuel Hela advised the media that 'those arrested would be charged with prostitution' because 'prostitution is the main cause of HIV/AIDS virus spreading like bushfire in the country' (Pilimbo 2004).

All the male patrons of the club were released, without charge, on the evening of March 12, but around 40 women, including several girls under the age of 18 and one infant, were held in Boroko Police Station for two days and eventually charged with 'living on the earnings of prostitution' under section 55(1) of the

Summary Offences Act. They were released on condition they appear in court on Monday 15 March 2004. As evidence of 'prostitution', referred to in the Statements of Facts that accompanied the Complaints on Information filed at the Boroko District Court, police largely relied upon sightings of condoms on the premises and in the possession of the accused women (cf Luker and Dinnen this volume).

The prosecution, however, collapsed. Nearly a month after the raid, on 8 April 2004, all charges against the accused women and girls were withdrawn on the basis that no warrant to enter the guest house premises had been obtained by the raiding police. Nevertheless, the impact of the Three-Mile raid on the PSP was profound, provoking intense security concerns for both project workers and participants. Also of grave concern to the NAC was that the police, and the media in their reporting of the case, associated the possession of condoms (most of which were Karamap condoms, funded by AusAID and distributed by the NAC, National HIV/AIDS Support Project and many NGOs and CBOs) so strongly with illegal activity and social stigma.

The Three-Mile Guesthouse case and similar events, before and after, have served to reinforce the authors' view that prostitution law reform should be a vital concern for public health institutions and practitioners concerned with the prevention of Sexually Transmitted Infections (STIs) in PNG, including HIV. Whilst the legal status of sex work was clearly not the only factor that gave rise to the raid, the view amongst police, the media and the general public that prostitution was illegal gave the police operation perceived legitimacy.

Is Prostitution a Criminal Offence in PNG Today?

On examination, does formal law really prohibit prostitution in PNG? The current PNG Criminal Code clearly criminalises 'brothel-keeping' (the ownership and operation of 'a house, room, set of rooms or place of any kind for purposes of prostitution') [6] and the detention or 'procurement' of women and girls for 'immoral purposes' including prostitution. [7] A set of recent amendments to the Code, enacted in 2002, also specifically criminalises the commercial sexual exploitation of children, which will be discussed later in this chapter. [8]

---

6   Ss 231 and 235.

7   eg. ss 221, 620 and 621.

8   ss229J-229V of the Criminal Code 1974, inserted by the Criminal Code (Sexual Offences and Crimes Against Children) Act 2002.

These laws (against brothel-keeping and procurement) mirror the archaic values underpinning Queensland and Australian laws on prostitution, inherited in turn from 19th-century English common law, according to which brothel-keeping and procurement were considered more serious offences than the practice of prostitution itself. For most of the 20th century, in contrast, 'soliciting for the purposes of prostitution' and other lesser, prostitution-related offences were often included in 'police', 'vagrancy' or 'summary offences' laws that drew together a range of 'street' offences such as obscene language and public drunkenness, for which fines were frequently available as an alternative to imprisonment.

Similarly, in New Guinea the colonial Police Offences Act (in force from 1925 to 1974) contained a grab-bag of minor offences including 'soliciting', [9] 'living on the earnings of prostitution' [10] (applicable only to men) and brothel-keeping. [11] In preparation for Independence in 1975, the PNG Law Reform Commission (LRC) conducted a review of these laws and recommended, controversially at the time, that the offence of 'soliciting' should not be included in the new nation's Summary Offences Act [12](Papua New Guinea Law Reform Commission 1975).

Jean Zorn, a US lawyer who at that time was Principal Projects Officer with the LRC, has stated that the Commission's intention was that prostitution should be decriminalised: while pimps, madams and others profiting from prostitution should be penalised, the Commission adopted 'the latest thinking of criminologists and social workers' in developed countries and advocated social services, not prison, for prostitutes (Ottley and Zorn 1983). The provisions of the LRC's proposed Summary Offences Act were therefore designed to criminalise 'pimps' and 'madams' were modelled on the NSW Vagrancy Act of 1902, though the LRC had one important difference: that the offence should be made gender neutral, so that both men ('pimps') and women ('madams') who knowingly live on the earnings of prostitution would be liable to prosecution. [13]

Section 55 of the Summary Offences Act of 1977 was enacted by the PNG Parliament precisely as recommended by the LRC. It provided, and still provides, that a 'person' who 'knowingly lives wholly or in part on the earnings of prostitution is guilty of an offence' and liable to a fine not exceeding 400 *kina* or imprisonment for a term not exceeding one year. Like the NSW provision, it further provides that proof that 'a person lives with, or is constantly in the

---

9   s 38.
10   s 79.
11   ss 80 and 81.
12   Later enacted as the Summary Offences Act 1977.
13   s 4(2)(o).. That Act, derived in turn from English law, provided that a man who 'knowingly lives wholly or in part on the earnings of prostitution' is guilty of a criminal offence and that proof that a man lives with, or is 'habitually in the company of' a prostitute and 'has no visible means of subsistence', is prima facie proof that he is knowingly living on the earnings of prostitution.

company of a prostitute', or 'has exercised some degree of control or influence over the movements of a prostitute in such a manner as to show that that person is assisting her to commit prostitution' is *prima facie* evidence that that person is knowingly 'living on the earnings of prostitution'.

Within months of the legislation's proclamation in 1977, four women (Anna Wemay and three others, unnamed in the law report) were charged with, and convicted of, 'living on the earnings of prostitution' under section 55. Mr Justice Wilson, the expatriate Australian judge who heard their appeal against the convictions in the National Court of Justice in May 1978, said they may have been 'the first prostitutes ever to be prosecuted in this country for any offence directly appertaining to their calling or, as it is sometimes called, their ancient profession'. [14] It is probably more likely that the case was the first reported prosecution of alleged prostitutes as there are no publicly available records of decisions in the lower courts dealing with summary offences.

According to the published report, Anna Wemay and her fellow appellants admitted to police that they were 'prostitutes' and that they received four *kina* per act of sexual intercourse. There was therefore no need for the prosecution to prove these facts and there is no information in the case report as to the circumstances of the women or their alleged offences. The only issue for the appeal was 'whether the prostitute herself, as distinct from the madam, the tout, the bully, the protector, or the pimp, may be convicted of a breach of s 55(1)' (per Wilson J in Anna Wemay & Others, p. 3).

In making his decision on that issue, Justice Wilson declined to look at the intention of the LRC, or indeed of the parliament, in enacting s 55. He argued that the language of the provision was clear and unambiguous and therefore should be interpreted according to its plain meaning. On this basis, and contrary to the intention of the LRC and parliament, he decided that 'the prostitute herself may be just as much a "person" for the purposes of s55(1) as the madam, the tout, the bully, the protector or the pimp' (per Wilson J, Anna Wemay & Others, p. 3). Thus the convictions of Anna Wemay and her three co-accused for 'living on the earnings of prostitution' were upheld by Mr Justice Wilson, although he reduced their prison sentences from five months to the six weeks they had already served.

The only other record of a prosecution of 'prostitutes' in PNG came two years after Anna Wemay's case. In August 1980 Mr Justice Narakobi in the National Court heard the appeals of three women, Monika Jon, Margaret Bima and Kuragi Ku against their convictions for 'living on the earnings of prostitution' (Monika Jon and Others v Dominik Kuman and Others 8/8/1980 (Unreported N253

---

14   (1978). Anna Wemay and Others v Kepas Tumdal [1978] PNGLR 173 N138. per Wilson J @ p5.

Narokobi J). Monika Jon and Margaret Bima had been questioned by police at a wharf in Lae in early 1980. Ms Jon had reportedly admitted she had 'slept' with a Filipino sailor in return for ten Australian dollars. Margaret Bima, too, had reportedly admitted to 'spending the night' with a Filipino sailor and the police had reportedly found an Australian ten dollar note in her wallet and another in her *bilum* (string bag). But details in the women's testimony seemed to indicate that they were unaccustomed to prostitution. Ms Bima had said in her evidence, 'That was our first time'.

The police case against the third woman, Kuragi Ku, as read to her at her District Court trial, stated that police had seen her at 'Eriku Bush... K2.00' ('two kina bush' is commonly understood in PNG as an outdoor or 'bush' setting where quick, anonymous sex occurs (see Hammar this volume)); under police instructions she had taken off her clothes whereupon two *kina* fell out of her vagina; she had then explained to the police 'that her husband did not give her some money so she sold her body'. But Ms Ku had told the District Court that the police case against her was 'half true and half lies'. From her testimony it was clear that she had been angry because her husband had given her no money that Friday night and was drinking, and she had heard that he was sleeping with another woman. 'I was angry and I took three men into the bush, and they paid me K2.00 each and after that, I returned and I was eating betelnut near Eriku Store and they arrested me.' She explained that she wanted to make her husband angry—and her behaviour and explanation make sense in many PNG contexts (see Wardlow 2004).

Mr Justice Narokobi upheld the appeal of all three women on the basis that the evidence did not indicate that any of the three were 'living on the earnings' of prostitution. Monika Jon and Margaret Bima, he said, admitted to sleeping with a sailor and receiving ten Australian dollars, but there was no evidence of any past association or 'work history' in prostitution. Kuragi Ku, he pointed out, was 'a married woman... who wished to *mekim save* her husband', that is, teach him a lesson. 'She wanted to punish the husband. There is no evidence that she was separated from him. Nor is there evidence that in the past she was in the habit of earning K2.00 in the bush.' In his view: 'Proof of repeated receipts of earnings of prostitution, enough to show that the accused was relying for bread and butter, or rice and tinned fish and smoke and buai on the earnings of her immoral associations are required to sustain a conviction under section 55'.

It is therefore arguable that, under current PNG legislation and common (judge-made) law, a *single* exchange of sex for money without a 'work history' of prostitution, is *not* a criminal act. Following Narokobi's reasoning, a 'prostitute' can only be convicted of a criminal offence if there is evidence that she or he depends on the income from prostitution for daily living. In the course of his judgment, Narokobi (unlike Mr Justice Wilson who had rejected the relevance of parliament's intentions) recalled the LRC's approach: that 'The act of prostitution would not be legalised, nor would it be made a crime'; and that neither the LRC nor Parliament 'ever intended this legislation to punish the so-called "K2.00 bush" lady' (Monika John v Dominik Kuman, per Narokobi AJ, p 12).

However, to establish beyond doubt the proposition that a single act involving exchange of sex for material recompense is not in itself a crime in PNG, there would need to be a successful test case in the National Court that directly addresses Wilson's reasoning and decision in Anna Wemay's case. Whilst Narokobi expressed clear differences with that reasoning, he stopped short of directly challenging Wilson's decision, accepting instead that 'Wilson J. made it plain that the [offence in section 55] includes the prostitute herself'. He distinguished his own decision in the Monika Jon case by pointing out that in Wemay's case the point as to whether an isolated occasion of prostitution fell within s 55 (1) was not at issue and therefore not part of that case's reasons for decision. A 'test case' on the criminal liability of 'prostitutes' is therefore one strategy that is worthy of consideration by those who advocate decriminalising prostitution in PNG (see also Stewart 2006, 19).

Child Prostitution Laws

Amendments to the Criminal Code introduced in 2002 were designed to toughen criminal penalties for sexual violence and child abuse. The Criminal Code (Sexual Offences and Crimes against Children) Act 2002 was sponsored by the PNG Family and Sexual Violence Action Committee of the Consultative Implementation and Monitoring Council and was introduced as a private members bill by Social Welfare and Development Minister Lady (now Dame) Carol Kidu.

Division 2B of the Act creates a number of new offences including 'obtaining the services of a child prostitute'; 'offering or obtaining a child for prostitution'; 'facilitating or allowing child prostitution'; 'receiving a benefit from child prostitution'; and 'permitting premises to be used for child prostitution'. But section 229Q provides:

> No person under the age of 18 years shall be charged with an offence under this Subdivision of any sexual service by that child for financial or other reward, favour or compensation.

This provision was intended by the sponsors of the bill, and by its mover Carol Kidu, to decriminalise prostitution by children less than 18 years of age (FSVC 2003).

The legal defence team in the Three-Mile case raised this provision. Mr Gonapa argued in the Boroko District Court that the prosecutions of the girls under 18 who had been arrested in the raid should be dismissed on the basis that child prostitution had been decriminalised. This argument was rejected by the Boroko magistrate on the basis that the new provisions did not amend or repeal section 55 of the Summary Offences Act and therefore only applied to 'an offence under this subdivision', that is, of the Criminal Code. It therefore appears that children under 18 may still be prosecuted under section 55 of the Summary Offences Act.

Further amendments to Division 2B of the Criminal Code are therefore required before it may be said that child prostitution has been decriminalised in PNG. This is a second issue ripe for attention from public health authorities and others concerned with prostitution law reform and the strengthening of laws to protect children.

Admissibility of Condoms as Evidence of Prostitution

As stated earlier, the PNG Criminal Code is based on the Queensland Criminal Code. In response to HIV prevention concerns, the Queensland code was amended in 1992 so that the presence or possession of condoms is not admissible as evidence that a place is being used 'for the purposes of prostitution'. Section 229N of the Queensland Criminal Code provides that the use of a place for the purposes of prostitution may be inferred from evidence of 'the condition of the place, material found at the place and other relevant factors and circumstances'. It goes on to provide, however, that 'evidence of condoms and other material for safe sex practices is not admissible against a defendant'.

This amendment has not been adopted in PNG. Yet in light of the starring role that condoms played in the Three-Mile prosecutions we recommend that a similar amendment to the PNG Criminal Code should be considered. The distribution of condoms is a key strategy for HIV prevention in PNG but changing attitudes towards them is proving difficult. Whilst the legal reform we are advocating will not act as a magic bullet, we submit that it will contribute to building an 'enabling environment' for such attitudinal change.

Decriminalisation, Legalisation and Regulation

In this chapter we have restricted ourselves to a discussion of the basic decriminalisation of prostitution, that is, the abolition of any laws that penalise an individual for providing sexual services in exchange for material recompense. The wider decriminalisation debate, however, is not so simple.

There are those who argue that decriminalisation of the prostitute herself (or himself) is not sufficient and that associated offences, such as pimping and brothel-keeping, should also be abolished. Proponents of this view argue that the existence of any laws against adult prostitution-related activities serve to reinforce negative attitudes towards adult sex workers (who, they argue, should be treated as workers and therefore subject only to the general laws to which all workers are subject) and thus legitimate abuse of their human rights (Banach and Metzenrath 2000). Others accept that prostitution should be decriminalised in some circumstances, for public health and/or human rights reasons, but favour strict regulation of the practice. This is the view that has been adopted in Queensland [15] where it is legal to operate a registered brothel under strictly supervised conditions and to work as a home-based, sole-operator sex worker.

While prostitution is a topic that incites heated controversy in PNG, the introduction of state regulation of legalised prostitution has considerable support amongst those who endorse the public health and human rights arguments in favour of decriminalisation but who believe the state can and should place some restraints on the 'sex industry'. [16] Indeed, the National AIDS Council's policy on prostitution commits it to considering both decriminalisation and regulation (Temu 2000)—and these issues are set to be debated afresh when the National AIDS Council brings forward specific options for law reform (Papik 2010).

Yet Lawrence Hammar (this volume; see also Stewart 2006, 17) identifies several deep problems with any proposal to regulate prostitution in the PNG context. One is that most exchanges of sex for money occur outside of any organised 'sex industry' and on a very broad continuum of sexual and economic behaviour. Any attempt to regulate the country's urban and camp-based brothels would leave the vast majority of acts of technical 'prostitution' criminalised and thus defeat the purpose of decriminalisation entirely. Even in Queensland, critics of that state's regulatory scheme have identified the continuing criminalisation of prostitution-related activities outside the state-approved brothels as the 1999 law's major weakness (Uusimaki 2002).

---

15   Prostitution Act 1999 (QLD).
16   Editors' note: Regulation of prostitution also has support among some clients of sex-workers. Certain soldiers interviewed by Pantumari and Bamne (this volume) favour the proposal.

Our view is that decriminalisation of the practice of prostitution is a desirable law reform goal, despite the controversy it would cause. We do not argue that this would 'solve' the problems that plague HIV prevention projects involving sex workers but we do argue that it would reduce those problems and open up new possibilities for effective work. However, broader decriminalisation and/or regulation of the emerging 'sex industry' in PNG is, in our view, a much longer-term project and the authors have not reached a shared view on whether such measures would ultimately be judged either beneficial or appropriate in the PNG context.

References

Anna Wemay and Others v Kepas Tumdal [1978] PNGLR 173 N138.

Monika Jon v Dominik Kuman Margaret Bima v John Mohin Kuragi Ku v Ilam Michael. 1980. National Court, Papua New Guinea (Unreported).

Banach, L. and S. Metzenrath. 2000. *Principles for Model Sex Industry Legislation.* Sydney: Australian Federation of AIDS Organisations.

FSVAC (Family and Sexual Violence Action Committee). 2003. *Rape, Incest, Child Abuse: The PNG Laws have Changed!!!* Port Moresby: Consultative Implementation and Monitoring Council.

HRW (Human Rights Watch). 2005. 'Making Their Own Rules': Police Beatings, Rape, and Torture of Children in Papua New Guinea. New York: Human Rights Watch. www.hrw.org

HRW (Human Rights Watch). 2006. Still Making their own Rules: Ongoing Impunity for Police Beatings, Rape, and Torture in Papua New Guinea. New York: Human Rights Watch. www.hrw.org

Jenkins, C. 2000. Female Sex worker HIV Prevention Projects: Lessons Learnt from Papua New Guinea, India and Bangladesh. UNAIDS Best Practice Collection. Geneva: UNAIDS.

Ottley, B. L. and J. G. Zorn. 1983. Criminal Law in Papua New Guinea: Code, Custom and the Courts in Conflict. *The American Journal of Comparative Law* 31:251–300.

Papik, John. 2010. PNG Civil Groups Prepare Gay, Sex Work Law Challenge. Pacific Beat, Radio National, Australian Broadcasting Commission. 29 January.

Papua New Guinea Law Reform Commission. 1975. Waigani: Report on Summary Offences.

Pilimbo, P. 2004. Police Arrest 80 in Brothel Raid. *The National*, 16 March 2004.

Stewart, Christine. 2006 Prostitution and Homosexuality in Papua New Guinea: Legal, Ethical and Human Rights Issues. Gender Relations Centre, RSPAS, ANU, *Working Paper No. 19*.

Temu, P. 2000. Statement on the Possible Decriminalisation of Prostitution in PNG. Port Moresby: National AIDS Council of Papua New Guinea.

Uusimaki, L. 2002. The 'Hypocrisy' of the Queensland Prostitution Act 1999. Paper presented at Social Change in the 21st Century Conference, Queensland University of Technology, 22 November.

Wardlow, Holly. 2004. 'Anger, Economy and Female Agency: Problematizing 'Prostitution' and 'Sex Work' among the Huli of Papua New Guinea'. *Signs* 29 (4): 1017–1039.

6. Sex Workers and Police in Port Moresby (1994–1998): Research and Intervention

CAROL JENKINS

The structure of the sex trade in Papua New Guinea and much of the rest of the Pacific differs from that in Asia in several important ways. For the most part, women are free-lancing. They are not under contract to a brothel or other manager, and can take their clients where they find them without need to share their earnings with others. Throughout the Pacific, ports, beaches, malls, night clubs, guesthouses, hotels and residences are common sites at which commercial sex is negotiated and/or carried out. In cities with crowded poor housing areas, sex is sold or exchanged for goods within those neighbourhoods and in local parks or open fields as well. At rural economic enclaves, such as logging camps, fisheries depots, mines and plantations, sex workers (SWs) are also present, particularly on pay days. Increasingly, urban sex work is becoming cell phone-coordinated in a number of cities of the Pacific region. In Suva, Chinese businessmen have instituted a more organised and controlled sex trade in brothels with imported Chinese women brought in to serve Asian sailors and fishermen. Anecdotal evidence suggests that Asian businessmen have been managing a certain portion of the sex trade in Port Moresby for a number of years.

In all countries, the organisation of the sex trade is very sensitive to pressures applied by legal forces. If sex workers are frequently rounded up and arrested, the trade morphs, moves elsewhere, goes underground and hides. Wherever sex work is illegal, the police are significant regulators of the sex trade and as numerous studies have shown, can become extremely abusive of their power (Blankenship and Koester 2002; Phal 2002; see also in this volume Hammar; Stewart; Fletcher and Bonapa). That is not inevitable, however, and in New York City, where an internal monitoring unit now tracks complaints of police abusiveness, a recent study showed that street sex workers are harassed and arrested, but not physically assaulted or raped (SWP 2003), as in Cambodia, Bangladesh and elsewhere (Jenkins et al. 2005; Government of Bangladesh

2000). Even in Ethiopia and Eritrea, NGO workers and fishermen clients of sex workers report that some police are willing to help sex workers by arresting men who refuse to pay them, or even intervene if clients refuse to use condoms. With enough good advocacy directed at those who abuse sex workers and an emphasis on sex workers' human rights, there is a good chance of improving their situation (Jenkins 2000).

Violence against sex workers, including rape, appears to form a pattern based on revilement of the public woman and is worse where women in general have little public power. In numerous Pacific nations, rape and violence against women is widespread though, as yet, not well documented. Many Melanesian societies, in particular, have the classic characteristics of rape-prone societies, that is, high levels of general violence, male dominance and the silencing of female sexuality (Sanday 1986; Buchanan et al. 1999; Goldberg and Unité 2005, 88; Pelletier 2002; see also Eves this volume; Hammar this volume), particularly after the imposition of Western Christian values. Traditionally, rape has been used to punish women for any number of transgressions in some Melanesian societies, and in contemporary life, gang rape has become particularly common as men use it to steal what they cannot (or will not) buy or to discipline women who challenge the existing gender power dynamics or simply to pay back the prior rape of their own group's women. [1] Gang rape appears to have unique social dynamics, different from any associated with intimate partner violence or other individually perpetrated rape, in that it can become a locally 'acceptable' expression of male bonding and homoeroticism without appearing to be connected with homosexuality at all (Jenkins 1996). In addition, where rape is common and HIV levels high, the contribution of rape to the spread of HIV is well documented (Donovan 2002; Smith 2003).

This chapter is based largely on data collected by the Papua New Guinea Institute of Medical Research from 1995 to 1998 as part of a project called the Transex Project (for transport workers and sex workers) funded by AusAID[2]. Additional funding was secured for one year from UNAIDS specifically to reduce the frequency of gang rape of sex workers by police in Port Moresby. At that time, inquiries in Lae and Goroka did not suggest a similar problem in those locations. However, preliminary work in Port Moresby identified gang rape, called *lainaps* or other terms, as a major problem faced by sex workers.

---

1   1Editors' note: The author is using the term 'gang' to mean any group of men, without some of the connotations of 'gang' as a highly organised body.

2   Editors' note: as indicated in the introduction to this collection, Carol Jenkins' chapter is best read in conjunction with the following chapter by McLeod and Macintyre, which puts the findings here in the light of more recent developments.

Methods

The work began in 1994 with an ethnographic study of the sex trade, including a total of 116 written observational sessions, 36 key informant interviews (mostly with owners or managers of houses in which rooms are rented for sex or men and women who act as *boskru*, a kind of protector to sex workers), and in-depth private interviews with 85 self-defined female SWs and 116 clients in six locations (Lae, Goroka, Highlands Highway, Ramu Sugar and Port Moresby).

From the observations and interviews with sex workers it was learned that police were their main source of harassment. Sex workers were rarely physically abused by venue managers, even though they were sometimes sent away from venues such as hotels or restaurants. Despite the fact that policemen were often paying clients of SWs, they also frequently beat and sexually abused these women. Out of 85 interviews, 12 discussed problems with the police and half of those stated they had been forced to give sex to the police in order to avoid being jailed. Usually, they were picked up for drunken behaviour, often in cars which were driven recklessly. Some were picked up for vagrancy and others had been harassed for selling betel nut since a ban was put in place against the sale of betel nut outside of designated markets within Port Moresby. One woman tried to lodge a police report about being raped but, because she was known as a SW, the police refused to help her. Several stated that women known as *tu-kina* and taken in by the police were at high risk of being raped by a large number of policemen. They stated that the policemen called over their car radios to different precincts asking if other officers wish to join in. When asked how their lives as SWs might be improved, one common response was to stop the police from beating and sexually abusing them. While not as frequent, the women also mentioned that security men working at various buildings at night also took advantage of them, and engineered *lainaps* in exchange for allowing them to sleep or rest at their post. This information led to the collection of seven in-depth taped interviews with police by trained ex-policemen, and the addition of eight interviews with security men. These interviews corroborated the women's stories. The following are excerpts from two such interviews with single policemen in their mid-20s. The various situations in which police can coerce women into having sex with them alone or with a group of policemen are described. It seems, in the case of the second interview below, that the man is making an argument based on the types of women, or types of circumstance in which they acquire these women.

Interview 1:

Yes, as best friends we do share some girls that they bring into the barracks. Well, girls like the ones that we pick up from the street side, outside the clubs while patrolling or other girls that policemen know very well of as regular providers to policemen. I mean those girls that we know very well and provide sex to us. We don't pay them, why do we have to pay for the stinking kan. Free Sex. No, she won't refuse. If she does, she will be in trouble. We always bash them up and so they know this very well. If such a girl is brought to the barracks, then that's for everybody.

Just last week I brought one. We picked her up next to PNGBC in town and it was time for me to sign off duty so I asked the driver to drop both of us off at Gordon Barracks and he did. I don't know but she told me that she was coming up from the wharf. She then told me that she was on her way to sleep and I forced her to jump on so. She got on and we went straight to the barracks. I think it was about 11.30 pm because I signed off duty at 11.00 pm. Anyway, some clever guys must have seen us going into my room, and not long after that I heard a knock on the door. As soon as I opened the door, I saw one of my friends standing right in the doorway. He then asked me, can you transfer her to my room as soon as you finish with her?

So I fucked her only twice and I sent her into another room. No, it did not take long. I think about 10 minutes only. No, she smelled very bad, why should I keep her there? She smelled of sweat, like she did not wash. I think she must have smelt of beer too. Good girls don't smell like that. She did not even sleep on the bed, she slept on the floor and I screwed her. Just normal position. Yes, I know, I have to use condoms. I used it twice because that was the only last one I have.

Yes that's right, she refused to go to the next room but I told her to fuck off from my room. She begged me to stay and I forced her to go outside. As soon as I closed the doors, I went off to sleep. I don't know what happened to the girl. I think they were watching so they just pulled her into one of the rooms.

Interview 2:

Bro, I think you have been in the system yourself and you know it. So I would tell you that I don't normally go out looking for girls for sex in night clubs or discos. The public is against us and I don't want to be beaten up in the night clubs. You mean pay for sex? That is quite new to me. I did not fuck a girl who demanded cash or money from me yet. I fuck for nothing, why pay? I'm telling you the facts. Policemen fuck like nobody's business. How many times we bring girls into this single barracks, they never demand for money. That's correct, we do group sex too. Well, you know the system yourself, brother boy!

Policeman can fuck at anytime, any place. Brother you listen, I will tell you. I get girls or women, no matter single or married so long as she agrees to fuck when she comes to the police station to lay complaints such as she was beaten by the husband, brother, father or their money was stolen or any complaints. Brother, any time, day or night, but most of the time is night. You just pay a visit to any of police stations in town and see. You will see that people are always there, some arguing, screaming and shouting at each other and others laying complaints at the duty counter. You know, any girl taken out by a police car to attend her complaint and to look for the suspect, the accused that she wants to be arrested, she has to be asked for a fuck. If she agrees, that's it, fuck her. No, we don't pay her too. If she smokes, we offer her cigarette or buai [betel net].

Yes, sometimes but sometimes not. Group sex does not apply in this case. Because we don't want to create trouble such as getting reported for rape or group sex and so on. As I've said you know the system. If she is forced against her will to have sex with all the policemen who are in the car then we expect rape charge next day. In this case the person who is in charge of her complaint or report only fucks. You sometimes see in the media, newspapers about policemen raping a woman, because they don't comply with what I've just said.

Also there are certain girls that we know of. They are regular faces to policemen and we fuck them whenever we meet them and that is when group sex comes in. Sometimes we see them and ignore them, we got tired of fucking them. We call them public toilets. When ever we feel like fucking, we go looking for them. As soon we spot them, we tell them to climb into the car or van. If they refuse, we use force to get them in. We always bash them up so they know our ways. We pick them up any place, on the streets, outside the clubs, any place. They seem to be everywhere. Yes, sometimes we bash them up and order them to get into the car. Well, where will they go and report or lay complaints? Every policeman and policewoman in town knows them very well. They are known as 'public toilets'. As soon as we see them coming to the police station and say that they have been raped, beaten or anything, we chase them away. Nowadays, they don't come to the police station because they know very well that their reports won't be heard. Yes, that's right, as we ask them to hop in, they just hop in because now they are frightened.

Here are some of the places where group sex takes place.

1: At the back of police station.

2: Police Van.

3: Dark and open fields around the city.

4: Police barracks.

Bro, I won't tell you how many times I get myself involved in group sex because I don't count it. It just happens at any time of the week or month. Well, as I've said any time once a week, twice a week. It is hard to count. You know, if any policeman brings a woman to the barracks, that's for the group. I mean apart from the regular girl friends. I don't know, it could be 8, 9, 10 men or more. I only go once and go to sleep. I don't know how many men go after me and go before me to fuck her. Well, because after fucking her, I don't stand there and count. Yes, now I'm using condoms. I use Protector condoms, the ones with the brown plastic cover. Because I'm frightened of getting AIDS. This disease is terrible and I don't want to be one of the victims of it.

No, I don't use it with my regular girl friend because we trust each other. It is true that when we get girls from the street, I sometimes don't fuck them when I don't have condoms.

In order to gain an estimate of how frequently these *lainaps* by police or security men took place, quantitative surveys were needed. After approaching the Police Commissioner with the problem and seeking his support for developing a special HIV intervention for the police, the funding was secured from UNAIDS and baseline surveys of policemen and policewomen were conducted as the training for peer educators begun. This was followed up nine months later, just before the UNAIDS funding ended, with a second survey of policemen. Baseline surveys were also carried out among security men from four major security firms. Work continued with police after this funding ran out but at a reduced level. An additional survey of policemen and security men took place at the end of the entire Transex Project in 1998. All questionnaires were written in Pidgin and pre-tested. Interviewers, male staff of the Transex Project, were trained and all data double-entered at the PNGIMR headquarters in Goroka. Interviewers for each of the follow-up surveys of policemen and security men were male staffers who had been working with other male groups, such as sailors, in order to reduce self-reporting bias.

Our sampling for the surveys aimed at geographical representativeness, but these cannot be considered probability samples. No statistical analyses were attempted except simple Mantel-Haentzel chi square comparisons using SAS 6.0.

Intervention

The intervention consisted, first, of sensitising high-level police officials to the risks revealed in the small qualitative studies and seeking their support for a targeted behaviour change program for the police. While there were no official statistics on HIV among the police available at the time, officials and others knew several policemen who had already died of AIDS. One HIVpositive policewoman was publicly vocal about the issues and repeatedly collaborated with the program. The police commissioner was very cooperative and wrote a letter to all precincts in the country instructing them to cooperate with this effort. Unfortunately, no funding was ever made available to cover police in any other section of the country, except Port Moresby, and then only for 18 months. The police welfare officer, a pastor, was assigned to attend the first training in peer education methods which was conducted by an experienced peer education/health promotion expert from Fiji. Following this, criteria were decided upon for the selection of policemen and policewomen to undertake peer education training. By mid-1998, 36 policemen from 14 stations had been trained as peer educators, as well as 16 policewomen from 10 stations, 14 wives of policemen, and 20 security men from firms that employed about 3,900 men. Considerable resistance from the managers of several security forms had to be overcome. Workplace policy workshops were organised with the largest of these firms and one was televised, a ploy that shamed the others and led them also to join in the HIV prevention effort for security men.

Special arrangements were made with the Medical Stores to release condoms to the projects and condom distribution to police stations began almost immediately, and remained in high demand throughout the project. The project delivered cartons of 100 gross boxes of condoms to each precinct in Port Moresby monthly.[3]

The high risk practice of *lainap* was highlighted both in the peer education training and in a specially developed and tested Pidgin comic book which had

---

3   As this effort could be integrated with other work in the Highlands, the same large cartons were also delivered by one IMR driver to several police stations along the Highlands Highway for a number of years. Post office employees also requested this service and large mail bags full of condoms were silently dropped off at the Goroka, Kainantu and Kundiawa post offices as well. Unfortunately, there were repeated stock-outs of condoms during those years.

a story of Susie, a sex worker caught in the nightly curfews in Port Moresby in those days. When police pulled her into their car and accused her of spreading AIDS, she showed them her negative results from a recent HIV test. That prompted the police to take her into their station and call on other policemen to join them in gang raping her (also known as *lainap*, 'single file', 'fuck 'n dump', and 'hit 'n run') until morning, when they tossed her out of the station in sad shape. The story then shows them receiving AIDS education as a group from a peer educator and many of the men realise they should be tested. In the doctor's office, one after the other receives positive results until finally the doctor asks one man why so many police were detected positive at one time. The policeman admits that a large number of them had sex with one woman but, he claims, she had a test result showing she was negative. The doctor then explains that that could have been true but they exposed themselves to the semen of the men before them in the *lainap* and could have been infected in that way. The policeman-patient begins to worry and tells the doctor that his wife is pregnant. The comic book ends up with a set of questions: Could this be you? Do you want more information? And then a set of phone numbers and addresses of a few places to reach for further help. The comic book proved to be very popular and very useful in educating the men about the practice.[4]

Results

The results are presented for policemen using data from the pre- and first post-test surveys. Results reported for policewomen derive from the baseline surveys only. Many questions were asked about knowledge of HIV and sexually transmitted diseases (STDs), but only those results pertinent to sexual behaviours are reported here.

The pre-test survey included 130 policemen at 19 sites (police stations, residential barracks, training colleges) interviewed in September-November 1996 and the first post-test survey consisted of 197 policemen interviewed in May-June 1997. The policemen sampled represented 18 percent high-ranking officers, 14 percent middle ranks, 62 percent constables and 6 percent auxiliary/ civilian police. They ranged from less than one year to 37 years on the job, with a mean of 9.2 overall. Their ages ranged from 19 to 51 years of age, with the majority between 25 and 34 and an overall average of 31 and they had between none and 13 years of education (overall mean 9.4). Marital status included 73 percent married, and 24 percent single, with a few percent separated/divorced or remarried. Demographic differences between the samples were not significant except for about 10 percent more single men in the second survey.

---

4   Editors note: see McLeod and Macintyre for later comment on 'Susie's story'

In the first survey, 33 (25 percent) men reported having had sex with 57 sex workers or *rot meri* (9 gave gifts but none reported having paid with cash) during the past week that included 76 events of penetrative sex, 51 percent of which had been unprotected. In addition, 84 (65 percent) men reported having sex with 85 non-sex working women (wives and more regular girlfriends) during the past week, which included 229 events of penetrative sex, 90 percent of which had been unprotected. Ten percent of men had joined at least one lainap in the past week, with an average of 3.6 men per *lainap* (range = 2–5). Following the first nine months of active intervention, in the post-test survey, 35 (18 percent) men reported having sex with 45 sex workers, including 77 events of penetrative sex, 30 percent of which had been unprotected. This time, more men reported paying the women (nine men spent K149 in cash for 14 women and 24 gave gifts (15 gave gifts only and nine both cash and gifts). In addition 123 (63 percent) men reported having sex with 134 non-sex working women, including 310 events of penetrative sex, 88 percent of which was unprotected. This time, 4.6 percent admitted joining *lainaps* the previous week with an average of 4.2 men per *lainap*.

Among the 154 security men surveyed, 55 (36 percent) reported having had sex with 79 sex workers or *rot meri* the previous week. These included 150 sex acts, 76 percent of which were unprotected. Unlike the policemen in 1996, 21 (38 percent) of the security men reported paying the women an average of 6 Kina each, while seven (13 percent) gave gifts. In addition 65 security men (42 percent) reported having sex with 88 non-sex working women (wives and regular girlfriends) a total of 246 times the previous week. Of these sex acts, 98 percent were unprotected. Further, 11 percent of the total sample reported being in a *lainap* the previous week, with an average of 5.3 men per *lainap*.

Among the 53 policewomen surveyed, while 86.8 percent said they had steady sex partners (including husbands as 45.3 percent were currently married), 30.2 percent had casual sex in the past week. Of the sample of 53 policewomen, 40 (75 percent) reported having sex with their main partner 105 times over last week, 96 percent of which had been unprotected. In addition, 15 policewomen (28 percent) reported having had casual sex 28 times during the past week, 75 percent of which was unprotected. Only 7.6 percent of these women considered themselves to be at high risk of getting HIV.

Comparing Key Results

Among policemen, the proportion seeking sex with *rot meri* (women of the streets) had increased between baseline and the second post-survey from 25 percent to 48 percent and for security men from 36 percent to 54 percent. Condom use, however, had risen, particularly with commercial and casual partners from 49 percent of sexual acts to 66 percent (p=.01) among policemen and from 24 percent to 53 percent among security men (p=.004). Among policemen, condom use rose from 10 percent to 13 percent with their regular partners (wives and steady girlfriends), but the difference was not significant. Among security men, condom use rose from 2 percent to 13 percent, a significant change.

When the second post-survey was conducted, one manager unfortunately made the decision to change the time period for the question on *lainaps*. Instead of maintaining 'the last week', he changed it to 'the last month', making direct comparisons very difficult. In the 1998 survey of policemen, eight percent of men reported involvement in a *lainap* the previous month. As a month is four times the length of a week, we assume that the proportion of policemen involved in *lainaps* continued to decrease, from 10 percent in the last week to 4.6 percent, to 2 percent; however, technically these results are inconclusive. No post-test results on *lainaps* among security men were reported.

Discussion

During the period of this research intervention, numerous nighttime curfews were set in Port Moresby due to the increasing gang violence. The intervention team was often under threat and a considerable amount of grant money (10 percent of total) was spent on security. Even so, the project car was stolen and destroyed when the driver was accosted at gunpoint and the project was greatly handicapped for months. Ambient violence is often associated with increased violence against women and perhaps that period in Port Moresby illustrates such an example. In addition, shortages of condoms occurred repeatedly as orders were not adequately or promptly submitted.

Nonetheless, the data from the surveys appear to show increased condom use by both security men and police with women they consider dangerous, that is, sex workers, but not with others.

Anecdotally, sex workers reported a decline in sexual harassment by policemen over the period through 1998. In one instance in August 1997, six policemen raped two sex workers during a guesthouse raid. The sex workers were arrested but managed to lodge a claim against the police who raped them. The women were released and all six policemen were jailed, pending trial. Over the years, newspapers report allegations of police rape but follow-up of the outcomes do not seem to be of importance. In 2004, a similar event gained international coverage, as 76 alleged sex workers were arrested at a guest house, now labeled a brothel (see Stewart this volume, Fletcher and Gonapa this volume). Interestingly, 35 alleged male sex workers (probably really clients and others) were released, presumably because the police do not think the law against prostitution covers males, while the women, nine of whom were juvenile, were detained, then later released on bail. AIDSTOK (Walker 2004) carried reports that the women were forced to blow up condoms and swallow them while being marched two kilometres to the police station. One woman was forced to swallow four of them. The police taunted the women saying they were responsible for spreading AIDS. If the women couldn't swallow the condoms they had the butt of a rifle smashed into their face. Some, mainly younger women, who were not rounded up as quickly, were raped at the guesthouse. Other reports of *lainaps* by police began to emerge.

While several individuals in PNG worked to help the women, little support was offered by the various concerned government bodies. Eventually all charges were dropped.

It is difficult to know if the reported reduction of *lainaps* during the 1996-1998 intervention was real.[5] As no funding was made available for continued targeted interventions with the police, it is no surprise that rape and harassment of sex workers by police and others continues. Research into the topic has also been dropped. HIV prevention projects in PNG seem no longer to be concerned with reducing violence against sex workers. Police in Port Moresby may simply be carrying out the denigration of sex workers that is desired by the public. If so, their entitlement to abuse these women is likely to continue for a long time to come.

References

Blankenship, K. and S. Koester. 2002. Criminal law, policing policy, and HIV risk in female street sex workers and injection drug users. *Journal of Law, Medicine and Ethics* 30: 548–559.

Buchanan, H. R., K. Konare and A. Namokari. 1999. *Chance Nao Ia! A situational analysis of STI and HIV in the Solomon Islands.* Honiara: Ministry of Health and Medical Services.

Donovan, P. 2002. Rape and HIV/AIDS in Rwanda. *The Lancet*, Dec 360: S17–S18.

Goldberg, M. and Unité 88, INSERM. 2005. Initial Results of the Survey on the Health, Living Conditions and Safety of Women in New Caledonia. INSERM, draft report.

---

5   The author left the project in mid-1997 and could not maintain oversight of the 1998 surveys. See also McLeod and Macintyre, this volume.

Bangladesh. 2000. *Report on the Second Expanded HIV Surveillance, 1999-2000*. Dhaka: Government of Bangladesh/UNAIDS.

Jenkins, C. 1996. The homosexual context of heterosexual practice in Papua New Guinea. In *Bisexualities and AIDS. International Perspectives, Social Aspects of AIDS Series*, ed. P. Aggleton, 191–206. London: Taylor & Francis Publishers.

Jenkins, C. 2000. Female Sex Worker HIV Prevention Projects: Lessons Learnt from Papua New Guinea, India and Bangladesh. UNAIDS Case Study. Geneva: UNAIDS. http://data.unaids.org/Publications/IRC-pub05/JC438-FemSexWork_en.pdf (accessed 27 April 2010).

Jenkins, C. 2006. *Violence and Exposure to HIV among Sex Workers in Phnom Penh*. Cambodian Prostitutes Union, Women's Network for Unity and Candice Stainsbury. Cambodia: POLICY Project.

http://www.researchforsexwork.org/downloads/Jenkins-CambodiaFinal.pdf (accessed 27 April 2010).

Pelletier, Y. 2002. *Qualitative Study on Domestic and Sexual Violence against Kanak Women in New Caledonia*. University of Paris and the Pacific Women's Bureau of the Secretariat of the South Pacific Community.

Phal, Serey. 2002. *Survey on Police Human Rights Violations of Sex Workers in Toul Kork*. [n.p]: Cambodian Prostitutes Union (CPU) and Cambodian Women's Development Association (CWDA). August/September.

Sanday, P. 1986. Rape and the Silencing of the Feminine. In *Rape*, eds. S. Tomasdelli and R. Porter. Oxford: Basil Blackwell.

SWP (Sex Workers Project at the Urban Justice Center). 2003. *Revolving Door. An Analysis of Street-based Prostitution in New York City*. New York: Urban Justice Center.

Smith, C. 2003. *Major SA study proves rape and AIDS are linked*. Health Systems Trust. http://www.hrw.org/en/node/11626/section/1 (accessed 27 April 2010)

Walker, S. 2004. But the men went free. Sex worker raid in Port Moresby. *AIDSTOK*, March 17.

Police, Prisons, Army and Mainstreaming HIV

7. The Royal Papua New Guinea Constabulary

ABBY MCLEOD AND MARTHA MACINTYRE

In Papua New Guinea, the police, being members of the Royal Papua New Guinea Constabulary (RPNGC), feature heavily in popular discussions of law, order and HIV. Most typically, the police are perceived as adversely impacting upon the epidemic, via the entrenchment of negative attitudes to prostitution, police brutality and the rape of victims and offenders in communities and police stations. In addition to these harmful impacts, the RPNGC has been actively involved in HIV prevention, both within the constabulary and the community at large. This chapter discusses the ways in which the RPNGC has, and continues to, impact both negatively and positively upon the course and management of HIV and AIDS in Papua New Guinea. The views presented in this paper emanate largely from the authors' experiences as gender advisers to the RPNGC during Phase III (2000–5) of the Royal Papua New Guinea Constabulary Development Project (AusAID/GoPNG).[1]

Perpetuating HIV and AIDS: Police Action and Inaction

In Papua New Guinea, as in many other countries, the police are implicated in the spread of HIV (see Luker and Dinnen this volume). Police actions such as rape and brutality directly contribute to the transmission of the virus, while police inaction in cases of rape and domestic violence allows such crimes to continue unchecked. As outlined below, police attitudes to violence and masculinity play a significant role in the ongoing occurrence of 'risk behaviours'.

---

1   The RPNGC Development Project was a 15 year institutional strengthening and capacity building project, which commenced in 1989 and ended in February 2005. The project was conducted in three distinct phases. Phase I, which was managed by Price Waterhouse Coopers, focussed upon organisational development. Phases II and III were managed by ACIL, with Phase II emphasizing operations support and training and Phase III concentrating on overall capacity building. Both police and civilian advisers were employed, with gender advisers responsible for promoting improved treatment of women employees and users of the constabulary being employed in all three phases.

Police Attitudes

Workshops held by both gender advisers, aimed at garnering (and challenging) police members' views about domestic and sexual violence demonstrate that the views of police differ little from those of many community members, despite their role as enforcers of laws that render domestic and sexual violence criminal offences. While police officers, by and large, are familiar with and understand the laws that they are paid to enforce (although some confusion has resulted from recent amendments to sexual offences legislation (see Stewart this volume)), the moral views of those officers are contrary to the morals embraced by these laws, which emanate from the Queensland Criminal Code as it has been adopted and applied in Papua New Guinea (cf. Fletcher and Gonapa this volume). For example, rape within marriage is entirely acceptable to many police, as women for whom bride-price has been exchanged are viewed as being required to 'give sex' to their husbands whenever it is demanded (see Eves this volume, Hammar this volume). Similarly, despite the fact that domestic violence constitutes assault under the Criminal Code, like rape in marriage, the vast majority of police officers deem violence within marriage to be perfectly reasonable.

Like many other Papua New Guineans, police share attitudes towards the use of violence as a way of 'resolving' disputes or solving problems that are often at odds with Western liberal values enshrined in law. Thus in a meeting with policewomen where the subject of training in 'mediation' and 'dispute resolution' was being discussed, the majority of women present endorsed the idea that a woman had the right to physically assault another woman who was having an affair with her husband. While some believed that it should still be considered criminal assault, most were of the view that it should be treated with leniency—effectively in a similar fashion to a murder that is *crime passionel* under French law. The women who participated in the discussion justified their use of violence (several indicated that they had physically attacked other women whom they thought were 'breaking up' their marriages) as both 'natural' and in terms of Papua New Guinea 'custom'. They were convinced that in administering a beating they were simultaneously venting their anger, ensuring that the woman would not continue her adulterous affair, and enacting a justifiable punishment (McLeod 2007, 80).

Similarly, in consultations on community policing strategies in villages and urban settlements, while many people complained about police brutality, on several occasions people emphasised the fact that they objected to unjust beatings of adolescent boys whom the police had designated *raskols*. They were not critical of all police violence and spoke approvingly of incidents where police had assaulted young men who were widely believed (or known) to be violent criminals. During focus groups conducted in the Highlands region in

2004, several community groups claimed that they respected the police more when they employed violence and displayed their guns.[2] The humiliation of prostitutes by police or the public use of violence in apprehending robbers in the 'Millennium Robbery' affront Western liberal sensibilities and ideals of justice (see Fletcher and Gonapa this volume, Jenkins this volume). [3] But for the many onlookers who jeered and cheered, these actions by the police were approved forms of 'justice'.

'Panel beating' is an anticipated and generally acceptable feature of police interactions with the community, occurring both publicly and within the confines of police holding cells (HRW 2005; 2006). Suspects are frequently beaten with fists, batons and firearms, in addition to being kicked and thrown. Not unexpectedly, police beatings often cause serious injuries, resulting in exposure to large amounts of blood. Given the prevalence of skin conditions such as ulcers, and the likelihood of violent police officers receiving wounds from retaliating suspects, police brutality poses genuine risks for the transmission of HIV and other blood-borne infections.

Police as Perpetrators of Rape

A survey of community attitudes to the police, conducted by the RPNGC Development Project, found that 50 percent of respondents (both men and women) were afraid of the police (RPNGC 2004; cf. PNG JAG 2008, 96–98). When discussing this fear with individual women and women in focus groups, they claimed that they were afraid of reporting crimes to the police, lest they become re-victimised. Many women relayed experiences of being told that their complaints would be investigated in exchange for sex, but not otherwise, and there is a widespread perception that policemen are often responsible for the rape of women on police premises (cf. Jenkins this volume). As such crimes are rarely reported (primarily due to fear of retaliation), it is difficult to ascertain the prevalence of rape by police. However, entries in the sexual assault registers of several stations throughout the country prove the existence of such behaviour (which rarely results in internal disciplinary or legal action), the incidence of which has been highlighted in widely publicised reports by Human Rights Watch (HRW 2005; 2006).

---

2 'Respect' for someone is often understood as involving 'fear' of that person's aggression and prowess (Macintyre 2008, 184)

3 On 17 December 1999, five armed men hijacked a helicopter and landed it on the roof of the PNG Banking Corporation in attempt to commit a robbery. The robbery failed when the police shot down the departing helicopter. All five suspects later died of bullet wounds, which the coroner attributed to police gunfire.

The issue of internal investigation and discipline was addressed in each phase of the AusAID police project. Training and advice has ensured that there is a high level of awareness about procedures and the standard of internal investigation is often high. But this does not mean that appropriate action proceeds from the findings of an investigation. Various forms of avoidance, incompetence and nepotism intervene and ensure that some people are not brought to justice. The impunity that prevails means that policewomen too are in some instances fearful of their male colleagues, resulting in requests by particular policewomen not to be rostered on shifts without other women, for fear of being raped or sexually assaulted by their colleagues. Policewomen have also expressed concern about situations in which men and women are simultaneously placed in police holding cells, as they claim that policemen turn a blind eye to the rape of female detainees by male detainees and that they themselves are too scared to intervene.

These ideas about female sexual 'availability', male entitlement and the use of rape as a form of punishment for female 'immorality' are not unique to police (see Eves this volume; Hammar this volume; Luker and Monsell-Davis this volume). In 2002, in community meetings about ways of reducing crime, people regularly suggested that women, especially young women, should not be permitted to walk about after dark; should be required to dress in ways that did not invite male attention; and on several occasions suggested that rape victims who had in any way transgressed had in fact invited the assault.

The RPNGC: Masculinity and Violence

The constabulary comprises approximately 5,200 sworn members, of whom only 5.4 percent are women. Consequently, the constabulary is an extremely masculine organisation. As previously mentioned, police violence is widely accepted and in some areas respected, rendering it an important part of police, particularly male, identity. So too, many policemen perceive themselves as powerful, by virtue of their profession (and access to guns)—a power that they seek to reinforce over women by rape and sexual harassment. While most police are aware that such actions contravene human rights, criminal law and the police code of ethics, they simultaneously enjoy the power conferred upon them as a result of their position, which is particularly attractive in a contemporary society in which there is deemed to be a 'crisis of masculinity'.

The resort to violence by men generally is not judged as a failure of self-control, but as an assertion of masculine authority. As such, whether the violence is in the home, on the streets of Port Moresby, or in the course of police duties, men who are able to successfully, if illegally, dominate others by force are in some respects admired. On both sides of the law, the image of 'Rambo' is positive (Macintyre

2008). Members of the mobile squads, police serving in Bougainville (as well as their opponents), 'tribal' warriors in the Highlands and adolescent boys swaggering around Lae or Port Moresby don headbands, shades and militaristic clothing and are enthusiastic consumers of videos that valorise muscular rough justice and the triumph of the hero who operates 'outside the law'.

Within the police force acts of violence are also justified in terms of 'frustration'. Many police think that the justice system favours criminals and thwarts their efforts at combating crime. Their efforts at pursuing and charging offenders are thus fruitless—and they feel diminished by the failures of prosecution. Violence and aggression are in many ways assertions of masculine potency. Defiance or 'lack of respect' from members of the public provoke responses by policemen that seem disproportionately brutal and are readily interpreted as indicative of fragile masculine egos—but such psychologising is of little comfort to a person who has been injured.

Working within the RPNGC enabled us to see at first hand the ways that frustration over working and living conditions sapped morale (cf. Pantumari and Bamne this volume). Once, after a discussion of the international human rights of those in custody (using images of clean police cells with electric lights, a bunk to sleep on and a toilet) one young policeman observed, 'If we had cells like that at the station, I'd move the prisoners into the barracks and live there myself!' The single men's barracks in which he lived had been condemned by health authorities, there was no married housing available and his wife and children lived in a squatter settlement. Wages are low; facilities often inadequate and there are often budget shortfalls that mean cars cannot be serviced or fuelled; phones do not work and fax machines or photocopiers cannot be maintained. Police resentment of Australian advisers often derives from their belief that the funds allotted to projects aimed at expanding training or 'capacity-building' would be better spent on infrastructure and maintenance so that they could perform their duties efficiently.

Arrogant and aggressive acts are thus often 'compensatory'. Policemen are able to wield power and authority in the communities where they work and they undoubtedly do so in a variety of ways—some petty, not all of them in areas that are related to their jobs. In some respects the abuses of power are a way of maintaining status and power in the context of low morale. Police in PNG (as elsewhere) can enjoy free meals, drinks and small 'perks' from members of the public who offer them in return for good relations or favours. Seizure of goods such as betel nut or cigarettes from unlicensed street vendors is sometimes conceptualised thus, especially if the vendors are not charged. Sex, is similarly perceived as a 'perk' of the job for some policemen (see Jenkins this volume).

By virtue of their profession, police will always be a mobile part of the community—literally in the case of members of the mobile squad. Their mobility in remote rural areas provides a form of social invisibility and disconnectedness, as there they are not recognisable members of a community, in the way that police working at a station are. Their actions in rural areas also escape media attention, as the media is concentrated in urban centres and people do not have ready access to complaint mechanisms, so that often breaches of discipline, administration of harsh 'rough justice' and even criminal offences go unrecorded. But stories abound and are sometimes elaborated in ways that ensure that the reputation of police as violent and unjust dominates the public image that circulates in both rural and urban environments. In areas of the Highlands provinces where tribal fighting has occurred sporadically (and sometimes continuously) for many years, the mobile squads are notorious for their acts of violence and punitive retribution against people and property. In some instances villagers have sued for reparation and won, at heavy cost to the government. Such cases are then publicised so that police notoriety is reinforced nationally.

Preventing HIV: RPNGC Initiatives

While members of the Royal Papua New Guinea Constabulary are most commonly associated with the transmission of HIV (through the aforementioned practices), the constabulary has simultaneously attempted to contribute to HIV prevention, both among its own staff and in the community. With the assistance of the Royal Papua New Guinea Constabulary Development Project (1989–2005), a number of initiatives were introduced, with a particular focus upon basic awareness-raising (see Patrick this volume).

According to O'Collins (2005), a previous gender adviser on the RPNGC Development Project, the constabulary began addressing HIV and AIDS in 1990, against a backdrop of rising concern about the epidemic and workshops such as the Health Department's 'HIV/AIDS and the Work Place' meeting (30 November 1990). At that time, constabulary members had reportedly begun dying of HIV-related illnesses and there was much misunderstanding about the disease, including its modes of transmission. Given cultural constraints upon the open discussion of sexual matters and the stigma attached to HIV and AIDS, early attempts to address HIV/AIDS within the constabulary were met with resistance and were hence undertaken as subtly as possible, being subsumed among the general activities of the RPNGC Welfare Unit.

In 1991, a policy entitled *AIDS in the Workplace: Policy Directives for the RPNGC*, based upon a Papua New Guinea Defence Force (PNGDF) policy directive, was released as Commissioner's Circular 13/91(see Pantumari and Bamne this volume).

Designed to equip members of the RPNGC with knowledge about the virus, its effects and prevention, the policy outlines training directives, precautionary measures, procedures for the supervision of HIV positive members, virus detection and screening measures and processes for maintaining confidentiality and respect. Throughout the 1990s, attempts were made to address HIV in most training courses and HIV considerations were incorporated into cell and custody procedures.

In Phase III of the RPNGC Development Project (2000–5), constabulary trainers, in collaboration with the project's training adviser developed a training package for use within the constabulary in order to educate constabulary members about the transmission and prevention of HIV. This package, which has also been used in police barracks, has been delivered to RPNGC members throughout the country, as have training packages on gender and human rights. In addition, an HIV/AIDS module was prepared for the competency acquisition program, which is a self-directed learning program for probationary constables. Posters aimed at raising awareness of HIV transmission and prevention are displayed in most police stations. While discussions suggest that they have aided awareness, their impact on actual behaviour remains unknown. In addition to training for members of the RPNGC and their families, the Community Policing division of the RPNGC actively participates in HIV awareness training in the community, using materials developed both internally and by the National AIDS Council. Training assumes a number of forms, including ad hoc verbal awareness raising at market places, seminar-style training for community groups, school visits and police-hosted theatre group presentations. Community police officers also distribute pamphlets on HIV and both male and female condoms to community groups. In addition to raising awareness of HIV specifically, the community police make reference to HIV when conducting training on both domestic and sexual violence. The constabulary is well networked with the National AIDS Council, the Provincial AIDS Councils and NGOs working on related issues, including the Family and Sexual Violence Action Committee.

As noted by Jenkins (this volume), members of the constabulary have previously participated in action research programs and more recently in a similar program with the European Union, which involves the training of peer educators. While there have been previous attempts to ensure that police officers working in high risk operations have been provided with plastic gloves, the provision of gloves is sporadic. This aspect of HIV prevention, namely occupational precautions, has been less substantially addressed than awareness-raising.

The constabulary has produced *Workplace Policy on HIV/AIDS* to supersede Circular No. 13/91. The policy, drafted in keeping with the HIV/AIDS Management and Prevention (HAMP) Act 2003 (see Stewart this volume), contains basic information about HIV and AIDS and condemns discrimination against HIV-positive people, including attempts to deny HIV-positive members access to training, promotions, housing or other entitlements. As per circular 13/91, the policy requires that applicants be screened for HIV as part of the standard recruitment medical test and disqualified from further consideration in the event that they test HIV positive (cf. Pantumari and Bamne this volume). The policy places responsibility for the dissemination of relevant information in the hands of the welfare and training officers and reinforces the need for confidentiality and privacy of information pertaining to members' HIV status. Despite much resistance to the idea, the policy states that 'the constabulary should ... provide or facilitate access to condoms for its officers, which can be obtained by personal choice', and that hand gloves should be supplied for members attending to incidents involving injuries and bleeding.

In addition to the constabulary's agency specific HIV/AIDS policy, attempts to address HIV at the sectoral level are being made by all law and justice sector agencies, in collaboration with the Law and Justice Sector Program (LJSP) (see Patrick this volume), aimed at supporting the development of sector-wide knowledge and involvement in the prevention and management of HIV and AIDS.

Police Attitudes to HIV

While there is little doubt that awareness-raising activities within the constabulary have contributed to gains in members' knowledge about the transmission and prevention of HIV, as no systematic research has accompanied the implementation of training programs, it is impossible to ascertain changes to attitudes and behaviours. Casual conversations and workshop discussions with police officers suggest that there is now general understanding of the ways in which HIV is transmitted and prevented, and of the need for non-discriminatory treatment of HIV positive people. There is however, an ongoing reluctance by police officers (particularly women) to carry condoms, lest their partners accuse them of being promiscuous. Policewomen, many of whom are married to policemen, express the desire to control their own sexual health by asking their husbands (whom they know to have multiple sexual partners) to use condoms. Simultaneously, however, they struggle with the violent implications of such requests and hence feel powerless to control their own bodies (cf. Eves this volume). This was aptly demonstrated by a policewoman, who, during an HIV workshop discussion of female condoms asked, 'How long can you leave these condoms in for? My husband comes home drunk early every morning and rapes me. Maybe I could put it in before I go to bed?'

Unfortunately, the change in attitudes to prostitutes documented by Jenkins (this volume), following work with the police in 1996, do not appear to have been sustained—few policemen and policewomen are sympathetic to prostitutes, and policewomen appear no more lenient in their views than their male colleagues. The HIV/AIDS awareness comic book produced in the context of the project discussed by Jenkins was used in workshops conducted in 2002. It was interpreted by some police participants as giving information about ways that HIV could be contracted in the context of their work; but equally was considered to be an official endorsement of the 'rights' of police to take known prostitutes into their barracks and require that they have sex with multiple partners. Many police officers, both men and women, do not accept that a prostitute can be raped, a view which is perpetuated by the belief that prostitutes attempt to lay charges for rape only when their customers have failed to pay for services rendered. In 2004, the public humiliation by police of prostitutes working in the Three-Mile Guesthouse serves to further emphasise their attitudes to the profession (see Fletcher and Gonapa this volume; Stewart this volume).

The images of modern masculinity in Papua New Guinea still entail gender distinctions that render liberal humanistic notions of the communication between men and women—especially over sexual matters—alien. Companionship between men and women is not an ideal embraced by many people, much less 'naturalised' as providing the basis for negotiating aspects of a personal relationship (cf. Pantumari and Bamne this volume; Wardlow 2009). In workshops on domestic violence, policewomen and the wives of policemen commented that it was difficult to discuss birth control, sexual needs and even domestic issues where there were differences of opinion. Often the living conditions prevailed against intimate conversation and notions of 'shame' (which encompasses 'shyness' in common usage) inhibited women. Asking a husband to use a condom was tantamount to accusing him of being adulterous, or admitting that one had engaged in extramarital sex and so might have contracted an infection. Either way, women who spoke of the problems facing them believed that condom usage in marriage was an unrealistic expectation, inviting violence from an affronted husband (see Eves this volume). Human rights approaches to HIV prevention require acceptance of notions of gender equity and that cannot be assumed.

In some communities people have neglected, rejected and even murdered people suspected of having AIDS. Links are made between witchcraft and HIV that have further stigmatised people with the infection (see Luker and Dinnen this volume, ch. 1; Haley this volume). The posters that were meant to ensure that the public recognised that people with HIV could look like any normal person and therefore accept sufferers as members of their community, in some ways reinforce the link. For just as witches can appear to be 'normal' while inflicting harm on those around them, so the person who transmits HIV to another can do so to 'innocent victims'.[4] The emphasis on patient confidentiality and its enshrinement in law strengthens both the existing association of secrecy, immorality and the wilful infliction of harm and the view that there are 'guilty' and 'innocent' people who contract the disease. Given the double standards in sexual morality that prevail, women who are considered sexually promiscuous are considered doubly guilty. They invite illicit sex and threaten the health of others—and so should be exposed and punished as anti-social and dangerous.

In discussions of human rights with police in 2002, several expressed the view that publicly exposing people with HIV or AIDS was a 'customary' way of making people safe and would 'deter' men from consorting with them. They were in effect reluctant to extend 'human rights' to those whom they considered immoral and socially irresponsible. Others were more accepting of the need to promote acceptance and support for people with AIDS—their position was expressed in terms of Christian ideals of charity and mercy. But such views often involved harsh moral judgements and the more evangelical were also more inclined to believe that 'repentance' and faith could cure the illness (see Hammar this volume; Wardlow 2008; Eves 2003). The emphasis on monogamous fidelity as the best means of preventing transmission effectively endorses the view that it is a disease of the immoral. These responses are not unique to members of the police force and reflect a climate of opinion and a dogmatic moralism that need to be acknowledged.

Conclusions

For almost two decades the RPNGC has been exposed to education and awareness programs aimed at improving understanding and compliance with basic human rights. By 2000 all members of the force were 'aware' of human rights issues. Aid programs implemented by AusAID, the European Union and the Red Cross have continued to emphasise the human rights of citizens and the international standards that must be maintained in a just society. More recently, senior police, including the police commissioner, have taken a leading role in advocating against gender violence. Measures introduced within the force include an equal opportunity policy, the promotion of female officers to senior positions, the establishment of a Victims Crimes Desk and changing the name of the Sexual Offences Squad to the Family and Sexual Violence Squad (Mabone 2009).

4　For a discussion of other unintended readings of AIDS posters, see Macpherson 2008, 233–240).

But such measures do not swiftly translate into actions at large that defend or uphold the rights of citizens. Indeed, in one session dealing with gender, several policemen who had demonstrated a thorough understanding of the principles underpinning policies on equality of opportunity insisted that 'such things cannot be accepted for perhaps twenty years in Papua New Guinea'. They were not hostile to the principles, they simply regarded them as unrealistic and unattainable. They were phlegmatic rather than pessimistic—attitudes that must be understood in the context of their own conditions of employment as much as the environment in which they work (McLeod 2007, 80–81).

Our analysis of the ways in which the Royal Papua New Guinea Constabulary impacts upon the course and management of HIV and AIDS in Papua New Guinea demonstrates the myriad ways in which a single organisation can be involved in both the transmission and prevention of the virus. Our aim has been to shed light upon the difficulties involved in tackling the epidemic in Papua New Guinea via Western analytical frames, such as human rights (see Reid this volume). In emphasising the multiple layers of cultural identity—both societal and organisational—that hamper the success of initiatives aimed at curbing police involvement in the transmission of HIV, we draw attention to the ways that police are simultaneously part of the communities in which they operate. Ultimately, however, the analysis points to the urgent need to bridge the gap between awareness and behavioural change, a challenge that is by no means unique to the constabulary.

References

Eves, Richard. 2003. AIDS and Apocalypticism: Interpretations of the Epidemic from Papua New Guinea. *Culture, Health and Sexuality* 5 (2): 249–264.

HRW (Human Rights Watch). 2005. *'Making Their Own Rules': Police Beatings, Rape and Torture of Children in Papua New Guinea.* http://www.hrw.org/en/node/11626/section/1 (accessed 27 April 2010).

HRW (Human Rights Watch). 2006. Still Making Their Own Rules: Ongoing Impunity for Police Bearings, Rape and Torture in Papua New Guinea. New York: Human Rights Watch.

Mabone, Travertz. 2009. Baki: I'll End Violence against our Women. *The National*, 25 March 2009.

Macintyre, Martha. 2008. Police and Thieves, Gunmen and Drunks: Problems with Men and Problems with Society in Papua New Guinea. *The Australian Journal of Anthropology* 19 (2): 179–193.

MacPherson, Naomi. 2008. 'SikAIDS: Deconstructing the Awareness Campaign in Rural West New Britain, Papua New Guinea. In *Making Sense of AIDS: Culture, Sexuality, and Power in Melanesia*, ed. Leslie Butt and Richard Eves, 224–245. Honolulu: University of Hawai'i Press.

McLeod, Abby. 2007. Police Reform in Papua New Guinea. In *Security in the Pacific Islands: Social Resilience in Emerging States*, ed. M. Anne Brown, 73–88. London and Boulder: Lynne Rienner Publishers.

O'Collins, M. 2005, Personal Communication, September 2005.

PNG (Papua New Guinea) JAG (Justice Advisory Group). 2008. Urban Crime Victimisation in Papua New Guinea 2004–2008: A Synthesis.

RPNGC (Royal Papua New Guinea Constabulary). 1991. *AIDS in the Workplace: Policy directives for the RPNGC*, Commissioner's Circular 13/91.

RPNGC (Royal Papua New Guinea Constabulary). 2004. Report on Community Perceptions of the Police in Papua New Guinea. Unpublished project document. Port Moresby: Development Project, Phase III.

Wardlow, Holly. 2009. 'She Liked It Best When She Was on Top': Intimacies and Estrangements in Huli Men's Marital and Extra Marital Relationships. In *Intimacies: Love and Sex Across Cultures*, ed. William R. Jankowiak, 174–194. New York: Columbia University Press.

Wardlow, Holly. 2008. 'You have to Understand: Some of Us are Glad AIDS has Arrived': Christianity and Condoms among the Huli, Papua New Guinea. In *Making Sense of AIDS: Culture, Sexuality, and Power in Melanesia*, ed. Leslie Butt and Richard Eves, 187–205. Honolulu: University of Hawai'i Press.

8. Prisons and HIV in Papua New Guinea

GREG LAW AND SINCLAIR DINNEN

The Prison System

Sinclair Dinnen

The modern prison system in PNG has a relatively short history. For much of the colonial period the imprisonment of offenders, usually for short periods, was administered as an integral part of the larger system of 'native administration'. Prisons were viewed by colonial officials as educational institutions in which prisoners learned about the ways of the Europeans and acquired respect for the authority of the colonial government. 'Education' consisted primarily of physical labour and prisoners were utilised in a range of public works from grass-cutting to road construction. Every government station had its own gaol under the control of the resident magistrate who served simultaneously as judge, jury, prosecutor and jailer. The first prisons provided important sources of recruitment for some of the early members of the 'native constabulary', as well as offering other Papua New Guineans employment in some of the only minor positions in the colonial government that were then open to indigenes (Reed 2003, 29–42).

The current prison system has its origins in the process of institutional modernisation that commenced in the late 1950s (Sikani 1994; Reed 2003, 42–48). This involved the gradual dismantling of the old administrative model of colonial control and its replacement with the institutional framework of a modern justice system in anticipation of eventual independence and statehood. The first stage of this process was completed in 1957 with the establishment of a separate prisons branch under the Corrective Institutions Ordinance.

Responsibility for the administration of Papua New Guinea's prison system now lies with the PNG Correctional Service (CS) which was established as a state service and disciplined force under the Constitution. The mission of the CS is to enhance the safety of the community by providing secure and humane containment and rehabilitating detainees. For many years, the CS was the most neglected of PNG's law and justice agencies. Unlike the police and courts, CS institutions tend to be located away from urban centres and, hence, from public view. The larger institutions have been described as 'green prisons', beginning as prison farms with large open spaces and barrack-type accommodation surrounded by high security fences.

Providing secure containment has been a major and growing challenge in the post-independence period with regular prison breakouts—often en masse. For example, around 60 inmates were reported to have escaped from Bomana prison in September 2009. According to an unnamed CS source, the escape occurred because of a shortage of warders who did not turn up to work due to a pay dispute (Anon 2009a). A month later, newspapers reported that almost 500 inmates who claimed that they had not been fed for two days scaled the four-metre fence enclosing Buimo prison but were quickly prevented from escaping by armed wardens (Anon. 2009b). After a daring breakout in January 2010 from Bomana prison, the Prime Minister dismissed the Minister for Correctional Services and suspended the Correctional Services Commissioner (Mercer 2010). Many mass escapes appear to have the tacit approval of prison staff and are often linked to industrial disputes between wardens and CS headquarters. These breakouts contribute, in turn, to localised 'crime waves' in the nearest town. Lack of adequate government support, overcrowded, outdated and poorly maintained facilities and sub-standard staff accommodation have contributed to low morale on the part of CS personnel. Approximately one-third of the prison population—rising to 50 percent in some institutions—consists of remandees awaiting trial. Some wait for periods of two years and upwards before their cases are heard. Delays in court proceedings have added greatly to internal pressures within the prison system. While correctional services have received significant levels of Australian aid (Moraitis 2008), many institutions continue to experience great difficulties in feeding, clothing and accommodating growing numbers of inmates.

Unsanitary conditions in some facilities threaten the health of staff, their families and detainees. Several facilities, including staff accommodation, have been condemned by health authorities as 'unfit for human habitation'. Similar conditions are found in police cells which are often used to hold inmates when space in CS facilities is unavailable. In September 2009, a detainee at Lae Central police station was suspected of having cholera, causing panic among the other 78 detainees and later the wider community when he escaped from hospital. Inspection of the police cells revealed blocked and overflowing ablution facilities, a condition shared among many police and prison cells (Anon 2009c). Prisoners in high-risk detention at Buimo prison in Lae told reporters that they had not had a proper shower for the previous three years (Korugl 2008). A number of deaths due to outbreaks of contagious diseases in prisons have recently been reported, but these problems are not new (Siaguru 2001, 208).

Convicted inmates and remandees have not always been separated in practice and resource shortages have also impacted on the capacity of the CS to provide separate facilities for juvenile inmates as required by law. Despite the 'correctional' tag and the commitment of many within the service to the ideal of rehabilitation, the rehabilitation of detainees remains undeveloped in many facilities and heavily reliant on church initiatives (Dinnen 2001, 52; Reed 2003, 52). Legal provisions also place constraints on the use of prison labour. Some prisons, like Port Moresby's Bomana prison, have active gang sub-cultures and, as with prisons elsewhere, significant numbers of inmates are released from PNG's prisons with a heightened commitment to criminal and anti-social activity (Dinnen 2001, 107; Reed 2003, 125–128; Goddard 2005, 101–105). Escapes and links between inmates and outside criminal activities have been attributed to prisoners' growing use of mobile phones. In February 2009, the Commissioner for Correctional Services banned visitors from carrying mobile phones following fears that a recent upsurge in armed holdups was being orchestrated from within prisons (Anon. 2009d).

There are currently 20 gazetted correctional institutions in PNG. These include Bomana (National Capital District), Buimo (Lae), Baisu (Mount Hagen), Kerevat (East New Britain), Kavieng, Manus (Lorengau), Lakiemata (Kimbe), Daru (Daru), Giligilii (Alotau), Biru (Popondetta), Beon (Madang), Boram (Wewak), Vanimo (Vanimo), Bundaira (Kainantu), Bihute (Goroka), Barawagi (Kundiawa), and Bui-Iebi (Mendi). The size of individual facilities and number of detainees varies considerably. At one end of the scale, Buimo has over 800 detainees, closely followed by Bomana. At the other end, Manus has about 40 detainees. Beon, just outside of Madang, is one of the larger facilities with a detainee population of around 350 in 2002. It has recently been upgraded as part of Australia's aid program (Moraitis 2008). There are also a number of smaller rural lockups that are administered jointly with the Department of Provincial and Local Level Government. The overall detainee population in 2002 was around 3200–3500 with around 92 percent of detainees being adult males, 4 percent females, and 4 percent being male juveniles. Data on the CS is difficult to obtain but some are available on the PNG government Law and Justice Sector Website: http://www.lawandjustice.gov.pg/www/html/7-home-page.asp.

Correctional Services has developed an HIV/AIDS and Other Infectious Diseases Strategy and introduced HIV awareness-raising programs among staff and detainees (see Patrick this volume). The first HIV behavioural study among prison inmates was conducted at the Bomana facility in 2005 (Pantumari et al. 2005) and prisons have been identified as high-risk settings that should be prioritised for the national response (NHASP 2006, 24–25). Among recent reported initiatives was a proposed pilot project at Buimo Prison to employ low-risk prisoners packing the new *Seif Raida* condoms, which was described as an opportunity to both rehabilitate prisoners and educate them about HIV while serving the national HIV response (Rai 2008). These and other initiatives for improving prison infrastructure, management and the welfare of inmates contend, however, with persisting funding and other difficulties. In January 2010, Prime Minister Somare personally took charge of the prison system, which he described as 'in crisis' (quoted by Mercer 2010).

Prisons

Greg Law

Prisons around the world are potentially among the unhealthiest places in our societies. They are places where peoples of varying ages and from different populations and backgrounds are compulsorily mixed, deprived of their freedom and are often exposed to direct threats of violence (including sexual violence) and infectious disease transmission.

The WHO publication, *HIV in Prisons*, notes that 'incarcerating people in prisons and denying them their freedom is supposed to be their punishment: exposing them to diseases which are often fatal is not part of their sentence and is unacceptable' (Bollini 2001, i). The US Bureau of Justice Statistics acknowledges that many researchers believe the number of prisoners with HIV is far higher than those officially documented (Clemetson 2004).

There are numerous risk factors for infectious disease transmission in prisons and police lock-ups in Papua New Guinea, including the usual scenario of intense overcrowding in the cell blocks (for both remandees and for those convicted and serving sentences). Overcrowded ablution blocks are another problem. With insufficient funds for maintenance, the septic systems do not cope with the load of excrement deposited in them and as a consequence, overflow into or in close proximity to the prison yard. Toilet blocks themselves are frequently awash with a mixture of urine and leaking water from damaged toilet pedestals and faulty plumbing. The potential for the transmission of infections such as typhoid, dysentery, hepatitis and tuberculosis in the prisons and police lockups is enormous and has been amply demonstrated in recent times (see, e.g., Korugl 2008).

Under the Correctional Services (CS) regulations every person admitted to a prison in PNG is required to have a medical examination to assess their physical fitness to serve the sentence they have been given. The examination is also to determine the presence of any infectious condition and enable management of that condition, to both cure the individual and to prevent the transmission of the infection in the prison setting. This examination is to be repeated on release from the corrective institution.

For three years in the early 1980s and another three years in the early 1990s, while the author was working in Madang, he acted as the visiting medical officer to Beon Prison just outside Madang town. This involved a half-day visit each week. All inmates admitted in the previous week and all to be released before the next week were given a limited medical examination and treatment was provided for any medical conditions found. During the first few visits numerous inmates were found to have STIs and these were treated. Included in this group were people who had been incarcerated for long periods of time yet who had acute STIs, indicating recent infection transmission within the prison setting. Once the medical visits became established, and included basic STI checks on admission to the facility, infections were identified on admission and treated. Following the instigation of this procedure, the numbers of new infections occurring within the prison dropped dramatically.

Beon Gaol is the only PNG prison where these medical checks have taken place in recorded history and since the mid-1990s have not happened there either. An audit of PNG's prisons conducted in 2008 called for the employment of more health and welfare professionals in CS institutions owing the the deaths of prisoners from outbreaks of contagious disease in recent years (Anon. 2008a).

The CS has provision in the records for each inmate for the recording of the medical examination of prisoners on admission and release but these examinations are not carried out due to the lack of trained medical staff. Each prison has a small aid post staffed by a Community Health Worker or Orderly, who provides basic medical attention for the inmates of the facility and the CS staff and families. The difficulty in getting the medical examinations performed routinely is in identifying medical staff from provincial health facilities who are (a) interested in prison health and (b) able to take enough time from their already heavy work loads to undertake prison health work on a regular basis.

Apart from the infectious diseases already mentioned, as in prisons all over the world, there is also great potential for the transmission of sexually transmitted infections (STIs) including the Human Immunodeficiency Virus (HIV). In prisons in PNG, the main types of behaviour that greatly increase the risk of STI/HIV transmission include:

- Tattooing with shared implements
- Skin cutting with shared implements
- Unprotected sexual intercourse.

We will look at each of these three groups of risky behaviour in turn. Injecting drug use, which is a major factor in the high prevalence of HIV among prison populations in many countries, is fortunately so far not a factor in PNG (Dolan et al. 2007)

Tattooing

It is common practice in PNG for prison inmates (especially sentenced prisoners but also remandees) to tattoo themselves and their fellow inmates. Tattoos vary in design but frequently there are recurring designs that are easily recognised by initiates for purposes of peer recognition in the community after release (see also Reed 2003). The common method of tattooing in prisons is to use either a razor to cut into the skin, or needles or thorns to make multiple stab wounds. After these lesions are made in the desired pattern, soot, usually from the base of the large cauldrons used for cooking over open fires, is rubbed into the wounds. Due to obvious lack of resources in the prison setting, it is common for inmates to share the cutting or piercing instruments. If any cleansing is done at all between uses, it usually consists of simply washing in tap water, but the more common scenario is to wipe the implement on cloth or clothing between uses. This practice clearly holds potential for the transmission of numerous blood borne infections including HIV, Hepatitis B and C and possibly syphilis.

Skin-cutting

Incising of the skin by inmates (either to themselves or to their fellows), is common in PNG prisons and is practised for several reasons. The principal two of these is either for decorative scarification or more commonly for penile modification. Decorative scarification may be anywhere on the trunk or limbs but is more commonly performed on the chest and consists of horizontal lines incised over the mid-chest at about the junction of the upper and middle thirds of the sternum. In some provinces pseudo-traditional scarification in the back, chest, buttocks and thighs may also be conducted in the prison setting, however these are rare as the practice is more easily noticed by CS staff and thus punishable.

Penile modification is traditional in some areas of PNG. For example, it is fairly common to perform circumcision on male babies and very young boys in parts of West New Britain. Likewise, dorsal slit of the prepuce is performed during initiation of adolescent males in the Rai Coast area of Madang Province. Over the past 20 years or so, techniques of modification of the dorsal slit, including insertion of foreign bodies between the layers of the slit prepuce and other skin of the penis, have been introduced, initially by Asians, especially those involved in the logging and timber industry. Anecdotal evidence suggests that these workers introduced the practice to local men in the areas in which they worked.

The practice of penile modification is common throughout prisons in PNG, as it is in some general communities, and is believed to be increasing (cf. Reed 2003,113–116; NACS 2006, 38). In prison, where communal bathing is the rule, male inmates who have not had some form of penile modification are often ridiculed, and submission to the practice by those prisoners (especially younger men) who have not previously undergone the procedure is often a rite towards being fully accepted into the 'community'. There are as many variations in reasons for undergoing the procedure as there are in the techniques of the actual procedure.

As mentioned already, one reason for submitting to penile modification procedures is the felt need for compliance with the sub-culture of the prison community. A further reason given for undergoing the procedure is the widely held belief that the dorsal slit of the prepuce and the resultant 'clean head' of the glans penis provides protection against STIs generally (cf. NACS 2006, 38). Others believe that the resultant scarring from the dorsal slit causes enlargement of the girth of the penis. The insertion of foreign bodies into the prepuce between the layers of the prepuce at the time of the incision and/or the insertion of foreign bodies below the skin of other parts of the penis is performed for the same reason. It is widely believed that the resultant bulges and general increase in the girth of the penis will greatly enhance sexual pleasure for the female partner during coital thrusting, so that she will always be 'coming back for more'.

The author has frequently been called upon to later surgically remove these foreign bodies and the resultant fibrotic tissue due to either recurrent infection or discomfort. Items inserted below the skin of the penis include steel ball bearings, glass marbles, plastic buttons, pieces of rounded carved wood, lids of tooth paste tubes, tooth paste itself (squeezed into the incisions and later hardening), rounded pieces of glass (often from the handle of brown glass coffee jars) and small key rings. In the prison setting, the most common material inserted into the penis is a part of the handle end (although the bristle end has also been used) of a plastic tooth brush. A piece about 1–2 cm long is broken off and rubbed against cement floors or walls until the edges and corners are smooth. This is then inserted through an incision either into the prepuce or other part of the penile skin.

In most cases incisions made by inmates in PNG prisons are made with razor blades. Since it is mandatory for all sentenced prisoners to shave daily, razor blades are available. However due to the rationing of these items, razors used in 'surgical' procedures are often shared and, again, if any cleansing is done between use on different people, it will usually only involve rinsing under tap water. Given the depth to which these incisions are made, should any antecedent 'patient' be HIV positive, the potential for HIV (and Hepatitis B and C) transmission in this scenario is high.

Sexual Transmission

Thus far we have looked at the potential for the percutaneous transmission of HIV in PNG prisons. Probably the greatest risks for transmission of HIV and other STIs exist in unprotected sexual intercourse. As in prisons around the world sexual intercourse occurs in prisons in PNG (see also Reed 2003, 116–119). At any one time the prison population in PNG is around 3,000 males and from 100–300 females (Karela, n.d.). In the case of the male prison population, both anal and oral sexual intercourse occurs. This may involve just two partners but may also involve group participation. As is the case internationally, men who do not identify as homosexual and who may not indulge in homosexual activities when outside the prison, do so when confined for periods of time away from their female partners. The reasons given by inmates for involvement in male homosexual activities whilst in prisons vary. In some cases it is voluntary and consensual, either from the natural inclination of the partners or as an acceptable substitute for their usual heterosexual activities. In others it may occur under coercion—either in exchange for protection from others, or for extra food or other items smuggled into the prison (often tobacco), or for the security of having a guardian. In these cases it is usual that the receptive (and rewarded) partner is a youth or at least considerably younger and thus more susceptible to abuse, than the other partner. Sometimes the sexually receptive partner may have been seen having sex with another inmate and is then coerced by threats of reporting to prison authorities to provide the same sexual service for other inmates.

The more traumatic of the 'sexual liaisons' that occur in the prisons is that of sexual assault (see, e.g. Kelola 2009). This sometimes happens when a younger male inmate is approached for sexual favours and may even be offered rewards but refuses to comply. It may also happen when the 'receptive' partner is caught by other inmates indulging in sexual activities with another prisoner, or is rumoured to have been involved and then refuses the approaches of other inmates. These attacks again may be by an individual prisoner, or may involve multiple assailants. In a recently reported case, prisoners retaliated against two fellow inmates who were serial rapists (Kelola 2009). Serious anal trauma is often the result of these sexual assaults. Whilst any form of unprotected sexual intercourse with an infected person is a risk of HIV and other STI transmission, it is well documented that unprotected anal intercourse, and especially as the result of sexual assault, constitutes the highest risk.

In PNG, sexual liaison involving female prisoners is less well documented. Certainly there are recorded cases of female detainees being involved in sexual activity (either consensually or allegedly forced) whilst in custody in lockups or other institutions (but see Reed 2003, 120–121). The author has also been consulted to extract from the vagina of female prisoners, pieces broken off from dildos made of available material. This matter has included pieces from 'carved' peeled raw sweet potato and other vegetable matter and also pieces broken from the deep fried wholemeal 'cakes' prepared for prisoner's breakfasts. It is highly unlikely though that these devices are shared and thus would not be seen as 'vectors' for the transmission of HIV or other STIs.

Summary

In summary then the most high-risk behaviour leading to the potential transmission of HIV (and other STIs) in the prison setting in PNG, includes skin-cutting or piercing with shared instruments and unprotected sexual intercourse. It is the oft-reiterated policy of the CS that condoms are not and will not be made available to inmates of corrective institutions. We have here a 'Catch 22' situation. The CS regulations that prevent the issuing of condoms to prisoners is based on the fact that the law in PNG makes sodomy and 'unnatural sexual acts' criminal offences, thus to issue condoms in single sex prisons is viewed as tacitly condoning those acts. Yet the HIV/AIDS Management and Prevention Act of 2003 (see Stewart this volume) clearly states that to deprive anyone of the means of protecting themselves against HIV is also an offence under that Act. Urgent discussion needs to take place at a national level to solve this seeming impasse.

Supervision of prisoners is clearly a major problem. Due to staffing shortages and inadequate ratios of CS officers to inmates in corrective institutions, it is obvious that close supervision of prisoners is not possible. On weekends especially, inmates are confined to the prison cell blocks and yards with minimal close supervision, which allows for hidden 'surgical' procedures to be performed with relative ease. Similarly after the evening meal, prisoners are locked up inside large open dormitory blocks each housing scores of inmates and there is usually no inspection or supervision until the doors are unlocked the following morning. It is unlikely that these conditions will change unless adequate funding is allocated to the CS to allow the raising of staffing ceilings and increased training of officers.

It is also imperative that younger prisoners be kept in separate accommodation from the other inmates to decrease the potential for sexual assault. Some inroads have been made to achieve this in the larger prisons, with the provision of separate juvenile blocks but a lot more needs to be done to expand existing facilities and to ensure that each prison has separate juvenile accommodation blocks.

Provision also needs to be made for the basic health checks to be carried out on each inmate on admission and prior to release from the corrective institutions. This may be possible by negotiation and collaboration with provincial health authorities and hospitals but it would also be helpful for CS to look at the possibility of recruiting trained medical staff at least on a regional basis to regularly visit Corrective Institutions in order to carry out routine and regular health checks on inmates.

At this stage voluntary counselling and testing (VCT) for HIV in prisons in PNG is limited. The lack of facilities and shortage of resources within prisons has curtailed the implementation of HIV prevention measures beyond awareness-raising (NHASP 2006, 25–26). Yet in response to education campaigns, prisoners have made regular requests in numerous prisons around the country for HIV testing. As the VCT programme is rolled out nationally, it is imperative that counsellors be trained to extend this service to the inmates of prisons as well as the general population. As the planned availability of HIV rapid test kits increases, the possibility of providing a VCT service to inmates of prisons in PNG will become more viable. As prisoners become aware of their HIV status, measures for the maintenance of confidentiality, easier access to health services and the supply of condoms will achieve even greater importance.

References

Anon. 2009a. *The National*, 28 September 2009.

Anon. 2009b. *The National*, 21 October 2009.

Anon 2009c. *The National*, 24 September 2009.

Anon 2009d. *Post-Courier*, 10 February 2009.

Bollini P., ed. 2001. HIV in Prisons: A Reader with Particular Relevance to the Newly Independent States. Copenhagen: WHO Regional Office for Europe.

Rai, Frank. 2008. Casual Jobs for Prisoners. *Post-Courier*, 31 July 2008.

Clemetson L. 2004. Links Between Prison and AIDS Affecting Blacks Inside and Out. *New York Times*, 6 August.

Dinnen, Sinclair. 2001. *Law and Order in a Weak State: Crime and Politics in Papua New Guinea*. Adelaide and Honolulu: Crawford House and Hawaii University Press.

Dolan, Kate, Ben Kite, Emma Black, Carmen Aceijas, Gerry V. Stimson. 2007. HIV in Prison in Low-Income and Middle-Income Countries. *Lancet Infectious Diseases* 7 (1): 32–41.

Goddard, Michael. 2005. *The Unseen City: Anthropological Perspectives on Port Moresby, Papua New Guinea*. Canberra: Pandanus Books.

Karela, K., Deputy Police Commissioner, PNG, personal communication.

Kelola, Todagia. 2009. Notorious Pair Beaten up over Sodomy Claim. *Post-Courier*, 20 February 2009.

Korugl, Peter. 2008. Buimo Inmates in 'Hell'. *Post-Courier*, 4 December 2009.

Mercer, Phil. 2010. Papua New Guinea's Correctional Services Minister has been Sacked following a Brazen Jailbreak. BBC News, Sydney, 21 January 2010.

Moraitis, Chris. 2008. Speech for the Official Opening of New Facilities at Beon Prison, 8th July 2008. http://www.png.embassy.gov.au/pmsb/Speech080708.html (accessed 27 April 2010).

NACS (National AIDS Council Secretariat). 2006. *HIV/AIDS Behavioural Surveillance Survey within High Risk Settings*. BSS Round 1. [Boroko]: National AIDS Council Secretariat.

NHASP (National HIV/AIDS Support Project). 2006. High Risk Settings Strategy Report: Moving beyond Awareness. Milestone 90.

Pantumari, Joachim, John Millan, Emil Ngansia, Joe Bunefa. 2005. *Human Immunodeficiency Virus Behavioural Study among Inmates, Bomana Prison, Port Moresby, Papua New Guinea*. Boroka: PNG National AIDS Council, supported by AusAID.

Reed, Adam. 2003. *Papua New Guinea's Last Place: Experiences of Constraint in a Postcolonial Prison*. New York: Berghahn Books.

Siaguru, Anthony. 2001. Prison Welfare in More Ways than One. In *In-House in Papua New Guinea with Anthony Siaguru*, by Anthony Siaguru, 207-209. Canberra: Asia Pacific Press.

Sikani, Richard. 1994. The Establishment of the Corrective Institution Branch and the Australian Colonial Detainee Rehabilitation Policies in TPNG Gaols, 1950-1975. NRI Discussion Paper no. 75. Boroko: National Research Institute.

9. HIV and the Papua New Guinea Defence Force: Risk Behaviours and Perceptions

JOACHIM PANTUMARI, PETER BAMNE
AND VICKI LUKER

Questions relating to the military's role in spreading HIV or the impacts of HIV and AIDS on armies place the epidemic in contexts traditionally central to national security (Barnett and Prins 2005; Whiteside et al. 2006; Kershaw 2008; O'Keefe this volume). In PNG, concerns have been raised about the potential for HIV to drain resources from the Papua New Guinea Defence Force (PNGDF), compromise operational capacity, and spread from HIV-positive personnel to their families and to the communities where their work takes them. Fortunately, the PNGDF can exploit certain advantages in tackling HIV, including the institution's organisational structure, an established interest and role in the health of soldiers, and the army's relations with the wider international military community that have facilitated the sharing of knowledge and other forms of cooperation (see e.g., NHASP 26–29; Kendino and Kaule 2005). The PNGDF has demonstrated leadership in aspects of the response.

This chapter focuses on risk factors of infection and perceptions of these within the PNGDF community, drawing on a study undertaken in 2001 and 2002. Its findings remain relevant to measures for limiting HIV's spread within the army, the uniformed services more generally, and the wider civilian population, for many of the behaviours and perceptions identified are not limited to the PNGDF—although some risk behaviours can be accentuated under military conditions (see Eves this volume; Hammar this volume; Jenkins this volume; McLeod and Macintyre this volume).

The PNGDF and HIV

The structure and role of the PNGDF were inherited from the Australian colonial administration and maintained after independence in 1975 (May 2004; Laki and May 2009). Under the Constitution, the principal functions of the defence force are to defend Papua New Guinea and its territory and to assist PNG fulfill its international obligations. In addition, the PNGDF is empowered to provide assistance to civilian authorities under certain prescribed circumstances. These include assistance in the case of a civil disaster; in the restoration of public order and security; in a declared national emergency; and in pursuit of national development and improvement. Due to downsizing, the PNGDF currently employs some 2,000 officers and lower ranks, but when this research was undertaken, more than twice that number were serving—in Headquarters, three battalions, an air wing and a maritime element. The major units are located at Murray Barracks, Taurama Barracks, Landing Craft Base and Kiki Barracks, all in the National Capital District; Goldie Barracks in Central Province; Igam Barracks in Morobe Province; Moem Barracks in East Sepik Province; and Lombrum in Manus Province.

Soldiers come from all over the country, usually from rural backgrounds, and are selected as youths on the basis of physical and academic criteria. As a result of the restructuring program commenced in 2002, the average age of PNGDF servicemen has fallen as many veterans (soldiers who enlisted during the Australian army or colonial eras) have taken the opportunity to retire. The first 21 female recruits were enlisted in late 2009 (Anis 2009), but the army remains an overwhelmingly masculine institution. At the time of the study, the number of soldiers' dependents, mainly wives and children, was estimated in the range of 12,000–18,000.

The first detected HIV case in a PNGDF soldier was recorded in May 1992, but statistics on HIV within the military are not freely available. In 2004, when concerns were aired about the impact of AIDS on the PNGDF, it was reported that within Port Moresby alone, 108 soldiers had AIDS and the defence force was incurring one or two AIDS deaths per month. Though testing of military personnel had only been limited, HIV prevalence within the army was said to be on a par with concurrent estimates for PNG's population as a whole (Steven 2004). [1]

---

1   HIV prevalence in some armies has been estimated to be much higher than in the general community (see, eg. Elbe 2003, 17–21). Yet it cannot be assumed that, as a rule, HIV prevalence in armies is higher than in the civilian population. Several factors can influence prevalence. In societies where sexual intercourse is the dominant mode of transmission, young men as a group often have low levels of HIV, and youthful recruits usually comprise a large proportion of the military population. Many armies also screen recruits for HIV (see Whiteside et al. 2006, 202–204).

Risk Factors and How they are Perceived

From December 2001 to January 2002 research was undertaken to identify the factors that may expose soldiers to HIV infection; explore the military community's perceptions of such factors; and provide qualitative information for preventive measures. Three methods of data collection were used: focus groups discussions (FGDs), in-depth interviews (IDIs), and document review. The FGDs and most of the IDIs were conducted at Taurama Barracks in Port Moresby. Two IDIs were done outside the Barracks. Part of the document review was done at the Murray Barracks where the Central Medical Records are located. Thirty-five people participated in the FGDs: ten soldiers; seven counsellors; six wives of soldiers; six non-commissioned officers; and six commissioned officers. Thirteen participants from the FGDs then participated in further IDIs. The discussions and interviews were conducted in a mixture of Pidgin and English. The study's findings are summarised below.

Environmental Conditions are Basic Influences on Behaviour

Participants identified housing as a big problem. Married quarters were chronically overcrowded. Most had been built by the Australian army for soldiers with two to three children, at a time when family planning was actively promoted by colonial authorities. Older soldiers, however, had on average four to six children, some of whom were adults with children of their own, as well as their own parents, residing within the barracks (F. Torova, Director PNGDF Health Services, pers. comm.). Many married soldiers were even worse off. They had no access to married quarters and remained in single barracks, while their spouses and children stayed in the village or in urban squatter settlements. The resulting separation of families had a noticeable impact on the behaviour of servicemen. As one officer remarked, 'You know, when a soldier has no home, wife and children with him, he goes looking for women'. Amenities were a further problem. The soldiers' club had been closed for a decade. Canteen and entertainment services were privately managed and relatively expensive. The gymnasium had no equipment. This lack of amenities, noted one NCO, 'leads to soldiers leaving the barracks and doing silly things'.

Inadequate institutional discipline compounded the problems of poor accommodation and facilities. Soldiers went out at night because there were no barrack bed checks and some resided away from the single barracks without lawful permission. Poor regulation of the movement of people in and out of both married and single accommodation was another cause of complaint. Females were regularly smuggled into the single barracks, contrary to the rules.

Low salaries contributed to difficulties. On average, a private earned about K150 ($A75) a fortnight. One wife remarked that because her husband was a sergeant and she earned a good salary in a bank, they could feed and clothe themselves and their children by pooling their wages. But ordinary soldiers whose wives were not employed and had three or more children could not cope. Moreover, many husbands did not pass their wages to their wives. One soldier suggested that perhaps PNGDF should establish a separate housewife's allowance. For extra money, some wives sold betel-nuts, cigarettes, twisties and alcohol in the informal sector, while a few sold sexual favours. As one counsellor remarked, 'Because the life is hard, the extra income from such affairs supplements the family income… often times the husbands allow it to happen'.

Lack of funding for annual leave entitlements was identified as another harmful factor. It prevented some soldiers from uniting with their wives and children, while others were unable to take their families to their home provinces during leave, thereby depriving children of the chance to learn the traditional values that participants thought could contribute towards their decent upbringing.

Nor was PNGDF providing incentives through further training, staff development, and promotion. The range of training opportunities had shrunk and stagnated since 1989, when the Bougainville crisis drained PNGDF's resources. Trade specialisation courses for caterers, medical assistants, storemen, signallers and the like, some of which had formerly been conducted in Australian military schools under the auspices of AIDAB (now AusAID) and the bilateral defence agreements, were no longer offered. The training repertoire had shrunk to military weapons handling, drills and military personnel management—largely incompatible with civilian service skill sets and therefore offering few opportunities for a livelihood beyond the PNGDF. With limited training opportunities combined with ineffective promotion procedures, many soldiers evidently saw little point in trying or planning for better things. Despite much reform since 2002, grievances about pay and conditions remain (Anon. 2007).

Awareness of STIs and HIV/AIDS

Among participants, understandings and perceptions of STIs varied, but all stated that STIs were transmitted through sexual intercourse and identified gonorrhoea as the most common infection. The discussions also showed the difficulties facing army wives. One recalled:

It took me about 3 years to become pregnant with our first child after our marriage. My husband did not have a house so I stayed in a girls' hostel in Port Moresby. He visited me at opportune times, usually when he was drunk… I had two abortions [miscarriages]. I was also treated for abdominal pain, going to the toilet frequently, pain on passing urine and offensive discharges from the birth canal. I was afraid to sleep with my husband … it was painful at times. On all occasions, the sisters diagnosed me as having PID [pelvic inflammatory disease]. I think, [tries to explain] it is a form of the illness. Twice I had to consult a medical officer. I am glad this is all over for me.

Another wife described how she would try to prevent an STI from getting into the family:

I would talk with him [husband]. We ladies, we have our own rights. Even if he beats you, you have to persist in talking to him… It is hard to stop it getting into the family, especially when the husband brings it … We just have to seek medical treatment. I cannot take up the issue with him directly. He is a man ah! In the white man's culture they understand each other – but for us Papua New Guineans, man [sic] say they are the bosses. They know everything and for the women they say, 'You are dirt. You belong to the home.' If I can't talk to him directly, personally myself, if I see him having affairs outside of the home, then I could go and seek counselling officer, or maybe I could get my family over … We ladies could feel, if the husband is having affairs outside the house. He normally gets angry over trivial things, he might belt you for no good reason and there is no more harmony … He could get all the money and spend it with ladies. The only way to sort this out with him, as a wife I should get my family over, maybe get the church members over, sit down and solve this [sic] things. As soldiers' wives we know that soldiers are not very faithful when they go for operations. As for my case, I normally tell my masta [husband]. If I see that something is not right I will tell my husband to go and get tested. We don't want to die quickly because we have kids. We ladies, we are strong. We can stay [i.e. be faithful] without husbands. It's only a few mothers who do things … majority of mothers we stay, ah. The only thing is our husbands, our husbands. They can't stay by themselves long. They want to enjoy themselves. For the safety of my kids, because I don't want to lose my kids, leave my kids hopeless, helpless, and motherless children, I will ask him to get tested… If he does not want to go, I could go on behalf of him and get tested. If I have it then it is him who gave it to me. 'I am an honest mother.' That's what I tell my husband. 'If you do not want to go, if [you] are staying in the house, then I will go on behalf of you.'

Participants knew that HIV is transmitted sexually, and some acknowledged other modes, such as mother to child. A few said that HIV is a curse from God for humanity's mischief, and one of the wives mentioned *buriburi* or magic by sorcerers, with which two others agreed (cf. Haley this volume). Beliefs concerning the treatment of AIDS differed widely. Some participants were certain that cure was possible by divine intervention and medicinal herbs (cf. Hammar this volume; Eves 2008). They understood that no cures for AIDS were available by conventional modern medicine and at that time antiretroviral therapies were hardly known and scarcely available in PNG.

All maintained that safe sex behaviours should be sex with one regular partner within marriage, use of condoms, adherence to Christian principles and avoiding places where sex is available. Soldiers accepted that their behaviours, in practice, were risky and one of the women expressed a common frustration of the wives:

> Anybody can contract HIV infection. I can get it from my husband or other way around. I do not trust my husband, he drinks and mixes around with his work-mates. I tried to discourage him but he cannot listen to me. He causes fights and go [sic] further non stop... At this point, I give up. I am fed up already. To be honest, I am very scared of my husband's behaviour. When he is drunk, he disregards the use of condom. I have to submit because he can be violent. I am in constant fear for my health and sometimes I am feel [sic] like committing suicide.

Risk Behaviours

Many of the risky behaviours of soldiers are no different from those of civilians. They include several forms of multi-partnering and the rejection or inconsistent use of condoms. Participants particularly discussed brothels and group-sex or *lainap* (cf. Jenkins this volume).

Close to the Taurama Barracks are a number of facilities for sex. One is at Three-Mile beside Port Moresby General Hospital, where soldiers go 'because the sex offered by commercial sex workers is cheaper at about K10.00 per go ... The other such outlet is in the precincts of Bisini Parade Ground where street vendors go for sex at a rate of K2.00 per go' (see Hammar this volume; Fletcher and Gonapa this volume; Stewart this volume). Habitual clients of sex-workers, noted one counsellor, 'are those with welfare problems such as separation and divorce, lack of institutional accommodation, and being rejected by their wives for fear of STIs and debilitating medical condition of their spouses'.

The practice of visiting brothels was not questioned by either soldiers or their wives. Soldiers felt that the government should legalise the sex industry so there could be controls in place to check the spread of diseases (cf. Hammar this volume; Fletcher and Gonapa this volume). As one of the officers commented, 'I would like to ask if the government could legalise things like brothels. This is to stop the little 'corner activities' which are done with a lot of risks'.

Lainap or 'line-up', also known as 'ATM' and by other terms, refers to several men having group sex with a woman. It can be a most effective way of spreading HIV (cf. Jenkins this volume; Jenkins 1996, 204) and appears to be commonly practised in the army. Condoms are sometimes worn, but the mood of the moment and the associated use of intoxicants militate against their use. According to informants in this study, pornography, and the consumption of alcohol and marijuana are often implicated in *lainaps* and other risky sexual activity.

To the question, what actually happens in *lainap*, one soldier explained, 'Doctor sir, *lainap* long unit XXXX, em everybody with pants down, some with condoms on, some "negative", "pure". *Meri em lie down long bed. Taim man i enterim room, em tok 'bend down', em meri bend down, em givim.* [Doctor, sir, line-up at unit XXXX is everybody with pants down, some with condoms on, others without condoms. When a man enters the room, he says, 'Bend down' and the lady bends down and he does it]... However some times three to one. *Wanpela long maus, wanpela long kan, wanpela long as* [one orally, one vaginally, and one anally].' If one man takes too long, they call "*Hariap, hariap, kapsait hariap na* next one" [hurry up, hurry up, release quickly and next one].'

The number of men said to be involved can range from a few to as many as a whole battalion. Soldiers in the FGDs commented, 'In a single barrack, the entire barrack's occupants could take part', up to 100 to 200 men, depending on the lady's attitude: 'Some would call out and stop the event but others can continue'. While the men participating could be either single or married, *lainaps* almost always occur in the single barracks.

The women involved, according to one counsellor, 'come from different sources':

> Sometimes it is daughters or relatives of soldiers living within the barracks... Some parents do not know of their daughters' activities. Some ... turn a blind eye.

Others are picked up at nightspots. Some come from brothels. Some, it was said, do it for fun and pleasure. Others do it for financial reasons but this seems rare. Others are forced. This force could be applied directly outside the barracks to bring the female in, or applied after she had entered the barracks voluntarily.

Condoms

Male condoms have a relatively long history in the PNGDF. They were originally introduced by the Australian army as a means of family planning and preventing STIs. At the time of this study they were provided as part of the standard ration pack, and were also available through the health service for soldiers, spouses and their teenage children. Most people in the study understood the use of the male condom. The female condom seemed less known. Health workers had never demonstrated it to the wives.

Male condoms were in some measure accepted by soldiers. As one NCO remarked, 'Carrying condoms in your ration pack is like wearing your boots. It is similar to any safety precaution you take like wearing your helmet or boots. Therefore carrying condoms as part of your ration pack is a good idea'. Wives too, as one of the extracts has already illustrated, saw condoms as providing some protection against STIs. But a number of qualifications about condoms emerged in discussion and reflect views held in the broader community.

Among men, the popular attitude of 'flesh to flesh is real sex' seemed to prevail: 'Still many soldiers are not using condoms despite being available free. Many soldiers prefer sexual intercourse without condoms because they say it is more satisfying. The common saying is "flesh to flesh is much better than *gumi* [condom] and flesh".'

Several participants, and nearly all the wives, thought that condoms did not offer 100 percent protection. They claimed to have witnessed STIs, pregnancies and lately HIV infections in couples who used them. It was unclear whether the study participants thought that a defect in the condoms was to blame, or human failing by not using them consistently (cf. Wardlow 2008, 196–197). As one of the quotes above has indicated, wives certainly saw alcohol as causing men to lose self-control and thus compromise the use of condoms, while more fundamentally both men and women described the male sex drive as precluding right thinking and careful action.

Wives also maintained that condoms promoted promiscuity and this view was prevalent among the soldiers themselves: 'With issue of condoms I feel that we are encouraging sex'; 'If they do not have condoms, the fear of acquiring sickness can act as a deterrent'; and 'Condoms should be discouraged. It encourages sex so government should do away with condoms'.

Male Bonding, Sexual Development and Sex Drive

Among the factors that male participants mentioned as influencing their sexual behaviour were: peer pressure; the way men developed sexually within the culture of PNGDF; and the male sex drive (cf. Eves this volume; Jenkins this volume). Soldiers acknowledged the irresistible force of male bonding. 'You will see that in the disciplinary forces, it's a bit different to the civilians. There is a kind of bond or comradeship among the troops. So when a mate brings a woman and tells his mate, and if his mate refuses, he will say, "You must be a woman. You talked of bringing women and you did not show up". This comradeship exists … If the mate refuses, that mate will be told, "You are not my good mate".'

The pressure to conform is almost impossible for a man to withstand. One soldier confessed, '*Mi pret long mi yet* [I am so very scared]. I cannot have that courage to say that, "Gentleman, No. Thank you for the offer, I have to go. I have a family to look after. Here is K5.00. Put it together and buy your beer but I have to go home". There is no courage in our soldiers. If only I had the courage.'

Soldiers also noted that the army shaped the development of soldiers' adult sexual behaviours. Recruits join the force as youths. Some have little prior experience of sex or of dealings with members of the opposite sex. If their sexual initiation takes the form of risky sexual acts, this will, they believed, affect the soldiers' later life. In the FGD, participants commented on the lack of sex education for kids and teenagers. For recruits, 'the sex education they get is the existing "sex culture" of the defence force'. In the army, young men do not have the opportunity to develop their character through civilian activities outside the military community and in day-to-day interaction with women. As one explained:

> We go out to do our shopping, banking, or military exercises and we come back. We do not have much association with women through civic exercise. That is why *planti taim yumi ol soldier go out long nait club na yumi* come across *long ol meri, yumi laik,* just go there and drink, *na* our aim is to grab a women, come back to our unit, *na enjoyim pleasures wantaim em* [That is why, often when we go out to night clubs, our aim is to go, drink, grab a women, come back to our units and enjoy pleasures with her.]

Soldiers (and their wives) also believe that men are subject to an overwhelming sexual drive. In the words of one soldier, 'Mi no tok body pleasure—body pleasure em in English. *Mi tok Pidgin, em body blong me needim. Body blong mi em needim tru* [I am not saying body pleasure… body pleasure, it's English. If I say it in Pidgin, my body really needs it. My body really needs it.] [Facial expression indicating a desperate need of something].' The remarks of another soldier also show one of the ways in which defence personnel may serve as bridges of infection in communities to which military operations take them:

> OK, the problem now comes back to us and our desires. How can we control our desires? Soldier is a colourful man in the world. When the soldier goes in full battle gear into a village all the ladies are saying, 'Look! That guy with the big bag – he is the medicine man, oh! That guy must be the boss!' [said with pointing fingers, eyes wide with wonder]. Three ladies will come to me, another four will go to another guy. How can I control myself?

The PNGDF's Response to HIV and AIDS

In many respects, the PNGDF has been in the forefront of the response to HIV in PNG. Army medical personnel, since their involvement in the care of the country's first reported case of AIDS in 1987, have contributed significantly both to the national response and more particularly to the PNGDF's. The army was the first government body to frame an HIV/AIDS policy, under which HIV-positive soldiers are protected from discrimination and allowed to remain within the force. When HIV-positive personnel are discharged, it is usually at their own request, and they are allowed to resign with full entitlements. In 2004 an HIV Committee was formed at PNGDF Headquarters to coordinate all levels of response.

Soldiers who are sick are cared for either in hospital or at home. Medical treatment for soldiers is free of charge. The PNGDF's medical capacity to deal with HIV has been building, through general efforts to upgrade army health facilities and training, for instance through the PNGDF's partnership with the Chinese National Defence Ministry (Gerawa 2008; Wakus 2005), and through specific measures targeting HIV and AIDS. Since 2005, the US Department of Defense HIV/AIDS Prevention Program (DHAPP), in collaboration with Joint United Nations Program on HIV/AIDS, AusAID, Family Health International and PNG National AIDS Council, has funded the renovation and outfitting of five voluntary counselling and testing centres for the military—at Taurama Barracks, Murray Barracks, Goldie Barracks, Igam Barracks and Moem Barracks—and necessary training for counsellors, pharmacists, nurses and physicians (DHAPP 2006). The PNGDF also supports a program for home-based care for people living with HIV that involves a cross-section of the PNGDF community while military sites have been targeted by major programs supporting community responses to HIV, such as the Tingim Laip ('Think about Life') Project (NHASP 2006, 26-29; Elder 2008, 12–19; 26–31). HIV initiatives within the army may have produced a relatively high awareness of HIV. Among adult male workers in private industries and the military surveyed for the National AIDS Council Secretariat, soldiers were the group with by far the most comprehensive knowledge of HIV and its prevention, and the most positive attitudes to people living with HIV or AIDS (NACS 2006, 31–32). The PNGDF has also assumed a role in the warehousing and distribution of condoms, following publicity about the fact that millions of condoms ordered by the National Department of Health had languished in storage and passed their use-by date (Taimbari 2009; Joku 2009).

The authors of this chapter remain grateful to the men and women who generously contributed to this study and to the PNGDF leadership for their response to HIV within the force. In conclusion we stress that many of the risks participants identified and the perceptions they shared, if often accentuated by army conditions, reflect risks and perceptions in the broader community too. In discussing some sexual behaviour as risky or destructive, many participants expressed personal ambivalence and even unhappiness. This in turn, suggests the possibility of traction for change in this difficult area.

References

Anis, Alison. 2009. Women Recruits Take up Duties as Soldiers. *National*, 7 December 2009.

Anon. 2007. Parade Called Off. *PNG Post-Courier*, 7 December 2007.

Barnett, Tony and Gwyn Prins. 2005. *HIV/AIDS and Security: Fact, Fiction and Evidence. A report to UNAIDS*. London: London School of Economics. Available. http://www.lse.ac.uk/collections/DESTIN/publink/barnett/asb06a.htm (accessed 27 April 2010).

DHAPP (DoD HIV/AIDS Prevention Program). 2006. DoD HIV/AIDS Prevention Program (DHAP) Activity Report January–March 2006. Papua New Guinea.

Elbe, Stefan. 2003. *Strategic Implications of HIV/AIDS*. International Institute for Strategic Studies, Adelphi Paper 357. Oxford: Oxford University Press.

Engels, John. 2008. *Tingim Laip: Success Stories from New Guinea*. Waigani: Family Health International.

Eves, Richard. 2008. Moral Reform and Miraculous Cures: Christian Healing and AIDS in Rural New Ireland, Papua New Guinea. In *Making Sense of AIDS: Culture, Sexuality, and Power in Melanesia*, ed. Leslie Butt and Richard Eves, 206–223. Honolulu: University of Hawai'i Press.

Gerawa, Maureen. 2008. Chinese Team Opens Clinic. *Post-Courier*, 13 June 2008.

Jenkins, Carol L. 1996. The Homosexual Context of Heterosexual Practice in Papua New Guinea. In *Bisexualities and AIDS: International Perspectives*, ed. Peter Aggleton, 191–206. Bristol, Pa: Taylor and Francis.

Joku, Harlyne. 2009. 2 Million Condoms go to Waste! *Post-Courier*, 4 March 2009.

Kendino, Gideon H and Ralph D. Kaule. 2005. HIV/AIDS Military Study Tour Report. National HIV/AIDS Support Project, High Risk Settings Strategy Report: Moving beyond Awareness. Milestone 90, Annex 7, 64–68.

Kershaw, R. J. 2008. *The Impact of HIV/AIDS on the Operational Effectiveness of Military Forces*. ASCI Research Report No. 4, April 2008, AIDS, Security and Confict Initiative. www.asci.ssrc.org.

Laki, James and R. J. May. 2009. Policy Making in Defence. In Policy *Making and Implementation: Studies from Papua New Guinea*, ed. R. J.May, 261–279. Canberra: ANU E Press.

May, R. J. 2004. Government and the Military in Papua New Guinea. In *Military and Democracy in Asia and the Pacific*, ed. R. J. May and Viberto Selodian, 148–175. Canberra: ANU E Press.

NACS (National AIDS Council Secretariat). 2006. HIV/AIDS Behavioural Surveillance Survey within High Risk Settings. BSS Round 1. [Boroko]: National AIDS Council Secretariat.

NHASP (National HIV/AIDS Support Project. 2006. High Risk Settings Strategy Report: Moving Beyond Awareness. Milestone 90. Revised July 2006.

Pantumari, Joachim and Peter Bamne. 2002. A Perception of Factors Associated with HIV/AIDS Infection among Soldiers in Port Moresby, Papua New Guinea. Masters of Public Health Thesis. Port Moresby: University of Papua New Guinea.

Steven, Charles. 2004. Epidemic Threatens Grave Ravages for our Defence. *Post-Courier*, 8th July 2004: 16.

Taimbari, Fredah. 2009. PNGDF Allocates Warehouse for Condom Storage and Distribution. *Bung Wantaim* 13: 2.

Wakus, Wanita. 2005. Training for Army Doctors. *Post-Courier*, 3 October 2005.

Wardlow, Holly. 2008. 'You have to Understand: Some of Us are Glad AIDS has Arrived': Christianity and Condoms among the Huli, Papua New Guinea. In *Making Sense of AIDS: Culture, Sexuality, and Power in Melanesia*, ed. Leslie Butt and Richard Eves, 187–205. Honolulu: University of Hawai'i Press.

Whiteside, Alan, Alex de Waal and Tsadkan Gebre-Tensae. 2006. AIDS, Security and the Military in Africa: A Sober Appraisal. *African Affairs* 105/409: 201–218.

10. Mainstreaming HIV and AIDS in the Law and Justice Sector

IAN PATRICK

The HIV epidemic in Papua New Guinea (PNG) demands effective responses from national leaders and public sector organisations charged with maintaining public health and more broadly promoting citizen welfare. These challenges are heightened in a complex sector such as law and justice—comprising six major agencies and two offices.[1]

This chapter explores opportunities and challenges for advancing a 'mainstreaming' response to HIV in the law and justice sector. [2] Mainstreaming requires an organisation to adapt its core business to address HIV and AIDS. This approach is equally applicable to public sector, private sector and civil society organisations. Mainstreaming is a key strategy in AusAID's support for strengthening coordination and capacity within partner countries for national responses to HIV (AusAID 2009, 23; AusAID 2006, 18, 21, 23).

What does a mainstreaming approach in the law and justice sector involve? How can development partners help this process? Two case studies concerning HIV initiatives within AusAID-suported law and justice projects will be discussed here. Although these initiatives were not designed as 'mainstreaming' measures they illuminate lessons for a mainstreaming approach. These initiatives were incorporated within the Royal Papua New Guinea Constabulary Development Project Phase III (2000–2005) (see also McLeod and Macintyre this volume), and the Correctional Services Development Project Phase II (2000–2003) and have informed LJSP's continuing response to HIV and AIDS.

---

1   Department of Justice and Attorney General, National Judicial Staff Services, Ombudsman Commission, Royal Papua New Guinea Constabulary, Correctional Services, Magisterial Services, Office of the Public Prosecutor and Office of the Public Solicitor.

2   This chapter draws on a review (Patrick 2005) conducted for AusAID in the period February to April 2005 that examined eight programs/projects supported by AusAID that had HIV/AIDS elements. These projects were located across a range of sectors including law and justice. Both of the case studies included in this paper were examined in the review. The review involved examination of AusAID and program/project documentation, and conduct of a wide range of interviews with stakeholders across government departments, managing contractors, AusAID, NHASP and NACS. The results of these interviews are used here.

Notions of Mainstreaming

Mainstreaming is 'a process that enables development actors to address the causes and effects of HIV/AIDS in an effective and sustained manner, both through their usual work and their workplace' (UNAIDS 2004, 4). It might, for example, involve an agriculture ministry adapting its extension work to focus on AIDS-affected families; or the judicial system introducing new codes of practice to protect the rights of people infected or affected by HIV or AIDS.

Throughout the 1990s, the limitations of a uni-focused, health-led response, typically delivered within a medical context, became increasingly clear. This led to the recognition that a universal, multisectoral approach to the epidemic was needed, involving many sectors such as education, law and justice, and infrastructure (United Nations 2001; UNAIDS and World Bank 2001; UNAIDS 2003, 2004). While a multisectoral approach retains specific HIV interventions, such as counselling and treatment, it also includes the adoption of a mainstreamed response that fundamentally requires sectors and their constituent organisations to adapt their core business to address HIV.

'Mainstreaming' challenges development actors to broaden their understanding and analysis of HIV and AIDS, including how they themselves can contribute, usually inadvertently, to HIV's spread. All sectors and their constituent organisations must answer the following questions:

- How might they be contributing to the spread of HIV?
- In what areas does their sector have a comparative advantage for limiting HIV's spread and mitigating the epidemic's impact?
- How is the epidemic likely to affect the goals, objectives and programs of the sector/organization?
- What context-specific actions, backed by sufficient resources, are required to address identified areas (UNAIDS and GTZ 2002, 5; SDC 2004,19)?

Good Practice in Mainstreaming

Good practice principles for HIV mainstreaming (eg. Wilkins and Vasani 2002; UNDP 2002; UNAIDS and GTZ 2002; Elsey and Kutengule 2003; UNAIDS 2004; SDC 2004) suggest that effective mainstreaming needs to

- be strategic and coordinated: initiatives in each sector must clearly link to a national HIV strategy, with active coordination between national/ sectoral coordinating bodies and implementing organisations. Partnerships for sharing knowledge and resources should also be developed and gaps in service provision filled.

- be based on a sector's or organisation's comparative advantage: initiatives should follow an analysis identifying areas of sectoral/organisational responsibility and how the most efficient and effective response can be made.

- occur in both the internal and external domains: for example, through an organisation both training its staff and working externally with clients/ beneficiaries in order to reduce risk and vulnerability to HIV.

- promote appropriate capacity-building: initiatives need to build the necessary commitment, knowledge and skills required for mainstreaming amongst staff and policy makers. Ideally, initiatives should strengthen existing institutional and community structures, rather than create new structures.

- address other cross-cutting issues: HIV responses need particularly to focus on and respond to issues of gender, participation and sustainability, because they critically inter-relate with HIV and the effectiveness of initiatives.

The above principles suggest that initiatives need to extend well beyond 'awareness raising' for staff which is the 'classic', superficial and limited response (Wilkins and Vasani 2002). Elsey and Kutengule (2003), for example, state that the range of organisational responses may include:

- putting in place policies and practices that protect staff from vulnerability to infection and support staff who are living with HIV and its impacts; ensure that training and recruitment consider future staff depletion rates; and consider the disruption caused by increased morbidity and mortality.

- refocusing the organisation's work to ensure those infected and affected by HIV are included and able to benefit from the organisation's activities.

- ensuring that an organisation's activities do not increase the vulnerability to HIV and other STIs in the communities with which it works, or undermine community options for coping with the epidemic's effects.

A Shift to a Multisectoral Approach and Mainstreaming

The two initiatives examined here were attempts to build organisational commitment and response to HIV within two major AusAID projects that were designed during the late 1990s and originally included no HIV provisions. Rather, responses were added during implementation, due to concern about

PNG's worsening epidemic and a new commitment to a multisectoral response. While this commitment was already growing generally in PNG, AusAID advocacy and the personal experience of individual consultants contributed.

A shift to a multisectoral approach was reflected in a series of national plans from the late 1990s (Government of PNG 1998; NAC 2004; 2006). Matching this intent, from early 2001 AusAID began actively working with contractors of existing projects across a range of sectors to promote responses to HIV. It also supported the appointment of a multisectoral advisor within its major National HIV/AIDS Support Program (NHASP) to initiate, in conjunction with the PNG National AIDS Council Secretariat (NACS), a broad range of responses across the country.

Commitment to HIV mainstreaming in different government sectors followed. While not reflected in the formal HIV/AIDS national plans, mainstreaming was informally endorsed by members of the National AIDS Council (NAC) and National AIDS Council Secretariat (NACS) from around 2004. Correspondingly, within AusAID a mainstreaming strategy was adopted for the PNG Branch in 2004, and a mainstreaming advisor was engaged in the same year to promote this approach. Because neither of the initiatives reviewed here was designed as a mainstreaming measure, they should not be judged on this basis in terms of performance. The experience of the projects, however, highlights potentials, shortfalls and continuing challenges for a mainstreaming approach.

Case Studies

Royal Papua New Guinea Constabulary Development Project Phase III (2000–2005)

This five-year project built on 12 years of Australian development assistance to the Royal Papua New Guinea Constabulary (RPNGC) with a focus on community policing, human resource management (including discipline processes), infrastructure refurbishment, and improved systems and training to enhance RPNGC capacity to analyse, prevent, investigate and prosecute crime (AusAID 2001). The project budget for Phase III was AUD 60 million.

In 2001, the project was redesigned to include an emphasis on 'integrating HIV/AIDS awareness into project activities' (see McLeod and Macintyre this volume). The redesign document acknowledged that the police community has a high HIV risk profile (see Jenkins this volume). The broader context for the introduction of HIV/AIDS initiatives in the Constabulary involved efforts to promote partnerships with the community, improve corporate planning, address gender bias and inequality in the police, and minimise crime against women.

Activities

The approach proposed to 'integrate' HIV into all appropriate project activities, and more generally into police training and operations. Major initiatives included the generation of a training package in conjunction with NACS. The focus was on awareness-raising and changing operational procedures. Areas covered included basic facts about HIV and AIDS; modes of transmission; relationship with other infectious diseases, particularly hepatitis; police operational contexts for HIV and AIDS, particularly cell hygiene; professional conduct; and gender issues. The package became a standard component of training for recruits. It also became the focus of dedicated in-service training and was incorporated into most other training, including community policing and decentralised training in the provinces and districts.

Other initiatives included a limited number of awareness-raising events with police families and policewomen; a review of police operational procedures to identify areas of HIV risk; promotion of linkages between the Constabulary and outside organisations also addressing HIV and AIDS such as NACS, Consultative Implementation and Monitoring Committee (CIMC) and its Family Sexual Violence Committee, Department of Health, Anglicare, and Individual and Community Rights Advocacy Forum (ICRAF) (an NGO with a gender and human rights focus); and several community theatre events that aimed to increase awareness of HIV together with other social issues.

Outcomes

The major outcome was the wide-scale incorporation of HIV issues into police training. Views of police management and consultants suggested that levels of awareness amongst police improved as a result and that police perceived a connection between their operational practice, personal behaviour and HIV and AIDS more clearly. [3] This perception may have extended to the connection between gender and HIV and AIDS. Some operational practices may have altered as a result of the training, for example safer handling of detainees. There was, however, far less certainty about whether training had led to a shift in personal attitudes and behaviours of police in relation to HIV and AIDS (see McLeod and

---

3 Interviews conducted as part of Review of AusAID Multisectoral HIV Initiatives in Papua New Guinea (Patrick 2005) that involved senior management of RPNGC, and consultants of RPNGC Development Project Phase II and Law and Justice Sector Program.

Macintyre this volume). Informants suggested that awareness-raising efforts among police families, particularly in the barracks, were less effective, largely due to their infrequency and didactic methods.

As a further outcome, management began taking HIV more seriously, leading to plans to develop an agency policy in response to the HIV/AIDS Management and Prevention (HAMP) Act (2003) (see Stewart this volume; McLeod and Macintyre this volume). Also discussed was the establishment of a designated coordinator position within the police based in the HR Division, to pull together and link various HIV initiatives across the agency. And a firmer basis was provided for further HIV initiatives, in peer education (supported by the EU), and awareness training in the National Capital District (supported by Save the Children Fund).

Issues

Despite progress, by the project's end a range of issues had become apparent. These included a perceived need to take HIV initiatives to a new level: to promote wider changes in attitudes, and operational and personal practice, in order to reduce HIV risk. Related needs included concern to have HIV issues better reflected in agency policy and strategy (for example in corporate plans and HR policy); stronger education on the link between HIV transmission and gender inequality; and the need to coordinate a range of HIV and AIDS activities across the agency funded by different donors and NGOs.

Correctional Services Development Project Phase II (CDSP) (2000–2003)

CSDP aimed to strengthen the operation and management of prisons (AusAID 2000). Phase II of the project was designed as an extension of earlier assistance to Correctional Services (CS) and had a major focus on 'increasing the responsiveness of the PNG justice system to community needs'. This reflected increased recognition of the inter-relationship and interdependence of many parts of the justice system in improving safety and security, and a desire to improve, ultimately, conditions for agency clients through technical assistance. The project budget for Phase II was AUD 20 million.

Activities

In contrast to the original design, Phase II of CSDP included specific HIV initiatives, one output of which was increased HIV awareness among staff, their families and detainees (see Law this volume). Major HIV-related activities included strategy development and training. The CS HIV/AIDS and Other Infectious Diseases Strategy (September 2001) was developed in close collaboration with NACS and included measures relating to human resources, education, prevention, treatment, counselling, testing and care for people living with HIV (PLHIV), and support for affected families. The strategy was distributed to all PNG government agencies as a model.

Training courses for staff and a small number of long-term detainees operated in 2001 and 2002. It was intended that the trainees would in turn lead awareness-raising activities in institutions. Training was developed in conjunction with NACS. Minor activities included preparation of a poster and distribution of other materials for display in institutions; a poster competition amongst detainees; and display of HIV awareness materials in prison vans.

Outcomes

The HIV/AIDS and Other Infectious Diseases Strategy represented the agency's strengthened commitment to respond to HIV, but results of implementation were inconsistent. Well-developed and enthusiastic responses occurred in some institutions, particularly larger institutions which also hosted formal training programs. In some cases, well-developed peer education programs and complementary awareness-raising sessions were mounted. Senior CS staff suggested that HIV activities may have led to better care of PLHIV in prisons and reduced stigmatisation. Support from institution commanders was essential for what was perceived as a sensitive topic. Attitudes towards the acceptability of condom distribution in institutions, for example, differed widely. Regrettably, staff families received little of the attention intended for them.

The initiatives implemented with support from CSDP provided a firmer basis for several subsequent initiatives with other donors or projects. These included a trial Peer Education project (EU), awareness-raising sessions by Anglicare (involving PLHIV) within all correctional institutions and surrounding communities, and activities under the Tingim Laip project (Elder 2009).

Issues

The need to translate aspects of the CS HIV/AIDS and Other Infectious Diseases Strategy into other areas of agency policy-making, particularly HR, and better implement the strategy became clear. Broader structural constraints within the agency—concerning resources, systems for monitoring and support, and developed management systems—hampered implementation. Subsequently initiatives have been introduced within CS to improve linkages between the centre and correctional institutions.

Unfortunately resources were inadequate for in-service training to reinforce HIV awareness and commitment, though an officer in CS who had a part-time, but dedicated responsibility for HIV and AIDS was valuable in stimulating concern. Historically, efforts to address HIV within the agency show a pattern of activity followed by subsidence, corresponding to receipt of donor funding. The lapse into relative inactivity reflects a lack of resources and stimulus by technical assistance, but also broader issues of competing priorities for management.

Assessment of Projects against Mainstreaming Principles

Both initiatives educated staff and raised commitment to respond to HIV within their respective institutions. Both also reflected the intrinsic value of a multisectoral approach through increasing the level of coverage and range of contexts in which HIV and AIDS are addressed. In general, however, the projects did not support a shift in their organisations' core business. Such a shift is fundamental to the mainstreaming approach. Rather, HIV was integrated into existing activities. The following analysis assesses the two initiatives against the principles of good practice in mainstreaming.

Responses are Strategic and Coordinated

The initiatives reviewed here were consistent with the support of national plans for a multisectoral approach to HIV and AIDS (Government of PNG 1998; NAC 2004, 2006). The CS attempted to align its HIV/AIDS and Other Infectious Diseases Strategy to national priorities, and both implementing organisations received material resources and developed training courses with assistance from the National AIDS Council. Yet, as suggested by key stakeholders in both implementing agencies, there appeared to be considerable potential for NAC to strengthen its coordinating and leadership role, by advising on the fit between organisational plans and national policy/strategy and facilitating partnerships between implementing and resource organisations.

Responses are Based on a Sector's/Organisation's Comparative Advantage

A mainstreaming approach based on comparative advantage requires a sector/ organisation to analyse its relationship and responsibility with regard to HIV and AIDS, and then define its most appropriate strategy. Modification or refinement of core functions, missions, objectives and programs may follow, in contrast to simply 'adding on' separate HIV components to existing programs. The generation by the CS of HIV/AIDS and Other Infectious Diseases Strategy came closest to this kind of approach, but to strengthen it, more was still needed from central planning functions within the CS, including its corporate plan and budget. For the Constabulary, undertaking a strategic analysis of its relationship to HIV and AIDS and identifying appropriate responses remained tasks for the future (see McLeod and Macintyre this volume).

Responses Occur in both the Internal and External Domains

The main strength and focus of the two initiatives was within the internal domain: staff education. The work of CS came closest to the best practice of acting in both internal and external domains by also educating its clients about HIV through staff and peer education. Consolidating this approach would involve a more explicit and detailed analysis of the range of HIV risks that detainees experience, within and outside correctional institutions, and developing appropriate responses to these contexts (see Law this volume). This would include preparation for release. For the Constabulary, the training programs emphasised personal protection of police, safe operational practices (such as in handling of bleeding detainees), and also warned against police engaging in unlawful assault and opportunistic sexual behaviour (see Jenkins this volume; McLeod and Macintyre this volume). As with CS, attempts to alter police behaviour and improve the quality of engagement with clients require a range of measures that extend well beyond training. These include attention to management, discipline and supervision, and direct learning from the community regarding concerns about HIV and AIDS.

In order to broaden organisational responses to HIV, the development and promotion of an organisational model for mainstreaming, adaptable to different contexts and needs, could cover areas such as training, policy and strategy development, developing service linkages and partnerships, and developing detailed implementation plans.

Reponses Promote Appropriate Capacity-building

Both projects involved capacity-building, introducing new awareness and commitment, and particularly in CS, new approaches to addressing HIV and AIDS. Achievements in building 'understanding' amongst staff were, however, limited to awareness-raising about the epidemic, how HIV is transferred, and personal protection measures. A broader challenge is to assist staff to develop analytical and planning abilities so that they can see the relevance of what they do in their daily work to the epidemic. This remains a challenge in both institutions, and more broadly across the law and justice sector.

Responses Address Other Cross-Cutting Issues: particularly Gender, Participation and Sustainability

While concepts of gender have generally been central to responses to HIV (see Eves this volume) and the Constabulary, with support from the RPNGC Development Project, introduced gender elements into training of police officers (see McLeod and Macintyre this volume), overall, the primary concern of training in both projects related to HIV risk and personal protection from a medical and/ or behavioural perspective. This tends to downplay the importance of broader social determinants of HIV, such as endemic gender violence and women's lack of power (see Eves this volume). The HIV/AIDS and Other Infectious Diseases Strategy developed by CS did contain some gender-sensitive initiatives such as recognition of the protection needs of female detainees. Overall, however, the initiatives showed limited appreciation of the connection between HIV and gender inequality and a need for explicit gender analysis in the design of HIV initiatives was highlighted.

The CS initiative demonstrated a participatory approach. The department sought to build support amongst staff and management through generation of its HIV/ AIDS and Other Infectious Diseases Strategy. The success of the integration of HIV training with the Constabulary relied on efforts to work closely with the training section as a whole and build the initiative into on-going work plans. A broader challenge in both implementing organisations is to build participation and coordination between different sections undertaking HIV-related work. The achievements of CS, albeit limited, in involving long-term detainees as peer trainers, reinforced the effectiveness of HIV initiatives and provided a basis on which to build. Both agencies also attempted to involve a broader group of stakeholders in awareness-building, particularly staff families who commonly reside in compounds surrounding institutions. While this outreach was limited, further extension promised to reinforce the value of educational work with staff.

Efforts to build staff participation and develop strategies to guide and legitimatise initiatives were perceived by stakeholders as reinforcing sustainability. The HIV/AIDS and Other Infectious Diseases Strategy in Correctional Services, for example, was seen as continuing to provide impetus for the HIV response within the agency. A tendency for HIV initiatives to wane with the cessation of direct donor and advisor support was noted. This trend highlights the need to reinforce the status of HIV in corporate and annual agency plans, and to seek core support in sector budgets.

Conclusion

This analysis of responses to HIV and AIDS in PNG, and specifically within two law and justice agencies, highlights a phase in the evolution of the sector's commitment and skills to respond to HIV—a sector that has potential to contribute vitally to the national response.

PNG's epidemic has been described as both generalised and concentrated. While mainstreaming promotes a systemic response that is particularly valuable for countries experiencing a generalised epidemic (AusAID 2009; UNAIDS 2004, 2), it also leverages the advantages that organisations, such as CS and RPNGC, have to influence the potentially concentrated epidemiological dynamics related to prisons, sex work and gender violence. Mainstreaming enables organisations to strengthen the ways in which they help reduce susceptibility to HIV infection among themselves and among the people they serve and implies that they too identify and minimise unintended negative effects of their own work.

The demand to mainstream HIV places additional strains upon public sector organisations in developing countries such as PNG that commonly have weak capacity and a poor service orientation. It may be regarded, however, as a pre-emptive step that addresses the underlying susceptibility and vulnerability of communities to infection (UNAIDS 2004). Experience in African countries highlights how the challenges of doing so are compounded in the context of epidemics which have progressed to higher level of HIV prevalence.

The good practice principles identified in this paper, although validated in the international literature, taken as whole do however represent a somewhat idealised response. Developing a mainstreaming approach in countries such as PNG is an incremental process requiring capacity-building within implementing organisations and clear starting points (UNAIDS and GTZ 2002). International experience suggests that organisations most effectively commence mainstreaming by promoting HIV awareness, knowledge and commitment among staff. Beginning with prevention activities, and in particular awareness raising and condom distribution (Elsey and Kutengule 2003), organisations then commonly undertake further and more ambitious planning, particularly in the external domain. Such a trend is suggested by the two case studies examined in this paper. As Butcher has stressed, 'Mainstreaming does not replace the need for AIDS work' (Butcher 2006, 5), such as awareness-raising, condom distribution and medical provision. Such work absorbs the bulk of AusAID funding, and is complementary to mainstreaming and is some senses a prerequisite.

The adoption of mainstreaming relies on developing a clear understanding of the meaning, intent and scope of the approach and its applicability to various organisations. This is likely to involve the incorporation and extension of initiatives such as those reviewed here within what will be a broader and more ambitious approach. A key aspect of this change will be for implementing organisations to move beyond 'integration'. Adding elements such as HIV training or curriculum development makes a start. The broader challenge is for organisations to assess their connection with the epidemic, identify their responsibilities, and delineate their responses in relationship to their core mandate. A mainstreaming response assists organisations to look outside their immediate institutional concerns and examine how they can assist in reducing levels of risk and vulnerability to HIV in populations with whom they work.

In the case of the law and justice sector, these issues are more obviously immediate and pertinent than in many other sectors. Safety and security in community settings, vulnerability of women, knowledge of legal rights and access to justice for marginalised people bear directly on the spread of HIV and the impacts of AIDS (see Luker and Dinnen, this volume). A significant enabling factor for mainstreaming in this sector will be access to viable methodologies, associated analytical tools and expertise. Donors such as AusAID play a role in this respect, but effective national leadership and coordination remain the basic, necessary precondition.

References

AusAID. 2000. Correctional Services Development Project—Phase II Extension Design Document. Port Moresby: AusAID.

AusAID. 2001. Royal PNG Constabulary Development Project Phase III Scope of Services. Port Moresby: AusAID.

AusAID. 2009. Intensifying the Response: Halting the Spread of HIV: Australia's International Development Strategy for HIV. Canberra: AusAID.

AusAID. 2006. Responding to HIV/AIDS in Papua New Guinea: Australia's Strategy to Support Papua New Guinea 2006-10. Canberra: AusAID.

Butcher, Kate. 2006. Mainstreaming HIV into AusAID's development portfolio in Papua New Guinea. Canberra: AusAID.

Elder, John. 2009. *Tingim Paip: Success Stories from Papua New Guinea.* [no place of publication stated] Family Health International.

Elsey, H. and P. Kutengule. 2003. *HIV/AIDS Mainstreaming: A Definition, Some Experiences and Strategies.* HIV-AIDS-STI Knowledge Programme and HERD. South Africa: University of Natal. http://gametlibrary.worldbank.org/FILES/454_ HIV%20mainstreaming%20experiences.pdf (accessed 27 April 2010).

Government of PNG. 1998. Papua New Guinea National HIV/AIDS Medium Term Plan 1998—2002. Port Moresby: Government of PNG.

NAC (Papua New Guinea National AIDS Council). 2004. *Papua New Guinea National Strategic Plan on HIV/AIDS 2004–2008*. Port Moresby: National AIDS Council.

NAC (Papua New Guinea National AIDS Council). 2006. *Papua New Guinea National Strategic Plan on HIV/AIDS 2006-2010*. Port Moresby: National AIDS Council.

Patrick, I. 2005. Review of AusAID Multisectoral HIV Initiatives in Papua New Guinea. Canberra: AusAID.

SDC (Swiss Agency for Development Cooperation). 2004. *Mainstreaming HIV/AIDS in Practice*. Berne: SDC. http://www.deza.ch/ressources/deza_product_en_1280.pdf (accessed 27 April 2010).

UNAIDS. 2003. *Progress Report on the Global Response to the HIV/AIDS Epidemic* (Follow-up to the 2001 United Nations General Assembly Special Session on HIV/AIDS). Geneva: UNAIDS. http://data.unaids.org/TOPICS/UNGASS2003/UNGASS_Report_2003_en.pdf (accessed 27 April 2010).

UNAIDS. 2004. Support to Mainstreaming AIDS in Development. *UNAIDS Secretariat Strategy Note and Action Framework 2004—2005*. Geneva: UNAIDS. http://www.afronets.org/files/MS%20Strategy%20Note.pdf (accessed 27 April 2010).

UNAIDS and World Bank. 2001. *AIDS, Poverty Reduction and Debt Relief: A Toolkit for Mainstreaming HIV/AIDS into Development Instruments*. Geneva: UNAIDS. http://data.unaids.org/Publications/IRC-pub02/JC536-Toolkit_en.pdf (accessed 27 April 2010).

UNAIDS and GTZ. 2002. *Mainstreaming HIV/AIDS: A Conceptual Framework and Implementing Principles*. Accra, Ghana: UNAIDS. http://www.afronets.org/files/mainstream.pdf (accessed 27 April 2010).

UNDP. 2002. Conceptual Shifts for Sound Planning. Towards an Integrated Approach to HIV/AIDS and Poverty. Pretoria: UNDP. http://www.sarpn.org.za/documents/d0000130/Conseptual_shifts_for_sound_plannig.pdf (accessed 27 April 2010).

United Nations. 2001. Declaration of Commitment on HIV/AIDS. United Nations Assembly Special Session on HIV/AIDS 25—27 June 2001, Geneva: United Nations.

Wilkins, Marissa and Dolar Vasani. 2002. *Mainstreaming HIV/AIDS: Looking Beyond Awareness*. VSO Experience in Focus series. London: Voluntary Service Overseas.

Governance, Rights and Security

11. Witchcraft, Torture and HIV

NICOLE HALEY

After questioning us further, they dragged me over to the Casuarina trees. They tied ropes around my hands and legs and tied me to one of the trees. I protested, 'I am not a witch, I have done nothing'. They then dragged my mother to the other side and tied her between two Casuarina trees as well. My mother said, 'I don't know what you have planned for me, but let me pray first'. While she was praying they were heating an iron bar. It was not just any piece of iron, they had fashioned it such that it was like a fishing spear with two hooks on the end. She prayed and just as soon as she said 'Amen' they got that iron bar and thrust it into her vagina. They cooked her vagina and ripped out her uterus. The smell was unbelievable. ....I couldn't do anything to help my mother as they had tied me up good and proper... That night it rained constantly. They left us there, just the two of us in the rain. While it was raining MP [a local pastor] came. He touched my body all over and said 'I was feeling sorry for you, so I've come to loosen the ropes' .... He continued touching me all over then said, 'Seeing you tied like this has aroused me. I want to fuck you'. He touched me and did terrible things to me. He then threatened me and told me not to tell anyone. That happened in the middle of the night. In the morning when the sun came up I saw clearly what they had done to my mother. Her legs were burnt and swollen, her vagina was cooked and buggered up completely, and she had lost plenty of blood. I knew then she was as good as dead... [1]

Accused Woman 2, 23 June 2004, Lake Kopiago, Southern Highlands Province

---

1 This quote is drawn from a much larger unpublished account concerning a witch trial that occurred at Lake Kopiago in December 2003. The young woman in her mid-twenties was held and tortured over a 13-day period, along with five other women including her mother, who died as a result of the injuries she sustained. Although the women involved wish their stories to be told I have protected their identities.

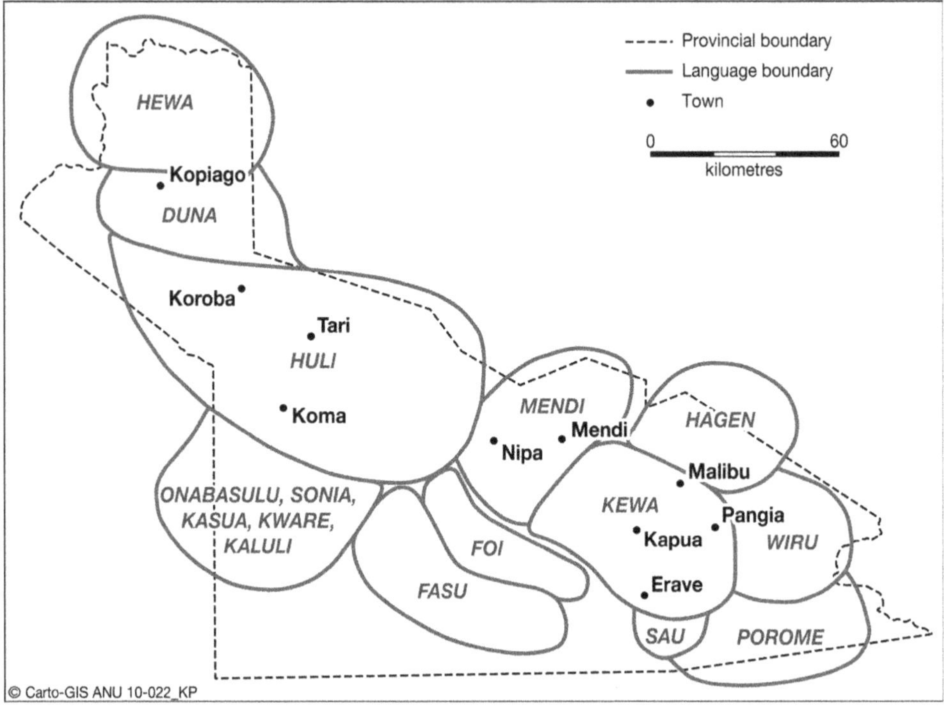

Map 3: Southern Highlands Province.

By Karina Pelling, Coombs Cartography, College of Asia and the Pacific, The Australian National University, Canberra, Australia.

Introduction

Accusations of witchcraft and sorcery, resulting in torture and sometimes death, appear to be increasing throughout Papua New Guinea and have prompted the current review of the nation's sorcery laws (Anon. 2009; Springler 2005, 68). Dozens of stories appearing in the *Post Courier* and *National* newspapers and carried by international news services give the impression that witch trials and killings are prevalent, especially in the Highlands, and on the rise.[2] At Goroka General Hospital in the Eastern Highlands Province, staff report growing numbers of patients with trauma from witch-torture. They also report that people are increasingly requesting post-mortem examinations in the hope of demonstrating sorcery or witchcraft as a cause of death (Kubu et al. 2004, 11). Dokup (2004) found that surgical wards in the Highlands were admitting more than 10 torture victims each week. These admissions do not, however, reflect the

---

2　Torture headlines from around the time of the Kopiago witch trials discussed here have included Anon. 2003a; Anon. 2003b; Anon. 2004a; Anon. 2004b; Anon. 2004c; Anon. 2004d; Anon. 2004e. More recent media coverage includes Anon. 2007; Anon. 2008; Anon. 2009; Muri 2009.

true extent of the problem. Dr Joe Aina of Kundiawa General Hospital has stated that only a fraction of those tortured and killed as witches come to the attention of medical services.[3] Perhaps even fewer come to the attention of police. For the most part these injuries and deaths go unreported.

Several observers, including the former Minister for Police and Internal Security, Bire Kimisopa, have directly linked this apparent increase in witchcraft accusations with PNG's growing HIV epidemic (Gerawa and Rheeney 2004). In many reported cases of witch-killing—such as the incineration of a young Mt Hagen woman in early 2009—AIDS has been explicitly implicated (Muri 2009; see also Anon. 2007). Classical analyses of witchcraft in fact correlate the efflorescence of witchcraft beliefs, in particular places at particular times, with periods of illness, misfortune and uncertainty (e.g. Marwick 1965), and have explained witchcraft and sorcery in terms of anxieties born of radical social change, suggesting that accusations arise when communities experience dramatic upheavals and conflicts precipitated by epidemics, labour migration and political insecurity. Certainly two of the most comprehensive studies of witchcraft/sorcery[4] in PNG, namely Lindenbaum's (1979) study of Kuru sorcery and Reibe's (1987) study of Kalam witchcraft, argued that particular PNG communities have used witchcraft and sorcery to explain sudden changes to mortality rates. Lindenbaum's study also showed that as the incidence of illness amongst the Kuru declined, so did sorcery accusations.

I too will argue that sorcery accusations and the HIV epidemic are linked, although on numerous occasions the torture or killing of an alleged witch is unrelated to any perceived or actual death from AIDS (cf. Durkheim 1952 on Suicide). I draw on material from Lake Kopiago, in Southern Highlands Province, where I have conducted research over the past 16 years. There AIDS deaths are being attributed to the agency of witches, while illness and death associated with HIV have heightened anxieties about witchcraft more generally. I shall provide an account of the Kopiago witch trials that occurred in the 18 months from December 2003 and ask why it is that AIDS deaths lend themselves to witchcraft accusations. I will not seek to explain witchcraft *per se* and, for the purpose of discussion, I will accept the view that witchcraft accusations have increased, without tackling the vexed question of whether the rise of

---

3 These claims were made at a workshop entitled *Sanguma in Paradise: Sorcery and Witchcraft in the Highlands of Papua New Guinea*. The workshop organised by the Melanesian Institute was held at Goroka from 7–11 September 2004. At the workshop Dr Aina reported that he himself had treated 44 people tortured as witches between 1996 and 2004. See Zocca 2009.

4 Following the work of Evans-Pritchard (1937) among the Azande, anthropologists have tended to distinguish between sorcery and witchcraft on the basis that witches are seemingly possessed of an innate and unconscious propensity to harm others, whereas sorcery involves the conscious and deliberate manipulation of objects and/or spells to achieve a desired outcome. This broad distinction is applied herein, however I note that witchcraft and sorcery are both subsumed under the term sorcery in the PNG *Sorcery Act 1976*, and that they tend to be used interchangeably in PNG media reports.

witchcraft accusations is actual or merely perceived.[5] Rather, I will explore how AIDS deaths contribute to witchcraft accusations in the Lake Kopiago area by attempting to elucidate the cultural logics and other factors which shape Duna people's experiences of HIV and AIDS. Finally, I will consider the implications for law and order in PNG.

Lake Kopiago—The Setting

Some 30,000 Duna speakers, alongside 5000 Hewa and 250 Bogoi, live in the Lake Kopiago sub-district, an area of about 3800km² in the far northwestern corner of Southern Highlands Province (SHP). Despite the SHP's lucrative natural resources, it is arguably PNG's worst-performing province (see Haley and May 2007). Service delivery has ground to a halt, human development indicators are among PNG's lowest (McKay, Lepani and Wagner 1999) and the province is riven by armed violence. A recent survey sponsored by the United Nations Development Programme (UNDP) and undertaken in collaboration with the Geneva-based Small Arms Survey found that the western end of the Southern Highlands is disproportionately affected by armed violence and its victimisation rates are amongst the highest reported anywhere in the world (Haley 2005, 25–26; see also Haley and Muggah 2006). Specifically 65 percent of households surveyed in the Kopiago sub-district reported victimisation, with respect to armed violence, in the six months to May 2005 (Haley 2008a).

Compounding this, demand for firearms in the province is robust and there are no police and no village court magistrates. In the absence of such formal dispute resolution mechanisms, compensation demands (now exacted at gunpoint) have escalated to the point of crippling livelihoods and fuelling renewed cycles of retribution and violence. The situation in the health and education sectors is equally disconcerting. Most public servants have absconded. Aid posts have closed down. Medicines are in short supply. Vaccination and other health programs, including disease surveillance, have ceased. Schools have shut. Road

---

5   Although anecdotal evidence suggests a recent upsurge in witchcraft activity, it should be noted that researchers in the 1970s and 1980s felt they too were witnessing 'a recent increase in sorcery and witchcraft beliefs in Papua New Guinea' (Lindenbaum 1981:119). In the 1980s, for instance, two edited collections concerning witchcraft and sorcery in PNG were published (Zelenietz and Lindenbaum 1981; Stephen 1987). The papers contained within both collections sought to document the emergence of new practices and the efflorescence of existing ones. Further research concerning contemporary witch hunts, combined with detailed historical and empirical accounts of witchcraft placed within local contexts, is therefore needed before we can say with any certainty whether witch killings are on the rise. Ethnographies from across the Highlands and the Highlands fringe make evident that witch trials and killings were certainly a feature of the recent past in many areas (Reay 1987; Glasse 1965; Kelly 1977; Maracek 1979; Poole 1981; Knauft 1985); that torture was often used to elicit confessions from suspected witches prior to execution (Poole 1981; Reay 1987:97–98); and that killings took place reasonably frequently. Steadman (1971), for instance, recorded 42 witch killings amongst the 460-odd Central Hewa in the period 1959–1969 alone, while Poole (1981:59) reported that the Bimin-Kuskusmin, who at the time of his fieldwork (1971–1973) numbered around 1000, could vividly recall 73 witch killings. He further noted (1981:59) that 'almost every adult' could 'recall having witnessed the public spectacle of the tortured confession and hideous execution, of a witch'.

closures, unchecked conflicts in the Koroba area, and the rising cost of air travel also mean that people can no longer access Tari Hospital. The cessation of passenger flights between Kopiago and Mendi (the provincial headquarters) prevent travel to the main provincial hospital too, so health services of any kind are very hard for people at Kopiago to reach. In addition, the cash economy has contracted, giving rise to an increase in transactional sex and the proliferation of polygamous, often short-lived marriages and unions through which Duna seek to access employment incomes and the benefits of resource development.

Men and women alike recognise that these changing sexual and marriage practices are a key source of violence in their communities. Household surveys and focus groups conducted with men and women separately in May 2005, as part of the UNDP sponsored Armed Violence Assessment (Haley 2005), revealed that family or domestic violence (*imanoni wei*, literally woman and husband fight) is the primary contributor to insecurity in the Lake Kopiago area. It was also found that in the six months to May 2005 domestic violence affected one-third of the 103 households surveyed and that 70 percent of the domestic violence reported had involved the use of a weapon.[6] Both men and women agreed that domestic or family violence arises, in one way or another, from tensions due to promiscuity, transactional sex, polygamy and marital infidelities (see also Haley 2008a). Against this backdrop people in the Lake Kopiago sub-district are experiencing the HIV epidemic.

HIV and AIDS at Kopiago

Although the Catholic Church has recently begun voluntary testing and counselling at Lake Kopiago, very few people know, even if they want to, their HIV status or have ever been tested. Accordingly there are few confirmed AIDS deaths at Kopiago and the overall prevalence of HIV infection remains unknown. Yet personal observation and anecdotal evidence suggests that growing numbers of men, women and children are living with HIV and dying from AIDS. Men are returning home from larger urban centres such as Moresby, Lae and Mt Hagen to die and many deaths 'in the village' appear to be AIDS-related. The officer-in-charge of the Lake Kopiago Health Centre reports a dramatic rise in tuberculosis since 2002 (Ekara Andape, personal communication 2004), which likewise suggests an increase in the prevalence of HIV.

In nearby Tari District, testing at Tari Hospital has confirmed a dramatic increase in the prevalence of TB and rising HIV. In 2005 Frank Kasahya, the pathologist

---

6 Further analysis of the Lake Kopiago data revealed that of the domestic violence cases in which a weapon was used, a bush knife or axe was used in all but one case, while firearms were used as well in 57 percent of the reported domestic violence events (Haley 2008a, 228).

at Tari Hospital, found a '2–3 percent HIV prevalence rate amongst those tested' with 'at least two new confirmed HIV cases each week' but pointed out that 'the majority of people are afraid to come forward for testing' and that 'plenty of people are dying without being tested' (Kasahya, personal communication May 2005). Figures released by the SHP provincial AIDS office reveal at least a five-fold increase in new HIV cases between 2003 and the first quarter of 2005,[7] while testing in Tari in 2006 was reported to show an HIV prevalence of 40 percent among people aged from 15 to their early 40s (Anon. 2006; cf. Wardlow 2008, 190–191).

Because health and education services are barely functioning and literacy rates are amongst the lowest in the country, people at Lake Kopiago are experiencing the epidemic with very limited public education about HIV and AIDS. The few national awareness messages in the electronic and printed media that have penetrated only bewilder the Duna, who are unsure about the nature of the virus, its modes of transmission and illnesses which accompany it (see also Eves 2003, 253). Even in cases where a person's HIV status has been confirmed, AIDS deaths, like all deaths, are primarily interpreted and understood with reference to local conceptions of illness and disease.

At Lake Kopiago, the HIV epidemic is unfolding within a cosmology characterised by entropy and a concept of the 'ground finishing' (*rindi itaraiya*). Duna hold that their world is bound up in a process of loss, with the fertile substance that sustains the universe tending, as Duna myths reveal, to dissipate. Declining fertility manifests in environmental degradation and in social and moral disarray. As fertility is morally constituted (cf. Ballard 1998; 2000), ongoing fertility must be negotiated through appropriate moral behaviour and proper social intercourse (Haley 2002). These underlying beliefs inform the way Duna interpret and understand environmental and social changes, including the manifestations of HIV (see also Haley 2008b).

Duna disease aetiology clearly links illness and disease with the erosion of traditional moral codes, such that deportment and physical wellbeing are seen to reflect the state of the world more generally. Accordingly Duna view HIV-associated illness and death as symptomatic of the 'ground finishing'. They talk about AIDS deaths alongside observations about corruption, the proliferation of small arms, incestuous marriages, gambling, the non-payment of bride-price, and the heightened immorality and promiscuous sexuality of youth—all of which are viewed as evidencing the social and moral decline of their world (cf. Eves 2003).

---

7 Figures released by the SHP provincial AIDS office reveal that there were 44 new cases of HIV reported in 2003, 66 new cases in 2004 and 56 new cases in the first 3 months of 2005. The 2003 and 2004 figures incorporate those from Tari, Mendi and Ialibu Hospitals, whereas the 2005 figures record only the new cases from Tari and Mendi (*Pacific Magazine*, 17 June 2005).

AIDS and Witchcraft

From a Duna perspective, the approaching apocalypse is also being hastened by an apparent upsurge in witchcraft activity. Duna hold that witches (*suwake*) threaten the flow of fertile substance. They devour it through the consumption of people's bodies and through their insatiable sexual appetites. Witches transgress social and moral boundaries. They are seen as mobile, greedy for food and sexually promiscuous (see Stürzenhofecker 1998, 158–183). Specifically they are said to consume a victim from the inside out, thereby draining them of their fertile substance.

Only those deaths that are sudden or seemingly unusual are attributed to malign causes such as witchcraft (cf. Yamba 1997, 219). For instance, deaths among the very young or the very old seldom result in accusation—they tend not to be considered unusual. Typically only those deaths that run counter to people's experiences—deaths among people of reproductive age, in the prime of their lives—are considered unusual. Duna assert that there have been many unusual deaths in recent times. They are cognisant of the small but steady stream of young men returning home from urban centres to die, and of the growing numbers of people succumbing to chronic respiratory problems.

Hence AIDS produces the kinds of death that lend themselves to witchcraft accusations. The spate of witch trials from December 2003 was triggered by several 'unusual' deaths in the Lake Kopiago area.[8] In these trials, three women were killed and nine others sustained horrific injuries. In the first trial, which occurred at Hirane in December 2003, six women were held captive and repeatedly tortured over a fortnight. These women, including the young woman to whom the opening quote is attributed, were blamed for a series of 'unusual' deaths including that of a young man who most likely died of HIV-related tuberculosis in early 2003. The accused women were beaten, stabbed, cut with bush knives and burnt with reinforcing iron. Two of the women were sexually assaulted and one, the mother described at the outset of this chapter, had her uterus ripped out with a hot iron hook. That woman died as a result.

> At the time this trouble came up two boys came to my house…. They took me to the men's house. When I got there I saw that they had cooked my sister and that other woman. I saw this and I was terrified. They ordered me to go and sit down with my baby. They said, 'Sit there and don't move, we haven't finished with these two yet'. With that they got some wire and tied my hands and legs. They tied me to a Casuarina

---

8   Research elsewhere has also shown that AIDS deaths were readily attributed to witchcraft as the HIV/ AIDS epidemic took hold in Zambia (Yamba 1997), South Africa (Ashforth 2002; Stadler 2003) and Haiti (Farmer 1990; 1992).

tree. While I was there, with my baby, they heated that wire. Then they burnt my breasts, my thighs, my backside. They burnt me all over.... The boys that cooked me were my husband's sons—the sons of his first wife. They blamed me for their brother's death.... The marks on my body bear witness to the things they did.... My body is completely wrecked...

Accused Woman 3, 26 June 2004.

In an unrelated trial two months later, two women (a mother and daughter) were killed at Horaile; in June 2004, four women were tortured as witches at Hagini; and in July 2005 a young man was accused and tortured at Kaguane. None of these incidents of torture were formally investigated and the perpetrators are unlikely ever be punished as there are no police or magistrates in the Kopiago sub-district.

In the Kaguane case, the accused was a young man rumoured to be practising a new form of witchcraft believed to have entered Kopiago from the Oksapmin area to the west in 2004. This new form of witchcraft, known locally as *kao suwake* 'white witchcraft', is thought to only harm young sexually active men. Its name reflects its alleged introduction by a white man, who is reputed to have trained and to command a band of local practitioners. These practitioners are supposed to drain their victims' blood and remove their internal organs for sale in Australia (cf. Englund and Leach 2000, 230).

Anxieties about 'unusual' deaths at Lake Kopiago are being played out in dreams which are publicly aired and often interpreted in terms of witchcraft:

I told you about that boy MW who died on Sunday.... Before he died HK had a dream. He saw a big cassowary behind MW's house. Another cassowary came and met it.[9] JK also had a dream. In his dream he saw a long drain. A line of young fruit pandanus was planted beside the drain. The first tree had fruit that was ready to be harvested. That man, the one they have accused, came and picked the fruit....The people are now saying that dream is proof that M was killed by witchcraft. M's death has proven that this kind of witchcraft is already here.... The young fruit pandanus in JK's dream are the young guys around here. In the dream only the first died, but they were lined up along the drain— one by one they will be harvested. They are truly worried this 'white witchcraft' will finish them all.

Richard Alo, 24 June 2004.

---

9   In myths and dreams witches are often paired and appear in the first instance in the singular and in the form of cassowaries.

The role of AIDS as a contributor to deaths and as a stimulant of witchcraft accusations is not, however, widely perceived among the people of Kopiago themselves. In fact, those who seek to attribute local deaths to the HIV epidemic are often ridiculed.

> About those deaths, they keep saying '*kao suwake, kao suwake*' ['white magic'], but I'm sure the thing that's killing the young guys around here is in fact this *sikAIDS* we have heard about. I told the people at Kaguane about that and told the people at the market today, but they didn't want to listen. They laughed at me and said, 'You are wrong. It's witchcraft we have the proof—it's in the dreams and on the skin.'
>
> Richard Alo 24 June 2004.

For people at Kopiago, witchcraft explains the deaths of young and middle-aged men who are usually considered strong, healthy and resilient to disease. In the context of AIDS, the witchcraft paradigm provides a readily accepted 'theory of causation' (Stadler 2003, 364).

While the burgeoning HIV epidemic can only fuel witch-killing at Kopiago, it does not, as I suggested at the outset, directly cause each witchcraft accusation or each witch-killing incident. On the contrary, the circumstances surrounding each case, their nature and the ad hoc explanations that emerge after the fact, remain much the same as they always have. This means it is typically women, especially those who are seen by men to have rejected their customary obligations or to have failed to conform to local gender and sexual stereotypes, who are accused. Of the six women tortured as witches at Kopiago in December 2003, three were widowed, one was divorced, and one was living apart from her husband. They were all living independently of their former in-laws, and were therefore viewed by many, including their in-laws, as having failed to fulfil their customary obligations.

For instance, one of the accused and tortured was a young widow, whose husband had died of cerebral malaria in 2000. Soon after her husband's death she had been accused of killing him using witchcraft. She and her relatives had denied the accusations, but had paid compensation to her dead husband's kin 'to solve the trouble'. In the course of the December 2003 witch trial she was targeted and tortured for failing to 'sit down good' with her in-laws and for her intemperate sexuality—that is for having a child with another man. She was tortured by her dead husband's older brother:

> ...the boys came. They dragged me to the men's house…. They dragged me back to the place where they had cooked [Accused Woman 1]... When we came up to that place I saw that they were already heating the wire…. They got rope and tied me and my small baby to a Casuarina

> tree. M2 said, 'Tie that bastard child to the tree with her!' After they had tied us both, he grabbed a bush knife and cut the baby's neck. I screamed, 'Don't cut my baby! If you want to cut me then go ahead cut me. Don't kill my baby'. The baby was crying. He pissed everywhere. With that M3 came and grabbed the baby. I said, 'If you are going to kill my baby then kill us both. Kill us both together'.... With that M4 came and grabbed my baby, he carried him off into the bush and left him there. I didn't know what they had done to him. They carried him away, then tied my legs and hands. They tied me to a Casuarina. Then M5 came and held a bush knife to my neck... While he did that M3 [her brother-in-law] was heating the wire in the fire. When it was red hot he came and shot me right here [just above her left buttock]. The wire went inside me. It went all the way down my leg and came out here [just above her knee]. It was hard for him to get it out again. My body bears the marks of this. This wire was no ordinary wire. They had sharpened it and fashioned a hook, two hooks, at the end. When it was hot really hot they shot it through my leg... Because of the hooks it was hard to remove.... I don't remember how they got it out. I passed out. When I woke they had removed it already... I saw that plenty of flesh and muscle had come out too....

Accused Woman 5, 26 June 2005.

The accused women were also held to have transgressed other gender codes. Indeed throughout their interrogation they were accused of behaving like men and of owning army uniforms, six-pocket trousers and high powered weapons—the accoutrements of contemporary masculinity in PNG (see Macintyre 2008).

Although they were held, questioned and tortured at the same time, the six women involved in the Hirane witch trial were tortured by different groups of men and subjected to accusations that differed in their particulars. For instance, AW5's mother, a widow in her late fifties, was accused of being a witch after publicly refusing the sexual advances of an old man who later became sick. Unlike her daughter she was tortured by the old man's sons, who saw fit to punish her insolence by burning her, stripping her naked and sexually assaulting her while she was tied to a Casuarina tree outside their father's men's house:

> They dragged me out from my house. They dragged me to the men's house. On the way they booted me. When we got to the men's house they hit me.... One of the boys got a bush knife and cut me.... Then they cooked me. They heated that wire till it was red hot and then cooked my thighs. They tied my hands and legs and told me not to move. Once they had tied me then they cooked me.... After doing that two of the boys,

tore my dress from me. I was completely naked. The boys then came touched my body all over. I couldn't do anything. I was still tied up. I couldn't do anything. I thought they were going to kill me....

Accused Woman 4, 26 June 2004.

The differences in the particulars of the accusations was underlined by the fact that it was possible for a young male torturer to assume contrasting roles in relation to the different accused women. For instance AW5's principal assailant (her brother-in-law) intervened to stop AW2 (his clan sister) from being burnt when it became evident that her attackers intended to burn her as they had her mother.

Law, Order and Governance Failure

Whilst it is not altogether surprising that AIDS deaths are now being attributed to the agency of witches, in that AIDS produces deaths of young, sexually active adults which are specifically the kind that attract witchcraft accusations, these Kopiago witch trials, involving prolonged pubic torture that did not cease upon confession, differ markedly from the traditional interrogation of witches. Formerly, accused witches were not ordinarily tortured, punished or killed.[10] Instead, they were publicly interrogated and urged to confess their misdeeds. The act of confession was thought to be disempowering, and they were then ordered to pay compensation. Only in the case of repeat offences were witches killed, and then by their own kin. Contemporary witch trials at Kopiago seem to be explicitly about punishment and retribution, rather than public confession. As such they have more in common with the way sexual impropriety was dealt with in the past. Traditional punishments for promiscuity and adultery included whipping the woman's genitals with barbed vines or branches, or lashing her to an ant's nest so her genitals would be bitten by ants.[11]

Another key difference is that the interrogation and punishment is being carried out not by community leaders, nor by the women's own kin, but by young men with guns, who would otherwise have very little standing in the community.

---

10   Whilst it was the case that Duna witches were not typically tortured, limited duress was sometimes used to extract a confession. Generally this involved having small slithers of bamboo inserted under their finger nails.

11   I am not aware of any cases in which the woman's genitals were actually burnt, and in fact Duna leaders assert that this did not happen in the past. That said it did happen in other areas. For instance Wagner (1972, 37) describes a Daribi form of punishment known as fire-genitals which was used on women who were found 'guilty of offences connected with intemperate sexual relations'. In it the woman was 'staked out on the ground, and a fire built at her genitals until they are *no goodanymore*'.

The boys who did these things, they came up like soldiers. Brandishing their guns they said to the leaders and to our relatives, 'No one can come inside the fence. We are going to teach these women a lesson. Do not come inside our territory'.

Accused Woman 4, 26 June 2004.

This has given rise to a great deal of community discord and division. Community leaders at Kopiago publicly decry the actions of these young men who have taken it upon themselves to seek out and punish suspected witches, but lament that they are powerless to intervene given the proliferation of marijuana and small arms.

There is no longer any law and order here. The young guys don't listen to the leaders. Instead they come with guns and threatening words. They smoke marijuana and take matters in their own hands. They are self-promoted leaders. They come with their guns. They threaten us, demand the leaders keep quiet and chase us away. They use their guns to threaten, to demand large compensation, to make their own laws. They say 'witch, witch' and cook the women they accuse. We reject what they are doing but they don't listen to us.

Sane Noma, 12 May 2005.

Kopiago's community leaders are firmly of the view that problems stem directly from service delivery failure and want the government to address them.

In my entire life I have not seen anything like this witch trouble before… Suppose we suspected a woman of being a witch, we would question her and order her to kill a pig. We never touched their bodies or spoiled them like that before. This practice of burning them, there's no law or custom to that effect around here…. That is the first time this has come up here. All this wouldn't have happened if there was law and order, proper medicines and proper health services here.

Jim Siape, 26 June 2004.

Kopiago is not like other districts. We don't have the services they have in other areas. We are without roads, schools and health services. This witch trouble came up here because we don't have police, magistrates or DPI officers [agricultural extension officers]. If we had police they could have investigated and charged those women and if we had DPI officers all these young guys would be busy with agriculture and making business. Instead they have nothing to do, so they grow marijuana and search for guns. We leaders reject what they are doing, but they don't listen to us or respect us. Instead they taunt us and say, 'When are you going to bring police and jail us?' We want a District Administrator, proper magistrate, police, village courts and good communication. Currently we have none of these things and that is why these problems came up.

David Lundape, 23 June 2004.

Undoubtedly governance failure and deteriorating service delivery play a big part in the way people at Lake Kopiago are experiencing HIV and AIDS. Service delivery failure in the health sector means that local aid posts have closed and the Sub-District Health Centre is without lighting, refrigeration, running water or basic medicines. Since 1997 there have been no health or immunisation patrols and disease surveillance has ceased. Sexually transmitted infections now go unchecked and untreated, increasing the likelihood of HIV transmission. Service delivery failure in the education and law and justice sectors is equally critical. School closures and the stalled implementation of elementary schools are behind falling literacy rates and formal education is at risk of disappearing, while police or magisterial services in the Sub-District no longer operate. Consequently witchcraft allegations are being dealt with locally and without reference to the police or courts. Increasingly they are being dealt with violently.

At Kopiago, as this chapter has argued, the HIV epidemic has contributed to the rise of witch-hunts and trials by torture. This has come about because of the culturally specific cosmological understandings Duna have of illness and disease; because AIDS produces the very kinds of deaths that attract witchcraft accusations; and because the illness and death associated with HIV add to a generalised anxiety about witchcraft. Interventions need to be carefully thought through and must take account of the cultural beliefs which inform people's experiences of HIV, for more awareness alone will not necessarily stop the accusations and killings. On the contrary, torture and killing may increase as part of new moralising projects, particularly if these projects accentuate existing beliefs about the potential of any women, who are perceived as insubordinate or transgressive, to do harm. Certainly there is evidence from Kopiago to suggest that recent awareness exercises, depicting women as agents of transmission, have focused much attention on the sexual practices of young women and cast them as predatory, leading to calls that they be 'punished' for their sexual misadventures (cf, MacPherson 2008). Thus PNG's HIV epidemic unfolds not merely as a public health issue of huge proportions, but also threatens to further impact upon law and order. Writing specifically about South Africa, Ashforth (2002, 136) observed that there are 'political implications for the state' when AIDS deaths are 'widely interpreted in terms of witchcraft'. He further cautions that democracy, the legitimacy of the state and the rule of law are threatened by the failure of government authorities to address the issue of witchcraft and witchcraft-related violence. Democracy in PNG, which has been described as disorderly, weak and in crisis (May et al. 2003) can scant afford such additional threats.

References

Anon. 2003a. Minister Horrified. *Post-Courier*, 19 June 2003.

Anon. 2003b. Deaths from Withcraft, Sorcery a Big Problem. *Post-Courier*, 29 August 2003.

Anon. 2004a. Seven Tortured. *Post-Courier*, 6–8 February 2004.

Anon. 2004b. Suspected Sorcerer Tortured and Killed. *The National*, 10 February 2004.

Anon. 2004c. Getting Away with Murder Every Week. *The National*, 16 February 2004.

Anon. 2004d. Belief in Witchcraft Causing Bloodshed: Inguba. *The National*, 8 March 2004.

Anon. 2004e. Two Killed in Sorcery-Related Violence. *The National*, 9 August 2004.

Anon. 2006. HIV/AIDS Prevalence Rate could be Higher. *Post-Courier,* 26 September 2006.

Anon. 2007. Witches Tortured over AIDS Deaths in PNG. *The National*, 27 August 2007.

Anon. 2008. PNG Police Recover Bodies of Women Killed after being Accused of Sorcery. *Radio New Zealand International*, 24 January 2007.

Anon. 2009. Battle for Sorcery Killings. *Post-Courier*, 7 April 2009.

Ashforth, A. 2002. An Epidemic of Witchcraft? The Implications of AIDS for the Post-Apartheid State. *African Studies* 61 (1):121–143.

Ballard, C. 1998. The Sun By Night: Huli Moral Topography of Myths of a Time of Darkness. In *Fluid Ontologies: Myth, Ritual and Philosophy in the Highlands of Papua New Guinea*, ed. L. R. Goldman and C. Ballard, 67–85. Westport: Bergin and Garvey.

Ballard, C. 2000. The Fire Next Time: The Conversion of the Huli Apocalypse. *Ethnohistory* 47 (1): 205–225.

Dokop, M. K. 2004. Research on Sanguma. *Post-Courier*, 23 February 2004.

Durkheim, E. 1952. *Suicide: A Study in sociology*. London: Routledge and Paul.

Englund, H. and J. Leach. 2000. Ethnography and the Meta-Narratives of Modernity. *Current Anthropology* 41 (2): 225–248.

Evans-Pritchard, E. E. 1937. *Witchcraft, Oracles and Magic among the Azande*. Oxford: Clarendon Press.

Eves, R. 2003. AIDS and Apocalypticism: Interpretations of the Epidemic from Papua New Guinea. *Culture, Health and Sexuality* 5 (3): 249–264.

Farmer, P. 1990. Sending Sickness: Sorcery, Politics and Changing Concepts of AIDS in Rural Haiti. *Medical Anthropology Quarterly* 4: 627.

Farmer, P. 1992. *AIDS and Accusation: Haiti and the Geography of Blame*. Berkeley: University of California Press.

Gerawa, M. and A. Rheeney. 2004. Sir Peter urges MPs to fight HIV. *The Post-Courier*, 13 May 2004.

Glasse, R. 1965. The Huli of the Southern Highlands. In *Gods Ghosts and Men in Melanesia*, ed. P. Lawrence and M. Meggitt, 27–49. London: Oxford University Press.

Haley, N. C. 2002. Ipakana Yakaiya: Mapping Landscapes, Mapping Lives— Contemporary Land Politics among the Duna. PhD thesis. Canberra: The Australian National University.

Haley, N. C. 2005. PNG Armed Violence Assessment. In *Small Arms Survey*. Final report for the United Nations Development Program. October/November 2005. Geneva: UNDP.

Haley, N. C. 2008a. Sung Adornment: Changing Masculinities at Lake Kopiago, Papua New Guinea. In Changing Pacific Masculinities, ed. J. P. Taylor, special issue 20, *The Australian Journal of Anthropology* 19 (2): 213–229.

Haley, N. C. 2008b. When There's No Accessing Basic Health Care: Local Politics and Responses to HIV/AIDS at Lake Kopiago, Papua New Guinea. In *Making Sense of AIDS: Culture Sexuality and Power in Melanesia*, ed. L. Butt and R. Eves, 24–40. Honolulu: University of Hawai'i Press.

Haley, N. C. and R. J. May. 2007. Introduction: Roots of Conflict in the Southern Highlands. In *Conflict and Resource Development in the Southern Highlands of Papua New Guinea*, ed. N. C. Haley and R. J. May, 1–19. Canberra: ANU E Press.

Haley, N. C. and R. Muggah. 2006. Jumping the Gun: Armed Violence in Papua New Guinea. In *Small Arms Survey 2006: Unfinished Business*, 165–187. Oxford: Oxford University Press.

Hanson, L. W., B. J. Allen, R. M. Bourke, and T. J. McCarthy. 2001. *Papua New Guinea: Rural Development Handbook*. Canberra: The Australian National University.

Kelly, R. 1977. *Etoro Social Structure: a study in structural contradiction*. Ann Arbor: University of Michigan Press.

Knauft, B. 1985. *Good Company and Violence: Sorcery and Social Action in a Lowland New Guinea Society*. Berkeley: University of California Press.

Kubu, T., Brother Andrew and P. Siba. 2004. Final Report into the Study of Sanguma in the Eastern Highlands and Simbu Provinces. Goroka: Goroka General Hospital.

Lindenbaum, S. 1979. *Kuru Sorcery: Disease and Danger in the New Guinea Highlands*. California: Mayfield Publishing Company.

Lindenbaum, S. 1981. Images of the Sorcerer in Papua New Guinea. *Social Analysis* 8:119–128.

May, R. J. ed. 2003. *'Arc of Instability'? Melanesia in the Early 2000s*. Canberra: State, Society and Governance in Melanesia Project, The Australian National University; and Christchurch: MacMillan Brown Centre, University of Christchurch.

Maracek, T. 1979. The Death of Koliam: A Witchcraft Killing in a Changing Environment. *Oceania* 49 (3): 221–225.

Marwick, M. 1965. *Sorcery in Its Social Setting: A Study of the Northern Rhodesia Cewa*. Manchester: Manchester University Press.

McKay, K, K. Lepani and T. Wagner. 1999. *Papua New Guinea Human Development Report 1998*. Office of National Planning: Port Moresby.

Muri, David. 2009. Hagen Girl Tied, Burnt to Death. *Post-Courier*, 7 January 2009.

Poole, F. 1981. Tamam: Ideological and Sociological Configurations of 'Witchcraft' among Bimin-Kuskusmin. *Social Analysis* 8: 58–76.

Reay, M. 1987. The Magico-Religious Foundations of New Guinea Highlands Warfare. In *Sorcerer and Witch in Melanesia*, ed. Michele Stephen, 83–120. Carlton: Melbourne University Press.

Reibe, Inge. 1987. Kalam Witchcraft: A Historical Perspective. In *Sorcerer and Witch in Melanesia*, ed. Michele Stephen, 211–245. Carlton: Melbourne University Press.

Stadler, J. 2003. Rumor, Gossip and Blame: Implications for HIV/AIDS prevention in the South African Lowveld. *AIDS Education and Prevention* 15 (4): 357–368.

Steadman, L. 1971. Neighbours and Killers: Residence and Dominance among the Hewa of New Guinea. PhD thesis. Canberra: The Australian National University.

Stephen, M. ed. 1987. *Sorcerer and Witch in Melanesia*. Carlton: Melbourne University Press.

Stürzenhofecker, G. 1998. *Times Enmeshed: Gender, Space, and History among the Duna of Papua New Guinea*. Stanford, California: Stanford University Press.

Wagner, R. 1972. *Habu: The Innovation of Meaning in Daribi Religion*. Chicago: University of Chicago Press.

Wardlow, Holly. 2008. 'You Have to Understand: Some of Us are Glad AIDS has Arrived': Christianity and Condoms among the Huli, Papua New Guinea. In *Making Sense of AIDS: Culture, Sexuality, and Power in Melanesia*, ed. Leslie Butt and Richard Eves, 187–205. Honolulu: University of Hawai'i Press.

Yamba, C. B. 1997. Cosmologies in Turmoil: Witchfinding and AIDS in Chiawa, Zambia. *Africa* 67 (2): 200–223.

Zelenietz, M. and S. Lindenbaum, eds. 1981. Sorcery and Social Change in Melanesia. *Special Issue Social Analysis* 8.

Zocca, Franco (ed.). 2009. *Sanguma in Paradise: Sorcery, Witchcraft and Christianity in Papua New Guinea*. Point Series No. 33. Goroka: The Melanesian Institute.

12. Community-building and Security: Case Studies

SINCLAIR DINNEN, JOHN CARTWRIGHT,
MADELEINE JENNEKER, CLIFFORD SHEARING,
ISAAC WAI, PAUL MAIA

Governance of Security

Sinclair Dinnen

Aral, Burris and Shearing argue that a shared sense of security from physical violence and interference with property contributes significantly to better community health (2002, 632; see also Burris 2006). Conversely, the absence of security can have devastating consequences for the health of individuals, communities and, indeed, nations. As well as its direct impact on the health of victims, violence has indirect effects that erode the quality of life and the ability to improve social and economic conditions (Emmett and Butchart 2000). These include, for example, the impediment that it presents to investment for economic development, its impact on tourism, and the way it can fuel the emigration of skilled citizens to more secure environments. Violence and conflict can corrode family and community ties, and disrupt the provision of basic health, education and other social services. High levels of sexual violence at home, or on the streets, undermine the freedoms and rights of women and children. In doing so, they deprive society and the economy of the full participation of a large proportion of the population. The manner in which any given society seeks to control crime, violence and other disputes—the governance of security—can thus be seen as a priority for public health research and intervention. Other chapters in this volume have shown how violence against women directly fuels HIV, which, in turn, contributes to conditions for further violence and insecurity.

In modern societies, the state has long been attributed the central role in the provision of security, as echoed in Max Weber's famous dictum about the state exercising a monopoly over the legitimate use of violence (Weber 1972). As far as internal security within designated territorial borders is concerned, this role has fallen traditionally to the state's law and justice system and the complex of associated agencies and institutions dedicated to the enforcement and administration of state law. These include, most obviously, the police, the courts and the prisons. Those suspected of infringing the law are apprehended by the police and taken out of their communities, prosecuted in the name of the state in the judicial system, and, if found guilty, punished. The interests of those most directly affected by their criminal behaviour are deemed to be satisfied by the imposition of state-administered retribution through the formal judicial and penal process. Civil dispute resolution is similarly removed from those most directly affected and managed by the judicial system and its cadre of professional officers—lawyers, magistrates and judges.

While few would disagree with the premise that states have a fundamental obligation to ensure a secure environment for their citizens, most would acknowledge that the governance of security is not exclusively a state function. State-centred approaches to the governance of security have undergone considerable scrutiny and reform in 'developed' countries as their inherent limitations have become more apparent and as recognition of the potential role of other stakeholders has grown. In many jurisdictions, emphasis is now placed on resolving small disputes through arbitration and other means in order to avoid costly and time-consuming legal proceedings. Recognition of the often harmful and counter-productive effects of imprisonment on offenders, as well as its considerable costs, has resulted in resort to alternatives to imprisonment for minor and juvenile offences, while the needs of 'victims' of crime are recognised in the expansion of restorative justice schemes in many countries.

Other harms, such as those caused to the innocent dependents of imprisoned offenders, appear to be an unavoidable consequence of the way the system works. Despite their universality and institutional complexity, criminal justice systems are, in fact, extremely crude instruments for deterring violence and settling conflict. They routinely exclude 'victims' from any meaningful participation in the resolution of disputes or offences that have affected them personally. In this sense, they steal conflicts away from those most directly involved and affected by them (Christie 1977). Experience of state-administered incarceration appears just as likely to accentuate criminal and anti-social attitudes on the part of individual offenders as 'rehabilitate' or 'correct' them in line with the rhetoric embraced by most modern penal regimes.

The Weberian depiction of the state and its pivotal role in the governance of security is, of course, an ideal and the reality in most societies is very different. In today's era of lean government and extensive out-sourcing, the monopoly over security functions of even the most long-established states has been diminished as a result of rising levels of private sector involvement in areas previously monopolised by the state. This is illustrated in, among other things, the massive growth of private policing and security (Shearing and Stenning 1987), including the controversial expansion of private military security (Singer 2001), as well as the increase in private prisons (Parenti 1999). In other less well-established states, centralised authorities have struggled hard to assert their writ successfully across the length and breadth of their designated territories. Law enforcement agencies, and other law and justice institutions, often have limited institutional capabilities and geographic reach in resource poor countries. In some cases, criminal justice agencies and processes designed to deter crime and disorder have themselves become a major source of harm and insecurity. Problems of corruption and serious abuse of human rights on the part of such agencies reflect, in part, a lack of adequate support and effective regulation by government. For example, prisons with insufficient funds and staff find it hard to maintain humane regimes and can become major incubators for violence and the transmission of deadly infections like HIV.

In countries, like Papua New Guinea, with predominantly rural populations, ordinary citizens may face significant difficulties in accessing justice, particularly when the state's justice facilities are concentrated overwhelmingly in urban centres. The prohibitive fees of lawyers and other associated costs provide further inhibitors. In such circumstances, the quality of 'justice' available may be determined more by an individual's wealth and place of abode than by idealised notions of equality of law. Moreover, where structural factors contribute to high levels of poverty, social exclusion and inequality, the operation of the criminal justice system can appear heavily weighted against those confronting the daily struggle to sustain themselves and their families. The targeting of disadvantaged communities for reactive policing and other repressive 'law and order' measures, as well as their over-representation in the prison population, can reinforce cycles of poverty and alienation rather than alleviate them. Criminal justice is designed to incapacitate and punish those who have or are likely to harm others. It affords little opportunity to acknowledge—let alone address—deeper structural factors that contribute to conflict, violence and anti-social activities in particular societies. The state system is oriented primarily towards control rather than prevention.

Where large numbers of people remain beyond the reach of formal justice processes or are otherwise disinclined to use them, informal responses to disputes and infractions of community norms are likely to prevail. In countries like Papua New Guinea, these include resort to older practices of dispute resolution and social control, associated with long traditions of self-regulation, as these have adapted to social and economic change. Reliance on local solutions is, in many cases, driven by the absence or weakness of state controls. It may also reflect a preference for familiar and socially attuned resolutions to local problems rather than reliance on external and impersonalised models. While some of these informal responses operate without any involvement of state or other external bodies, most others work with the explicit or tacit approval of relevant bits of state, NGOs, churches, or private sector bodies.

Informal approaches can work well in relatively cohesive communities. However, in other cases they can infringe seriously upon the rights of vulnerable groups such as women and children, thereby compounding their existing disadvantage. Likewise, in the absence of linkages to the formal regulatory system, informal responses can become the norm for dealing with all manner of disputes, including serious criminal matters, such as rape and murder, which legally should only be dealt with by the state through its higher courts. Informal approaches are also susceptible to capture by powerful local interests, such as older men whose actions are legitimated in the name of 'traditional' or 'customary' authority or, in seriously fractured and militarised environments, by younger men in possession of guns or other means of intimidation. In some parts of the world, including South Africa, informal self-policing has sometimes deteriorated into violent vigilantism.

Without effective regulation and accountability, informal approaches—as with their formal counterparts—can become quickly 'corrupted' and 'brutalised' and, thereby, a source of further injustice and insecurity. In addition, where informal approaches include the payment of monetary compensation, as in many parts of Melanesia, profit can become the predominant motive, thereby contributing to the further distortion and corruption of such practices (Fraenkel 2004). This is evident where relatives of a victim of gender violence or sexual abuse project themselves as the principal victims and seek to profit from the offence. In such circumstances, the actual victim is often left without any effective remedy.

In 2000, the PNG government endorsed a National Law and Justice Policy (GoPNG 2000) that recognised the need to develop partnerships between community-based organisations and state agencies aimed at enhancing safety and security at local levels. These have resulted in a flurry of activities including support of local dispute resolution mechanisms such as peace committees, human rights and law awareness initiatives, cooperation between police and community-based peace and safety processes, and increased support to the Village Court system operating at local levels throughout the country (Goddard 2009). Informing the policy was the long and frustrating experience of trying to respond to the growth of violence and conflict that has marked the past three decades in many parts of the country. While the need to improve the effectiveness of the state's formal deterrence system provides a major pillar of the new policy, it is accepted that the task of enhancing community safety also requires the active participation of community and civil society actors. Reflecting the thinking of the seminal Clifford Report on Law and Order (Clifford et al. 1984), the policy acknowledges that sustainable peace cannot be imposed on communities by state agencies acting alone. What is also needed is the building of local capacity that will enable community organisations to take more responsibility for solving their own problems.

Building the governance capacity of local organisations (or 'community-building' as the policy puts it) is thus seen as a key strategy for violence reduction and conflict prevention in PNG's diverse communities, as well as for enhancing their overall health and wellbeing. This would include a focus on addressing some of the underlying factors that contribute to violence and conflict in particular areas, such as lack of sustainable livelihoods or recreational facilities for local youth, as well as on strengthening community-based conflict resolution mechanisms. There is an implicit acknowledgement that problems of crime and violence reflect the weakness of both formal (state) and informal (non-state) controls, as well as the absence of pathways out of poverty, marginalisation and criminality.

Developing partnerships between state agencies, such as the police, and local organisations involved in addressing conflict would, in theory, have other mutually beneficial outcomes. For example, they could serve as vehicles for infusing informal approaches with respect for human rights and awareness of public health issues including HIV, while simultaneously rendering the police and other formal agencies more responsive to local needs and accountable to ordinary citizens. Available evidence suggests that community policing initiatives in different parts of the country, often involving police working with local peace or law and order committees, have achieved some success in enlisting young men at risk of engaging in criminal behavior and working with women's groups around issues of violence and public health (JAG 2004).

The alarming (alarmist?) portrayal of Papua New Guinea as uniformly beset by an expanding epidemic of crime and wanton violence inevitably overlooks the diversity of local experiences and responses. Given the predilection for 'bad news' in the local media and many external representations, it is hardly surprising that the rich array of problem-solving initiatives that are to be found throughout PNG, including in some of the most seriously disadvantaged rural and urban areas, are rarely reported (Hegarty and Thomas 2005; James et al. 2009). These would include the remarkable peace-building efforts of the Kup Women for Peace in a part of Simbu Province that had suffered from many years of violent inter-group conflict (Garap 2004; Hinton et al. 2008). There are also plenty of examples from post-conflict Bougainville where innovative community-based approaches to reconciliation and peace-building have met with considerable success (Howley 2002; Boege 2009).

Many of these initiatives have taken place far from the view of the urban-based media, national policy community, international donors, centres of commerce and foreign embassies. Without understating the challenges they face in sustaining themselves over time, it is important to acknowledge the agency and ingenuity of local actors in practical attempts to overcome adverse circumstances, including efforts to transform their own systems of governance in order to address better the problems of violence and conflict (Regan 2005). More significantly, it is important to study these cases in order to learn from their successes and failures and extend this learning to other communities facing similar problems.

The following two case studies examine local responses to problems of human security in disadvantaged urban communities—one in South Africa, the other in Port Moresby. Cartwright et al. outline the rationale and workings of the Zwelethemba model in South Africa, a model of what they call 'local capacity governance'. It offers a mechanism for communities to govern their own security while avoiding the problems associated with both formal and informal approaches to conflict and violence. At its core, the Zwelethemba model is a locally driven attempt to build community cohesion by connecting local and translocal structures. It seeks to mobilise capacity and knowledge within poor multi-ethnic communities in order to enhance the governance of their own security while simultaneously attracting the resources needed to support community-building through, for example, income-generating schemes. Resolving disputes through the agency of local peace committees is thus viewed as a window through which to address deeper social and economic problems, such as lack of local capacity and legitimate economic opportunities.

As noted earlier by Luker and Dinnen (this volume, chapter one), the Zwethelemba model is designed for a particular environment and would not necessarily work everywhere. However, the basic principles underlying the model could, in theory, be adapted and transferred elsewhere, as, indeed, they are in other South African cities and parts of Argentina. The Zwelethemba model clearly articulates certain features of interest to the present volume, including:

- Defining an effective, strategic but nevertheless limited role for the state. As described below, this includes conformity with state law, including the National Constitution; good working relations, with the South African Police Service and Department of Justice, as well as with individual police station commanders and magistrates in the areas where the Peace Committees operate. Many other possibilities exist for developing appropriate forms of state cooperation, including a light regulatory role, such as the use of state facilities or requiring the keeping of records.
- Utilising locally abundant resources: knowledge and time.

- Delivering a two-tiered 'peace dividend': two-thirds of payments to Peace Committees are divided among committee members, thereby acknowledging and valuing individual local expertise; while the remaining one-third goes into a community development fund to be spent on local projects collectively determined by members of the community.

- Operating on two tiers of prevention: resolving conflicts before they escalate; and potentially preventing some conflicts before they arise, through initiating and funding community projects which address local needs.

- Linking peacemaking and peacebuilding in a way that co-generates a new civics and new forms of community development.

- Enfranchising women and youth: according to the statistics provided, 59 percent of participants were women and 17 percent were youth.

The Zwelethemba model has also benefited from the research and monitoring work undertaken by the University of the Western Cape and the considerable international interest in its innovative approach. This has enabled a process of learning and development, as well as critical linkages and support from a range of external stakeholders including state agencies, like the police, and donor organisations.

While there is no evidence of any direct communication between them, it is striking that the second case study from Saraga settlement in Port Moresby demonstrates important similarities to the South African initiative. As with the Zwelethemba model, the fundamental aim of Saraga's peace committees is to build community cohesion and use conflict mediation to address some of the community's more fundamental challenges. It is also a locally driven approach that seeks to mobilise local knowledge and capacity in addressing local problems and develop supportive relations with external (translocal) bodies on the community's own terms. One of the practical challenges it faces, along with similar self-help initiatives in PNG, is how informal mediation by local groups relates to the mediation services provided by the government-administered Village Courts system. There is the risk that informal mediation services might undermine the authority and role of the more formal Village Courts. Efforts have been made by agencies like the Community Justice Liaison Unit (see below) and NGOs involved in providing mediation training to ensure that informal community-based approaches such as those developed in Saraga operate in a complementary manner with the Village Courts.

Unlike the South African case, Saraga has not been the subject of extensive research or international interest. Indeed, it remains relatively little known beyond the immediate community itself and individual supporters in a number of external agencies, companies, and NGOs. As a result, it remains essentially a one-off initiative that is unique to Saraga and highly dependent on the energy and leadership of a small group of community members and external supporters, mainly from the business sector. This makes it vulnerable to changes in key personnel or supporters, as happened when Downer Construction closed down. It also makes the task of developing a sustainable model, whose principles can be applied elsewhere, more difficult. The Zwelethemba model has been more successful in linking the economic incentives for conflict resolution to community development. Likewise, it has been more effective in institutionalising the necessary linkages between local and translocal structures.

Many of the ideas informing the Zwelethemba model correspond with those underlying the AusAID-supported Democratic Governance Strategy in PNG that aims 'to help articulate demands for democratic processes and institutions in PNG, and support the required reforms of the state and civil society to meet that demand' (AusAID 2007). The related initiative *Strongim Pipol Strongim Nesen* (Empower People: Strengthen the Nation) aims 'to enable civil society, together with the state and others, to better meet the needs and priorities of men, women and children in communities across PNG' (SPSN n.d.) . Its main components comprise:

1. Strengthened practice and promotion of democratic governance by key partners;
2. Communities working together to address identified priorities;
3. Improving local governance in selected geographic areas;
4. Strengthened collaboration of men and women stakeholders for the promotion of democratic governance;
5. Strengthened human capital of men and women for the practice of democratic governance (SPSN n.d.).

The thinking behind these initiatives as described by one of their key advisers (Goudsmit 2008) includes the need to use the limited local capacities of the state to greatest effect; to better mobilise existing local resources; to link peacemaking and peacebuilding with real development; and the need to develop a new 'civics', drawing upon a hybrid of local and state forms. These ideas appear to resonate with recent community policing and locally initiated peace strategies in different parts of PNG, some of which have also explicitly involved HIV education efforts,[1] gender violence initiatives, as well as the enlisting of women[2] and male youth.[3] Instead of trying to impose a top-down

---

1 A story in the PNG *Post-Courier* (23 August 2006) reports the efforts of Detective Sargeant Dianne Uro'o of the Royal Papua New Guinea Constabulary (RPNGC) in carrying out HIV/AIDS and other community policing awareness in collaboration with NGOs in the Markham area of Morobe Province.

2 The PNG *Post-Courier* (23 September 2009) reports 22 women participating in training to become community auxiliary police in Buka with a particular emphasis on dealing with problems of sexual abuse and domestic violence experienced by women in rural Bougainville.

3 The PNG *Post-Courier* (30 January 2009) reports that more than 400 youths from Port Moresby South graduated with certificates of recognition for community policing. The youths had been attached with the police in the National Capital District during the festive period in partnership with the National Capital

model of governance at local levels, there is a growing acknowledgement of the need for limited and strategic interventions by external actors (whether state, donors, private or non-government organisations) that do not undermine the spontaneity, autonomy and self-direction of local initiatives. The state should ideally provide an enduring structuring element with a focus on enabling and helping to sustain state/community partnerships aimed at promoting community safety and wellbeing.

Hybrid justice initiatives are, of course, nothing new in PNG. The Village Courts established shortly after independence represent the most prominent institutional example and simultaneously source their authority and legitimacy in both state law and local norms. Village Courts were established as a pragmatic response to the need for a bridging mechanism between the normative orders and modus operandi of community and state. They also serve the practical purpose of diverting cases and individuals away from the congested formal court system. The creeping formalism in these courts highlighted by some critics (Paliwala 1982) reflects their adaptation to local expectations and the fact that they are resorted to when other informal methods of conflict resolution are considered inappropriate to the case in question. Given their serious neglect by successive governments, including failure to provide financial support in the decade following the enactment of the Organic Law on Provincial and Local Level Government in 1995, these courts generally do a good job and have proven to be remarkably resilient across a range of diverse local contexts (Goddard 2009). Moreover, despite longstanding criticisms of Village Courts on the grounds of their lapse from international and PNG constitutional standards of human rights and gender equity, recent moves to increase the number of women officials, including magistrates, and enhance conformity to these standards appear to be meeting with some success.[4]

Community engagement of the kind envisaged in the national law and justice policy is clearly not without risks and tensions will continue between local sociality, the state, and values promoted by global human rights discourse. Ignoring these localised forms of 'doing justice' in the hope that they will be progressively supplanted by a uniform system of state administered justice is, however, totally unrealistic, not least given the limited fiscal capacity of the PNG state. Ultimately the most important things are to work out what kind of 'hand' the state extends to community peacemaking/building, reliable systems

District's *Yumi Lukautim Moresbi* (Lets Keep Port Moresby Safe) program.
4   Speaking at the launching of the second phase of the PNG-Australia Law and Justice Partnership (PALJP), the Australian High Commissioner noted successful efforts to revitalise village courts and increase the number of women magistrates (PNG Post-Courier 9 June 2009).

of incentives to foster conformity to acceptable standards, and some latitude with respect to the 'rights' outcomes as purism in this respect will invariably cast local initiatives in the worst of lights (cf. Reid this volume, chapter 13).

A Grass Roots Governance Model: South African Peace Committees

John Cartwright, Madeleine Jenneker and Clifford Shearing

Introduction

In the first chapters to this volume Luker and Dinnen draw attention to a model that has been developed in South Africa, and tested in Argentina, and that has established a simple and routinised set of institutional arrangements for bringing people together in deliberative forums to create 'a better tomorrow' in response both to specific disputes and more general issues of community development. They also mention the work of Aral, Burris and Shearing (2002) who have argued for the applicability of this model in responding to sexually transmitted infections. The editors have asked us to set out briefly the nature of the model's arrangements and the way in which they are being used in South Africa.

This model was developed by researchers at the Community Peace Programme (a unit of the School of Government at the University of the Western Cape) using a methodology that involved them working closely with members of a pilot community in a trial and error 'experimental' fashion to shape a workable set of procedures that operate within a regulatory framework that identifies and promotes liberal-democratic values embodied by the South African state.

The Community Peace Programme

The Community Peace Programme coordinates, facilitates and supports people engaged in re-imagining and transforming the way in which governance generally—and safety and security in particular—is accomplished. In doing so, it develops, reflects upon, and makes available, innovations in governance.

Its aim is to facilitate the validation, and effective application, of local knowledge and capacity as a massive but under-valued resource, making it possible for communities of 'ordinary' citizens to enter into effective partnerships of mutual respect with state agencies and specialist professionals.

In doing so it seeks to overcome the marginalisation of local knowledge that often occurs in governance programmes in poor and disadvantaged communities in ways that ensure that it is recognised and related to other forms of knowledge used to build community harmony and safety.

The Challenge

- Whose knowledge and experience is valued?

- By what means, and through which agencies or institutions, is security with justice produced in any given community?

- How can the knowledge and experience of civil society organisations and actors be effectively and sustainably mobilised to promote legitimate common interest?

- How can broad-based concepts of justice and human rights be integrated into social projects?

- What, in these circumstances, are the responsibilities of the state? What forms of cooperation or partnership between the state and civil society give most effective expression and implementation to their varied strengths and capacities?

The Post-Apartheid South African Context

Questions of this kind became especially prominent in public life in South Africa in the early 1990s following the collapse of the apartheid regime. Anything seemed possible, and there was—and to some extent continues to be—an exceptional opportunity to think freshly about the kind of society South Africans wished to live in. 'Reconstruction and Development' was a key slogan of the new government for the first few years, and—encouraged by the enlightened guidelines laid down in the new national Constitution—a great deal of energy and creativity went into developing policies and strategies aimed at social transformation.

For example, in the area of safety and security—crucial issues in a period of radical social change—the concept of 'policing' was revisited. There was general agreement that policing ought not to be viewed as the exclusive responsibility of the police, or, indeed, of the state. A broader conception was preferred that viewed security as the collective responsibility of networks of state agencies and commercial and non-commercial 'partners'. The possibility was thus opened up of taking more seriously the capacity of communities to contribute to their own safety and security, and, of course, other aspects of their wellbeing (Dixon 2004).

The Beginnings

In late 1997, with the active encouragement of the then Minister of Justice, the Community Peace Programme launched a deliberative model-building experiment in Zwelethemba, a suburb of the rural town of Worcester in the Western Cape. The Xhosa name for the suburb, Zwelethemba, means 'place of hope'. Specifically, the focus was to be on questions of safety and security in the local context, and the aim was to build a sustainable model of governance, based on the mobilisation of local knowledge and capacity around issues of dispute resolution and community-building.

This work was concerned with developing structures and ways of doing things that could be sustained over time and that enable poor and disadvantaged people to:

- Play a significant role in directing what happens in their communities;
- Rely on their own knowledge and capacity in their planning and in implementing these plans;
- Coordinate this knowledge and capacity with state agencies, and
- Access money to support their planning and the implementation of these plans.

Governance and Security

The Peace Committee model is designed to enable people to manage their own lives more effectively. Although its aims are general (that is, the whole of people's lives), it approaches general things in very specific and concrete ways by giving priority to disputes. The model sees most disputes as problems that are usually small in themselves but which, if not dealt with, can quickly escalate to disastrous proportions. It also regards disputes as related to more generic issues.

There are two main processes in this model—'PeaceMaking' and 'PeaceBuilding'.

PeaceMaking

Peace Committees operate according to a Code of Good Practice (see below). When a dispute is brought to a Peace Committee, an agreed set of procedures is followed. A 'PeaceMaking Gathering' is arranged, usually within days. Its purpose is to bring together the disputants and any other people who may be in a position to help understand and resolve the dispute. In this process, the role of the Peace Committee members is to facilitate what happens at the Gathering. They do not see themselves as problem solvers but as persons who facilitate problem solving by the parties to the dispute. The Gathering is guided through several stages, with all those present being encouraged to take part. In the first place, statements and discussion are heard on what happened and its consequences. This is followed by an attempt to identify the root cause(s) of the problem. Finally there is discussion aimed at producing an appropriate action plan, agreed to by all and designed to ensure that the problem does not recur. The focus of the Gathering, therefore, starts with the past problem and moves progressively towards ensuring a better and more secure future. Unlike formal criminal justice procedures which are concerned with past events, it is essentially a future-focused process. [5]

Here is a more detailed account of the PeaceMaking process:

- People in communities establish groups of 5–20 people, who call themselves a Peace Committee. The purpose is to create a sustainable institutional structure that people in the community, government agencies and others can relate to.

- The Peace Committee announces itself within the community as a group who will facilitate the resolution of disputes. When this happens the Peace Committee tells the community about their values. They do this by stating and making available a Code of Good Practice that says 'Here are our values; here is what we are committed to'. One of the most fundamental of these is that 'we don't use force to solve problems'. The purpose of the Code is to ensure that people know the key values of the Peace Committee and, thereby, what to expect if they opt to take their dispute to a Committee.

- Why would people choose to bring a dispute to the Committee? People usually do this because they do not want the blaming and punitive approach that underpins the operations of the criminal justice system, but also because they do not wish to take the vigilante route which is relatively common in poor communities in the larger South African cities.

- Once a dispute has been brought to the Peace Committee, it assigns two or more members to facilitate a dispute resolution.

- Once the Peace Committee understand what has been going on, they organise a PeaceMaking Gathering that includes the disputants and other people who they think will be able to contribute to solving the problem. Selecting members of the Gathering is very important as these people bring with them knowledge and resources that can help solve problems. Having the right people from the community involved ensures that solutions will be

---

5 For a discussion of the implications of this way of resolving problems for an experience of justice see Shearing and Johnston, 2005.

community-based and that decisions taken will respect peoples' values and the way they live.

- Gatherings usually take place in the house of a Peace Committee member, in a room at a community centre, or in a Community Peace Centre (see below under Project iThemba). Wherever it is held, the atmosphere is informal and non-threatening.

- After reading the Code of Good Practice, the first thing that facilitators do is to hear from the disputants separately as to what the dispute is all about. The reason for this separation is to ensure that a single account by one or more of the disputants does not frame the events. The purpose, at this stage, is not to decide who is right and who is wrong but to try and identify the causes of the problem and to find out who is likely to be able to help in solving it. No one is labelled as a victim or an offender. Rather they are seen as people who have a dispute in need of resolution.

- At a Gathering (whether for PeaceMaking or for PeaceBuilding) the focus is always on the future. The question asked is 'what can be done to reduce the likelihood of this and similar problems happening again?' As already noted, this does not mean that participants do not talk about the past. The past will be discussed in order to discover what can be done to ensure a better tomorrow.

- Once a plan of action has been finalised, it is recorded in writing and everyone signs to show his or her commitment to it. If specific actions are required, the plan will list them and identify who is responsible for doing these things. The purpose here is to ensure that everyone knows exactly what has been decided so that they can make sure that it is subsequently acted upon. One or more people at the Gathering are assigned the role of following up to see that the plan of action is followed.

- At the end of the Gathering disputants might apologise to each other. They may also choose to shake hands or hug each other. But this is not seen as essential. It is useful insofar as it contributes to people being able to move forward. However, the disputants may also decide that this is neither necessary nor helpful. When this happens there may be no apology.

- The close of a Gathering will invariably be accompanied by an act that symbolises the commitment of those present to what has been decided. This might be a dance, a song, a prayer, holding hands, or a combination of such things.

Peace Committee members who participate in a PeaceMaking Gathering prepare a report on what has happened. This goes to a central office where statistics are prepared, and feedback is then given to each Peace Committee on a monthly basis.

Code of Good Practice

Members of this Peace Committee use these guidelines in the course of their work as peacemakers:

- We help to create a safe and secure environment in our community.
- We respect the South African Constitution.
- We work within the law.
- We do not use force or violence.
- We do not take sides in disputes.
- We work in the community as a co-operative team, not as individuals.
- We follow procedures which are open for the community to see.
- We do not gossip about our work or about other people.
- We are committed in what we do.
- Our aim is to heal, not to hurt.

Disputes and other problems brought to PeaceMaking Gatherings for facilitation include such matters as unpaid loans and child maintenance, insults and fighting, theft and domestic violence. The coming together of appropriate local people in a facilitative environment is the key to the resolution of these dispute and the preparation of an agreement based on practical and effective plans of future-oriented action.

Payments

Before proceeding to the PeaceBuilding part of the model, we need to consider the matter of payments. For every Gathering that is completed according to the rules agreed upon, a payment is made to the Peace Committee. This is in recognition of the value of the work that the Committee does and responds to the common complaint that while professionals are always paid, poor people are usually asked to volunteer.

A proportion of this payment—currently two-thirds—goes to the individual Peace Committee members who facilitated the PeaceMaking Gathering, while one third goes into a PeaceBuilding Fund. This Fund is used to finance projects or individuals who have developed responsible entrepreneurial schemes for addressing some of the long-term problems in the community. This ensures that communities have money of their own. It is not a grant or a handout. Rather, it is money that they have 'earned' and is to be spent on activities aimed at building a better future for the community.

PeaceBuilding

PeaceBuilding works in the same way as Peacemaking except that the Peace Committee is here addressing broader generic problems rather than dealing with individual disputes. When there is an emerging pattern of local disputes or where the findings of regular base-line surveys indicate the existence of underlying problems confronting the community, the Peace Committee may decide to arrange a Solutions Gathering. Such a Gathering—often consisting of a series of meetings—is held to work out a long-term solution to these deeper problems and to establish who is to carry out the necessary work. The idea is to pay for this service out of the money accumulated in the PeaceBuilding Fund and to ensure that as much of this money stays in the community as possible. In addition, the Peace Committee might negotiate with others to increase the funds available for a project—for example, through a contract with a local municipality.

The PeaceBuilding process develops the model from a conflict management orientation to a broader governance focus. Individual disputes are seen as starting-points, issues that bring people together and mobilise their local knowledge and experience. Disputes in this sense constitute a 'window' through which one can proceed to identify and then address more general governance issues.

Many of the projects that emerge out of Solutions Gatherings are ones that, in one way or another, involve public health, for example, feeding schemes, touring drama groups to educate people about health issues, food gardens, first aid training, clearing public recreation areas of debris such as broken glass and so on.

Outcomes

By February 2005, there were 20 Peace Committees in South Africa, and together they had facilitated the resolution of over 11,000 Peace Gatherings. These Gatherings generated about R2,500,000 in revenues for Peace Committees. All of these revenues have been spent in these communities.

The authors of this chapter have analysed the reports of some 7000 Gatherings, which took place over the four years prior to 2005. Approximately 60,000 people had participated directly in solving problems in their communities through the 'window' of Gatherings. That is, 60,000 people have had the experience of shifting their stance from one of dependency on external agencies to one of assuming responsibility for resolving their own problems and, in the process, have moved from an orientation of blame to one that is focused on creating a new future. On average, 5.6 Peace Committee members were involved in each gathering.

In the Gatherings analysed, 59 percent of the participants were women, and 17 percent were youth. Of the Peace Committee members who facilitated Gatherings, 62 percent were women. The most frequent issues (36 percent) dealt with by Gatherings were to do with money (e.g. money-lending disputes, non-payment of loans or for goods and misappropriation of funds). Insults, threats and gossiping made up 17 percent of the total number, while property offences made up 20 percent. In 96 percent of the Gatherings, the participants developed a course of action and people committed themselves to implementing it. In a little under three-quarters of the gatherings some gesture marking the end of the conflict took place. At times this involved everyone present making a commitment to peace. At other times only the disputants were involved.

Relations with State Agencies

The continuing evolution of the Peace Committee model takes place against the background of a very important question. That is, what kind of partnership can be built between the state and civil society, in which the resources, knowledge, capacities and responsibilities of each party can be given practical and effective expression?

From the beginning of the pilot project in Zwelethemba in 1998, a good working relationship was established with the South African Police Service (SAPS) and the Department of Justice at both national and the provincial levels. Similarly, informal relationships of mutual referral have since been established with the Station Commissioners and magistrates in areas in which the Peace Committees operate. However, an important further step in improving cooperation has been taken with the establishment of Project iThemba, as described in the following section.

Project iThemba

In April 2002, the Community Peace Programme was approached by the SAPS Area Commissioner in the Boland (a region of the Western Cape) to consider the possibility of a cooperative venture in the township of Nkqubela, Robertson. The satellite police station in Nkqubela had been closed for some time owing to lack of resources and the Commissioner was under pressure from the local community to restore services.

After extensive negotiation, the principles and outline of a cooperative agreement became clear. In effect, the new Nkqubela Peace Committee would provide a conflict-resolution and community-building service, while the police would provide a contact point for reports and enquiries, an emergency response service, and a conduit for bringing appropriate cases to the courts. The former police station would be refurbished and extended and would reopen as a Community Peace Centre. An important feature of the refurbishment was the re-branding of the building by using both the emblems and colours of the SAPS and the Peace Committees.

After appropriate community consultation, the Nkqubela Peace Committee began work in late June 2002. Twenty-two police reservists were trained with Community Peace Programme and Peace Committee input. The Nkqubela Community Peace Centre was formally opened on 19 October 2002, in the presence of representatives of the Finnish Embassy (who provided some financial assistance to the project), the SAPS Western Cape management, the Mayors of the Boland District Council and the Breede River-Winelands Municipality, and the Western Cape Committee for Community Safety.

Project iThemba ("iThemba" means "hope") in Nkqubela was seen explicitly as a pilot project, with the intention of extending the model in due course throughout the Boland SAPS Region. Subsequently, the Zwelethemba Community Peace Centre was launched on 28 February 2004, and the Mbekweni Community Peace Centre was formally opened on 1 April 2004.

This Partnership Works as Follows:

- The SAPS carry out regular police work—that is, law enforcement, emergency response and detective services;
- The Peace Committees facilitate the resolution of disputes, conflicts and problems that do not require police action;
- Community members may take their problems directly to the Peace Committee for facilitation;
- Alternatively, the SAPS shift officers in the Community Peace Centre may offer disputants the option of taking the matter to the Peace Committee rather than opening a docket or following some other formal bureaucratic route;
- The Peace Committee may also refer matters to the SAPS where appropriate;
- The SAPS notes referrals to the Peace Committee, while Peace Committees complete a detailed report-form for all facilitations that they carry out.

In addition to providing an effective service to the residents of these communities, this Project is intended to demonstrate the feasibility and sustainability of an active partnership between state agencies (the police and local government) and a civil society organisation, as well as between professional or 'expert' knowledge and local community knowledge. This is a partnership whose practices are premised on respect for each other's culture, capacity and experience. In particular, and in relation to national policy on policing, the Community Peace Centre model gives effective expression and implementation to the principles of Sector Policing which is the process being used by the SAPS to implement the principles of community policing.

Extension of the Model

Other communities are being encouraged to adopt the model, provided they recognise a copyright (which is provided free of charge) and constitute themselves as an Implementing Agency willing to have their activities certified on a recurring basis through audits to ensure that the integrity of the model is preserved.

Conclusion

The model outlined here has now been tested well beyond the original pilot site. Moreover, procedures have been developed for ensuring sustainability and the utilisation of local knowledge and capacity. In addition, detailed operational procedures for managing Peace Committees on a wider scale are being constantly refined as the network is extended. As part of this process, it has been agreed that the Community Peace Programme should adopt a regulatory role, in relation both to financial accounting and to the monitoring of the PeaceMaking and PeaceBuilding procedures.

This is being done through a deliberative crucible of practice, which ensures that local people are part of the process by which the applicable principles and procedures are developed. This insistence on the full participation of civil society is matched by an insistence on pursuing mutually respectful partnerships with state agencies.

To conclude, the strength of this model lies in:

- the lawful and effective mobilisation of local knowledge and capacity around local conflicts and generic community problems;
- the development of complementary civil society-state agency relationships in promoting public goods.

Building Community and Peace in Saraga Settlement, Port Moresby

Isaac Wai and Paul Maia [6]

Background

Saraga was once a traditional Motu Koitabuan village on land that was later to become part of the modern city of Port Moresby, the capital of Papua New Guinea. It is now a sprawling urban settlement in the area known as Six-Mile, indicating its approximate distance from the commercial centre of the city. As Port Moresby grew, Saraga became home to many migrants from other parts of the country. The first groups of settlers from the mountainous and undeveloped Goilala region to the north of the capital arrived in 1949. Settlers and customary landowners agreed that, in return for rights to use the land, the former would provide the local Motu Koitabuans with security and labour. These first settlers arrived at a time when the colonial administration in Port Moresby was recruiting casual labourers for a variety of tasks. Labourers were recruited from different districts in PNG and usually arrived in Port Moresby unaccompanied. As the years went by, relatives of these labourers began to join their *wantoks* in urban settlements like Saraga. This movement of people from rural areas, along with new births, contributed to the growth of the urban population and the extension of *tambu* (in-law) relationships between different groups of people. Saraga developed in this way and the current population includes third and fourth generation residents who now identify themselves as Saraga people. In 1999, the Saraga Peace, Good Order and Community Development Association undertook a community survey that indicated that the settlement had a population of approximately 17,000 people representing around 34 ethnic groups.

From the 1970s, Saraga acquired an unfortunate reputation among Port Moresby residents as a breeding ground for criminal elements—an urban Wild West populated by gangs and other lawless characters engaged in a range of illicit and violent activities including murder, tribal fights, rape, *raskolism*, car thefts, break and enters, and armed hold-ups. The general public, and even the police, avoided going near Saraga, particularly at night. Among the urban population, Saraga was a place that primarily inspired fear and insecurity.

---

6   At the time of writing, Isaac Wai was the Deputy Chairman and Paul Maia was the Chairman of the Saraga Peace, Good Order and Community Development Association based at Six-Mile in Port Moresby. This account of peace-making in Saraga is based on an article by Isaac Wai and Paul Maia and is reproduced here in edited form with the permission of the authors and the *Development Bulletin.*

Association Formation

On 9 February 1998, a nine year-old girl from Rigo in Central Province was shot dead by young criminals on the Magi Highway in the vicinity of Saraga. Prominent leaders from Central Province, the national government, Motu Koitabu landowners, and many members of the public called for the immediate removal of all settlers from Saraga and their repatriation back to their provinces of origin. This was a difficult and worrying time for many law-abiding residents of the settlement who feared for their future and that of their families.

The broader context to the high levels of crime and violence engaged in by some members of the community was one of chronic unemployment and a large and growing body of alienated youngsters with little to do and limited access to legitimate economic activities (cf. Luker and Monsell-Davis this volume). Following the 1998 murder, an anti-crime campaign was initiated in Saraga by the then Central and National Capital District Police Commander, Jeffrey Vaki. The essence of this police initiative was to persuade criminal and anti-social elements to desist from their predatory and destructive activities and to threaten eviction and repatriation for those who did not. Following the campaign, Paul Maia, a long-term resident of Saraga and co-author of this account, called an urgent meeting of all community leaders with a view to establishing a mechanism that could help develop a vision for the future wellbeing of the community, while becoming an important forum for residents. It was at this meeting that the idea of establishing a system of committees to represent each of the community's ethnic groups and help foster and sustain peace and harmony within the settlement was first conceived. Subsequently each group established its own law and order committee. The response of community leaders at this initial meeting was overwhelmingly favourable and an overarching body—the Saraga Peace, Good Order and Community Development Association— was established with the aim of developing strategies to combat law and order problems occurring, or originating, in the community, while simultaneously building community cohesion and capacity.

The Association's broad aims and objectives were stated as follows:

- Promoting Good Governance—helping to achieve good governance, respect for human rights, and the promotion of conflict prevention. One of the ways in which this was to be achieved was through the establishment of a community coalition comprising community representatives, business houses, and government officials, working together to help restore and maintain law and order.

- Promoting human development—helping people achieve higher levels of education and widening the opportunities for disadvantaged members of the community.

- Promoting the status of women—contributing to the removal of gender discrimination and encouraging greater participation of women in all aspects of community life. Pursuing this goal would involve liaison, coordination and enhanced networking between all collaborating agencies and organisations to ensure that high levels of violence against women were addressed.

- Prevention of delinquency—diverting community youth into lawful and socially useful activities. This would entail fostering more respectful and socially responsible attitudes on the part of young people—as well as attitudes towards young people—in order to counter criminal and anti-social tendencies. In this regard, PNG's Juvenile Justice Act should be immediately implemented to provide for an effective system of juvenile justice that, in conformity with PNG's international obligations under the UN Convention on the Rights of the Child, is respectful of the rights of juveniles and responsive to their specific needs.

- HIV prevention—promoting the use of *Karamap* (locally produced) condoms as part of a community-based safe sex and HIV awareness campaign.

- Protection of the environment—contributing to the protection and sustainable management of the local environment. Strategies included tree-planting in the community.

- Conflict mediation—undertaking peace mediation between parties in dispute following restorative justice principles aimed at conflict resolution, reconciliation and community harmony.

- Skills training for engagement in the informal sector—training for sustainable livelihoods in the informal economy and enhancement of formal employment skills.

Activities

Following its establishment, the Saraga Peace, Good Order and Community Development Association embarked on a series of planning exercises relating to law and order issues, started monitoring community activities and liaising directly with local groups and external agencies and organisations in the promotion of its broader agenda for community regeneration. Among other things, association members approached a number of neighbouring business houses with a view to eliciting support for community sports activities and securing casual or part-time employment for local youth. These efforts met with some success and sports equipment was provided by commercial sponsors, while job opportunities were presented to a number of local youngsters. The Association's activities are described in more detail below.

Community Sports Sponsorship

Sports sponsorship secured by the Association helped create new opportunities for community youth to socialise and engage in healthy recreational activities. These sporting activities initially involved 355 participants and approximately 35 supervisors. They also attracted large numbers of spectators and provided additional income-generating opportunities to members of the community who sold home-made produce at the sides of the two sports fields.

Sponsorship was provided by a locally based firm, the Downer Construction Company, with a package of K25,000 distributed at K5000 per year. At a ceremony announcing the sponsorship, the company's general manager, Greg Wright, said that the community's reputation as a home to criminals reflected the limited work opportunities available, serious overcrowding, and the proliferation of *raskol* gangs. These factors contributed to the urban law and order problems identified by government, police and the private sector. Mr Wright said that his company was proud to sponsor community sports activities in Saraga. The sports program was a way of breaking down barriers between Saraga's different ethnic groups and building community cohesion and harmony.

Law and Order Awareness

The British High Commission also provided support to the Association to conduct law and order awareness in the community. Leaflets were prepared containing basic legal information and subsequently distributed among the 34 ethnic groups by their respective committees. Issues covered included domestic violence, laws about alcohol, home brewing, marijuana, sexual offences, recent changes to PNG laws, child abuse and children's rights.

Peace Mediation and Restorative Justice

Peace mediation according to restorative justice principles has deep roots in Melanesian cultures and has been adopted by the Saraga Good Order and Community Development Association as an appropriate technique for mediating conflicts within the community. Mediation training had been provided to some community leaders by the Port Moresby-based NGO—Peace Foundation Melanesia—and was subsequently adapted for use in Saraga. This technique was used to mediate conflicts between different ethnic groups in the settlement arising from six murders that occurred in the period 1997–2004 and continues to be used today. Association members involved in mediating conflicts sought to address the underlying grievances between different groups in the community and reconcile their differences. Emphasis was placed upon the reintegration of offenders after reconciliation with their victims and making suitable reparation.

Individuals are encouraged to take responsibility for their actions and change their attitudes accordingly. The ultimate aim is to increase respect between different groups and individuals and thereby enhance peace and harmony in the community. Upon completion of a successful conflict mediation process, *Peace Declared Memorandum of Understanding* forms are drawn up by Association members with specific conditions attached. All parties to the conflict agree to these conditions and sign the forms confirming that peace has been restored. The mediation panel also signs the forms, thereby sealing the peace agreement, and, where possible, a police station commander witnesses the signing. Upon signing the peace agreements, the parties to the conflict become solely responsible for repairing any damage caused in accordance with the conditions specified in the agreement.

This approach has proved to be extremely useful and, as an alternative to going through the formal criminal justice process, provides some relief to the already overburdened police, courts and prisons. The Association has developed a good working relationship with the local commander at the Six-Mile police station. Minor summary offences committed in the settlement and cases involving juveniles are registered in the police occurrence book and are often referred back to the Association for mediation. After the mediation group has dealt with a case, it reports back to the Six-Mile police who then finalise the incident reports at the station. Cases mediated by the group have included stealing, bag-snatching, conflicts relating to alcohol consumption, tribal fighting, gossiping, domestic violence, child abuse, false allegations, adultery, broken marriages, bride-price, attempted rape, land disputes, non-payment of credit and possession of marijuana.

Major Sponsors

The association has received support and encouragement from a number of government agencies and NGOs, as well as from some business houses. The Community Justice Liaison Unit—a donor-funded initiative with the law and justice sector—aims to foster partnerships between government agencies and civil society groups involved in crime prevention and conflict resolution like the Saraga Association. Recognising the merits of the Association's work, the Unit has contributed K12,874 towards community sporting activities. Small income-generating activities—such as the sale of food and drinks—have also benefited from this support to community sporting events. The Community Justice Liaison Unit has also agreed to fund a multi-purpose community hall in Saraga. This will allow all the community groups involved in crime prevention and violence reduction activities to come together under the one roof. Downer Construction and a local security company, Pacific Corporate Security, have provided financial and logistical assistance since the establishment of the Association. The security company has also provided employment opportunities to members of the different ethnic groups in Saraga. It has also provided an efficient community communication system linked to its radio network that has been an invaluable resource in enabling the Association's committee network to respond in a timely manner to crime and conflict in the community. While Downer Constructions has subsequently ceased its operations in PNG, its successor company—Omni Limited—has continued to provide the association with logistical support.

Looking Ahead

Planned activities include:

- Building a multi-purpose community hall;
- Installing electricity and streetlights in selected areas
- Installing and extending water supply in selected area and increasing water pressure;
- Building sewerage blocks to improve hygiene in the community;
- Establishing poverty alleviation schemes such as food gardens; poultry keeping; and flower planting;
- Improving the mobile clinic service;
- Vocational skills training for local youth (boys and girls);
- Environmental work in the community and elsewhere in the city;
- Preparing leaflets and promoting community awareness about sexual violence, alcohol and drugs;
- Increasing participation in sports and developing competitions with other settlements and villages.

The Association remains focused on community-building as the essential foundation for improving safety and harmony in the settlement. Considerable efforts are directed at developing and maintaining partnerships and linkages with relevant government agencies, NGOs, and the private sector, in order to assist the Association's work.

Conclusion

Association leaders appreciate that addressing law and order problems is not only a task for government and police. It is also an issue that requires active participation by ordinary members of the community, drawing on local knowledge and expertise. Building partnerships for change between community organisations, government agencies and business houses, is an important aspect of building stronger and more stable communities.

The Association is committed to developing strategies that will include all of the various ethnic groups making up Saraga and develop a strong sense of belonging to the same community. Meeting regularly to discuss issues affecting the community and working together to devise appropriate solutions to identified problems has helped overcome some of the divisions and suspicions that have undermined community cohesion in the past. It is also about empowering the community to take responsibility for the challenges it faces on a daily basis and devising approaches that build on local knowledge and expertise.

References

Aral, S., S. Burris and C. Shearing. 2002. Health and the Governance of Security: A Tale of Two Systems: Crime Control and Sexually Transmitted Diseases in Russia. *Journal of Law, Medicine and Ethics* 30: 632–643.

AusAID. 2007. Democratic Governance Program. Information Note – July 2007. Canberra: AusAID

Boege, Volker. 2009. Peacebuilding and State Formation in Post-Conflict Bougainville. *Peace Review* 21 (1) January-March 2009, 29–37.

Burris, Scott. 2006. From Security to Health. In *Democracy, Society and the Governance of Security*, ed. Jennifer Wood and Benoît Dupont, 196–216. Cambridge: Cambridge University Press.

Christie, Nils. 1977. Conflicts as property. *British Journal of Criminology* 17 (1), 1–14.

Clifford, W., L. Morauta and B. Stuart. 1984. *Law and Order in Papua New Guinea* (Clifford Report). Port Moresby: Institute of National Affairs and Institute of Applied Social and Economic Research.

Dixon, B. 2004. Cosmetic Crime Prevention. In *Justice Gained? Crime and Crime Control in South Africa's Transition*, ed. B. Dixon and E. van der Spuy, 163–192. Cape Town: University of Cape Town Press and Willan Press.

Emmett, Tony and Alex Butchart eds. 2000. *Behind the Mask: Getting to Grips with Crime and Violence in South Africa*. Cape Town: HSRC Publishers. www.hsrcpress.ac.za

Fraenkel, Jon. 2004. *The Manipulation of Custom. From Uprising to Intervention in the Solomon Islands*. Wellington, NZ: Victoria University Press.

Garap, Sarah. 2004. *Kup Women for Peace: Women Taking Action to Build Peace and Influence Community Decision-Making*. State Society and Governance in Melanesia Discussion Paper 2004/4, 1–16. Canberra: Australian National University.

Goddard, Michael. 2009. *Substantial Justice. An Anthropology of Village Courts in Papua New Guinea*. New York and Oxford: Berghahn Books.

Goudsmit, Into A. 2008. *Nation Building in Papua New Guinea: A Local Alternative*. State Society and Governance in Melanesia Discussion Paper 2008/9, 1–15. Canberra: Australian National University.

Government of Papua New Guinea (GoPNG). 2000. The National Law and Justice Policy and Plan of Action: Toward Restorative Justice.

Hegarty D. and Pam Thomas eds. 2005. Effective Development in Papua New Guinea. *Development Bulletin* No. 67 April 2005. Canberra: Development Studies Network.

Hinton, R., M. Kopi, A. Apa, A. Sil, M. Kini, J. Kai, Y. Guman, and D. Cowley. 2008. The Kup Women for Peace approach to peacekeeping: taking the lead in the Papua New Guinea national elections. *Gender & Development* 16 (3): 523–533.

Howley, Pat. 2002. *Breaking Spears and Mending Hearts: Peacemakers and Restorative Justice in Bougainville*. London and Sydney: Zed Books and Federation Press.

James, Paul, Victoria Stead, Yaso Nadarajah, Karen Haive. 2009. Projecting Community Life, themed issue, *Local Global: Identity, Security, Community* 5.

Justice Advisory Group (JAG). 2004. *Community Justice Situation Audit*. Report prepared for JAG by Lawrence Kalinoe.

Paliwala, Abdul 1982. Law and order in the Village: the Village Courts. In *Law and Social Change in Papua New Guinea*, ed. D. Weisbrot, A. Paliwala and A. Sawyerr, 191–217. Sydney: Butterworths.

Parenti, C. 1999. *Lockdown America: Police and Prisons in the Age of Crisis*. London and New York: Verso.

Regan, Anthony. 2005. Clever people solving difficult problems: perspectives on weakness of the state and the nation in Papua New Guinea. *Development Bulletin* 67, April 2005, 6–12.

Shearing, C. and L. Johnston. 2005. Justice in the Risk Society. *Australian and New Zealand Journal of Criminology* 38 (1) April 2005: 25–38.

Shearing, C. and Stenning, P. eds. 1987. *Private Policing*. Newbury Park, CA: Sage Publications.

Singer, P.W. 2003. *Corporate Warriors: The Rise of the Privatised Military Industry*. Ithaca, NY: Cornell University Press.

SPSN (Strongm Pipol Strongim Nesen). [n.d.] 'Empower People: Strengthen the Nation'. Draft Executive Summary.

Wai, Isaac and Paul Maia. 2005. What We Do in Saraga: Building Community Peace and Harmony, *Development Bulletin*, No. 67 April 2005, 53–55.

Weber, Max. 1972. Politics as a vocation. In *Max Weber*, ed. H. H. Girth and C. W. Mills. New York: Oxford University Press.

13. Re-thinking Human Rights and the HIV Epidemic: A Reflection on Power and Goodness

ELIZABETH REID

The discourse on human rights in the context of the HIV epidemic has been drawn from a legal paradigm of human rights for which international human rights law provides the theoretical and legal framework. As a result, the HIV and human rights discourse has focused on the ways in which human rights law has been violated in the context of the epidemic. Extensive descriptions of HIV-related human rights violations in different cultural, economic and political contexts have been documented. These inventories are then used to confront and shame the perpetrators, a classical legal practice and the dominant practice of human rights activism. This chapter upholds the importance of respect for and promotion of human rights in general and in the context of the HIV epidemic. The issue it explores is how best this can be done.

The legalistic approach to human rights and HIV has had positive outcomes. However, neither the confronting of transgression nor the discourse of a human rights based approach to HIV seem to have been as effective as desired in bringing about greater respect, greater dignity or lives less harmed by stigma or blessed with greater wellbeing. Heywood has pointed out some achievements (Heywood 2004). It has resulted in changes in policies and behaviours. In many countries there is now legislation and policy protecting the human rights of people infected/affected by HIV. Human rights arguments have had an impact on global thinking, the conduct of pharmaceutical companies and, in some cases, the practices of governments. However he acknowledges that the degree to which these protections have benefited people is patchy and they have had little tangible impact on the lives of poor women and children. To this list, one should also add men.

The prominence given to the legalistic and violations approach to human rights has meant that little or no work has been done to document and analyse the ways in which HIV-related human rights have been respected and upheld. Early in the epidemic, at the First International Conference on Health and Human

Rights, held at Harvard University in 1995, those present were challenged by Slobadan Lang, the Professor of Public Health at the University of Zagreb, to develop an activism of praise. He pointed out that, where, as in his region, human rights violations are widespread, a practice of praising those who honour and respect human rights might be developed. This, he argued, would reinforce such behaviour. It provides guiding narratives, accounts of respect and support across difference, of defiant bravery, of quiet resistance.

A practice of praising builds on and strengthens the goodness in people. It is an activism of respect. Respect differs from rights. It is not an entitlement that people have or something that can be claimed. Respect must be earned. An activism of respect and praising gives hope to those who want to live according to the values embedded in human rights. It gives an account of the exercise of responsibility and creates the possibility of collective integrity. Through reinforcing the individual and collective practice of human rights and values, this approach could bring about the benefits and social changes, the lack of which Mark Heywood laments. A practice of praising would also bring a different moral dimension to the legal paradigm. It offers an alternative to its confrontational forms of advocacy and activism.

A further consequence of the practice of the violations approach is that the focus on identifying and confronting transgressions means that less attention is paid to understanding the social and economic conditions which create the violations. Paul Farmer writes: 'The struggle to develop a human rights paradigm is one thing; a searching analysis of the mechanisms and conditions that generate these violations is quite another. Without understanding power and connections, how do we understand why rights are abused?' (2003, 11). Farmer argues that violations of human rights are symptoms of deeper pathologies of power 'linked intimately to the social conditions that so often determine who will suffer abuse and who will be shielded from harm' (2003, 7).

The pathologies of power that determine who, amongst those infected, affected or in danger of infection by HIV, will suffer from violations of their rights have not formed a part of the human rights discourse on HIV. The discourses of vulnerability, women's vulnerability to infection, the vulnerability of the marginalised, are power neutral, divorced from the pathologies that create the conditions of vincibility. Nor are these pathologies of power often addressed in HIV programming. The social conditions in which they are embedded and expressed give rise to the abuse of rights but are usually considered to be slow and difficult to change, too slow for the response to the HIV epidemic.

Consider the pathologies of power which shape women's lives within the epidemic. Violence and the fear of violence, rape, incest, bride price, marital subjugation, child brides, death in childbirth, ignorance of one's body and sexuality, misogyny, covert HIV testing in pregnancy, the abduction of women, the lack of valuing of women, and more—practices such as these spread the epidemic, assign the duty of care and concern to women, and often constrain women's access to HIV prophylaxis and antiretroviral therapies. They cause untold trauma to women and their children.

The attempts to capture these pathologies in a language of the infringement of women's human rights has often miscarried. Claims of violations of women's rights provoke various responses from men, including: What about *our* rights? And: Why are *we* being blamed? Both are reactive and close down dialogue; neither open up the possibility of reflection and growth. Men often experience the discourse on the rights of women as a form of social exclusion resulting in their 'loss of respect and dignity' (Colvin and Robins 2009). Women have been told that these rights violations are difficult if not impossible to address in the timeframe of HIV. What is needed is an understanding of the forces and double standards in a society which are manifested in these pathologies of power, for these are the same forces which drive the HIV epidemic.

An approach to HIV-related social change which, drawing on the work of Paulo Freire, attempts to address these driving forces of the epidemic has been developed. Stephen Lewis has singled it out as 'the stunning revelation of community conversations' (Lewis 2004). In a visit to rural Ethiopia mid-2004, Lewis sat with two communities, listening to them converse about the social conditions which were spreading the epidemic. One conversation involved 200 villagers who had been meeting once a fortnight for a couple of months; the other involved 15 or 20 people, with dozens of onlookers, who had been conversing for more than a year. Both communities were in a predominantly Islamic region.

The community conversation approach draws on traditions of talking things through and collectively deciding how to handle them. Community conversations are structured approaches to helping communities become aware of the ways in which their social norms, values and practices can bring the epidemic into their community, marginalise and humiliate those affected, and lessen the community's capacity to survive the epidemic. The methodologies used to stimulate conversations create a consciousness of these dynamics and then assist the communities in deciding how to respond.

The community conversations approach is based on a theory of social change which posits three areas of focus in building community capacity to change: community understanding of the issues it faces, community knowledge of itself, and community skills for changing. It facilitates conversations structured to assist in bringing about the changes in community norms, values, practices and power relations which help create communities in which conflicts can be resolved, in which HIV-affected and other socially marginalised people are supported, and in which the HIV epidemic struggles to gain a foothold.

The subject matters that Lewis heard publicly discussed in these community conversations 'without so much as a touch of embarrassment or shyness' included female genital mutilation, sexual violence, bride sharing, child abduction, early marriages, condoms, living with HIV and women's rights.

The results were astonishing. In one community, where female genital mutilation had been universally practised, it was down to 10 to 15 percent within a year as a result of the understanding gained in these conversations. An Islamic leader and 130 other men decided to be tested for HIV in order to set an example for others. Young girls talked openly about their rights as women and strategies they had adopted to protect themselves from HIV infection. Lewis commented:

> It was all quite extraordinary. We talk forever about countries where the level of awareness of HIV is very high but behaviour change is negligible. These community conversations have resulted in huge behaviour change. I have always believed that it would take generations even to show a willingness to address gender equality. Here it seems to have happened virtually overnight! (Lewis 2004)

What makes these community conversations so effective in addressing the pathologies of power? The answer lies in the creation of a structured environment in which communities are able to reflect together upon their norms and practices, inclusive spaces in which all their members—irrespective of gender, age, class, articulateness, status, ethnicity—are able to voice their concerns and opinions, and in which together, as a group, they seek to find ways to change, to protect themselves from the epidemic.

These conversations harness the power for good in a community and build on human potential and human virtues. They acknowledge human frailty without seeking it out to shame or confront. They enable practices of collective integrity and responsibility to arise.

They are, in the words of Michael Ignatieff, a practice of human rights as aspirational. They assume that people aspire to a world in which all human beings are respected, where their persons should be inviolable, and where they have enforceable rights by the very fact of being human beings (Ignatieff 1999). These aspirations are made more possible through the shared spaces of these conversations, spaces which form sanctuaries within which the pathologies of power can be confronted and changed.

The pathologies of power that determine who, amongst those infected, affected or in danger of being infected by HIV, will suffer from violations of their rights include the norms and practices of communities but encompass a multitude of other offences against human dignity: deprivation, neglect, indifference, racism, unemployment, sexism, corruption, ill-health, illiteracy and under-education. Can these be addressed and changed through methodologies of community 'conscientisation' and empowerment?

Many of these offences are not amenable to community-based problem-solving approaches alone. Their roots lie beyond communities as well as within them. Within communities the roots are found in systems of social relations and cultural practices; within societies, structural violence is embedded in the institutions of the society and economy. In what ways can these structural pathologies be understood and addressed?

We have been reminded recently that, as long ago as 1969, Johan Galtung wrote of the condition of structural violence in which people are denied decent and dignified lives because their basic physical and mental capacities are constrained by hunger, poverty, inequality and exclusion (Galtung 1969; Uvin 1998, Farmer 2004, 307). Structural violence is systemic violence carried out by those belonging to a certain social order. In these situations, neither blame nor praise can be attached to individual actions alone.

Violence of this type is built into the structure and functions of a society. Hence, it manifests itself differently in each society, for it depends on each country's historical, political and cultural circumstances. Structural violence leads to acute violence. Genocide might be its manifestation in Rwanda in 1994 (Uvin 1998), or it might be the violence, aggression and corruption in Papua New Guinea in recent years.

In PNG, there is a rapidly expanding and generalised HIV epidemic; there is a breakdown in law and order; there is the constant threat of violence; increasing numbers of politicians and senior bureaucrats are being named as corrupt. To outside eyes, these are often seen as local tragedies locally derived.

The concept of structural violence helps us see it differently. It traces how inequity is structured and legitimised over time. It renders visible the structural power relations which have contributed to how the present has come to be and who within the present benefit or are debased. It enables the question to be posed: who are the untimely dead? In PNG, these include the women dead in childbirth, the women raped and discarded, those dead of treatable diseases and conditions, the burnt, the children defiled, those killed in ethnic conflict, the murdered, and, increasingly, the dead of HIV. These are the victims of structural as well as local violence, those whose human rights have been violated in multiple ways.

Paul Farmer's challenge to undertake a 'searching analysis of the mechanisms and conditions that generate these violations' raises the question of how we understand this world of hostility and degradation. Too often it is 'seen' and understood through the creation of 'the Other'. From the description of what is—brutality, lawlessness, quickness to anger, vengeance, insecurity—an elision is made to They: 'They are a violent people'; 'They have little or no respect for human life'; 'They are rascals and rapists'; and so on. The state of their world is ascribed causally to them. This way of understanding their world justifies the neglect of their human rights. Moral scrutiny focuses narrowly on them rather than encompassing the factors which shape and determine their world and their behaviour.

The concept of structural violence provides us with a way of understanding such violence and lawlessness which refuses the elision from description to the predication of these qualities to people. Rather, anger, despair, frustration, cynicism, normlessness, confrontation are seen as outcomes of deprivation, as manifestations of structural violence, rather than as existential states, ways of being in the world.

The validity of such an analysis is borne out by a study of crime in NSW. A report prepared by the NSW Bureau of Crime Statistics and Research showed that falling crime rates in NSW (12 out of 16 major categories in the two preceding years) can be linked to higher wages among young men and a drop in long-term unemployment. The Director of the Bureau argued: 'Low wages and long-term unemployment are significant contributors to crime. When they improve crime tends to fall' (quoted in Nicholls 2004). Cowboy teaches us that this is as true in Port Moresby as in NSW (McLaren and Stiven 1991).

Historical and political conditions in PNG have created the systems and institutions which create deprivation and dysfunctionality. The social outcomes include a paucity of social mechanisms for dealing with conflict, concepts of women as disposable property, and pervasive and chronic unemployment, especially among young men. These deprivations contribute to the violence, aggression and corruption which fuel the HIV epidemic.

In such a context, it is not difficult to assemble an inventory of human rights transgressions. Nor is the confronting of perpetrators unusual. Practices of blaming, threatening, finger pointing and demands for vengeance are pervasive.

However, a legalistic approach to human rights in such settings does not create a moral discourse, stimulate the desire for change or craft the courage to speak into the silence of taboos, tradition or allegiance.

How then might human rights be addressed and honoured? Would practices of respect and praising work? Because, in PNG, one's identity, ways of behaving, the borders of one's world are communal rather than individual, it was decided to convene two workshops to critically reflect on approaches to community mobilisation to determine their relevance and possible effectiveness in the context of the HIV epidemic and its driving forces (PNGSDP 2007).

The methodology of community conversations privileges working with groups and communities, builds on the goodness in people and communities, and strengthens social capital. For these reasons, participants at the workshops decided that it should be developed for the PNG context. The community conversations approach resonates with people's view of the PNG way of doing things: community and clan discussion of problems, story telling as a form of moral guidance, a strong sense of reciprocity and of concern for the well being of the group. The methodology strengthens the skills required to understand problems and to look for ways through them: the ability to see and understand the consequences of actions, to make the transition from talking or 'storying' to addressing problems, to resolve differences and tensions in non-violent ways, to experience empathy and concern across differences, to accept responsibility and the hard work of thinking as a collective duty rather acquiescing to traditional or modern forms of knowledge and authority.

As the methodology for PNG was being developed, a pilot phase was begun. Community conversations teams have gathered and been trained in communities across seven provinces. The interest in the work is great. Stories are emerging of women feeling able to talk at community meetings, of communities coming together to talk about problems caused by drug use, of young people re-thinking their brewing and drinking activities, of parents talking to their children, of husbands and wives talking together. It is too early to determine if communities, as well as individuals, will be able in a sustained way to identify and respond to the forces of disharmony, exclusion and deprivation, the pathologies of power, in their midst and to develop the socio-cultural norms, values and practices that create caring and HIV protective communities.

Even if they can, pathologies of power are not only found within communities. They also arise from and cause structural violence. An HIV-related human rights discourse, in this analysis, would encompass social and economic rights such as the right to gainful employment, the right to adequate wages/incomes, to education, to health and more. People have a right not to be systemically and chronically deprived of their capacity to lead decent and dignified lives, a right, in Galtung's words, to fulfill to the extent possible their physical and mental capacities.

Such an HIV-related human rights discourse could also encompass a practice of praising. The praise stories could create an understanding of how people resist being overwhelmed by structural and local violations in their society. Such an understanding refuses an analysis in terms of human faults and failings and is open to a belief in human goodness.

A discourse on HIV and human rights which builds on human goodness and integrity could lead to effective approaches to addressing the HIV epidemic and the pathologies of power, local and national, which drive it. It would allow us to aspire to a world where human rights are respected and to an activism of praising, emulating and supporting goodness.

References

Colvin, Christopher and Steven Robins. 2009. Positive Men in Hard, Neoliberal Times: Engendering Health Citizenship in South Africa. In *Gender and HIV/AIDS: Critical Perspectives from the Developing World*, ed. Jelke Boesten and Nana Poku, 187–188. Farnham, UK: Ashgate Publishing.

Farmer, Paul. 2003. *Pathologies of Power: Health, Human Rights, and the New War on the Poor*. Berkeley: University of California Press.

Farmer, Paul. 2004. An Anthropology of Structural Violence. *Current Anthropology* 45 (3): 305–317.

Galtung, Johan. 1969. Violence, Peace, and Peace Research. *Journal of Peace Research* 6:167–91.

Heywood, Mark. 2004. Human Rights and HIV/AIDS in the Context of 3 by 5: Time for New Directions? *Canadian HIV/AIDS Policy & Law Review* 9 (2): 6–12.

Ignatieff, Michael. 1999. Human Rights: the Midlife Crisis. *New York Review of Books*, May 20. 46 (9).

Lewis, Stephen. 2004. Press Briefing Notes: Recent Trip to Ethiopia. June 1 2004. The Stephen Lewis Foundation. http://www.stephenlewisfoundation. org/news_item.cfm?news=342&year=2004 (accessed 27 April 2010).

McLaren, Les and Annie Steven. 1991. *Cowboy and Maria in Town: Stories of Urban Drift in Papua New Guinea*. Australian Film Commission with the assistance of the Australian Broadcasting Corporation and the PNG National Research Institute, Cultural Studies Division.

Nicholls, Sean. 2004. Crime Linked to Economy. *Sydney Morning Herald*, 23 November 2004.

PNGSDP (PNG Sustainable Development Program) 2007. Report of the Learning Workshops on Strengthening Community Engagement with the HIV Epidemic and its Driving Forces. http://www.pngsdp.com/images/documents/cci_learning_workshop.pdf (accessed 27 April 2010).

Uvin, Peter. 1998. *Aiding Violence: The Development Enterprise in Rwanda*. Connecticut: Kumarian Press.

14. Enabling Environments: the Role of the Law

CHRISTINE STEWART

The 'Enabling Environment'

In the context of HIV prevention, a distinction may be drawn between approaches which aim to persuade individuals to change their behaviour, and approaches which enable behaviour change by focusing on the social and environmental factors which assist or impede that change. These enabling approaches are directed towards removing barriers to protective and preventive action, and constructing barriers to the taking of risks (Tawil, Verster and O'Reilly 1995). The provision of an enabling social environment becomes all the more necessary when we consider how much the success of individual 'persuasion' approaches depends on a vast range of socio-cultural, historical and psychological factors—factors which vary not only from country to country, but between individual communities in a country as culturally diverse as Papua New Guinea, and which often sabotage even the most well-designed prevention efforts.

Why 'Enabling'?

It is generally considered by the international community that repressive measures to combat HIV simply drive those affected underground and fuel the epidemic (Jenkins and Sarkar 2004; UNHCR /UNAIDS1996). Thus people who know that their HIV status will not be kept confidential will not come forward to be tested. People who know that they will be thrown out of their homes, workplaces or communities will not seek medical or counselling assistance. People who have already suffered HIV and AIDS discrimination face increased economic burdens of health care and providing for dependents, and will turn to risk behaviours for survival. People who are members of criminalised groups, such as sex workers, are unable to assert their rights in situations of violence and exploitation.

But it has proved incredibly difficult to persuade the general Papua New Guinean community of this simple message: that repressive measures do not stop the epidemic, they actually assist its spread. Even in the most informed and articulate sectors of society, and despite the passage of the HIV/AIDS Management and Prevention Act (HAMP Act) through parliament in 2003, which recognised the counterproductivity of repressive measures, objections are still often raised to almost every proposal for an enabling environment. 'Mandatory testing is essential in the workplace, for planning purposes.' 'Sex workers should be all locked up, because they spread infection.' 'Giving condoms to teenagers will simply encourage them to experiment with sex.' 'Decriminalising homosexuality is not necessary because it is an expatriate import and not part of traditional Papua New Guinean culture.' 'Infected people should be driven from their homes and communities because contact with them or any of their possessions will cause infection to others.' 'Women spread HIV and should be raped as punishment.' 'Positive people should all be banished to a remote island.' And so on.

The Role of the Law

It has often been said that law cannot change behaviour. And it is true that law, even when properly implemented, often has little direct effect on people's choices, as has been realised by generations of criminologists attempting to discover why deterrence has not had the hoped-for effect of stamping out crime (Norrie 1993). But law, in whatever form, has always been seen as central to social existence and in recent years, social theorists have increasingly acknowledged the crucial role of law in shaping societies, particularly in colonial and post-colonial conditions (Merry and Brenneis 2004). Law, with its purpose of regulating, by its distribution of power and legitimacy, by its affording or denying certain resources to society for the resolution of conflict, has a significant role to play in the erection or removal of barriers to social action, and hence in the creation of the enabling environment we are aiming for.

The importance of law reform in the provision of an enabling environment for HIV prevention and management has been acknowledged at the highest levels. In 1996, an International Consultation on HIV/AIDS and Human Rights produced the *HIV/AIDS and Human Rights International Guidelines*. These Guidelines are aimed at providing

> an environment in which human rights are respected [which] ensures
> that vulnerability to HIV/AIDS is reduced, those infected with and

affected by HIV/AIDS live a life of dignity without discrimination and the personal and societal impact of HIV infection is alleviated (UNHCR/ UNAIDS 1996, 2).

The Guidelines recommend a national approach of widespread reform of laws and legal service provision, with an emphasis on anti-discrimination, protection of public health and improvement in the status of women, children and marginalised groups. They were followed in 1999 by a joint publication of UNAIDS and the Inter-Parliamentary Union, the 'Handbook for Legislators' (UNAIDS/IPU 1999) which fleshed out many of the recommendations in the Guidelines. The principles contained in these two documents were adopted by the South Pacific Commission in its *Regional Strategy* (SPC 1997) and by Papua New Guinea in its national plans (PNG/UN 1998; PNG/NACS 2006) as well as the HAMP Act.

Nevertheless, it must be acknowledged that law reform has its limitations. For a start, a legal regime is at best no more than an enabling device. It is only the first step in a three-stage process. The second is implementation. The third is the monitoring and, where necessary, enforcement of implementation. Even the best law reform cannot achieve, by several strokes of the pen, such wholesale social change as the empowerment of women. Nor can law reforms reach all levels of society. This is all the more so in a country such as Papua New Guinea, with over 800 different societies, most of them located both physically and conceptually far from the centre of government power; where the provision of government services is inexorably deteriorating and economic opportunities are limited; where the introduced common law system competes with or has achieved uneasy syncretism with custom and its more modern manifestation 'customary law'; and where state law, if it has penetrated to any degree at all, is ill-understood and inadequately applied by law and justice institutions and enforcers. However, this is no reason to ignore the potential of law reform to assist change, while nevertheless recognising its limitations and the external factors upon which it depends for effect.

Law Reforms which can Promote an Enabling Environment in Papua New Guinea

A case study is provided by an incident, now known as the Three-Mile Guesthouse Raid, which took place in Port Moresby one Friday afternoon in March 2004 (see Fletcher and Gonapa this volume; Jenkins this volume). [1] The

---

1   This account is drawn from newspaper reports and statements from various people involved at the time (Pilimbo 2004, Yiprukaman 2004a, Yirpukaman 2004b, Hershey 2004).

police raided a guesthouse which also operated a bar with gaming machines. There are a number of these guesthouses in Papua New Guinean towns providing short- and long-term accommodation at the lower end of the socio-economic scale. [2] Along with the higher-class hotels and motels, they frequently serve as contact points for the negotiation and conduct of commercial sex (Jenkins 1994; UNAIDS 2000; see Hammar this volume, Pantumari and Bamne this volume). But not everyone at the Three-Mile Guesthouse that afternoon was involved in the buying and selling of sex. Many were there simply to enjoy a beer from the bar and listen to the live band. Some of the young women were related to band members and turned up to support their kin in typical Papua New Guinea fashion. Some were there for the first time, brought by a girlfriend or relative. Some could not even afford the two kina [3] entry fee and peeped in through the gate to the yard, where older women sold cooked food, cigarettes and *buai* (betel nut). Some, men and women, were guesthouse staff; entire families, including children, were in long-term residence.

The raid was conducted in the style often used for raids on urban settlements, which involves a dramatic 'code-name', advance notification to the press, and other high-profile display tactics, all designed to bring to the attention of the public the job the police are doing in maintaining law and order (for a description of such raids, see Goddard 2001). In this case, that public display involved not just a lot of violence, looting and rape at the guesthouse itself, and mass arrests of almost everyone on the premises, but a public parade of those arrested through the streets of Boroko to the police station. The women were forced to chew and swallow condoms, blow them up, and wave them above their heads while a crowd of onlookers heckled them.

The Metropolitan Police Commander claimed that the raid was designed to prevent sex workers from contracting and spreading HIV. The women and girls arrested were charged with 'living on the earnings of prostitution', a charge which is the basis of the current criminalisation of sex work (see Fletcher and Gonapa this volume). The evidence produced in support of this charge was that condoms had been found on the premises and in their possession, which supposedly proved that the premises were a brothel and the women were prostitutes. [4]

What could the law do to mitigate this tragic event? What could it do to redress the wrongs committed that day, and to prevent any recurrences? Did it, could it, have any role at all?

---

2   Some 15–20 in Port Moresby at present.

3   Around AUD80¢. One PGK (Papua New Guinea kina) = approximately 0.42 AUD (January 2005).

4   This term is used because it is the language of the law. For some of the difficulties defining 'prostitute' or its loose synonym 'sex worker' in the Papua New Guinea context, see Hammar this volume.

As it turned out, the charges had to be dropped, but only on a technicality—the police were so eager to embark on their (law enforcement?) mission of social reform that somebody forgot to obtain the necessary search warrant (Anon. 2004; Yiprukaman 2004d). So the women went free. Apart from a condemnatory statement by the Internal Security Minister, who is responsible for the police (Yiprukaman 2004c), there has been no public announcement of any repercussions against those who ordered and conducted the raid. But was there, is there, anything further that could be done?

First, of course, is the possibility of action for abuse of human rights. The constitutionally-guaranteed rights to liberty and freedom and specifically freedom from inhuman treatment and from arbitrary search and entry have all possibly been infringed. In Papua New Guinea, any person can take an action in the National Court on behalf of any other person whose constitutional rights have been infringed, even without that other person's consent. So, for example, a rights advocacy group or church-based support group could easily take action on the women's behalf. Damages could be claimed, and importantly for present purposes, the whole matter of the police action, its style and its motivation, could be thoroughly examined in open court.

Action could also be taken for any number of criminal offences, such as assault and theft. But given the history of persecution of sex workers by the police in recent years (UNAIDS 2000), it is unlikely that such action would have serious repercussions for those involved. Although complaints of police mistreatment of prostitutes have on occasion been successful in the past (PNGIMR 1997, 9; cf. Jenkins this volume) overall, the chances today of a group of alleged prostitutes bringing successful complaints against the police are not good. This view is reinforced by the fact that prostitution is still criminalised in PNG. Although decriminalisation might not bring about an immediate reform in police attitudes, it might nevertheless remove the legal basis for police regarding their actions as justified. This is not to say that the treatment of the women by the police, including their being forced to suffer the indignity of the 'condom parade', was legitimate. But criminalisation can produce a simple equation in the minds of many people, including the police: these people are criminals and police protect society by apprehending criminals. 'Do what it takes to achieve this', so runs the thinking, 'we have the authority of the State on our side, as manifest in the law' (cf. Luker and Dinnen this volume, chapter one).

In fact, the law criminalising prostitution is somewhat shaky (see Fletcher and Gonapa this volume). Shortly after independence, the Law Reform Commission sought to abolish any offence of prostitution or soliciting and recommended the retention only of the related offences of operating a brothel and pimping or touting, described as 'living on the earnings of prostitution' (Law Reform Commission 1975). In 1978, however, an expatriate judge decided that this applied to the prostitute herself. [5] However, it is hard to imagine, in the Three-Mile Guesthouse Raid, how the police intended to sustain a prosecution for living on the earnings of prostitution when the only evidence of this was to be possession of condoms. It could have made for an extremely interesting case, in which the 1978 decision could possibly have been challenged if a conviction had gone on appeal to the National Court.

Decriminalisation of prostitution was advocated in the Medium Term Plan 1998–2002 (PNG/UN 1998, 34) and has been urged by the National AIDS Council since 2000. Action in this regard is underway, with draft changes to the legislation governing sex work and homosexuality prepared for preliminary discussion in 2010 (Papik 2010). But it may be a long and hard road (see Fletcher and Gonapa this volume). Political will in this regard is almost non-existent, and this is a classic example of the difficulties of persuading the general community that repressive laws merely add fuel to the epidemic. Even if the law were to be successfully amended, the stigma would remain, and Hammar (this volume) and Fletcher and Gonapa (this volume) allude to other difficulties.

But decriminalisation of prostitution would not assist in relation to other criminalised or stigmatised activity. Homosexuality, for instance, in the form of a charge of sodomy, is still a crime in Papua New Guinea (Criminal Code Section 210), and although there are few cases actually brought to court, the threat, and the very real possibility of being framed for ulterior motives, such as dismissal from employment, is enough to make life quite uncomfortable for gay men, both national and expatriate, in Papua New Guinea. Abortion too is illegal (Criminal Code Section 225). This denies a woman control of her sexual and reproductive rights, an issue that was mentioned in the International Guidelines regarding HIV/AIDS (UNHCR/UNAIDS 1996). It is all very well advocating drug supply for pregnant women, but what of an HIV-positive woman who does not wish to bring a potential AIDS orphan into the world? In the Papua New Guinea context, she can hardly rely on a guaranteed supply of drug therapy to sustain her until her child attains majority.

Efforts so far

One almost-successful move towards the creation of an enabling legal environment for epidemic management was the passing by Parliament in 2003 of the HIV/AIDS Management and Prevention Act (HAMP Act). After considerable consultation in 2001, this law was prepared to reflect, as far as was possible, the recommendations of the International Guidelines.

---

5   In Anna Wemay & Ors. v Kepas Tumdual: [1978] PNGLR 173.

The first and principal aims of the Act are to reduce the barriers to beneficial change caused by discrimination and stigmatisation. HIV/AIDS discrimination may be directed not only against those infected, but also against their relatives and associates. So the scope of those to be protected may be likened to a series of widening circles: first, a person with HIV or AIDS; next, a person presumed to have HIV or AIDS; next, a relative or associate of a person with HIV or AIDS; then a relative or associate of a person presumed to have HIV or AIDS; and last comes a particularly important category, that of people who are or are presumed to be members of or associated with groups, activities or professions or living in environments, which are associated with or presumed to be associated with HIV infection or transmission. This last category is so important because it provides a 'back-door' way of protecting those involved in or with criminalised or stigmatised activities and groups, such as prostitutes, gay men, urban 'squatter settlement' residents, even as broad a social category as 'women'.

The second measure is the prohibition on withholding, without reasonable excuse such as unavailability, any means of protection against infection. This could include HIV/AIDS awareness materials, condoms and lubricant, sterile skin-penetrative equipment, and so on.

Next, the HAMP Act prohibits any kind of mandatory, coerced or otherwise involuntary HIV testing. This was a matter of the greatest concern to the framers of the National HIV/AIDS Medium-Term Plan 1998–2002 (PNG/UN 1998), so care was taken to ensure that testing without full voluntary informed consent could only be carried out in the most limited circumstances.

The final significant enabling measure in the Act is the protection of confidentiality regarding a person's HIV status. Obviously this restriction cannot be applied to the whole of society, but it is applied to anyone who comes by the knowledge of HIV status in the course of his or her official duties, even if these are not directly related to health or other care. Courts have the power to close their doors where appropriate. Contact-tracing and partner-notification are discretionary and may only be carried out by professional carers in limited circumstances.

So how can these grand statements of dos and don'ts be made effective? The first step is to set out what should happen if they are breached. The Act allows a wide range of remedies, depending on what particular wrong has been done. Redress can be obtained by civil or criminal court action, or where appropriate, through professional misconduct or disciplinary hearings. The range of civil remedies is very wide: as well as orders for damages, restitution and apologies, the courts may make orders to do what has not been done or to refrain from doing that which was done; to provide what has been withheld; to restore what has been taken away; to do whatever is necessary to redress any loss or damage suffered.

But court action is not always appropriate, or even feasible. So the Act permits another avenue, that of inquiry by the Ombudsman Commission, in accordance with its jurisdiction over discriminatory practices. This is possibly the single most significant feature of the Act. Although the Commission has no power to take direct action, it can nevertheless make recommendations as appropriate, whether to public authorities or private persons. And the Ombudsman Commission of Papua New Guinea has, over the years, established a reputation for fearless and forthright investigation and action. It is a force to be reckoned with.

Unfortunately though, the Act was not in force at the time of the raid, so it will be of no assistance to the aggrieved victims of the Three-Mile Guesthouse Raid. However, the Raid does seem to have galvanised efforts to progress the legislation, and the Act was finally gazetted for commencement in September 2004. The only actions taken so far as a result of the commencement were a charge, enabled by the Act, of manslaughter for an accusation of infection by injection, (dismissed in January 2005 for lack of evidence (Faiparik 2005)) and the conviction of a man for proclaiming that his formar girlfriend was HIV positive (Kelola 2009). Further tests of its efficacy are sure to come. What usually happens with a new legislative regime is that after one or two good test cases, or in this case Ombudsman Commission inquiries, with appropriate media attention, the message starts to get out. Gradually, employers might stop sacking positive employees. Doctors and laboratories might stop giving out test results to third parties. Access to condoms might no longer be barred. And the police may no longer think they have a right, in the name of preventing HIV and AIDS, to swoop on suspected brothels, empty the tills, use violence and march women in a parade of humiliation through the streets of the nation's capital.

Another recent move towards improving the legal situation as regards sexual offences has been the Criminal Code (Sexual Offences and Crimes Against Children) Act of 2002. This Act was drawn up by the Family and Sexual Violence Action Committee headed by Lady (now Dame) Carol Kidu. It is a sad comment on the state of law reform in Papua New Guinea that Carol Kidu, although she is the government Minister for Community Development and therefore deeply involved in the social aspects of matters such as sexual violence and child prostitution, could only get this law through Parliament by proposing it as a Private Member's Bill. Why? Because it amends the Criminal Code in several significant ways; the Criminal Code is part of the Justice Minister's portfolio; and the Department of Justice and Attorney-General are not overly concerned with the promotion of social welfare amendments.

However, the Act did pass Parliament. It is the only major amendment to the sexual offences aspects of the Code since its first introduction into Papua New Guinea some hundred years ago. It makes such overdue amendments as rendering many of the sexual assault offences gender-neutral, whereas previously, for example, it was impossible for a male person to be raped. It makes marital rape a crime. And it inserts two new Divisions dealing with sexual offences against children and offences of child sex trafficking. A new Section 229Q makes it an offence to prosecute a child under the age of 18 years for prostitution, but unfortunately the amendment was worded so as to restrict its ambit solely to prostitution offences under the new law. When the legal team assisting those arrested in the Three-Mile Guesthouse Raid attempted to have the charges against nine under-aged girls dismissed, they were unsuccessful, as the charges had been laid under different legislation, the Summary Offences Act (Chapter 264). This is one small example of the power of the law, and the form of the law, in dictating the fundamental ways in which people's lives are shaped, and in this case, maintaining a barrier against effective social action.

Conclusion

This chapter has tried to demonstrate that the law, despite significant shortcomings of implementation and access, has a role to play in shaping society and social action. The law can enable—and disable—many things. This is essentially the role of any law. It can provide the legal characteristics of an enabling environment by removing legal barriers to effective action and by establishing legal barriers to adverse outcomes. Stigma and discrimination may remain, but at least they will no longer be reinforced by repressive legislation. The task for law reformers now is to identify further law which needs changing or improving, and to support as far as possible the creation of social and political environments in which law can take effect.

References

Anon. 2004. Police Withdraw Case against 40 women. *The National*, 8 April 2004.

Faiparik, Clifford. 2005. Manslaughter Charge against Soldier Dismissed. *The National*, 23 January 2005.

Goddard, M. 2001. From Rolling Thunder to Reggae: Imagining Squatter Settlements in Papua New Guinea. *Contemporary Pacific* 13: 1–32.

Hershey, Christopher. 2004. *Statement of Facts on Police Raid at 3-Mile Guesthouse 12 March 2004, and Related Incidents*. Statement made on behalf of Poro Sapot Project, Save the Children in Papua New Guinea, 20 March 2004.

Jenkins, C. 1994. *Situational Assessment of Commercial Sex Workers in Urban Papua New Guinea*. Prevention Research Unit/GPA. New York: World Health Organisation.

Jenkins, C., and S. Sarkar. 2004. Creating Environments that Care: Interventions for HIV Prevention and Support for Vulnerable Populations (draft). Policy Project (USAID) and UNAIDS.

Kelola, Todagia. 2009. Hefty Penalty. *Post-Courier*, 26 May 2009

Law Reform Commission of Papua New Guinea. 1975. *Report on Summary Offences*. Report No. 1. Waigani: Law Reform Commission of Papua New Guinea.

Merry, S. E. and D. Brenneis. 2004. *Law and Empire in the Pacific: Fiji and Hawai'i*. Santa Fe, New Mexico: School of America Research Press.

Norrie, Alan W. 1993. *Crime, Reason and History: A Critical Introduction to Criminal Law*. London: Weidenfeld and Nicolson.

Papik, John. 2010. PNG Civil Groups Prepare Gay, Sex Work Law Challenge. Pacific Beat, Radio National, Australian Broadcasting Commission. 29 January.

Pilombo, Peku. 2004. Police Arrest 80 in Brothel Raid. *The National*, 15 March 2004.

PNG and NAC. 2006. *Papua New Guinea National Strategic Plan on HIV/AIDS 2006–2010*. Port Moresby: Government of Papua New Guinea and PNG National AIDS Council Secretariat.

PNG/UN. 1998. *National HIV/AIDS Medium Term Plan 1998–2002*. Port Moresby: Government of PNG with assistance from the United Nations System.

PNGIMR. 1997. *Final Report to UNAIDS: Police and Sex Workers in Papua New Guinea*. 12 October 1977, Goroka: Papua New Guinea Institute of Medical Research.

http://www.walnet.org/csis/papers/jenkins_papua.html (accessed 27 April 2010).

SPC (Secretariat of the Pacific Community). 1997. Regional Strategy for the Prevention and Control of STD/AIDS in Pacific Island Countries and Territories. Noumea: South Pacific Commission.

Tawil, O.A. Verster and K.R. O'Reilly. 1995. Enabling Approaches for HIV/AIDS prevention: can we modify the environment and minimize the risk? *AIDS* 9: 1299–1306.

UNAIDS. 2000. Female Sex Worker HIV Prevention Projects: Lessons Learnt from Papua New Guinea, India and Bangladesh. In *UNAIDS Best Practice Collection*. Geneva: UNAIDS.

UNAIDS/IPU. 1999. Handbook for Legislators on HIV/AIDS, Law and Human Rights: Action to Combat HIV/AIDS in View of its Devastating Human, Economic and Social Impact. Geneva: Joint United Nations Programme on HIV/AIDS and Inter-Parliamentary Union.

UNHCHR/UNAIDS. 1996. *HIV/AIDS and Human Rights: International Guidelines*. New York and Geneva: United Nations Commissioner for Human Rights and Joint United Nations Programme on HIV/AIDS.

Yiprukaman, Michelle. 2004a. Sex Workers on Parade. *Post-Courier*, 15 March 2004.

Yiprukaman, Michelle. 2004b. Males 'Freed' … but 31 Suspected Female Prostitutes Charged! *Post-Courier*, 16 March 2004.

Yiprukaman, Michelle. 2004c. Police Actions Damned. *Post-Courier*, 19 March 2004.

Yiprukaman, Michelle, 2004d. Police Withdraw Prostitute Case. *Post-Courier*, 8 April 2004.

15. HIV and Security in Papua New Guinea: National and Human Insecurity[1]

MICHAEL O'KEEFE

Introduction

Much of the discussion in this volume focuses, understandably, on particular experiences and responses to HIV and AIDS in PNG, just as much of the international discourse focuses on the immediate needs of prevention, treatment and care. Yet the impact of the epidemic is potentially felt across all of society, and an unchecked epidemic will further challenge the collective viability of Papua New Guinea.

Such a broad analysis might be expected in the field of International Relations, attempts to provide this overview of the epidemic have been made (e.g., Altman 2003; Brower and Chalk 2003; Eberstadt 2002; Barnett and Whiteside 2002). Most mainstream International Relations research, however, concentrates on threats to states—particularly military threats—and the implications of a full-scale HIV epidemic are not developed in their calculations, although for political reasons the epidemic may rate a cursory mention. There are, of course, exceptions: indeed US intelligence agencies were among the first to begin this broad sort of analysis (CIA 2000).

This chapter reflects on larger strategic questions about the overall impact— social, political, economic and cultural—of the epidemic on an already fragile state where national cohesion is very weak, and society is mainly organised at kin and local levels. Studies of the strategic effects of HIV (particularly on its possible economic impact (e.g. CIE 2002, HEMIS 2006)) have not linked this to more general research on the development in PNG and various factors that threaten political and social stability. The following discussion is framed by the concept of human security and the application of this framework to the epidemic in PNG. At the same time an 'apocalyptic' view of HIV and security

---

1 Thanks to Dennis Altman and the editor for comments on this chapter. Of course, any errors are my own.

will be avoided. As evidence from sub-Saharan Africa suggests, the worst affected societies are remarkably resilient even when infection rates reach 30–40 percent of the young adult population (e.g. de Waal 2005, 119).

Notwithstanding problems of surveillance and reporting (PNG National AIDS Council 2008, 75–77), the epidemic clearly has become entrenched in PNG and has the potential to become significantly worse. Ben Reilly has written of the potential for the 'Africanisation of the Pacific' (Reilly 2000), and if this prediction is accurate then HIV and AIDS will be a central part of this process. However, much of the 'African experience' may not be relevant to PNG and many objections to the 'Africanisation' thesis have been raised (e.g. Fraenkel 2004a; Chappell 2005) and these objections may similarly apply to HIV (O'Keefe 2008; Hammar 2007; Hammar this volume). For instance, PNG is at a much earlier stage in the epidemic than the countries of southern Africa and local factors always affect the epidemic's course. Therefore, in the following discussion the relevance of the 'African experience' will be treated with caution.

Regardless of these qualifying statements, the following overview highlights the major challenges that PNG society and the state are facing, with an emphasis on what can be learned from the broader international experience. This chapter does not seek to make all the connections with the situation on the ground in PNG but rather, to make some key connections and to provide a frame that PNG specialists can use to judge for themselves the relevance of various aspects of the international experience.

The Meaning of Security

Various types of insecurity are often conflated, which causes some confusion, especially when it is unclear whether the discussion refers to the security of the most affected states, societies or people, or to the wider international system. In very simplistic terms one might posit a tension between a narrow, state- and military-centred vision of security, and one that places an emphasis on human welfare and survival. The Cold War policy of 'Mutually Assured Destruction' (MAD), which would sacrifice all human life to 'defeat' an enemy, is symbolic of a view of security that is totally centred on the state.

Mainstream International Relations theorists regard the state as the primary unit of analysis. Statehood involves the possession and maintenance of formal sovereignty, which has internal and external dimensions. Theoretically, a state must acknowledge the legitimacy of international law, and is recognised by the international community of states as the legitimate authority over a designated geographic area.

Territory must be held, borders must be protected against encroachments by other states, and authority must be maintained within these borders. That is, a state's 'monopoly of violence' must be maintained. These aspects of formal sovereignty explain why military security forms the basis of much debate in international relations and why most non-military issues are excluded from analysis.

In the contemporary world there are many 'states' whose control over their territory is in fact limited. For instance, state sovereignty in PNG has been challenged by the secessionist movement in Bougainville, the 'porous' borders with West Papua and the Solomon Islands and, in some areas, by the breakdown in law and order—but not by epidemic disease. Shocking as HIV statistics may be, few International Relations scholars see AIDS as a direct threat to states and, more specifically, to PNG as a state.

The primary source of orthodox state-centric threats is invasion and internal conflict (civil war), the former possibly removing the existing state altogether, the latter creating instability that could lead to state fragility. Internal conflict could be sponsored by another state or be caused by domestic rebellion. The likelihood of these types of threats developing in PNG is as follows:

Cross-border Threats

Strategic forecasts paint a benign picture: there are no external military threats to PNG likely for the foreseeable future (Australia 2005). If there were to be any such threat, then it would be more likely to be over the land border with West Papua. There is a paucity of commentary on this diplomatically sensitive topic but all indications are that an invasion by Indonesia is extremely unlikely. Cross-border incursions are more likely but would not threaten the PNG state (they would however erode its legitimacy).

The Threat of Civil War and/or Rebellion

Due to signs of internal instability in other South Pacific states, the threat of coup or rebellion might appear the most likely state-centric threat to security in PNG (May 2004). Several movements of a micronationalist character preceded and followed Independence in 1975, and over the last 30 years challenges to the PNG state have been launched from within. The Bougainville conflict and Sandline Affair are two of the most noteworthy, though tensions have also arisen from attempts to reform the PNG defence force (see Pantumari and Bamne this volume). However, so far these have not amounted to serious threats of a military coup. The key issue is that governments have changed in PNG in a relatively orderly fashion and national institutions have proved surprisingly resilient (if limited in capacity). Besides, the PNG military is small and multi-ethnic, and in recent years has been reduced in size (see Pantumari and Bamne, this volume).

HIV as an Unorthodox State-centric Threat to PNG

In fragile states such as PNG non-military sources of insecurity, such as natural disasters, transnational crime, and major epidemics can have a real impact on the ability of the state to function. For most people HIV and AIDS pose a greater threat than an orthodox military one, but analysing this requires a comprehensive 'threat matrix' that includes individual, societal and national/ state security. A similar debate has occurred over global warming. Critics of remedial actions to counter global warming, such as signing the Kyoto Protocol, are fighting a similar rearguard action against the orthodox military perspective of security. An extended treatment of human security would be out of place here although a valuable discussion of this concept can be found in Tow et al. (2000; see also Reid this volume).

It has been posited that HIV may prove a threat to the survival of the state in a number of ways. The most obvious is if increasing HIV rates lead to civil conflict. A causal link has been postulated between conflict and increased transmission of HIV in Sub-Saharan Africa, for example in Rwanda and the Congo, although there is also evidence that some conflicts may actually slow HIV transmission (Whiteside et al. 2006). (However, as noted earlier, PNG is unlikely to face the sort of intense levels of armed conflict that has plagued some African states.) The unlikely prospect of invasion or rebellion in PNG effectively removes the most credible link between HIV and state-centric threats.

More serious is the possible impact of HIV on domestic forces of law and order. It is often asserted that HIV prevalence in the military in some African states is disproportionately high (as in Angola and the Congo), especially during early stages of the epidemic, thus making the military a source of instability (Kendino 2005a; 2005b; Elbe 2003, esp. chapter 2). This instability could result from either rebellion or because the military is so weakened it can no longer defend the state. More recent research, however, has qualified the assertion that military populations tend to experience higher HIV prevalence than their civilian counterparts (Barnett and Prins 2005; Whiteside et al. 2006) and available prevalence figures suggest that the military in PNG has infection rates comparable to those of the general populace. [2] Many observers actually see the Papua New Guinea Defence Force (PNGDF) as a source of stability, rather than a threat to the state. This puts paid to threat perceptions focused on increasing prevalence in the military as a source of instability but does not represent the end of the story. The PNGDF does take responsibility for its members and the rising costs of treatment and funeral expenses will impose a burden on its already tight budget (see Pantumari and Bamne this volume).

Of more concern is the effect of HIV and AIDS on the Royal Papua New Guinea Constabulary (RPNGC). The police have not been able to maintain law and order, or halt the declining law and order situation. Indeed, as several chapters indicate, many observers see the RPNGC as too often actively implicated in the escalation of law and order problems, including in sexual assaults (e.g. Luker and Dinnen this volume; Jenkins this volume; McLeod and Macintyre this volume). While there is little evidence suggesting that HIV is among the factors currently impacting on police efficiency, increased infection rates will presumably weaken the effectiveness of the force over time. As with the PNGDF, the diversion of resources to cover medical expenses will also have an impact on the RPNGC.

Higher HIV rates can increase and compound instability by limiting the ability of the law and order agencies to do their jobs. Assuming that criminal groups, refugees, illegal immigrants, and even neighbouring states might take advantage of any military and police ineffectiveness, even in the narrow terms of state-centric security, HIV becomes a concern. However, this assumes that these challengers to the state are not afflicted by similar prevalence rates as the forces of law and order, which is an improbable outcome. Clearly evidence of HIV as a state-centric threat is patchy and incomplete. By contrast, if we understand security to mean human and social development the picture is more complex. HIV poses a human-centric threat that bears further examination.

The global spread of HIV is shaped by local political, economic, cultural and societal attributes, and while concerns about the possible growth of HIV in PNG are legitimate there is also no inevitability about it reaching the adult prevalence of around 26–28 percent found in, say, Swaziland or Botswana (UNAIDS 2009, 27–28). Some parallels can be drawn with the political weaknesses of a number of African states, in that the many peoples within PNG have arguably never been cohesively united by a national identity—clan and *wantok* groups prevail and are only united in so far as they all attempt to use the PNG state to further the interests of their group (see Luker and Dinnen this volume, chapter one). Coincidentally, however, it is this diversity that also limits the threat of state collapse through coup or rebellion because 'ethno-linguistic fragmentation'

---

2   There are many reasons to question the accuracy of prevalence figures, both PNG-wide, as alluded to above, and for the military (see Pantumari and Bamne, this volume).

means that small groups lack the resources to threaten the state, regardless of its weaknesses (Reilly 2004, 484). Yet as Reilly and Phillpot, among others, have argued: 'ethnic fragmentation, while ensuring the continuity of formal democracy at the national level, has undermined the development of social capital at the local level and effectively created a massive collective action problem' (Reilly and Philpott 2002, 927).

The state in PNG can be viewed as a large patronage network that divides and distributes the resources of the state but within which the players do not comprise sufficiently large groups to independently challenge the state. It is this form of instability that much of the scholarship on state failure in Africa has highlighted. Reno and others identify internal security challenges as being at the root of the problem of state failure in African 'quasi-states'. That is, internal conflict destabilises the patronage networks that many African states rely upon to maintain domestic law and order but not formal 'external' sovereignty. Historically, attempts to develop new networks often led to an over-reliance on external groups. However, in the post-Cold War environment the superpowers are no longer interested in proxy wars and blocs of allies so new relationships need to be built, be they with governments, investors or aid organisations (Reno 1997).

The relationship between the state, patronage networks and external actors described above was also evident in the Solomon Islands but has not had the same impact in PNG (Fraenkel 2004b, 5). The African experience does not necessarily translate to the South Pacific. For instance, a key element in the loss of superpower support mentioned above is a drying up of external aid, which must be supplemented from other sources. The opposite has been the case in PNG where Australian aid and intervention has increased markedly (O'Keefe 2005). Furthermore, external aid has become more tightly focused on state capacity-building and governance, rather than over-reliance on foreign investment primarily aimed at relieving the debt burden.

Human Security and HIV

So far we have discussed the state-centric perspective of the security implications of HIV. While the virus may have devastating consequences, HIV does not fit into the orthodox security paradigm. However, if one's starting point is human security rather than state survival the emphasis will be quite different (Altman 2003; Brower and Chalk 2003; Reid this volume).

In the early 1990s the UN Development Programme undertook a major review of the nature of security. The UNDP acknowledged that 'security symbolize[s] protection from the threat of disease, hunger, unemployment, crime, social conflict, political repression and environmental hazards'. Human security was defined as 'safety from such chronic threats as hunger, disease and repression… [and]…protection from sudden and hurtful disruptions in the pattern of daily life.' Therefore, human security involves economic, food, health, environmental, personal, community and political security (UNDP 1994, 22–5).

Clearly the concept and application of human security is drastically different to state-centric perspectives. One of the benefits of taking this broader approach is that it more accurately reflects the day-to-day reality facing most people. As stated earlier, for most people HIV is a greater threat than those of an orthodox military nature.

Discussion of the impact of AIDS must focus on the untimely deaths and incapacitation caused by epidemic HIV. Laurie Garrett has noted that 'the HIV/AIDS pandemic is having severe demographic effects on hard hit societies, producing a so-called youth bulge, and reversing gains previously made in life expectancies and infant and child mortality rates' (Garrett 2005, 11). This situation points to a demographic imbalance that can only have long-term ramifications on state stability.

The long period between infection and death, often a period involving serious illness, is crucial to understanding the full impact of the epidemic on people and the states they live within. Well before a person living with HIV dies of HIV-related disease, he or she often cannot work, and will require high-intensity care. The Brazilian example suggests that providing the best available treatments is actually a cost-effective measure for those states with sufficient means (*Economist* 2005, 69), though providing even the most basic level of medical care for people with HIV is very costly, especially in terms of human resources. In PNG, the burden of providing this care falls on the informal sector, and as prevalence rises, the existing shortage of skilled personnel in PNG will become more acute, just as the number of HIV patients requiring treatment increases.

Societies characterised by strong relationships of kin underpin traditionally weak states in Africa and the South Pacific, and PNG is a particularly good example. The loss of an able-bodied family member is a tragic circumstance with devastating interpersonal and familial consequences. In the absence of strong state services, death or disablement affects considerable numbers of dependents, families and communities. This contributes to the breakdown of the family and communities that form the fabric of society. Gender inequality in PNG is already stark (Eves this volume), and the impact of HIV is to increase the burden on women as both carers and providers of income. Of particular concern is the rising number of orphans who are growing up in increasingly fractured societies with little hope for the future. These children are likely to survive through marginal activity and not attend school (UNGA 2005; HEMIS

2006, 56–57). Elderly people requiring care will also suffer as they are denied the benefits of the traditional social compact. When the cause of death and disablement reaches epidemic proportions it is no longer a matter of isolated family suffering—the fabric of society is strained and the resilience of the kin bonds that underpin the state in PNG will be tested.

As bread-winners require care or themselves become carers, household income drops, affecting the prospects of all members of the household. The poor get poorer because AIDS can exacerbate existing poverty and push low-income earners below the poverty line. In this manner AIDS is implicated in increased poverty and social inequality in Africa (UN 2001; UNAIDS 2008, 162). For instance, the burden of large numbers of burials is often mentioned as one of the real consequences of the epidemic at a household and community level. Many of those infected by the virus are, however, the ruling elites and middle classes who have received the largest per capita investment in human capital. These doctors, teachers, government officials are very difficult to replace. The institutional memory of the civil service can become incomplete (Pharoah 2003, 6). The loss of scarce human capital represents a loss of education, health, productivity, living standards and physical security (UNAIDS 2008, 174–177). Similar impacts have been modelled for PNG (CIE 2002; HEMIS 2006, 53–80).

Life expectancy in Sub-Saharan Africa is lower today than it was 30 years ago, with catastrophic drops in the most heavily AIDS-affected countries—falling, for example, by 16 years in Swaziland and 20 in Botswana (UNDP 2006, 265). This means that many people with a great deal of experience will die before they can pass their knowledge on and many others will become infected or die before they gain experience relevant to the effective functioning of families, communities and societies. The loss of the possessors of kinship knowledge can only alter and undermine the societal bonds that buttress the state in PNG. When HIV prevalence among younger people and amongst productive members of the workforce is high, population replacement and composition will also become an issue (Eberstadt 2002). A disproportionate number of infections occur amongst 15 to 49 year olds and due to 'equality of infection' it is commonplace for mothers to pass HIV on to their children (UN 2001, 31–32). Successes in reducing infant mortality in the 20th century have already been wiped out in some countries (WHO 2003, 7, 10–11). Similar projections have been made for PNG (CIE 2002; HEMIS 2006).

As AIDS exacerbates social fragmentation it becomes more and more difficult to mobilise the resources, human and material, to address the epidemic. Some African studies have posited a connection between AIDS and increased crime rates (Schonteich 2000, 57–66). Social dislocation caused by the potent mixture of the epidemic, conflict or state fragility increases 'survival' crime. Orphans may be forced onto the streets of large metropolitan areas where petty crime and commercial sex provide a means of survival (Fourie 2003). Furthermore, the usual response to crime is punishment but this can be counterproductive in the extreme as prisons are well known incubators for the disease (See Law this volume). In fact, in countries such as Russia and the US the single most effective means of HIV prevention may be to drastically reduce the prison population (Altman 2005). The link between AIDS and increased crime can only become stronger if the organs of law and order begin to fail.

State Capacity and Security in PNG

For states that function reasonably well to begin with, the HIV epidemic can degrade the capacity to provide basic services. However, these states usually have the capacity to marshal resources to head off any major threat. For states that have limited penetrative power within their societies and can be said to be already fragile, AIDS can limit the potential for capacity-building that can improve services. Law and order can break down and health and social welfare safety nets, already weak, can fail. The loss of human capital and economic growth has the potential to undermine the maintenance of various functions of government, especially highly technical areas (such as the medical services, economic management and taxation) or areas involved in maintaining law and order. Under these conditions the most basic medical treatments cannot be guaranteed, let alone treatment for HIV. Even the ability to provide basic technical services, such as sanitation and clean water, can be affected.

The preceding summary applies to many fragile states in Africa but is not readily transferable to PNG. As we have seen some government instrumentalities in PNG, such as the military and police, have not followed the African experience and been disproportionately degraded. They may be under-resourced and ineffective, AIDS is not the cause. Moreover, the PNG state has not reached much beyond the main population centres and many areas lack the most rudimentary services. In the presence of an expanding epidemic there can be little hope that this situation will improve—although it is unclear whether an improvement would occur in the absence of the epidemic.

Civil disorder and armed conflict, through such consequences as displacement, unregulated population flows and scarcity of essential foodstuffs, are likely to raise the incidence of HIV infection in some circumstances (Hankins et al. 2002). The lawlessness in PNG provides the potential for similar conditions to develop in certain locations. In many countries, injecting drug use (IDU), sexual violence and commercial sex, all of which exacerbate the spread of HIV, are becoming more widespread, even as the capacity for HIV prevention declines. In PNG, IDU is not an issue but the other factors are present.

While a state's inability to provide physical security for its citizens is the most visible form of human insecurity, there are other implications, especially for the provision of essential services in health and education that are taken for granted in wealthier sates. As large employers in many countries, the government is most likely to introduce HIV testing of employees (as is definitely the case for the military). If they are lucky, those who are deemed unfit will receive health benefits. This adds a further burden to governments and society, one that appears unsustainable in many African countries (Quattek 2000).

Although estimates of the overall impact of the epidemic on the economy often vary widely,[3] there is no doubt that AIDS has an impact on economic growth and inequality in fragile states. Premature death and disablement on epidemic levels also cause a major reordering in community and family support mechanisms, which in turn can lower agricultural productivity (du Guerny 2002). It is estimated that the agricultural workforce in the most affected African states has declined by between 3 and 13 percent due to AIDS. The resultant impact on food security could not be worse for societies where nutrition and clean water are problems and few reserves are in place to allow for the ever-present threat of famine (Fourie 2003).

As the Commission on AIDS in the Pacific (CAP) has noted, little research has been undertaken to date on the economic impacts of HIV in the Pacific or more specifically in PNG (CAP 2009, 46). Those studies that are available (e.g. CIE 2002, HEMIS 2006) are based on modeling, rather than measuring effects that have occurred. CAP however found that both public and private sector superannuation schemes in PNG reported an increase in claims due apparently in part to morbidity and mortality from AIDS (CAP 2009, 46). Also, a quarter of companies surveyed in 2009 reported that their operations in PNG had been negatively impacted by HIV over the previous five years, while three-quarters anticipated negative impact in the coming five years (CAP 2009, 49-50). Because only a minority of adults can find work in the formal sector, the sickness and death of a wage-earner affects the large number of dependents that employee usually supports. Effects of HIV and AIDS on the informal and subsistence sectors, which support the vast majority of the population, are even harder to track, but geographers expect that AIDS may affect food security, with communities in the most marginal and least endowed environments being most vulnerable (Hanson et al. 2001, 13).

---

3   Many studies focus on individual states and while illuminating about that state they do not provide a useful comparison with other states within the region or outside. See for instance Quattek 2000 and Shell 2000.

Conclusion

The orthodox focus on military security that dominates International Relations limits our ability to analyse the implications of 'new' security threats, such as HIV and AIDS, for fragile states, such as PNG. This in turn creates a structural weakness in external responses to 'new' security threats in fragile states. As Dinnen and others argue, a state-centric view of security leads to the '*securitisation of aid*, whereby the priorities of donor assistance are increasingly shaped by an external, and questionable, security agenda, rather than by domestic priorities' (Dinnen 2004, 5; italics in original). From this perspective serious domestic sources of instability are sidetracked by the donor's agenda focused on the external threats to sovereignty (Dinnen 2004, 14).

The epidemic poses a serious human security threat to Papua New Guineans. The combined effects of a growing epidemic have the potential to further weaken the state's capacity to provide basic services and public goods—from the maintenance of law and order to the provision of education and health services. As a consequence HIV transmission is likely to increase, and HIV programs will be further weakened.

Papua New Guinea is a weak state built upon societies that rely heavily on the strengths of kin and local community. It faces many challenges emanating from the combined effects of decolonisation and globalisation. Issues such as endemic crime and corruption have further reduced the capacity of the state to protect and promote the interests of its citizens. Some observers believe that PNG is teetering on the brink of collapse—that living conditions are degrading and that indigenous efforts to halt this malaise are not working. Even in the absence of the HIV epidemic Papua New Guineans would face a challenging future. Nevertheless, national institutions have proved to be surprisingly resilient. However, it is the ability of HIV and AIDS to weaken those strengths of society upon which the state rests that will make the epidemic so destructive in PNG.

References

Altman, Dennis. 2003. HIV and Security. *International Relations* 17 (4): 417–427.

Altman, Dennis. 2005. Rights Matter: Structural Interventions and Vulnerable Communities. *Health and Human Rights* 8 (2): 1–11.

Australia, Commonwealth Government of. 2005. *Australia's National Security: A Defence Update 2003*. Canberra: Commonwealth Government of Australia.

Barnett, Tony and Gwyn Prins. 2005. *HIV/AIDS and security: fact, fiction and evidence. A report to UNAIDS*. London: London School of Economics. http://www.lse.ac.uk (accessed 27 April 2010).

Barnett, Tony, and Alan Whiteside. 2002. *AIDS in the Twenty First Century*. Houndmills, Basingstoke: Palgrave Macmillan.

Brower, Jennifer, and Peter Chalk. 2003. Global Threat of New and Reemerging Infectious Diseases: Reconciling U.S. National Security and Public Health Policy. Washington D.C.: Rand.

Chappell, David. 2005. 'Africanization' in the Pacific: Blaming Others for Disorder in the Periphery? *Comparative Studies in Society and History* 47 (2): 286–316.

CIA (Central Intelligence Agency). The Global Infectious Disease Threat and its Implications for the United States. Washington DC.

CIE (Centre for International Economics). 2002. *Potential economic impacts of an HIV/AIDS epidemic in Papua New Guinea*. Report prepared for AusAID. http://www.ausaid.gov.au/ (accessed 27 April 2010).

CAP (Commission on AIDS in the Pacific). 2009. *Turning the Tide: An OPEN Strategy for a Response to AIDS in the Pacific*. Suva: Commission on AIDS in the Pacific.

De Waal, Alex. 2005. HIV/AIDS and the Threat of Social Involution in Africa. In *Towards a New Map of Africa*, ed. Ben Wisner, Camilla Toulmin and Rutendo Chitiga, 113–122. London: Earthscan.

Dinnen, Sinclair. 2004. Australia's 'New Interventionism' in the Southwest Pacific. In *Governance Challenges of PNG and the Pacific Islands*, ed. Nancy Sullivan, 59–71. Foreign Policy, Governance and Development: Challenges for Papua New Guinea and Pacific Islands. Madang, PNG: Divine University Press, and Caberra: State, Society and Governance in Melanesia Project, Australian National Univeristy.

Du Guerny, Jacques. 2002. *Agriculture and HIV/AIDS*. Bangkok: UNDP South East Asia HIV and Development Program.

Eberstadt, Nicholas. 2002. The Future of AIDS. *Foreign Affairs* 81 (6): 22–45.

Economist. 2005. Roll out, roll out. *The Economist*, 30 July 2005:69.

Elbe, Stefan. 2003. *Strategic Implications of HIV/AIDS*. Oxford: International Institute for Strategic Studies/Oxford University Press.

FAO. 2001. *The Impact of HIV/AIDS on Food Security*. UN Food and Agriculture Organization, Committee on World Food Security, Twenty-seventh Session, Rome, 28 May–1 June 2001. http://www.fao.org/docrep/meeting/003/Y0310E.htm (accessed 27 April 2010).

Fourie, Pieter and Martin Schonteich. 2001. Africa's New Security Threat: HIV/AIDS and Human Security in Southern Africa. *African Security Review*, 10 (4). http://www.iss.co.za/pubs/asr/10no4/fourie.html (accessed 27 April 2010).

Fourie, Pieter. 2003. *Die, The Beloved Countries: Human Security and HIV/AIDS in Africa*. Pretoria: South African Regional Poverty Network. http://www.heart-intl.net/HEART/100507/DIE,TheBelovedCountries.pdf (accessed 27 April 2010).

Fraenkel, J. 2004a. The Coming Anarchy in Oceania? A Critique of the 'Africanisation' of the South Pacific Thesis. *Commonwealth and Comparative Politics* 42 (1): 1–34.

Fraenkel, J. 2004b. Political Instability, 'Failed States' and Regional Intervention in the Pacific. In *Redefining the Pacific; Regionalism; Past; Present and Future*, ed. Jenny Bryant-Tokalau and Ian Frazer. Dunedin: University of Otago.

Garrett, Laurie. 2005. *HIV and National Security: Where are the Links?* New York: Council on Foreign Relations.

Hammar, Lawrence. 2007. Homegrown in PNG – Rural Responses to HIV and AIDS. *Oceania* 77 (1): 72–94.

Hankins, C., S., Friedman, T., Zafar, and S. Strathdee. 2002. Transmission and Prevention of HIV and Sexually Transmitted Infections in War Settings: Implications for Current and Future Conflicts. *AIDS* 16 (17): 2245–2252.

Hanson, L. W., Allen, B. J., Bourke, R. M., and T. J. McCarthy. 2001. *Papua New Guinea Rural Development Handbook*. Canberra: The Australian National University.

HEMIS (HIV Epidemiological Modelling and Impact Study). 2006. *Impacts of HIV/AIDS 2005-2025 in Papua New Guinea, Indonesia and East Timor*. Canberra: AusAID.

Kendino, Gideon. 2005a. Current Developments in the Management of HIV/AIDS in the PNG Defence Force, 15th Asia-Pacific Military Medicine Conference (APMMC XV) in Hanoi, Vietnam May 8–13, 2005.

Kendino, Gideon. 2005b. PNG: 38 Soldiers Die Of AIDS in PNG. *Pacific Magazine*, 25 February 2005.

May, R. 2004. A Brief Overview of Pacific Security Issues. Foreign Policy, Governance and Development: Challenges for Papua New Guinea and Pacific Islands. Madang, PNG: State Society and Government in Melanesia.

O'Keefe, Michael. 2005. Australian Intervention in Its Neighbourhood: Sheriff and Humanitarian? In *Righteous Violence: The Ethics and Politics of Military Intervention*, ed. Tony Coady and Michael O'Keefe, 75–98. Melbourne: Melbourne University Publishing.

O'Keefe, Michael. 2008. State Fragility and AIDS in the South Pacific. In *AIDS*. The Hague: Security and Conflict Initiative, Netherlands Institute of International Relations Clingendael. http://asci.researchhub.ssrc.org/state-fragility-and-aids-in-the-south-pacific/attachment (accessed 27 April 2010).

PNG National AIDS Council Secretariat and partners. 2008. *UNGASS Country Progress Report. Reporting Period: January 2006–December 2007* Port Moresby: PNG National AIDS Council Secretariat.

Pharaoh, Robyn and Martin Schonteich. 2003. AIDS, Security and Governance in Southern Africa: Exploring the Impact. *Institute for Security Studies,* Paper no. 65. Johannesburg: Institute for Security Studies.

Quattek, Kristina. 2000. *The Economic Impact of AIDS in South Africa: A Dark Cloud on the Horizon.* Occasional Paper. Johannesburg: Konrad Adenauer Foundation South Africa.

Reilly, Ben and Robert Phillpot. 2002. 'Making Democracy Work' in Papua New Guinea. *Asian Survey* 42 (6): 906–927.

Reilly, Ben. 2000. The Africanisation of the South Pacific. *Australian Journal of International Affairs* 54 (3): 261–268.

Reilly, Ben. 2004. State Functioning and State Failure in the South Pacific. *Australian Journal of International Affairs* 58 (4): 479–493.

Reno, William. 1997. African Weak States and Commercial Alliances. *African Affairs* 96: 165–185.

Schonteich, Martin. 2000. *Age and AIDS: A Lethal Mix for South Africa's Crime Rate.* Occasional Paper. Johannesburg, Konrad Adenauer Foundation South Africa: 57–66.

Shell, Robert. 2000. Halfway to the Holocaust: The Economic, Demographic and Social Implications of the AIDS Pandemic to the Year 2010 in the Southern African Region. Occasional Paper. Johannesburg: Konrad Adenauer Foundation South Africa.

Tow, William, Ramesh Thakur and In-Taek Hyun eds. 2000. *Asia's Emerging Regional Order: Reconciling Traditional and Human Security*. Tokyo: United Nations University Press.

UNAIDS. 2008. *Report on the Global AIDS Epidemic*. Geneva: UNAIDS. www.unaids.org

UNAIDS. 2009. *AIDS Epidemic Update. December 2009*. Geneva: UNAIDS. www.unaids.org

UN. 2001. *Global Crisis – Global Action Fact Sheet*. New York: United Nations.

UNDP. 1994. *World Development Report*. Geneva: UNDP.

UNDP. 1999. *World Development Report*. Geneva: UNDP.

UNDP 2006. *Human Development Report 2006: beyond scarcity*. New York: UNDP

UNGA (United Nations General Assembly). 2005. High Level Meeting on HIV/AIDS, Discussion Paper for the Round Table on Orphans and Children Made Vulnerable by HIV/AIDS. New York: United Nations.

Whiteside, Alan, Alex de Waal and Tsadkan Gebre-Tensae. 2006. AIDS, Security and the Military in Africa: A Sober Appraisal, *African Affairs* 105 (409): 201–218.

WHO. 2003. *Annual Report 2003*. Geneva: World Health Organisation.

Conclusion: Civic Security

VICKI LUKER

This book's overriding aim is to advance the goal of 'civic security'. Joan's story that was reproduced at the beginning indicated some of the term's meanings in reverse. An abused and ostracised woman with HIV, civic security was lacking from her life and death. Within the terms of this volume her experience was one result of the vicious circle produced conjointly by HIV and the complex factors that come under the rubric 'law and order'—and contributors have outlined others. Because the introduction and first chapter argued that civic security would offer both some immunity to such harms and a means of facilitating virtuous circles, this conclusion returns to the case for 'civic security' while flagging some big difficulties that do not, however, negate the general thrust.

Civic security, as earlier discussed (see Luker and Dinnen this volume, chapter one) in one narrow but influential sense refers to the security of person that states in the Western democratic pattern nominally guarantee their citizens. But if 'citizenship' is used more loosely for 'membership' of a political community—local, national, global, or whatever—civic security can designate that safety and regard granted to an individual by virtue of his or her inalienable 'belonging' to that group.

The governance of civic security—where 'governance' refers to the institutions, processes, and values that regulate social life—in most nations involves disparate actors. In PNG the role in this played by a young state is important and necessary, even if less effective than it could be within its limits; but in most parts of PNG and for most people, the state's role is small, if not absent. Hence for most citizens this task will de facto remain largely the activity of the communities, however configured, where they live. The governance of civic security thus falls within two often tenuously related domains: that of the state, and that of community. The connections between local and national governance are thin, like the waist of an hourglass; and the institutions that link them at this juncture—police, schools, aid-posts, village courts—are stressed.

Several chapters in this volume address HIV and 'law and order' through a focus on state law and the state's law and justice sector. PNG's state, its laws, its agencies, can be more visible to the international community, and better connected to it by flows of information, symbols, personnel and money than it is visible or connected to most of its citizens. This is perhaps most painfully demonstrated with respect to state law. Former Australian High Court judge and human rights advocate Michael Kirby has quipped that shortly after HIV was identified, so was the problem of internationally epidemic HIL: highly ineffective laws (Kirby 2009, 5). Certainly law reform can have irresistible justification, many benefits incidental to its primary purpose, and in some circumstances a change of law does lead promptly to changes in practice: but, as contributors note here, in PNG law reform is only the first step, and hard though that step may be, the further steps that would make new law effective can be even harder and also dependent on favourable terrain (Fletcher and Gonapa this volume; Stewart this volume). In the year 2010, as this book goes to press, law reform relating to sorcery, sex work and homosexuality is likely to be debated in some fora in PNG (Anon. 2009a; Anon. 2009b; Papik 2010) and the long-anticipated Lukautim Pikinini (Child) Act 2009, including provisions for children infected or affected by HIV is due to be gazetted (Aggleton et al 2009, 14; HELP 2005, 103–104). But PNG's experience so far with the HIV/AIDS Management and Prevention (HAMP) Act cautions against expectations of great impact on the ground. Although the HAMP Act is the best HIV legislation in the Pacific and intensely appreciated in some informed (and many transnational) circles, too few people in PNG know or care about it, and those who do have too few resources to implement it (CAP 2009, 56; Aggleton et al. 2008, 25–26; Stewart 2009). To date only one solitary and relatively minor conviction under the HAMP Act appears to have been made: in 2009 a jilted man was fined for slandering his ex-girlfriend as HIV positive (Kelola 2009).[1] In the meantime, assaults, rapes and killings occur (including assaults, rapes and killings of people targeted because of some association with HIV), the majority probably with no reference to or consequence from any state law in PNG.

Several chapters have also highlighted the geographically limited reach of the state and the limited capacity of state agencies, even within their zones of operation (e.g. Patrick this volume; McLeod and Macintyre this volume; Dinnen and Law this volume; Hammar this volume; Haley this volume; Luker and Monsell-Davis this volume). The most publicised cases of civic insecurity involving criminal abuse and HIV unsurprisingly have happened near administrative centres, where the chances that these deeds will be heard about, seen and reported are greater. Joan's story of abuse and rejection unfolded within and on the edges of Goroka, the capital of the Eastern Highlands Province. Two other stories from the capital of the Western Highlands Province, Mount Hagen, retold from press accounts (see Boxes 1 & 2) also suggest the relatively small and inactive part of state law, its machinery and enforcers in these ordeals.

---

1   To say this is a 'relatively' minor charge does not deny its seriousness, or that serious consequences can follow from such slanders.

Box 1

The Hagen 'Lass'

On 6th January 2009, at about 2 am, a truck, laden with firewood and used truck tyres, drove into Kerebug Dump in Mt Hagen. Suspects laid out the tyres and firewood, placed a young woman—naked, blindfolded, gagged, and strapped to a log—on top, poured on petrol and set the pile alight (Muri 2009a). According to a witness, the girl could not cry for help. She was said to have HIV and to be a witch. Several days later, two different groups, insisting that she was two different people, claimed her body. A police officer explained to the press that establishing the girl's identity was hard, for unfortunately incidents such as these were not uncommon. The Director of the National AIDS Council Secretariat was reported to say, 'If anyone is caught and found guilty of burning the woman in Mt Hagen they can be prosecuted under the AIDS Prevention Act [sic] of 2003' (Noho 2009).

Box 2

Rose

On the eve of 2007 general election, Rose Kombe, then 16, was dragged from Mt Hagen and raped several times. Her attacker released her the following day. Considerably later an AIDS counsellor heard Rose's attacker boasting to some men that he had spread the virus to several 'young virgins' and mentioned Rose's name. The AIDS counsellor contacted Rose, who was now sick, and suggested that she take a blood test, which proved positive. This was a blow to her family, because young girls are 'precious' in the Highlands. Her family wanted to keep her, but because the community that hosted them (Rose and her family were immigrants) feared AIDS, Rose moved into a house in Mt Hagen for people living with HIV (Muri 2009c).

In September 2009, Rose was raped again. A grade 11 student, son of a prominent Hagen family, broke into the house. He was drunk and demanded sex. She warned him she was HIV positive and not to have sex with her. He punched her. She then offered him condoms which he threw away before he raped her. The landlord, on hearing her screams, was able to alert police, who arrested the young man. But charges were dropped when the PLHIVs received K1150 from the boy's mother (they had initially asked for K2000). When asked why she accepted compensation, Rose reportedly explained, 'Because we didn't want the young boy to go through a lot of trauma and agony. He knew very well that he had sex with an AIDS victim and that this memory will psychologically kill his mind if he was going to jail' (Anon. 2009b). Rose later told the paper that she and the other girls were subject to frequent attacks and rapes at the house. They wished it could be fenced: 'This place has got no fencing. That is why men enter the area at will and force us to have sex with them' (Muri 2009). NACS warned the public to refrain from this abuse of people living with HIV and said that NACS would pursue the matter under the HIV/AIDS Management and Prevention Act (Gerawa 2009).

Partly in recognition of the state's shortcomings, increasing attention has focused on the potentials of community to ensure the safety of its members. In this volume, Reid has argued for 'community conversations' as a way for people to identify the challenges that they collectively face, understand the role of deeper structures particularly with respect to HIV and violence, and realise what they need to think and do for their shared future (Reid this volume; see also Gibbs 2009). The Tingim Laip ('Think about Life') project, the national HIV intervention program that commenced in 2005 and targeted 34 high-risk settings in PNG, has focused on building and mobilising communities (Katz et al. 2007; Engels 2008). In the law and justice sector, recent initiatives in community policing and the village court system have reinvigorated efforts to enlist and support local resources—and also strengthen connections between community and state (PNG 2007, 19, 35; cf. MacDonald 2008). More broadly PNG's government and development partners have directed policy and resources towards new paradigms for 'community-centric' development (Jacka 2007; Kidu 2008; James et al. 2009). Many of these draw inspiration from existing examples of successful grass-roots creativity (Jacka 2007; Wai and Maia this volume). Attempts have been made to theorise a new national and democratic civics rooted in the politics of kin (Goudsmit 2008). Others call for the forging of links between understandings of HIV, citizenship, and community responsibility (Aggleton et al. 2008, 22).

Therefore the thesis, articulated by Aral and her coauthors, that forms of community governance in primarily fostering civic security can also foster health warrant some further final thought (Aral et al. 2002; Luker and Dinnen this volume, chapter one). They specifically argued that the Zwelethemba model for community governance, while preventing community conflict and promoting cohesion, could be predicted to limit the spread and ameliorate the effects of STIs such as HIV. Without recapitulating at length the earlier discussions (Luker and Dinnen this volume, chapter one; Dinnen this volume, chapter 12; Cartwright et al. this volume, chapter 12), the model can be said (even if its proponents do not use quite these words) to work on two levels of prevention against conflict and HIV: one deliberate and closer to the 'surface', the other incidental and 'deep'. The deliberate peace-making prescribed by the model prevents minor conflicts from escalating. Under the model's design, the monies earned by peace-making not only personally remunerate individuals who participate, but a proportion of the small financial dividend goes to a fund that the community can spend on specific projects—including, if the community decides so, initiatives in health. At this level of prevention, problems are self-consciously identified and deliberately 'nipped in the bud'. At a deeper, unconscious level, the social cohesion created, collective knowledge articulated, conflict prevented, resources acquired, and the direction of these resources and human energy into other goal-oriented occupations for collective and individual benefit, may prevent some types of conflict and harmful behaviour before they have even 'seeded'. People, in effect, are otherwise engaged. It should be stressed that this model (like the kinds of community governance propounded by Goudsmit (2008)) explicitly links peace-making to tangible material rewards and real opportunities for locally formulated development projects: the personal remuneration for participants and the monies paid to the community fund are clearly incentives for individual and collective participation in the virtuous circle of the Zwelethemba process. Although the role for the state is limited, it is clearly defined and there is scope for its strategic enhancement.

This rosy picture at first glance 'makes sense'. Speaking loosely and generally, and without limiting the discussion to the community level of governance, the thesis that security—if defined as a condition of shared existence in which individuals can live with a high degree of confidence in peace, collective respect for cardinal social norms, and freedom from violence—seems logical. Conversely, the harmful effects of insecurity on health can be plain: witness deaths, sickness and social breakdown due to war. It is also easy to imagine a range of possible health benefits that might derive from enhanced security for any society—for example, lower morbidity and mortality due to injury; lesser costs associated with injury and traumatic death; better access to health services unimpeded by ambient violence; better health services because work-places are safe for staff; better health services because levels of internal corruption are low; and so on. The prevention of gender violence should also reduce, for instance, HIV transmission through violent or coerced sex as Eves argues (this volume), acknowledging the large international literature on this nexus. And despite the specific focus of Aral and her coauthors (2002) on the potential benefits of the Zwelethemba model for HIV prevention, the model is implicated in a body of work that more generally explores the potentially beneficial impacts of security on health (see e.g. Burris 2006). There is also a considerable literature postulating that measures primarily to foster health can also secondarily foster security, build peace, and legitimate states (Grove and Zwi 2009; Eldon et al. 2008; Zwi 2004).

But shadows cross this picture. Perhaps counter-intuitively, there are many examples of conditions of insecurity that correlate with health, and conditions of security with ill-health. For instance, the endemic warfare in precolonial Papua New Guinea may have helped to create *cordons sanitaires* that impeded the transmission of infectious disease and contributed to the health of populations (Denoon 1989, 9–17). Conversely, the peace that typically followed the introduction of colonial rule coincided with the spread of diseases and the very steep demographic declines of some societies in PNG and elsewhere in the Pacific (Luker 2008, 254–257). Certain work on HIV in Africa has also challenged assumptions that war or even rape necessarily spread HIV or correlate with high

HIV prevalence (Whiteside et al. 2006, 212–214; Anema et al. 2008). The point to stress is that processes outlined in models are abstracted from the many processes with which they would interact in real life. Specific health data relating to the health effects of the Zwelethmeba model in the communities where it operates are also lacking. Burris, while insisting that the model indeed delivers health benefits, notes that these effects would anyway be hard to measure (Burris 2006, 210).

There are other shadows too. Many donors and governments that partner communities in projects of local governance subscribe to a set of Western democratic ideals and the principles of human rights. Yet these ideals and principles may not always neatly accord with local values. The village court system in PNG for example has been vigorously criticised by some commentators for judgements inconsistent with human rights or PNG's state law, but which arguably reflect local sociality and concepts of justice (Garap 2000; Goddard 2009, 13; cf. McLeod and Macintyre this volume). Contrasts are moreover often popularly drawn between grassroots moralities that prioritise 'community' versus a type of globalised morality that highlights 'the individual'; one that emphasises 'responsibilities' versus another that stresses 'rights'; one that supremely honours 'reproductive sexuality' versus one that, if not celebrates, at least forefronts 'non-reproductive sexuality'. These contrasting tendencies can sometimes correspond to differing conditions for social survival. In many communities in the world residents would depend for survival more on local politics, close cooperation among neighbours and the production of children than, for instance, do residents of the Canberra suburb where I live.

These contrasting tendencies can open up further differences—and those concerning roles and ideals for women are particularly raw. Women's heavy contribution in most PNG societies to child-bearing, production and service to others can often seem to their menfolk right and necessary. Without denying varied and changing views, many women agree and find their sense of self-worth and social influence in the hard work of motherhood and its associated roles (see, e.g., Sepoe 2000, 160).[2] Differing measures for the scope of legitimate violence are also implicated. Although major donors may be based in countries where popular culture is saturated with commodified representations of violence and where governments exercise blood-spilling military might, salient Western attitudes allow much smaller scope for legitimate violence in every

---

2   It is worth noting that the mistreatment of women like Joan, the 'Hagen lass' and Rose easily yields to a kind of gender analysis in which they can be taken as embodiments of the multiple disadvantages that women can suffer in PNG. Following from such analyses, it may often be assumed that if women were given more power in political decision-making, such mistreatment would be challenged. While there is clearly a need for women to participate in formal decision-making from the local to the national level (see, e.g. Sepoe 2000; Sepoe 2007; Kidu 2009), subscription to the cluster of female ideals that centre on the maternal role seems to make many women very critical of others perceived to be anomalous.

day and domestic life than accepted in some PNG contexts (see, e.g., McLeod and Macintyre this volume). As Michael Goddard has noted, a Western ethos that values social harmony, and sees it as necessary for community life, may actually be predicated on the experience of frail social bonds, so that some of those who subscribe to the 'harmony ethos' often have difficulty appreciating how stronger community ties may enable, ideologically and in practice, the accommodation and legitimation of violent acts that would permanently rend weaker communities (Goddard 2009, 4). Of course, as with the comments concerning women's roles, in PNG attitudes understood as 'traditional' with respect to violence differ, while modes of violence and associated perceptions are also changing, particularly where communities can no longer cope (see, e.g., Haley this volume).[3] Finally, these contrasting tendencies, at the utmost opposition between the rights of the community versus the rights of the individual, can clash over the belief that, in the interests of the collectivity, a member or members can be disowned, discarded, or killed.

Divergent discourses about HIV draw attention to such contrasts and differences. Some, particularly over the supposed interests of the social collectivity versus those of the individual, have wrestled within Western HIV discourse from its early days (see, e.g. Scheper-Hughes 1994; Thôrn and Follér 2008, 282–283), notwithstanding the global ascendancy of the rights-based approach and forceful arguments that in fact it serves the interests of both. But Joan's story, and accounts of 'the Hagen lass' and Rose (Box 1), appear to exemplify the plight of individuals who are pushed outside the pale of social safety seemingly created by those values at the 'community' end of the series of popular contrasts outlined above, and often through acts perpetrated on their persons over which they had no control. Their membership of the group, and entitlement to its protection, were not inalienable but conditional. Their civic insecurity suggests the risk that new institutions of community governance might authorise the very values, or those people within the community who espouse them, that led to their mistreatment, rejection, and, in the case of 'the Hagen lass', murder. Indeed, despite examples of successful local governance, promising community conversations, and public education campaigns about human rights, some communities and spokespersons, in PNG and elsewhere, have called for stronger local powers to use means such as shame and expulsion to deal with the challenges of HIV and lawlessness, or for forms of 'guided democracy' out of temper with state principles or the democratic ideals upheld by key donors (see, e.g., Gigmai 2005).

---

3   The influence of Christian churches over the contrasting tendencies and tensions outlined in this discussion are often ambivalent. Some churches have locally strengthened the 'harmony ethos' (see, e.g. Goddard 2009, 6–7). On the other hand, most churches tend to endorse local values that centralise community and reproductive sexuality (see, e.g., Eves this volume).

The greatest challenges for strengthening community governance pertain to those communities that need it most: 'intra-community', where members do not perceive a common interest with others in their midst, may feel poorly connected to neighbours by kin and culture, or would be difficult to draw into a common process with any available carrots or sticks; and 'inter-community', where a strong sense of community identity and cohesion can often be generated by conflict. In such settings the roles played by potentially a range of community actors and bridging agents, including representatives of the state, can be crucial in local political transformation. But it is also worth thinking about tangible 'peace dividends'. In the Zwelethemba model, money earned through peace-making activities is a vital element; some recent recommendations for local governance in PNG similarly stress the importance of a real 'peace dividend' (Goudsmit 2008); and as Dinnen and Braithwaite have noted (2009, 165–167, 169–170), colonially the system of mobile colonial officers or *kiaps*, dovetailed the administration of justice with the rewards of local development projects. Yet one could ask: in some communities, would the possibly small pickings from peace-making activities or the prospect, for instance, of a functioning health clinic motivate those members who might want much more excitement or profit from criminal activities? Would the continuing pursuit of intergroup conflict offer key participants richer satisfactions than peace? Could a community deal with members beholden to powerful, translocal criminal organisations?

And civic security has macro-economic dimensions. This book has stressed that uneven development in PNG is a driver of many law and order problems and also HIV (Luker with Monsell-Davis, this volume). Competition for resources is a factor in inter- and intra-group conflicts; unemployment is a factor in property crime; labour migration is a factor in the spread of HIV; and so is the commodification of female sexuality that in turn responds to the pressing need for finding ways and means of tapping the cash economy. As Hammar's chapter (this volume) abundantly demonstrated, one cannot reduce 'transactional sex' to the narrow profile of a 'sex worker': it is a big and internally diverse category that can encompass bride-price and *plet kaikai* (sex for a plate of takeaway food), brief and long-term relations, reproductive and non–reproductive sex, the coercion of girls and women and, within the often severe limits on their life-choices, their agency.[4] While much attention focuses on 'sex work' more narrowly defined and on the undoubted role that sexual violence can play directly and indirectly in the transmission of HIV, the array of economic pressures for and mulitifarious character of transactional sex is often more difficult to comprehend (see Epstein

---

4   The push factors for the commodification of female sexuality are richly illustrated in the disturbing 2005 report by HELP on the sexual abuse and commercial sexual exploitation of children (2005, see esp. 88–93); The monetary value that girls represent, through bride-price, is implied in the newspaper reports regarding the shock of Rose's family (Box 1) to learn that she had been raped, because girls in the Highlands are 'precious'. The subtext here is that her rape discounted the value she could command for bride-price.

2007, 244–247; Barnett 2008, 8; see Luker with Monsell-Davis this volume). Thus the interests of civic security, not least with respect to HIV, property crime and violent competition for resources, are enmeshed in patterns of macro-development over which institutions of community governance may have very little influence indeed.

Given the profound character of these concerns and others not flagged, is the goal of civic security worth pursuing? The obvious answer is: of course. As Anne Brown has remarked, 'The safety and relationships of trust that security implies are fundamental to good development, as they are to all forms of community well-being' (Brown 2007, 1). And despite the multiple actors that may be involved in its governance, the role of the state in realizing this public good is, in the words of Loader and Walker, both 'necessary and virtuous' (Loader and Walker 2006, 167). While PNG's young state has very limited capacity to ensure the security of its citizens through the arms of the law and its other agencies, it does have a cardinal responsibility to foster it.

Yet the special emphasis in this volume on the *local* governance of security is warranted: it is an inevitable consequence of the social realities in which most citizens live—as numerous community leaders, development practitioners, policy-makers, parliamentarians and social researchers have insisted. Strengthening the local governance of security involves mobilising resources at hand and also tapping resources from further afield (cf. MacDonald 2008). A range of local actors can contribute to these tasks, but state representatives, even if they are few and constrained, can potentially play vital roles in enabling and sustaining, bridging and channelling. As suggested in chapter one, perhaps too much talk of failed, fragile or failing states has muffled the possibilities of an 'enabling state'.

What would the 'civic security' resulting from such processes of localised political evolution look like? The question reminds us that any outcomes involving multiple sites, shifting circumstances, changing thought-worlds, and the mixing of endogenous and exogenous elements will be impossible to predict in detail; and it is hard to imagine that local, community politics in PNG could be otherwise. Various words—syncretism, fusion, hybridity, indigenisation—can denote ways in which local and more recently imported concepts and practices combine. Some of these terms have been applied to the adoption of Christianity in PNG and elsewhere. Political orders fashioned from local and translocal, indigenous and exotic elements in nations where state capacity is limited have also been described as 'hybrid'. These hybrid modes of governance, as Boege and his coauthors argue, can work, citing Bougainville as one example (e.g. Boege et al. 2008).

Such processes however pose difficulties for purists, even when there is no alternative. Goddard addresses this in relation to PNG's village court system, which could be described as a 'hybrid' institution: though judgements may not always chime with state law or global rights discourse (and these discrepancies, particularly regarding women, can be abysmal (see, e.g. Garap 2000, 162–168)), he argues that village courts have by and large delivered 'substantial justice' in the estimation of their communities, women included, and have met a need (Goddard 2009, 13). The system moreover is evolving (Goddard 2009, 277–279). Reid (this volume, chapter 13) suggests other ways for working towards human rights in the prevention of violence and HIV. Like others (e.g. Cartwright et al. this volume, Barnett 2008), she puts heavy stress on looking ahead, on hope. Community conversations are a means of learning for change that is geared to the future: it is in the light of the good to which participants collectively aspire that current practices and values are reviewed. In this methodology, an impulse towards human rights serves, not condemnation, but local motivation to move forward. And many facilitators have noted that an appeal to the future of the clan, the *lain*, the community is in many settings a more effective motivator than an appeal to the individual, so sharply etched in the Western consciousness of human rights (see, e.g., Regan 2004; Kelly et al. 2008, 10; cf. Lepani 2007).

Nor are these processes for the impatient. HIV and 'law and order' pose challenges in PNG that are long-term, entwined and endemic: in important respects, as discussed in chapter one, common connotations of the term 'epidemic' and its related rhetoric are misleading when applied to HIV and, metaphorically, such problems as crime. In the absence of quick fixes, these require longer term thinking, which in turn require a broader and deeper consideration of context: not just to create social and political environments which 'enable' deliberate responses to HIV and 'law and order', but which are simply, inherently, safer. 'Civic security', as an ideal, encompasses these goods.

References

Aggleton, Peter and Shaline Bharat, Felecia Dobunaba, Roger Drew and Steve Wignall. 2008. Independent Review Group on HIV/AIDS: Report from an Assessment Visit 27 August–9 September 2008.

Aggleton, Peter and Shaline Bharat, Alex Coutinho, Felecia Dobunaba, Roger Drew and Tobi Saidel. 2009. Independent Review Group on HIV/AIDS: Report from an Assessment Visit 23 April–9 May 2009.

Anema, Aranka, Michel R. Joffres, Edward Mills, Paul B. Spiegel. 2008. Widespread Rape does not Directly Appear to Increase the Overall HIV

Prevalence in Conflict-affected Countries: Now so What? *Emerging Themes in Epidemiology* 5 (11), http://www.ncbi.nlm.nih.gov/pmc/articles/PMC2527307/ (accessed 27 April 2010).

Anon. 2009a. New Law to Curb Sorcery Killings. *Post-Courier*, 9 January 2009.

Anon. 2009b. Battle for Sorcery Killings. *Post-Courier*, 7 April 2009.

Anon. 2009c. Rapist Pays Price. *Post-Courier*, 1 September 2009.

Barnett, Tony. 2008. *Hoping or Discounting the Future: A New Perspective on the Transmission of HIV/AIDS*. World Institute for Development Economic Research, WDP 2008/08. Helsinki: United National University.

Boege, Volker, Anne Brown, Kevin Clements and Anna Nolan. 2008. On Hybrid Political Orders and Emerging States: State Formation in the Context of Fragility. Berghof Research Center for Constructive Conflict Management. [no place of publication given] www.berghof-handbook.net

Brown, M. Anne. 2007. Security and Development: Conflict and Resilience in the Pacific Islands Region. In *Security in the Pacific islands: Social Resilience in Emerging States*, ed. M. Anne Brown, 1–32. London and Boulder: Lynne Rienner Publishers.

Burris, Scott. 2006. From Security to Health. In *Democracy, Society and the Governance of Security*, ed. Jennifer Wood and Benoît Dupont, 196–216. Cambridge: Cambridge University Press.

CAP (Commission on AIDS in the Pacific). 2009. *Turning the Tide: An OPEN Strategy for a Response to AIDS in the Pacific*. Suva: Commission on AIDS in the Pacific.

Denoon, Donald. 1989. *Public Health in Papua New Guinea: Medical Possibility and Social Constraint, 1884–1984*. New York: Cambridge University Press.

Dinnen, Sinclair and John Braithwaite. 2009. Reinventing Policing through the Colonial Kiap. *Policing and Society*, 19 (2): 161–173..

Eldon, Jack, Catriona Waddington and Yasmin Hadi. 2008. *Health System Reconstruction: Can it Contribute to State-building?* London: HLSP Institute.

Engels, John. 2008. *Tingim Laip: Success Stories from New Guinea*. Waigani: Family Health International.

Epstein, Helen. 2007. *The Invisible Cure: Why We are Losing the Fight against AIDS in Africa*. New York: Picador.

Garap, Sarah. 2000. Struggles of Women and Girls. In *Reflections on Violence in Melanesia*, ed. Sinclair Dinnen and Allison Ley, 159–171. Leichardt and Canberra: Hawkins Press and Asia Pacific Press.

Gerawa, Maureen. 2009. NACS Upset on Rape. *Post-Courier*, 8 September 2009.

Gibbs, Philip. 2009. Making Sense of HIV and AIDS: Community Conversations in the Papua New Guinea Context, in AIDS; Belief and Culture in Papua New Guinea, ed. Hermann Springler, special issue of *Catalyst: Social Pastoral Journal for Melanesia*, 39 (2): 56–70.

Gigmai, Freddy. 2005. AIDS Warning: Highlands Leaders Call for Condom, Nightclub Ban. *The National*, 21 November 2005.

Goudsmit, Into A. 2008. *Nation Building in Papua New Guinea: A Local Alternative*. State, Society and Governance in Melanesia Project Discussion Paper 2008/9. Canberra: State Society and Governance in Melanesia Project, Research School of Pacific and Asian History, Australian National University.

Grove, Natalie J. and Anthony B. Zwi. 2009. Beyond the Log Frame: A New Tool for Examining Health and Peace-Building Initiatives. *Development in Practice* 18 (1): 66–81.

HELP. 2005. A Situations Analysis of Child Sexual Abuse and the Commercial Sexual Exploitation of Children in Papua New Guinea. Prepared by HELP Resources, Inc. with the support of UNICEF PNG.

Jacka, Marion. 2007. Local Solutions: Security and Development in Papua New Guinea. In *Security in the Pacific islands: Social Resilience in Emerging States*, ed. M. Anne Brown, 33–64. London and Boulder: Lynne Rienner Publishers.

James, Paul, Victoria Stead, Yaso Nadarajah, Karen Haive. 2009. Introduction: Projecting Community Life. In Projecting Community Life, by Paul James et al., *Local Global: Identity, Security, Community* 5: 6–16.

Katz, Che, Lesley Bola, Florence Bundu, Caroline Bunemiga B. Bus, Berit Gustafsson, Nayer Kaviani, Deborah McSmith, Romanus Pakure and Darryle Raka. 2007. Putting the Community at the Center of Measuring Change in HIV Prevention in Papua New Guinea: The Tingim Laip (Think of Life) Mobilisation. *Health Promotion in the Pacific* 14 (2): 133–138.

Kelola, Todagia. 2009. Hefty Penalty. *Post-Courier*, 26 May 2009.

Kelly, Angela, Frances Akuani, Barbara Kepa, Lawrencia Pirpir, Agnes Mek, Martha Kupul, Rebecca Emori, Somu Nosi, Lucy Walizopa, Brneda Cangah,

Kritoe Keleba. 2008. *Young People's Attitudes towards Sex and HIV in the Eastern Highlands of Papua New Guinea*. Monograph 1/2008. Sydney: National Centre for HIV Social Research.

Kidu, Carol, 2008. The Power of Partnerships: Reflections on Addressing PNG Social Challenges. Presentation to the Lowy Institute, Sydney, 7 May 2008. Available http://lowyinstitute. org/ (accessed 27 April 2010).

Kidu, Carol. 2009. Rhetoric to Reality: Trying to Break the Gender Barrier in Papua New Guinea. *The Parliamentarian* 90 (3): 222–225.

Kirby, Michael. 2009. Foreword. In *Criminal Transmission of HIV: A Guide for Legal Practitioners in New South Wales—May 2009*, by Gina Mitchell, 5–6. Sydney: HIV/AIDS Legal Centre Inc. and DLA Philips Fox.

Lepani, Katherine. 2007. 'In the Process of Knowing': Making Sense of HIV and AIDS in the Trobriand Islands of Papua New Guinea. PhD thesis. Canberra: Australian National University.

Loader, Ian and Neil Walker. 2006. Necessary Virtues: The Legitimate Place of the State in the Production of Security. In *Democracy, Society and the Governance of Security*, ed. Jennifer Wood and Benoît Dupont. 165–195. Cambridge: Cambridge University Press.

Luker, Vicki. 2008. Papua New Guinea: Epidemiological Transition, Public Health and the Pacific. In *Public Health in Asia and the Pacific: Historical and Comparative Perspectives*, ed. Milton J. Lewis and Kerrie L. MacPherson, 250–275. Abingdon: Routledge.

MacDonald, Rosita. 2008. Safety, Security, and Accessible Justice: Participatory Approaches to Law and Justice in Papua New Guinea. Pacific Islands Policy No. 3. East West Center. Honolulu: University of Hawai'i.

McLeod, Abby. 2007. Police Reform in Papua New Guinea. In *Security in the Pacific islands: Social Resilience in Emerging States*, ed. M. Anne Brown, 73–88. London and Boulder: Lynne Rienner Publishers.

Muri, David. 2009a. Hagen Girl Tied, Burnt to Death. *Post-Courier*, 7 January 2009.

Muri, David. 2009b. HIV+ Plea: Protect Us. *Post-Courier*, 4 September 2009.

Muri, David. 2009b. PLWHA Contracted Virus through Rape. *Post-Courier*, 8 September 2009.

Noho, Bola. 2009. Don't Hate HIV Victims: Pakure. *Post-Courier*, 12 January 2009.

Papik, John. 2010. PNG Civil Groups Prepare Gay, Sex Work Law Challenge. Pacific Beat, Radio National, Australian Broadcasting Commission. 29 January 2010.

PNG (Papua New Guinea) 2007. *A Just, Safe and Secure Society: A White Paper on Law and Justice in Papua New Guinea*. Port Moresby: Office of the Secretary for Justice and Attorney General.

Poiya, Johnny. 2009. Woman's Body yet to be Identified. *Post Courier*, 20 January 2009.

Regan, Mary Walta. 2004. Report on Youth to Youth Theatre Troupe—Action for Change—Bougainville—Papua New Guinea. Caritas Australia with assistance of New Zealand Government AID.

Scheper-Hughes, Nancy. 1994. An Essay: 'AIDS and the Social Body.' *Social Science and Medicine* 39 (7): 991–1003.

Sepoe, Orovu. 2000. Changing Gender Relations in Papua New Guinea: The Role of Women's Organisations. New Delhi: UBS Publishers' Distributors Limited.

Sepoe, Orovu. 2007. Power, Gender and Security in Papua New Guinea. In *Security in the Pacific islands: Social Resilience in Emerging States*, ed. M. Anne Brown, 65–72. London and Boulder: Lynne Rienner Publishers.

Stewart, Christine. 2009. Posting on AIDSTOK listserve. 3 September 2009.

Thörn, Håkan and Maj Lis Follér. 2008. Governing AIDS: Globalization, the State and Civil Society. In *The Politics of AIDS: Globalization, the State and Civil Society*, ed. Håkan Thörn, and Maj Lis Follér, 277–296. Houndmills: Palgrave MacMillan.

UNAIDS. 2009. AIDS Epidemic Update: December 2009. Geneva: UNAIDS.

Whiteside, Alan, Alex De Waal and Tsadkan Gebre-Tensae. 2006. AIDS, Security and the Military in Africa: A Sober Appraisal. *African Affairs* 105/419: 201–218.

Zwi, Anthony 2004. Health and Peace-building: Securing the Future. The University of New South Wales Health and Conflict Initiative Issues No. 1. Sydney: School of Public Health and Community Medicine, University of New South Wales.

Epilogue: Ela's Question

ELIZABETH REID

In late 2003, the Howard Government announced that it was sending police, military personnel and senior public servants into PNG under a programme of expanded cooperation. The announcements and subsequent discussion on talkback radio were in terms of 'restoring law and order' in PNG and of 'propping up the country'.

As this was being reported in the papers in both countries, Ela sought advice: 'My parents want Willie to go back to the village and go to school there. What do you think?'

At the beginning of 2003, Ela had brought her six year-old son to Port Moresby to go to school. He had loved his life in the village: catching fish in the river, playing soccer, going to the garden, hunting for birds, swimming. But nobody was making sure that he was going to school, and he was being beaten up by the bigger boys.

The school year had started when he arrived in Moresby. There was just one place left in the preparatory grade. He was of the age group but lagged well behind in school work. He had virtually no English, the language of teaching. 'Let him try it', advised the school.

Willie flourished. He plays soccer, gets into fights in the school yard, learns English and maths, and is beginning to absorb the values that lie behind learning. He does his homework, more regularly than not. Ela or one of her sisters walks him to school, up and down and across the roads of the settlement, and back again at midday.

He lives in one small rented room with Ela and two of her sisters, three young women around their twenties. They are in Moresby to be educated.

'Dad says that the school in the village is OK and they want him back with them.' She paused, thinking out loud.

'If he stays here, he will finish school and then what? There are no jobs, even if you are clever and speak good English. He will become a rascal. Most boys who go to school in Moresby become rascals and take drugs.'

How does Ela think her way through this dilemma? Ela had Willie when she was very young and her parents brought Willie up. She feels an indebtedness to them. She knows that they miss him and are growing sickly. There is no-one else to look after them, although this is not a traditional role for a boy. And looking after Willie in town is not easy for her.

He could do his schooling in the village school, but who would make sure that he attended and help him with his books? Education is not highly valued since it seems to be an investment of very scarce resources with little or no return. Scarcity and poverty give a clarity to decisions.

The village school teaches in the local language and its standards are minimal. But what use could he make of an education in the village? Men's traditional roles, hunting, fishing, horticulture and governance, are dwindling and there are few modern roles or jobs for them. Village life centres on the land, the weather, conflicts, both traditional and new, news from town, rumours, remittances and gatherings. It is absorbing.

What life might Willie make for himself in this village nestling up the side of the mountains, far from the sea, three hours from Moresby, by a road thick with bandits? He will grow up playing soccer, warding off violence and sorcery as best he can, and living a life fashioned by *kastom*, by customary ways of doing things. He will speak in language and be of the village. His identity will be formed by the belief systems and traditions of his clan. He will have no sense of himself as a citizen of a nation, little horizon beyond the surrounding villages and the bus stop to Moresby. Family business will take him there regularly but it will be as a foreign territory, generating fear or aggression. He will be untouched by modernity. He will have been denied the possibility of living in the modern world.

He is thriving at school in Moresby. He has flourished, academically and as a person. It has been pure joy for all to watch. His capacity to learn had, up to then, been restrained by the lack of decent rural schools, health services, communications and other structural factors. He is, in some sense, the same person but as if set free. In Moresby, he is gaining a sense of himself as part of a larger whole as he lives side by side with and comes to know people from different customary groups: a diverse local world, perhaps the makings of a nation. If Willie were to stay on in school in Moresby, his pathway to an interconnected world might be less fraught than that of the girls.

But meanwhile, Ela asks, will he survive the lawlessness of Moresby? Will this education lead to employment? Estimates of youth unemployment in Port Moresby approach 70 percent. In 1990, only 18 percent of the labour force worked for wages, were self-employed or running businesses. Less than a fifth of these were women. Opportunities for employment in the formal sector have shrunk since then.

The informal sector, small-scale trading, retailing, manufacturing and services, is the site of coping and survival in such economies. Yet regulations introduced at the time of Independence made most small-scale trading illegal. The 2004 Informal Sector Development and Control Act introduced into Parliament by Dame Carol Kidu has created spaces in which an informal trading sector can begin to flourish. Already people are flocking to the footpaths to trade, and survive, creating sites of extraordinary energy and vitality.

If Willie remains in town, with or without gainful employment, will he succumb, as so many others, to the addictions of home brew, of pack rape, of gambling, of confrontation, of seemingly wanton violence? Will he become infected with HIV? The growing youth movements, of which Ela and her sisters are members, might provide a sanctuary for him in which other ways of living become possible. Committed youth leaders and groups are springing up in the settlements but they remain without support, their leaders unpaid, and so unable to settle down and establish families.

It is a hard struggle for Ela to have her son in town. There are no hostels in Moresby for women with children. They were lucky to find the small room that they have. Affordable accommodation is hard to find, especially in the safer areas. Landlords want public servants, not students or women alone. Not single mothers.

They consider the settlement neighbourhood where they live too dangerous for Willie to walk home from school by himself, yet their study schedules make it very difficult some days for one of them to pick him up. Arrangements are often *ad hoc*, relying on the good will and availability of friends or neighbours. There is no after school care, even if they could afford it.

It is extremely expensive to live in town. The cost of education is high. So too is health care. Student bus fares keep increasing. The price of rice keeps rising. Meat meals, even with tinned meats, are rare. Rice and greens and bananas or rice and noodles are the staples.

Their situation is precarious. They are imposed upon by *wantoks* from the village, and pressured for money by street boys and friends. They have suffered sexual harassment, physical abuse and accusations of loose behaviour, sorcery and lesbianism from landlords, security guards and neighbours. A family of sisters without a man in the house arouses hostility, suspicion and jealousies.

They are buffeted by misogyny, exploitation, the difficulties of accessing education, youth unemployment, appalling health services, and one of the most inequitable and corrupt distributions of wealth in the Asia and Pacific region.

How does Ela decide, when these are the options? Village life would give Willie the best of the traditional systems of social support, and embed him in the Papua New Guinea way of doing things. It would also diminish his world. Schooling in Moresby will mean that moving into modernity remains a possibility, but it does not follow that that is where he will end up.

Ela and her sisters live on the cusp of two worlds: traditional village life and modern urban life. They travel constantly, literally and metaphorically, between these worlds, drawn to the advantages of each, but returning each time so far to the city, with its access to education and footholds into modernity. Once there, however, they are harassed by its demands: the need to be able to manage money, to actively seek for jobs, to find and negotiate accommodation, to move about safely, to interact with and befriend different people, and to think through *kastom* in this different setting.

In town, the boundaries of their moral universe are expanding. They are developing a tentative sense of belonging to a larger whole, although still referring to their neighbours as 'that Kerema man' or 'that Sepik woman'. This enforced and growing openness to difference is the precursor to curiosity about others, a mark of modernity. They have come to understand that they may have obligations to people beyond their language group, a pre-requisite of modernity and a pre-condition for the possibility of human rights activism.

The Howard Government was accurate in its talk of lawlessness and violence in PNG. The question is whether the way they decided to set the world to rights will address the complex fabric of the society in which Ela and her family struggle to survive.

The interventionist remedy, no matter how successful the outcome, humiliates and renders childlike its addressees. It provides grounds for people to consider their self-respect injured. As a form of the resort to authority, it diminishes human beings. The humiliation and infantilisation inherent in such a relationship leads to anger, cynicism or frustration rather than to working partnerships.

Ela's question reminds us that what we do and what decisions we take are often determined by the way we see the world. This is as true for the Australian Government as it is for Ela. It also holds true for the Papua New Guineans who watch bemused as their country is flooded with 'advisers' and 'personnel', all there to 'prop things up' and 'build their capacity'. They ask one another: 'What are they looking for? Why did they come? Don't they have enough food in their place? Have they run out of land there?'

The justification for the placement of Australian civil servants in PNG came perilously close to an elision from a description of unrest and violence to an ascription to a populace: 'they are a violent people', 'they have little or no respect for human life', 'they are rascals and rapists' and so on. The state of their world ascribed causally to its citizens. 'Seeing' the world in this way justifies intervention as an end in itself: Order needs to be re-established, the Rule of Law restored, and They are not capable of doing it themselves.

In this creation of the Other, lawlessness and violence are implicitly portrayed as local tragedies, locally derived. They are not seen as carrying within them their root causes in the structures, ambitions and values of the past, traditional, colonial and national.

Ela and her sisters, as they move towards modernity, understand that they must struggle to resist ascribing qualities to people as a group: 'The Goilala are like that', or 'Europeans are like that'. At the same time they are caught up in the systems and structures, traditional and modern, colonial and national, which perpetuate abuse, disempowerment, disenfranchisement and hopelessness. The same systems and structures are fuelling the HIV epidemic.

This is not the profile of a country in need of propping up. Rather the most pressing need is for a deeper analysis of the factors which have led to lawlessness and violence, which shape Willie and Ela's lives, and of how change might occur.

Index

www.ingramcontent.com/pod-product-compliance
Lightning Source LLC
Chambersburg PA
CBHW040402240726
48664CB00013B/1708